'One of the greatest things is walking back in after
winning a test match to see his face, and how proud
and happy he is – it's like a window into how
the nation feels ... Rala's room is a safe haven from
coaches and management. It's like going to
your granny's where you can be yourself instead
of a professional rugby player'
Donncha O'Callaghan

'He's one of my favourite people'
Keith Wood

'An institution in his own right'
Peter Clohessy

'What a guy, what a legend, what a servant
to Irish rugby, what a friend'
Paddy Johns

'The ritual of going to Rala's room before an international
to polish boots, have a chat and a cup of tea was always
something to look forward to'
Rob Henderson

'When he does retire, I think the Irish team might fall
apart. He's a legend' Tommy Bowe

Patrick 'Rala' O'Reilly has been the bagman for the Irish senior rugby squad for nineteen years and, during that time, he has toured every major rugby-playing nation. He was also the bagman for the British and Irish Lions in South Africa (2009) and Australia (2013).

He has been a member of Terenure College RFC since 1967 and he lives in Dublin with his partner Dixie.

John O'Sullivan is a sports writer with *The Irish Times*.

RALA
A Life in Rugby

PATRICK O'REILLY
with
JOHN O'SULLIVAN

HACHETTE
BOOKS
IRELAND

First published in 2013 by Hachette Books Ireland

Copyright © Patrick O'Reilly 2013

The right of Patrick O'Reilly to be identified as the author of the work has
been asserted by him in accordance with the Copyright, Designs and
Patents Act 1988.

A CIP catalogue record for this title is available from the British Library.

ISBN 978 1444 743 319

Typeset in Bembo Book ST and Myriad Pro by Bookends Publishing Services.
Printed and bound by CPI Group (UK) Ltd, Croydon, CR0 4YY.

Hachette Books Ireland policy is to use papers that are natural, renewable
and recyclable products and made from wood grown in sustainable forests.
The logging and manufacturing processes are expected to conform to the
environmental regulations of the country of origin.

Hachette Books Ireland
8 Castlecourt Centre
Castleknock
Dublin 15, Ireland

A division of Hachette UK Ltd.
338 Euston Road
London NW1 3BH

www.hachette.ie

To Dixie

And rugby lovers everywhere

Foreword

I got the call from Rala about fifteen years ago. He asked me if I would sing for the Irish rugby squad and I jumped in like a ferret. The then Ireland team manager, Brian O'Brien, gave the nod and I showed up in Greystones with my guitar in one hand and jockstrap in the other.

Rala welcomed me to the fold and Malcolm O'Kelly offered to be my minder for the night. Some of the squad were well up for the gig, whilst others were a bit perplexed by this baldy ex-prop in their midst. That first night, Trevor Brennan joined me for a full-on version of 'Ordinary Man'. This got the session rightly revved up. Then Keith Wood had a go at 'Clare to Here', but the Claw soon put an end to that racket.

This was to be the start of a series of gigs that has continued on and off ever since. Over the years, many of our great rugby players have displayed hidden talents with some fine singing performances.

Rala himself turned in a few good shimmies, ROG a tuneful 'Ride On', Big Donncha might have strayed slightly offside on 'Joxer', but who's going to argue with him? Denis Leamy excelled one year with a great version of 'The Contender' too.

I always knew who to call on as Rala would have me well

primed beforehand – he always knew who might be rehearsing 'on the sly'. Those who have joined me on stage over the years include Luke Fitzgerald, Peter Stringer, Drico, Reggie Corrigan, Felix Jones, Gert Smal, Mick Kearney, Frankie Sheahan, Fergus McFadden and Damien Varley.

Thanks to Rala, I have some great rugby memories. I have been following the Irish rugby team since my boyhood and I've even got to sit near the bench on a few occasions. I remember David Humphreys coming off the field, shaking my hand, saying, 'It's good to see you here.'

This (then) sixty-year-old man was like a schoolboy once again. I was there for Paulie's first cap against Wales, when he came off concussed. I remember the inspiring words that Declan Kidney offered after Declan Sinnott and I played for the squad in Maynooth.

I also recall the night in Citywest when my brother, Luka Bloom, sang 'A Song for John Hayes', the lyrics suggesting that The Bull might play on the wing. And I fondly recall the night that I brought Paul McGrath to Killiney Castle and witnessed the Irish rugby squad give him a hero's welcome.

All of this came about as a result of Rala inviting me to sing for the squad. I look forward to reading of Rala's exploits and I am delighted to write these few words of introduction. Ride on, Rala …

Christy Moore
(ex-prop for Bective Rangers, Cashel and Galway Corinthians)

Introduction

My name is Patrick O'Reilly, or at least I thought it was but that's a story for another time. Most people know me as Rala. I've been the bagman to the Ireland rugby team for the past nineteen years (and still counting), and have also been fortunate enough to fulfil that role on two Lions tours, to South Africa in 2009 and Australia in 2013.

People are curious about what I do for a living, the minutiae of it. 'Fascinated' would be too strong a word. It's not rocket science – but, then again, there is only one job that is. In broad terms, my responsibility is to ensure that the Ireland players and coaches have everything they need to train and play the game.

I am responsible for, amongst others things, all the playing paraphernalia, like jerseys, socks, shorts, spare studs, laces, gumshields, rugby balls, kicking tees, cones, body shields, communication headsets for the coaches, and other items, like toiletries, tea, coffee, sugar, milk, drinking chocolate, biscuits, water, protein shakes, recovery drinks and music, to give you a short long list of the spectrum in my remit.

I'm first to a training venue and last to leave it, ditto for test matches. I am the man in the white van, arriving at a training session about three-quarters of an hour before the team bus. For internationals, I'd be in the ground seven to eight hours before kick-off.

Being there so far in advance is not mandatory – I have come across several of my peers who could get their preparations done in a couple of hours – but I like to work at my own pace, to take time for casual conversations with old friends and new, the security men, ground staff and those whose responsibility it is to look after the dressing room area.

When the team arrives about an hour and a half before kick-off, I'll have their jerseys hanging and their kit neatly folded, along with their anthem tops, towels and programmes. There are some players who I know like specific bits and pieces – for example, I'd always have put a red apple with John Hayes' kit, George North and Stephen Jones likes a small tub of wine gums. Apart from all the gear, I'd have cones, footies and tackle shields for the warm-up in the corridor.

I've come a long way, literally and metaphorically, from the clapped-out player propping up the bar in Terenure RFC, who, when asked if he'd take on the role of bagman to the first team for the 1983–1984 season, shrugged and said, 'Why not?' I blame the pints.

I had no idea what the job entailed, but at that point I did realise that as a thirty-five-year-old hooker-cum-second-row with high mileage, my best days, such as they were, were barely visible in the rear-view mirror.

My education as a bagman began with instruction from some of the best in the business and continued with the practical experience gleaned from ten years of travelling the highways and byways of the Irish club scene.

Opportunities knocked and I was there to answer the door. I got an invitation to work with the Leinster under-20s, moved to the senior Leinster side and then, in 1994, Ireland. For a brief moment in time, I was bagman to the Terenure, Leinster and Ireland teams while holding down a day job – rugby didn't turn professional for another year. I took a gamble and discovered I'd got the winning docket.

People say that I am very fortunate, and you certainly won't get any argument from me. I'm privileged to have travelled the world and met some wonderful people. Some are players, some aren't – I'm not too fussed whether you're a pauper or a prince. I've been granted a ringside seat to some of the greatest moments in Irish and Lions rugby – the Grand Slam in 2009 and the Lions test series victory in 2013 to name but two.

While I want the players to achieve their hearts' desire, I don't become overly fixated on the match results. When I look at a player, I see the person first and the player second. Rugby for me is about people, places and experiences. Winning and losing are the core elements of sport but if they are the only things that shape your mood, sport becomes a pretty soulless experience.

Every time the team takes to the pitch, I have the same thought. I watch twenty-three players run out and I want twenty-three to come back in under their own steam. That's more important than anything to me. I have witnessed shattered limbs and ligaments ripped from the bone, and seen careers threatened by injury where the pain goes far deeper than the physical wound.

Maybe I can afford to hold that view because my position is not determined by winning or losing – or at least I don't think it is. I have shed a tear or two but not simply because Ireland have lost, but for the impact on the people involved. I see the dedication, the desire, the work ethic and the sacrifices. I know what it means to the players to wear the green jersey and how much they invest emotionally and physically to try to make the country proud.

Players talk about great matches or venues, whereas I refer to wonderful hotels and their staff, great liaison officers and van drivers without whose help I would be floundering. My father gave me one bit of advice that I have always held dear: 'It doesn't matter what job you do, all that matters is you do it to the best of your ability.' I've tried.

This book isn't a series of match reports – I'll leave it up to others, better qualified, to examine the victories and defeats – it's about incidents and accidents, tall tales and short stories about people, some of whom happen to be very good rugby players. It's a story about a boy from Inchicore who won life's lottery.

NOTE ON THE TEXT

When we're in camp before a match, part of my job is to write up the daily itinerary sheets, which are given to each member of the team (players, management and backroom staff) so that everyone knows where they need to be and what they need to do the following day.

On the bottom of these sheets, I always add a quotation or saying to help motivate everyone – or just to make them smile. One of my favourites is: 'Even a cat can look at a king.' They're only mine occasionally, though, mostly they're plagiarised from other sources. Donncha O'Callaghan comes up with a few, so did Mark Tainton – sometimes the hotel receptionists come up with them. There are lot of contributors, but even if Einstein unwittingly provided one, it would still be pencilled in under 'Rala's quote of the day'.

I thought it only right that these should be included here too, and so I've used them to title the chapters.

The publisher also thought it would be a good idea to include a few words from the players – to give them a chance to tell a few stories, and their contributions are in between the chapters.

Preface

The Electric Light Orchestra (ELO) sang 'Hold on Tight to Your Dreams', a tune that sprang to mind following a phone call I received towards the end of January 2009. Gary O'Driscoll, the current Arsenal and former Lions team doctor, phoned to give me a tip-off that I'd be getting a call to interview for the position of bagman to the British and Irish Lions for their tour to South Africa later that year.

I was pretty sceptical about my chances. Looking back, I realise it was because I desperately wanted the gig and was afraid to invest too much hope in it for fear of being disappointed. I'm pretty sure no child dreams of being a bagman, but having embarked on that career path, my ideal world was now shaped a little differently to how it had been in my youth.

The prospect of travelling to the southern hemisphere with the Lions had huge personal appeal, but I considered it a bit of a pipe dream until I took a phone call a week later from Guy Richardson, the logistics manager for the tour to South Africa.

We had a very pleasant chat without getting into any specifics and he finished the conversation by saying he'd be in touch. He rang back two days later and invited me to meet him at Murrayfield – he was Scotland team manager at the time – on what I presumed would be a more formal footing. When I arrived at the ground, Guy came down to the gate and whisked me away to a wee hotel nearby where we had 'the interview'.

I'd done a little research into his background. As he had spent twenty years in the army with the Royal Scots Regiment, reaching the rank of major, I anticipated a certain type of process. I couldn't have been more wrong. Guy immediately put me at ease to a point where I suspect I might have blurred the line between an interview and a chat. On the journey home to Dublin, I thought about all the things I should have said.

The interview took place on a Tuesday and Guy promised to ring me no later than Friday with the news – good or bad. The Irish first XV had a camp in Limerick that weekend and, as is my wont in those circumstances, I headed down early. Dixie, my better half in every respect and the person whose support makes it possible for me to immerse myself in the world of rugby, came down too.

Even though Peter and Anna Clohessy were away, we were staying chez Claw with their children, Harry, Jane and Luke, my erstwhile helper, as our hosts.

Geraldine, a friend who worked with Claw, brought us to his Crokers pub, where we met up with a crowd from Claw's other watering hole, the Sin Bin, on a night out.

I was sipping and chatting away when I noticed my phone light up and dance a little jig across the table – I nearly upset a pint or three in my panic to get to it. I hurried outside to the children's play area at the back of the pub. I can still remember Guy's exact words: 'Me and you, big fella, are going to South Africa.'

Dreams do come true.

On returning to the fireside in that part of the pub known as 'Johnny's cottage', I wore a big, sloppy grin, so Dixie knew instantly that the news was good. Sworn to secrecy by Guy, I couldn't tell anyone else for a while, but news eventually filtered out and the slagging started. Marcus Horan would tell anyone who'd listen not to bother asking me for a lace or a stud unless they had at least fifty caps and were a former Lion.

But the Lions tour was four months away, and I had to park all thoughts of it because Ireland were about to embrace the Six Nations Championship. It was a wonderful year to be involved in Irish rugby, with a team that gave birth to a Six Nations title, a Triple Crown and a Grand Slam. Then there was a Heineken Cup for Leinster and Munster's ultimate triumph in the Magners League. Declan Kidney took an Ireland A side to the Churchill Cup that summer and returned with the trophy. They were heady days.

On a personal note, one other image sticks in my mind from that late spring. Terenure College hosted their neighbour and fiercest rival St Mary's College for the Dublin 6 bragging rights, which were almost as important as the league points. They erected a marquee for the day and about 500 people attended the pre-match lunch. I was charged with bringing along the 'guests of honour', aka most of the trophies listed above. Young and old clambered to have their pictures taken and get their own private snapshot of rugby history.

By the end of March 2009, with the Six Nations over and a Grand Slam won, I could start to think about going to South Africa.

The orientation process for the tour involved the odd day in London during April for various meetings and incorporated a little required reading, kindly provided by Lions CEO John Feehan and Communications Officer Christine Connolly. My homework was to read a couple of books on the history of the Lions and they gave me an insight into the ethos of the red-clad troubadours.

The Lions pre-tour base was the magnificent Pennyhill Park and Spa Hotel in Bagshot, Surrey. It's where the England team prepares for matches, and it's easy to understand why. It's picture-postcard perfect. The accommodation is luxurious, the food Michelin-star quality and a real threat to the waistline – added to that, the facilities include a rugby pitch less than 100 metres from the front door of the hotel.

I remember the first training session. I was pitch-side about an hour and a half before the players were due to arrive. I'd laid out three trestle tables, complete with white linen cloths. Two contained food and drink – tea, coffee, drinking chocolate, milk, cups, spoons, sugar, recently baked biscuits (not my work, I hasten to add), serviettes and sweets – while the third, which I referred to as the 'healthy table', was choc-full of water, protein shakes, other supplement drinks and Viper belts (a bungee-style rope used in training that promotes the development of speed, balance and power).

Then, on an adjoining table, I had my iPod and Bose speakers, spare training jerseys (three colours), along with spare training socks, shorts (two colours), laces, shin guards, scrum caps, various other bits and pieces of Adidas kit and my trusty stud box, which contains studs of varying sizes and a tool to affix same.

Dotted around the pitch were two different brands of ball (for commercial reasons), tackle shields, cylindrical tackle shields, belly shields, cones and bibs (six different colours, three sizes). A marquee beside the pitch housed weights and a machine that replicated the effects of playing at high altitude.

It was my first day in the new job, so to speak. I was nervous.

I had my back to the entrance from where the players and coaches would come, preoccupying myself with a smoke, a cup of coffee and listening to music. I just happened to turn around as they approached, this human sea of green (unexpectedly for they Lions, they were training in green that day).

Immediately flustered, I simultaneously tried to put out the coffee and drink the cigarette. I turned off the music.

I was promptly told to turn it back on. I was playing a sixties compilation album and England's New Zealand-born centre Riki Flutey proved to be a big fan of the genre. I'd put the music on for the training warm-up and after the session had finished, in fact during the seven weeks of the camp, the only time it was switched off was when the players were out training. We'd also crank it up in the team room or bring it to where the lads were doing weights.

I have about 7,000 songs on the one iPod and it's fair to say it's an eclectic mix from traditional Irish to the more modern stuff –

garage, house, techno and all that noise – it's not my cup of tea, but it's not about me. In fairness to the players, they were pretty easygoing when it came to the tunes.

For me, that first training session brought back memories of the insecurity and uncertainty of my first day at primary school.

Obviously I knew the Irish players and they knew me, but there were plenty of others, household names and some of the best players in northern-hemisphere rugby, who I was meeting for the first time. Keith Wood had given me a bit of advice – 'Be yourself, Rala. No fancy stuff' – and that was the formula by which I worked.

It took me a while to put names to all the faces of the players, management, commercial team and the media – I was never good at remembering names at the best of times – but I'd like to think I established a rapport. I also remember the induction meeting for the backroom team. Everyone sat in a room one evening and one by one offered a little bit of information about themselves. I was furiously trying to think about what I would say. When Guy Richardson had tried to introduce me before that meeting, he'd called me 'the Lions' baggage master'. I had corrected him, 'I'm a bagman. The day I become a master is the day I'll stop.'

I didn't have to speak that evening, much to my relief. Guy stood up and said, 'Also on board my team is Rala, who hopes one day to become a bag master.'

The players would probably say that I still have a long way to go to get that badge.

Injuries are the bane of a sportsperson's career. There's never a good time to sustain one but sometimes the timing can be particularly cruel. That was certainly the case for Tomás O'Leary,

Jerry Flannery and Tom Shanklin, who were all ruled out of the tour having been originally selected. Jerry sustained his elbow injury during a training session at Pennyhill Park. There is very little you can say in those circumstances – you offer your condolences, but it doesn't even scratch the surface.

Alan Quinlan was slightly different. There's no point in rehashing the events surrounding his suspension but, on a personal level, I felt sorry for him and his kitbag seemed to haunt every leg of the trip, offering a constant reminder of his absence.

We were due to fly to South Africa less than a week after the training camp finished. I couldn't help but be amazed by how far I'd come in a career that I was already in the middle of before I even realised it *was* my career.

Chapter 1

'The mind is a parachute – it doesn't work unless it's opened.'

I was born on 15 April 1948 – the same year as Ireland's first rugby Grand Slam – at 18 Woodfield Cottages, Inchicore, one of Paddy and Helen O'Reilly's nine children. It was a little row of *Coronation Street*-style houses up a hill from the Model School, with the railway cottages behind us. We lived in a cosy, three-bedroom house, always piping hot thanks to my father, who was a central heating and plumbing contractor. An incredibly hard worker, he built up a very successful business employing many people.

Looking back, I realise how blissfully happy my childhood in the company of my siblings was. I have four sisters, June, Pauline,

Jeanette and Geraldine, and four brothers, Brendan, David, Brian and Christopher – or Rasher as he was known because of his fondness for bacon, but he wasn't born until after we moved to Templeogue.

My earliest memories include visits to Granny O'Reilly in Mount Brown where we would be treated to custard tarts and tea by her fireside. My granny was never seen without a black shawl draped across her shoulders. She would later join us in Templeogue.

Woodfield was a place where neighbours looked after one another. The front-door key was left in the lock day and night, and someone's arrival was heralded by a brief knock before they pushed open the door.

Children played on the street and there was a community care attitude to their welfare. It didn't matter who belonged to who when it came to meals. Mothers just fed whoever sat at a table. Every now and then Travellers would arrive to mend pots, colourful balloons attached to their carts and long red scarves billowing from their necks.

The first dead person I saw was Mr Gibney. We were marched military fashion to his house, two doors down, to pay our respects.

Our street was quiet, a secluded playground, as you had to go down a cobble-stoned hill to get to the main street. If you went up the main street, you came to an area called 'the Ranch'. After that was Ballyfermot. Heading the other way, you would be going to James Street and Kilmainham. There were people living up the road from us called the O'Briens. Paddy O'Brien bought our house from my dad when we left for Templeogue. Paddy used to drive the Pacific Showband around the country, but then he got a job with my da.

Some years ago, I went back and knocked at his door. There was no answer and I was just on the point of leaving when I heard the door opening. Paddy was old and frail, but he looked at me and said, 'Paddy Reilly.'

I replied, 'It is.'

He brought me in. Because of his age, he'd moved downstairs. He immediately started speaking about my parents, which made me a bit weepy. He recalled the day I was born, pointing to a corner of the room where my mother gave birth. He recounted a story about another neighbour, Mrs Keegan. She had a son who made his Confirmation on the day I was born. He went into showbusiness, joining a group called the Four Ambassadors. His daughter Beverley went on to marry a former All Black Mike Brewer, and their son Harrison went on to be a standout player for Terenure on both the junior and senior cup teams.

I made my Communion in St Michael's Church in Inchicore, and one of the highlights of the day was buying a Crunchie. It's been my favourite since. Someone once asked me in an interview what my favourite bar was and so I said, 'Crunchie.' Yer man looked at me like I had two heads. He thought I was going to say Kehoe's or some other pub.

Another cherished memory is of going to the cinema – we called it 'the pictures' – and to this day Westerns are my favourite.

We were a tight-knit family, but you had to be able to give and take a bit of slagging. I suppose we got our sense of humour from our parents. I remember a row between my father and mother. Leaving for work, he turned to her and said, 'Goodbye, mother of nine.'

Quick as a flash she replied, 'Goodbye, father of four.'

My father did a great deal of country work in those days and on a Friday night men would converge on number 18 Woodfield Cottages to collect their wages. They would usually end up in Cleary's pub. They'd return later with brown bags bearing bottles of Guinness. Then the singsong would start and I would creep from my bed to the top of the stairs to listen. To this day, I like to have background noise when I am drifting off to Lala land.

My introduction to the plumbing and heating game was more by accident than design. My dad had to go back into overalls to do a job in a school assembly hall that involved welding radiators. My brothers would have been more proficient, but were possibly too young at the time, so I was chosen to assist him. Now, I know some might consider me pedantic when it comes to compiling lists and completing tasks in a regimented manner, but there is no doubting that it wasn't from the stones I licked it. The auld fella was fastidious in his preparation. I had to help him lay out the rods in a proper fashion, find him something to kneel on and ensure that the two bottles for the acetylene torch were on hand along with his goggles. Everything had to be in the right place. I definitely wasn't made for the heating business, but we completed the job on time.

Dad was generous, on one occasion loaning some money to a friend to buy a motorcycle after the bank had turned down the friend's loan application. My dad was a member of Newlands Golf Club and liked to squeeze in eighteen holes from time to time, but he wasn't consumed by the sport – or any sport for that matter. To my knowledge, he only ever came to watch me play rugby once – a league final between Terenure and Wanderers at Templeville

Road. It was freezing and I found out a few weeks later that he'd left after half an hour.

One Friday night, when I was about eight years old, we kids were told to pack up our bits and pieces and assemble on the street outside the house. We were moving to Templeogue. We'd spent the odd Sunday out there looking at a house being built, but I hadn't twigged that a change of address was on the cards. Templeogue was a proper village in those days with a lot fewer houses. I love the place, always will. In my mind's eye, I can still see it all as it was when we moved there – the Troys' (post office), the Hollingsworths' (bicycle shop), the Ryans' (pub, now known as the Morgue), McDermotts', McCanns', Byrnes', Grahams', Bradys', Mick and Rusty Egan, who I used to hunt rabbits with, and Templeogue Tennis Club, where I also learned the difference between chasing and catching girls.

Rasher arrived to swell our family numbers. A Sunday dinner of roast chicken was quite an event, considering there were eleven mouths to feed, and my only concern was how I could get more of the bird. I don't know how Ma managed it, but we all got enough.

It reminds me of a story. My parents went away on holidays when I was on the junior cup team in Terenure, and left my sister Pauline in charge under instruction to feed me with steak every day. Now Pauline had other ideas and decided that my lack of knowledge would enable her to choose a less expensive part of the cow. She opted for hearts and pocketed the difference. The plan worked without a hitch until she fell out with one of my other sisters, who spilled the beans. A war of sorts broke out for several days but eventually I had to accept defeat. My sister had driven a heart through my steak.

My ma was very funny, a real comedian with a great turn of phrase, although getting on her wrong side would earn you a filleting. Once the phone rang and I could hear her saying, 'I'm sorry but there's no one here by that name.' She came back in and said, 'A lot of people keep ringing here looking for a Raja.'

I couldn't suppress a giggle. 'Rala is it? That's what they call me.'

She didn't understand why.

Soon after moving to Templeogue, my schooling took me to Terenure College under the educational baton of the Carmelites. I loved my time there and made friendships that have endured a lifetime.

I wouldn't say that I was the brightest bulb in the factory, but I tried to be diligent. Then again, they voted me past-pupil of the year in 2000, so I must have done something right. To say I was surprised to be asked to be past-pupil of the year (especially in the millennium year) would be something of an understatement. Over the years, many of the school's illustrious former students have held the title, including Donal McCann, Mike Murphy, Niall Hogan, Lorcan Cranitch and Girvan Demsey, and I was hugely honoured to take on that mantel.

Our geography teacher, who we called 'Johnny Bear', used to single me out occasionally for praise. He was big into his colours when it came to drawing maps, and I played up on that – marking rivers in blue and mountains in brown, although not always with great accuracy. I remember him saying to me one day, 'That's lovely work, Rala – top notch – but you might want to move the Mississippi out of Alaska.' Thankfully my attention to detail has improved slightly since then.

Being Terenure, there wasn't much choice about what sport you played and rugby has been a passion and the central tenet in my life from the day I walked through the gates of the college as a boy. The first team I played for was the under-9s in 1956. I was chosen as a second row but the following year was moved to hooker, a position I principally occupied for the remainder of my career.

In those days, there were four houses in Terenure College – St Patrick's, St Simon's, St Columcille's and St Elisa's. Fr Hegarty decided which house you joined and I wore the blue jersey of St Pat's. 'Hego', as we referred to him, was to have a profound effect on us, instilling a love of rugby that endured long after we walked out of the school gates for the final time.

By the age of fifteen, a team began to take shape. The lads – Michael Mahony, Michael Smyth, Colm Jenkinson, John Gleeson, Pat Tormey, Paddy Devlin and Dominic Fusco, who were later joined by the likes of Shay Ruane – played a huge part in my life. Pat Tormey is still my dentist, Michael Mahony was my bank manager until he retired and the late Michael Smyth was my doctor.

One day many years after we left school, I arrived at the AIB in Dundrum to meet Mick Mahony, who I knew as 'Slick'. The bank was closed, but Slick had told me to just knock on the door. When a guy opened it I asked him if he would mind telling Slick that Rala was here to see him. He replied, 'I am sorry, sir, but we don't use names like that. Give me your real name and the person you are looking for.' I had to think about it for a few minutes before I remembered.

It was in Terenure that I was given the name to which I answer to this day. It came about in pretty innocuous circumstances. I was trying to spell my name in Irish on the blackboard, I think I was about ten at the time. I managed R-A-L-A and then stopped, stumped. Dominic Fusco, whose family owned a chipper in Crumlin, started laughing, 'Good old, Rala.' The name stuck.

There is a slightly bizarre sequel to the tale. I thought I had been christened Paddy because that's what I'm called by my family and it's also on my passport. Then, one day a couple of years ago, I had to go in to collect my birth certificate and gave the lady at the counter my name, Paddy O'Reilly, and birth details. She came back a few minutes later and said, 'Your name is not Paddy, it's John.'

I told her there must be some mistake, but then got to thinking that my father had been called Patrick John (P.J.) O'Reilly, so maybe my parents had christened me John Patrick and decided to call me Paddy because my father was always known as 'P.J.'. The lady behind the counter quickly exploded that theory. 'No,' she said, 'you were christened John O'Reilly. There's no mention of the name Patrick.' So I have been operating under an alias all my life.

Rugby dominated my childhood by design and possibly because other activities had a short shelf life. I joined the Scouts but was expelled after a couple of weeks following an incident on a trip – we were asked to light a fire to cook a stew and rather than collect firewood, I set fire to a bush, which got a bit out of hand. My next vocation was as an altar boy but I received my marching orders after an episode at mass. My FCA experience lasted slightly longer, but asking for a lift home in a general's staff car when we were on manoeuvres in the Dublin Mountains because I didn't fancy walking sealed my fate. When I volunteered for the Christmas play, I usually ended up stuck at the back of the choir, the front-of-stage action being left to Donal McCann (though he did go on to become one of Ireland's most famous actors).

There was very little festive cheer when a handful of us were caught out late on an rugby away trip just outside Reading in England when I was about eighteen.

We were trying to sneak back into the dormitory when the lights went on and Fr McCuaig, all six foot six inches of him, stopped us in our tracks. He told us that we were all dropped for the following day's game. At the time, it didn't occur to us that we would have to play because there wouldn't be sufficient numbers otherwise. We spent a sleepless night and apologised in the morning.

Fr Mc coached us at junior cup level but we suffered the heartbreak of a semi-final defeat to Castleknock after three replays. In my first year on the senior cup team, I didn't fare much better as we went out to Blackrock College, a Mick Kelly drop goal sealing our fate. We bulldozed our way through the friendly matches the following year and there were great expectations when it came to the cup, but we went out 5–3 to a Shay Deering-led St Mary's College in a match everyone considered to be the final. The actual final saw Mary's beat a Newbridge College side captained by Tom Grace. I shared a pint or two with Shay over the years. I was very fond of him, probably dating back to our time on the Leinster Schools side.

Time passed so quickly in Terenure but those easy, fun-filled days had to come to an end. From an academic perspective, sixth year was a bit of an eye opener. There was no mollycoddling any more and we were expected to work on our own initiative.

I'll never forget the words of our history teacher – his name was Tom, but we all called him 'Beatnik' – on my last day as he gazed out the window, 'Well, Rala, it's over. Out there is a big world, which you have to join. Good luck, as you'll certainly need it.'

He was right. I lacked focus and that's probably why I jumped at the opportunity to accompany a friend, Richie, to London – his sister had offered us temporary lodgings. My first place of employment was a shampoo factory but I quickly got shown the gates because of my inability to concentrate on the task in hand. My job was putting caps on the bottles, but I was too easily distracted by the excellent piped music in the background. I was called over by my supervisor who pointed out that I had missed a few bottles. When it happened twice more, I was fired.

Then Richie got us work with a builder from Tipperary who was constructing an outdoor swimming pool in the shape of Africa for a wealthy client. Payday was Friday and I rambled up to Mr Jones. The boys were sitting around obviously aware that all was not well. He handed me an envelope and then a second one, saying, 'Son, I am going to be very generous to you here. There are your wages. I'm giving you a second one with your fare home. Take my advice and go home because you are not going to make it here.'

I did what he suggeseted.

I remember telling that story to Brian O'Driscoll, Denis Hickie and Shane Horgan – or the 'Golden Triangle' as I call these three amigos – and it was all very solemn until I let slip that my emigration to England had lasted the full two weeks and not the ten years they'd anticipated. The convulsions of laughter lasted quite a while.

Richie stayed on in Romford and after a while took an assisted passage to Australia, settling in Brisbane. I met him for a few beers when we were touring there with Ireland.

The prodigal son's speedy return forced my dad, who had branched out into a few different businesses, to give me a job. I then worked with the Bear's brother Noel, travelling the roads of Ireland as a sales rep, selling hair-care products to pharmacies. After a year, I switched to Colet Products, headed up by Brendan Murphy and his aide-de-camp the Prince, aka Niall Sweeney, who is still a great mate.

My rugby education also continued as I made the short journey from the school pitches across the far side of the lake to Lakelands, home of Terenure College RFC. It seemed a natural progression and it was undertaken alongside many of the boys who I had started playing with at under-9 level. We were welcomed into the bosom of the club under the watchful eye of the late Joe Milroy, Paddy Lyons, Ronnie Marsh, Ted Holt and Paddy Murphy – stalwarts one and all, and guardians of Terenure's traditions. I was occasionally given a clip on the ear and a dressing down by one of these gentlemen, being a bit younger and wilder in those days.

During my time as a rep for Colet, I used to call into O'Sullivan's pharmacy in Ballymount. Mr and Mrs O'Sullivan were very good to me, providing a bite to eat, a mug of tea and, perhaps most importantly, an order for products. They had three sons – Declan and Knick Knack, both living at home at the time, were the two that I got to know best.

I was playing with the firsts for Terenure and Knick Knack, who had just left school, was called in to play for that team. He was a talented, brave full-back but not the biggest in stature.

We were playing a Blackrock side that included the Ireland and Lions colossus Willie Duggan. Mrs O was a little concerned about her pride and joy, so I undertook to reassure her that I would let nothing happen to KK. She seemed mollified by my commitment.

As I mentioned, KK wasn't the biggest and there were times during the match when I struggled to see him tending his lonely outpost. Everything went according to plan until a moment near the end of the game when I found myself way too close to a huge up-and-under that was coming down in our twenty-two. I spotted Knick Knack in my peripheral vision, and a quick reconnaissance told me that Willie Duggan would be arriving at the same time as the ball. I shouted 'your ball' to KK and slipped away from what I knew could end up as a crime scene.

KK caught the ball, Duggan and half the Blackrock pack, and my only contribution after the whistle went was to pull bodies from the top of the wreckage to try and find KK. Dazed, he just looked up at me and tried to smile, but that soon turned into a grimace. Needless to say, I steered clear of the shop for a while until the heat had died down a little. KK is involved in the airline business in London now, and we relive that story every time we meet.

My debut for the Terenure first team saw me come up against the Ireland and Lions legend Ken Kennedy. My abiding memory is of the last scrum when I got twisted badly and damaged some ribs and was out for six weeks. I didn't fare much better when I came up against another Irish hooker, that son of Limerick, Pa Whelan. We would subsequently be reunited as manager and bagman for the Ireland team and I'm surprised how good Pa was to me on the strength of what I did to him that day in Lakelands. It was a wet and windy afternoon, Terenure had a lineout and the obvious thing in those conditions was to throw the ball to the front, or the number two position to use rugby parlance. Sure enough our coach, Eddie Thornton, ran up and whispered, 'Low and hard at number two.' Now Pa was standing with his back to me, the number two on his jersey, so I threw the ball at him, striking him squarely on the back of the head.

He turned to me and said, 'What the f★★★ did I do to you?'

I spent the rest of the afternoon trying to avoid him, a difficult task when you consider we were cheek-by-jowl for every scrum. At the post-match meal, Eddie was sitting in our company and at one stage he turned to me – my steak was obscured by the mountain of mashed potato – and said, 'That's the difference between you and Pa, about four stone of potatoes.'

Paddy Murphy was a great character who captained Terenure in the 1948–1949 season to a Leinster junior league and cup double. Joe Milroy, a founding member, was another club captain and the esteem in which he was held can be gleaned from the fact that he was twice president, on the latter occasion in the club's Golden Jubilee year (1990–1991). These men would be the first to drive you to or collect you from the train station for away matches. Other names from my club rugby days come to mind, like the great scrum-half Frankie Crossan, full-back Gimper O'Donovan, Jerry, McFriendly O'Sullivan, Johnny Connolly, who emigrated to Skerries, and another second row, Kevin, forever known as Gilly and sadly no longer with us. He was a premier league messer.

On one occasion, I found myself sitting alongside Gilly in the dressing room at 2.30 p.m. for a J1 league match against Edenderry.

Kick-off was at 3 p.m. and he leaned over and whispered, 'If anyone asks, tell them I'm in the toilet. I forgot to back a sure thing in the 3.15' – I can't remember the race meeting – 'and I'm just going to nip down the town and put a few quid on it.'

He slipped away in his gear and boots, borrowed a car and headed off, to return about five minutes before the match was due to start.

There were others like Sean Crossan, who formed a half-back pairing with his brother Frankie, Nicky Moore, Johnny Thornton, Mike 'Flower Power' Barrett, Fangio, Niall 'Flash' Morrissey, Aidan '7–6' Neill (so called because he scored all the points in a J1 league final victory over Blackrock College at Donnybrook), Willie Flynn, Ronan 'My Left Foot' Browne, Terry Doyle and Shay 'the Bear' Ruane.

I first met the Bear in 1965 when his parents decided to send him to Terenure to finish his schooling. He was incredibly strong and, in those days, fast – unfortunately, wine, women and song might have sapped a little speed. Mick O'Carroll, who dedicated his life to rugby on and off the pitch and went on to be President of the IRFU in 1985, a Triple Crown year, presided over the rabble that we were in a coaching capacity. The Doyles were a famous Terenure family and Terry, a prop, was a terrier and not afraid of confrontation – how he managed to hold up my eighteen-stone frame is the eighth wonder of the world.

In mentioning that J1 final victory over Blackrock, I couldn't leave out a tale about our illustrious captain Barry Roche, whose nickname was Rover. His family lived behind mine in Templeogue village and included a brother Mick, who went on to do well for himself in the newspaper business. Anyway, Rover lived up to his name in scouring the pubs on the eve of a match to make sure no players were around – but he'd end up having several himself along the way.

I used to do some additional training with the Leinster squash club on Tuesdays and Thursdays in Rathmines. Ben Cranwell was one of the internationals in that sport who I trainded with, so I had to have been pretty lively to try and keep up. Gerry Martina was the training coach and didn't suffer fools or late-comers gladly. He would be standing there waiting for the clock on the street to sound six bells and he'd start the training even if it meant talking to invisible people. He'd wrestled for Ireland at the 1956 and 1960 Olympics.

My personality on the pitch was easygoing, although I suspect others would say I lacked a bit of focus given that I was dropped more times than I care to admit – the primary reason was that I spent too much time hanging out on the wing. It wasn't really a good look for a hooker in those days. Maybe I was a little bit ahead of my time. I wouldn't shy away from the physical and if someone threw a punch, I would reciprocate. I once lost a tooth following a row just before a match ended. After the whistle blew, I put my arm around my opponent, we shook hands and then got locked in the clubhouse in the time-honoured tradition.

It was only after I'd visited the dentist a few times for him to fill in gaps that I realised I needed to duck more often or I wouldn't be having too many steak dinners in the future.

There was an obligation to attend training and several times I received a phone call to ascertain my whereabouts. One of those was from Liam O'Dea. I told him I was watching *Emmerdale Farm* and from that night on, he referred to me as Amos. Liam was a good friend and I remember ringing him in hospital not long before he died – I couldn't bring myself to go there. His phone went to voicemail and to be honest I was a little bit relieved because I didn't know what to say or whether I could hold it together. I was just walking past Brian O'Driscoll's room in the Killiney Castle when my phone went. It was Liam. 'Amos, don't be worried, just make sure the lads beat Scotland on Saturday.'

He was buried on the day of the game, something I didn't tell Girvan Dempsey, who was full-back that day, before the match because I knew how upset he'd be. Terenure is family.

Rewinding a little, while I'm talking about my younger days, it would be remiss of me not to say more about the Doyle family or recall the role that they played in claiming the 1968 Winters Cup with a 7–3 victory over noisy neighbours St Mary's in the final. Mick McKenna led a team that included my good self and one Marty 'Party' Doyle, or Noddy as his mum used to call him. We happened upon a pre-match routine and we stuck to it rigidly in the belief that it was central to our run of success.

For a 6 p.m. kick-off, I would arrive down to Mrs Doyle's house at 1 p.m., just in time to share dinner with Marty Party. We had the works, finishing off with apple tart and ice-cream. A short siesta would be required. The next port of call was down in Dartry, where Flower Power, one of my props, lived. His mum would provide several thick slices of fruitcake washed down with a mug of steaming tea. Another nap was part of the regimen before heading down to the ground for about 5 p.m. I firmly believe that these kind ladies thought that we might have ambitions of playing for Ireland. After the match, Marty Party and I would slowly make our way to the cinema in Grafton Street to watch a few cartoons and close our eyes for a little while. The night would conclude at the Imperial Chinese restaurant. There was no drink taken on the assumption that we didn't have medals in our pockets. We did not deviate from that match-day routine for many years.

I played in nine finals for Terenure, at a variety of levels, winning six and losing three. The defeats are etched in the forefront of my mind. We lost to Wanderers in the Leinster Senior League final and Lansdowne in the Leinster Senior Cup final, both in 1978. They were the only defeats that season under the captaincy of the late and much loved Dr Mick Smyth. There was never a dull moment when the doc was in charge – I remember turning to Dixie one night proclaiming that a finger was killing me and that I was off to see Mick in the army barracks where he happened to be on duty. Mick insisted that the consultation should take place at the bar. One pint led to ten, by which time the room had become misty and my vision fuzzy. I was drinking with my left hand to emphasise my poor finger, but that fact got lost in the maelstrom of drink. A cohort of the good doctor's army buddies came up to tell stories and I felt obliged to listen to every single one of them. It was 3 a.m. when I begged to take my leave and order a taxi. No taxi could be found, so I went home in an ambulance that happened to be going in the general direction of where I lived. I woke the following morning with a throbbing headache and a finger that had swelled to twice its original size.

That defeat by Wanderers was the day my old fella came to watch and left after half an hour because of the freezing conditions.

Mick blamed me for losing the Lansdowne match. We were leading at the time and I had a bit of a foot rush going towards their line. Lansdowne's scrum-half Donal Canniffe picked up the ball behind his own line, sold me a dummy and thirty seconds later, we were standing behind our own posts. Dr Mick mentioned that dummy over a pint or two down through the years.

My third losing final saw me up against another Irish hooker in Harry Harbison, whose UCD team hammered us in a J2 decider.

I managed to amass six winners' medals over the years, but was only trotting after the likes of Terenure legends Willie Flynn and Frankie Crossan, who had twenty plus, as did others like Tojo and Frank Kennedy in St Mary's and the Wesley prop who was known to all and sundry as Twenty Major and a Box of Matches.

Smythy was my doctor from the day he qualified to the day he was tragically killed, aged forty-nine, in a car crash on Kill Avenue near Foxrock in Dublin. We also lost our full-back Pat 'Pop' Sparks, prematurely at forty-seven. He was another great character. His son was on a Terenure senior cup team when I did the bags for them. I remember going into the changing room for the first time when Des Thornton told me that the little fella in the corner was Pop's son, Robbie. I had to go outside the room and compose myself because it made me very tearful thinking about his father. In the years that followed, Robbie would have to listen to my stories about his old man – I think I might have got the better part of that deal.

Then there were the players who carried the club's name to the far-flung corners of the rugby world. I can recall the day in 1971 when Mick Hipwell was called into the Lions squad to tour New Zealand.

I was also playing the day former Ireland scrum-half Brendan Sherry donned the Terenure colours for the last time. Gerry Tormey wore the green of Ireland in South Africa but never got capped, whilst wing Paul Haycock, whose son is now a referee, stared down a mighty England team and David Corkery, Kevin Flynn and Ciaran Clarke represented Ireland when they were with the club. Niall Hogan captained every team on which he played, including Ireland, and has been equally successful in his medical career.

Then there is Girvan 'Mad Dog' (he was given this title because he was one of the nicest, gentlest people you could meet) Dempsey, who has represented Terenure, Leinster and Ireland with great distinction and who has been a fantastic ambassador. For a good deal of his career, I was able to witness his talent from close range, and a particularly fond memory is the try he scored against England at Twickenham to guarantee a Triple Crown in 2004, a first since 1985.

Terenure has produced many other fine footballers – including Paul Hennebry, Michael Costello, 'Ponty Boots', Peter Walsh, Matt D'Arcy and John O'Brien – who, with the rub of the green, might have made the national team.

Of course everything wasn't rosy in the garden at the club all the time, and I sometimes overstepped the mark. Two occasions spring to mind. The first involved a tour to Wales when our travelling party was divided into two groups, each with their own hotel. After the match, I fell in with a crowd of hardened drinkers, trying to punch well above my weight in alcohol terms. I soldiered on manfully trying to keep up, but then whiskey was produced with disastrous consequences for yours truly. I ended up in the wrong room, in the wrong hotel with the quietest member of the touring party. The specifics of the havoc I wreaked escape me – selective amnesia – but the following morning, the manager of the hotel was waiting for me at the foot of the stairs with a sizeable bill in hand. I didn't have the money to pay for the damage to the room and it was only the intervention of the club to settle the account that ensured I could leave with everyone else. Back at the club, I was brought before the committee and they pointed out the error of my ways. I was grateful that I was only given a dressing down.

My second transgression occurred when I was acting as a touch judge. A fight broke out and I lost it, ran onto the pitch and attempted to strike an opposition player with my flag. The referee ordered me to surrender 'the weapon' and sent me packing. My actions necessitated an appearance at the Leinster branch offices where I had to stand before the disciplinary committee. I was banned from the sideline for a year.

Drink might lead some people astray but it's also the company you keep. One evening after a match in Lakelands, several of us consumed a little too much Liffey water and someone, not me, came up with the bright idea that it would be funny for me to bury my boots in the in-goal area. I was happy to go with the flow, in every respect, and on looking in my gear bag later that week wondered where I'd put my boots. It took a little bit of time before the exploits of the previous Saturday night all came back in glorious Technicolor. I had to go and buy myself another pair and it cost me £30. It was an expensive bit of devilment (and all Ponty Boots' fault). I've occasionally thought of going back with a metal detector to see if I can locate the old pair. To the best of my knowledge, they are still there.

Off-field shenanigans didn't always end in calamity and they have given me some fantastic memories. There was probably a great deal of drink taken when a group of us decided to put on a Demis Roussos tribute. The Bear played the main man and Marty Party, me, Denis Doyle and Mr Massey acted as the backing singers. Benny Doyle was our art director, some of the wives and girlfriends provided the costumes and we got down to rehearsing the show, which would contain other acts. On the night in question, we arrived early to imbibe some Dutch courage, pints for most of us; but the Bear and Massey took to a bottle of Bacardi. We hit the stage about 9 p.m. and mimed our way through six songs. It went down superbly in the packed hall of members and friends. Looking back, that was the rock on which we perished because a few weeks later – following a drinking session in the Sisters pub and at my instigation that we could raise more funds for the club by putting on a Maureen Potter sketch – we reclaimed our inner thespian. The club hall would again provide the backdrop.

I went to source the script from Peadar Burke's famous theatre shop. The next task was to sell the idea to the cast and, having accomplished this, we set about rehearsing. I'd love to have a video of those rehearsals. We spent most of the time in a heap, laughing.

The Bear reprised Maureen Potter's role as the mother, I played her son Christy while Marty Party was the butcher. He even got his hands on an old till to further authenticate his part. The scene was set in Moore Street and revolved around buying a chicken on Christmas Eve. Benny was once again the director.

The first inkling of trouble on the night of the show was when I realised that the boys were getting seriously stuck into the alcohol. The witching hour arrived and we were very much the worse for wear. Benny got us on stage but not in the rehearsed order. In fumbling around for our microphones, we kept bumping into one another.

The audience thought this hilarious and the noise was deafening. We had lost the plot, literally, when one of the lads decided to leave the stage because he needed the toilet. I don't think he ever came back. We started to speak our lines but not in order. Denis concluded that the mic system had been switched off but it hardly mattered because we couldn't hear anything with the laughter. We staggered off the stage and were back in the changing room when I heard the Bear's voice. He was still out there, on his own, performing his lines, the sketch still swirling around in his head. We ran to rescue him.

For some reason known only to the intelligentsia in the club, I was once asked to judge a ladies' 'best pair of shoes competition', at a particular lunch prior to a league match – which one escapes me, but it was some time in the early 2000s. I regarded it as a poisoned chalice on the basis that there were about 150 entrants and there could be only one winner so there were going to be 149 disappointed ladies, who were not going to be too enamoured with the judge. Now Dixie would have been a much better choice to adjudicate but there was no way that they were letting me off the hook. I decided to play the odds a little by extending the number of prizes to three – first, second and third. It gave me a little more wriggle room and meant that there were only 147 ladies who could question my fashion sense.

I don't know how Dixie has put up with me for all these years. She's not sure either. I'd be lost without her. She is my best friend, my soul-mate and someone who understands me and my ways. I am happiest when she is beside me.

How we first met is actually two stories rolled into one. I shared a two-roomed apartment with the Bear in Ranelagh. A week after moving in, the Bear decided that he would move his bed out into the kitchen area. He took the curtains too, creating a draped effect over the bed – think sheikh's boudoir in a Bedouin tent, although that sounds a little too exotic. The Bear's decision to reposition his sleeping quarters made access to the cooker quite tricky. It was just as well we never used the appliance. This was a man who when faced with a hangover used to lie on the floor and put his head in the fridge.

One particular Good Friday, Marty Party and Benny Doyle called in offering the prospect of a game of cards in the flat. The game was called Slippery Sam but I can no longer remember how to play it. I won the money, a rarer occurrence than a sighting of Halley's Comet, and, as Marty was heading to a car rally in Killarney, I used my winnings and we all went along with him.

We left straight away, the Bear and I, in his gleaming MGB GT. I was given map-reading responsibilities. You learn a lot of things as you journey through life – I've learned that I'm not cut out for orienteering. We ended up in a traffic jam on Patrick Street in Cork.

The Bear cursed me out of it, but he must share partial responsibility because he was driving the car and might have paid attention to the odd signpost. Extricating ourselves from the traffic, we covered the last sixty miles without further misadventure and managed to find the cottage that had been rented for the occasion. The old lady who owned it lived next door. The cottage slept four and there were ten of us with close to the same number of cars outside. When she used to ask how many of us were staying, we'd reply, 'Just the four of us.'

'How come there are so many cars?'

'Ah they're just visitors.'

She might not have believed us, but she turned a blind eye to the comings and goings.

Marty knew a girl called Maureen Shudel – he might have been going out with her – who was on holiday with a bunch of her friends and he'd arranged to meet her in the Three Lakes Hotel in Killarney. One of the bunch was Dixie from Dublin's Liberties. A couple of weeks after returning to Dublin, I invited Dixie for tea in the apartment. The Bear was still in possession of the kitchen and I had to borrow cups, saucers and side-plates. I went to the shop and got four slices of ham, a couple of tomatoes, a loaf of bread and half a pound of Kerrygold butter. I took down Shay's soft furnishings and moved his bed. Dixie never turned up.

I wasn't put off, though, and was relentless in my pursuit and she eventually gave in. We hooked up again a couple of weeks later. The rest as they say is a mystery.

Terenure RFC has been very good to both myself and Dixie, and it's not overstating our feelings to describe it as a home from home. I have been there man and boy as the expression goes and so I was rather overwhelmed recently when the committee approached me and asked me to become junior vice-president. Imagine having me as president of anything, let alone Terenure. As Groucho Marx once said, 'I wouldn't want to be a member of a club that would have me as a member.' It is a massive honour and I'll do my best to live up to their expectations and not down to my shortcomings. I've spoken a few times at dinners and been honoured to do so but to be recognised in that fashion is very humbling.

In May 2011, a group of like-minded people got together to

create a long-term pathway that they wanted the club to take. It's called 'Terenure 2020'. The primary goal is the improvement of the structure of the rugby club but the idea behind the project is the creation of a club that the community at large can be proud of and one of which people want to be a part. So far, seventy volunteers have committed around 10,000 hours, which equates to 250 weeks of work or what a paid full-time staff of six people might manage. The core group continues to try and deliver on the outstanding support they have received in helping to provide direction.

At one of those meetings, I was asked to equate Terenure to a car and I chose a Lamborghini. It wouldn't have been typical of the offerings. When I was asked why, I told the story about Ferruccio Lamborghini, whose company originally made tractors, and very fine ones by all accounts. But he had a weakness for sports cars and bought his fair share of Maseratis, Alfa Romeos, Lancias, Mercedes Benz and Ferraris. One day, a clutch broke on one of his Ferraris and he discovered that it was the same clutch that he used on his tractors. The story goes that he went to Enzo Ferrari and asked for a better replacement. Ferrari responded by pointing out that Lamborghini only built tractors and what would he know about sports cars. The Lamborghini motor car was born soon after. Ferruccio took the perceived snub and turned it into a positive; he refused to be cowed by his peers. I believe that Terenure rugby club is doing, and has done, an excellent job since its foundation but there is no upper ceiling to what the club can achieve. A club is limited only by ambition or drive and Terenure has plenty of both.

I look forward in my year as president of Terenure College to playing a part and giving something back to a club that has shaped my life on and off the pitch, enriching it in equal measures. The ledger will always show that Terenure College RFC, just like the school before it, gave me far more than I could ever repay, even if I lived to be 200, but that won't stop me trying to chip away and make inroads into the debt.

MIKEY JORDAN
School friend

I've known Rala since we were eight years of age and sat beside each other at school. He was a bit of a pet as far as the teachers were concerned, and was meticulous even then – if we had to draw a map of the world, he'd come in with a colour-coded version to demonstrate, say, main crops from different countries. He took his rugby seriously and was always well turned out with his boots polished.

As a person, he'd have time for everybody. If Rala agreed to meet you at 3 p.m. in Grafton Street, he'd leave his house in Arnott Street at 1 p.m. on the basis that he'd bump into people he knew. It meant that if someone asked him to go for a cup of coffee, he'd always make time. He's never late.

I remember when he started with Colet Products, his first day involved visiting a host of pharmacies in Cork city. He didn't know his way around, so I volunteered to go with him. We arrived at the first stop at about 8.50 a.m., just as the girl pulled up the shutters. On my suggestion, he waited several minutes to allow her to prepare to open the shop. He spent twenty minutes inside and emerged with his first order: six toothbrushes.

I said to him, 'But, Rala, they come in packets of twelve.'

He replied, 'She only wanted six.'

That's him to a tee. He never forced people to do something they didn't want. The following month, the shop took two dozen toothbrushes, and the month after, four dozen. He was subsequently voted Salesman of the Year during his time with Colet.

He told me a story about the time he promoted a library

amongst the Ireland players where they'd each bring a book and he'd assemble them on a window ledge in his room. On one particular occasion, the door to his room opened at 4 a.m. and a player, who obviously couldn't sleep, tiptoed across to get a book.

Just as the player was gently closing the door, Rala said, 'Geordie [Murphy], don't forget to sign out the book.'

Chapter 2

**'Have patience. All things are
difficult before they become easy.'**

I was standing at the bar in Terenure RFC downing a blonde with a black dress, when I was interrupted by the arrival of two club stalwarts, Paul Joyce and Barry Coleman. They had been charged with taking over the running of the first XV and were planning their backroom team for the 1983–1984 season. The previous year, Niall Williamson, known as 'Bleach' because of his hair colour, had been captain while Greg Ward had acted as the bagman for the club. I was still slobbering into my pint of Guinness as they explained my role in the new set-up. They thought I would make a good bagman. I had no real concept of what the position entailed but it didn't take much to persuade me to accept the invitation.

On Paul's advice I sought out 'Rainbow', Jimmy Smyth – father of Peter – who was bagman to the Blackrock College club and Leinster senior teams at that time. He was a great help in advising me on my new vocation. I also spoke to Dave Gargan (Guggs) from Old Wesley RFC.

They laid out a plan for me, imparted knowledge and I have been indebted to them ever since. Little did I know that what started as a part-time venture would turn into a career that has enabled me to travel the world with the national team and the Lions, occupying a very privileged seat.

In any job, you must learn from your peers, either through observation or consultation, and that's what I did. As I criss-crossed Ireland for ten years, I was the benefactor of many a kindness from other bagmen.

One thing that I realised quite early on was the value of making a list. I still write it out by hand, although it's expanded quite a bit from the brief notes I jotted down back then.

Dixie's mum, Mrs Roche, had a fruit and vegetable shop in Meath Street – trading since before 1913 – which is still run by her son Jack, and she provided me with the most magnificent basket of fruit, containing whatever was in season. The players didn't know they were born. I'd nip down on a Saturday morning to collect it. Over the course of the next decade, the club's playing fortunes ebbed and flowed. I remember the day we were relegated from Division One. We lost to Blackrock at Stradbrook. Niall Woods scored a brilliant try for our hosts and Terenure laid siege to the

Blackrock line in the dying minutes of the game but could not find salvation by scoring the points they so desperately needed.

T.P. Morrissey, a Terenure man, was responsible for me broadening my duties as a bagman. The Leinster under-20 team were looking for someone to fill the role and I was recommended. In the squad at the time were Crow (Niall Woods), Munch (Shane Byrne), Fla (Paul Flavin), Caesar (Conor O'Shea) and Martin Ridge amongst others, who would all graduate to the Leinster senior squad. I relied heavily on the support of former Munster and Ireland wing Jimmy Bowen and Leinster and Old Wesley second row George Wallace, who were selectors at the time. They kept me travelling in the right direction.

There were many times when I surprised myself by how quickly I adapted to a situation I wasn't expecting – one game stands out, because it occurred in two locations. Leinster were due to play Munster in the curtain-raiser to the senior game at Thomond Park. I arrived at the ground about two hours before the noon kick-off and had set things up for the arrival of the players. At about 11.30 a.m., George Wallace walked in the door of the changing room, told me to sit down and not to ask any questions. I noticed that he had pulled his car up outside the entrance and the engine was still running. George swept up the backs' jerseys in one swoop of his large arms and threw them into the boot. He returned and did the same with the forwards' set, the water and the biscuits – in five minutes he had reduced my beautifully kitted-out room to an empty shell. He even scooped up my John Player Blue in his haste. George turned to me, 'Right, Rala, jump in the car. The venue has been changed to the Killing Fields [home of Young Munster] and we haven't any time to lose.'

I was breathless even though I hadn't moved a muscle since he arrived. We made it to the new venue about two minutes ahead of the players. A Munster team containing Fester (Keith Wood) kicked a late penalty to earn a draw and a share of the under-20 interprovincial series. Woody would have a profound effect on my life.

I was bagman for the club (ably assisted by my good friends Micky Lloyd, Roger and Mallarkey), the Leinster under-20s and also retained the day job for Colet Products. Dave Gargan was due to become President of Old Wesley and it was felt that he could no longer maintain his role as bagman to the senior Leinster team, one he had taken over from Jimmy Smyth. I was invited to take over the role. True to form, and being the man he is, Guggs gave me a crash course in my new responsibilities. I couldn't have done it without his assistance. Jim Glennon, Paul Dean and Willow Murray were involved in the management and many of the under-20 side who I had worked with had graduated to the senior ranks. There was a good mix of experience in the form of players like Chris Pim, Robbie Love, John 'Spud' Murphy, Neil Francis, mixed with some youth in Niall Hogan, Alan McGowan and Conor O'Shea.

There were plenty of characters including our physical therapist, the self-styled Great AK, aka Alan Kelly. He used to say to me, 'Rala, don't mind all that business about the jerseys, laces and studs, just make sure there are plenty of French fancies and strawberry tarts to go with my cup of tea.'

On one occasion during a pre-season tour, we were staying at Loughborough University in England. The boys had gone off to the amusements and Johnny O'Hagan, who had come on board the set-up, and I were left to mind the shop. We were sorting through the washing that had been returned after cleaning, and noticed that AK had some particularly expensive underwear.

There were a couple of trees outside our dormitory and I got some rope and hung his underwear on the makeshift line. There was great laughter when the bus pulled up and the boys noticed AK's CKs fluttering in the breeze.

It was during my time with the province that Victor Costello and I endured what become known as 'the plane incident'. Leinster were flying to Edinburgh to play a match and because of ice on the wing, the plane returned to Dublin. We were both petrified so on landing proceeded to drop a few brandies before re-boarding and continuing on to our destination. It's remarkable that Victor overcame his fear of flying to become a commercial pilot. You would have got long odds on that as a future career in those days.

There was a memorable trip to Saint Jean-de-Luz. The great Irish wing Alan 'Dixie' Duggan – he's why I christened my Dixie, Dixie and it made her year when she received a Christmas card from the real Dixie – was manager and there were nine players from the St Mary's College club in the squad. If two were caught talking together they were fined. We raised a tidy sum invoking that rule.

In 1994, Ireland returned from a summer tour to Australia and during that trip my name was apparently mentioned for the position going forward as bagman. Eddie Coleman, who was on the IRFU executive, rang Dixie in O'Reilly's Auction Rooms, where she works to this day, and asked her to get me to ring Gerry Murphy, who was Ireland coach at the time. I arranged to meet

Gerry a few days later in the Burlington Hotel. Walking in the door to what was ostensibly an interview situation, I was giving out to myself about not preparing properly.

Gerry was a gentleman and quickly put me at my ease. I must have been convincing enough because I was given the gig and my first match in the Irish set-up was a charity game in Mallow between an Irish President's XV and a Munster President's XV. Noel Murphy was Ireland team manager and I can still hear his perplexed tone in that lilting Cork voice as he walked into the dressing room for the first time to view my handiwork, 'You've more stuff here than I have in my shop.'

The players have also been incredibly generous to me in my role in every way conceivable. I could not have done – could not do – my job without their co-operation. One of my first instructors was Nick Popplewell (Poppy), a man of Greystones, Newcastle, Ireland and the Lions, an outstanding prop, athlete and person.

During that first Irish training camp at which we met, he sat down at dinner and patiently explained the ins and outs of life on the road with the national team. It proved an invaluable education. At the time, even though I was involved with Ireland, I knew I would not be going to the 1995 Rugby World Cup in South Africa because, in those days, the host nation provided two bagmen for each of the competing teams. On the eve of departure, I remember being numbed when the great Young Munster and Munster colossus John 'Paco' Fitzgerald failed a fitness test at Kilkenny RFC, which ended his tournament before it had begun.

Out of the blue, at the going away dinner that night, the captain Terry Kingston called me up to the top table to present me with a watch on behalf of the squad. It was only later that I discovered that Poppy was the driving force behind that presentation. His last involvement with Ireland came in the 1998 Five Nations Championship. His final cap was against France when he came on as a replacement at the Stade de France. Two weeks later, Ireland lost at home to Wales — he wasn't involved — but there was an injury issue at prop for the match against England at Twickenham on Saturday, 4 April, the final weekend of the tournament. An Irish squad of twenty-three players travelled to London with twenty-two to tog out for the game. On the eve of the match, Poppy came to me and asked what time I would be heading to the ground the following morning. I thought it was a strange question at the time but, distracted by my preparations, didn't dwell on it unduly. I told him I'd be jumping into the van at 9.30 a.m. He said he'd meet me in the lobby.

The next morning, he appeared at the appointed time, carrying his kitbag and suit carrier, the latter containing his number ones (blazer, tie, chinos, etc.). I had semi-forgotten the conversation of the previous night and asked him where he was going at that hour of the morning. I knew the team wouldn't be leaving for about another three hours or so. He told me he'd like to come with me and help prepare the changing room for the boys. I was aghast at the very notion, but he insisted. We arrived at Twickenham, unloaded the van and he carried many of the bags through the players' entrance and into the changing room. Having completed the task, he asked me what way I wanted the jerseys hung: 'Left to right, one to twenty-two,' I replied. It was about 12.30 p.m. before everything was done and Poppy just picked up his kitbag and suit carrier, slung them over a shoulder and headed for the exit.

I can't remember the exact conversation but the gist of it was he felt that it was time to go in every sense of the word – and with that he walked out the gates at Twickenham as the supporters began to arrive. No one batted an eyelid, oblivious to the circumstances. It was the last time I saw Poppy in the team environment, but it left a powerful memory of a selfless person, someone who I had the utmost respect for.

It's one of the reasons why I address the players as gentlemen at the top of their daily itineraries. I have always found that to be the case and will continue to do so until my experiences are otherwise.

I received another wonderful gesture during 1995 – one of the nicest gestures of which I have been the beneficiary, and I've been spoiled for choice in that respect during my time in rugby. Because I wasn't going to South Africa for the World Cup in an official capacity, Niall Hogan and Peter Walsh organised a collection amongst the Terenure players to raise funds to send me anyway.

They approached the IRFU about their plan and the union offered their support. I could not go in an official capacity, but the lads felt I should travel in any case. I'm not sure whether the story is apocryphal but there was a suggestion that Ireland coach Gerry Murphy was willing to share his room with the bagman.

I was thrilled on the one hand and certainly humbled by the lengths people were going to on my behalf but, on reflection, I felt it was better that I didn't travel. Everything had been booked at that juncture, and I didn't think it would be fair to be hovering around in the background. I would have been travelling a fair bit by myself. The Terenure boys insisted that I have a holiday so instead of South Africa, a group of us, including Dixie and the Bear, ended up in the Parador Hotel in the beautiful town of Nerja in Spain.

I was now bagman for Terenure, Leinster and Ireland, three extracurricular activities that I was trying to hold down alongside my day job. It was an untenable position. I decided to take a six-month sabbatical from Colet Products, something Niall Sweeney as sales manager kindly granted. I was destined never to go back to the world of the travelling salesman and the last position I held down before I became a full-time bagman was that of doorman at the Conrad Hotel in Dublin. I was dressed like Sergeant Pepper. There were several positives in that it paid well, I could walk to work and I got to meet some interesting people – Ben Dunne, Christy Hennessy, Martin Sheen and Billy Connolly spring to mind.

There was great camaraderie and craic amongst the front-of-house staff and that led to a challenge. A certain ambassador visited the hotel once a year and no one had ever managed to get a tip from him. The boys invited me to try my luck. His car pulled up and I was quickly out of the traps. Unfortunately, as I opened one door, he got out the other, thwarting my ambition.

I spent five happy months working at the Conrad but a chance encounter with long-time IRFU Treasurer John Lyons changed my circumstances once again. Rugby had officially made the transition from amateur to professional and he asked me if I would be interested in dedicating myself full-time to the union. I didn't have to think too hard or long to come up with an answer. The only downside was to have to tell Michael Governey, the general manager at the Conrad. He is someone who I have a great regard for, and he has been very good to me. Leinster were due to go to Milan about that time but I had to decline because I wanted to serve out my two weeks' notice. I felt that not to do so would be disrespectful to Mr Governey. I also gave up my bagman duties with Terenure and Leinster – Johnny O'Hagan took over with the province. Ireland was now the only team for me.

One of the first overseas tours I went on with the Irish team was the 'Lucky Man' tour to South Africa in 1998. Paddy Johns, our captain on that expedition, and his wife Kirsty are amongst my favourite people and I have been fortunate to sample their generous hospitality in Dromore on several occasions. However, whenever I visit before I can sit down and talk to them, I must observe a ritual involving their son Christopher where I am obliged to square off against him in several codes, including rugby, soccer, Gaelic football and basketball to name but a few – he will definitely play for Ireland in one of these disciplines.

Allow me to digress for a second. One gesture I have never forgotten was on the occasion of Paddy's thirty-ninth cap in Paris. Victory got away from Ireland in the end but the next morning I got a call to go to his room whereupon he presented me with his kit from the match. I was speechless. These boys earn every single one of their caps, through talent, hard work, dedication, blood, sweat and tears. I was overcome by emotion for him to give me his kit. There have only been five occasions during my time as bagman that this has been done – by Paddy, Peter Clohessy, Simon Geoghegan, Shane Horgan and Jamie Heaslip.

Paddy was part of an Ulster crew that included David Humphreys, Denis McBride and Maurice Field. Others would come and go but I established a close relationship with the boys and every now and again when talking to the likes of Tommy Bowe, Andrew Trimble, Paddy Wallace and Rory Best, I reminisce about the old days, telling stories about travelling north to visit the boys.

This would invariably lead to me being slagged, accused of not being willing to travel to meet anyone unless they had fifty caps or more.

My old pal Reggie Corrigan inadvertently allowed me to christen that tour. He was in charge of the music and chose 'Lucky Man' by The Verve as our theme song. Paddy Johns had arranged for the purchase of a huge ghetto blaster and Mike Mullins was directed to carry it round on his shoulder. Nowadays it's all iPods, but I loved that music box.

Keith Wood was on that tour. It was twelve months after the Lions had won the test series against the Springboks 2–1 and he had been a pivotal player. There are plenty of Keith Wood stories floating round, tales of derring-do on a global scale, but the one I would choose to capture his essence on a rugby pitch involves a hot, dusty day in Kimberley.

Ireland were playing Griqualand West, my old club-mate Derek Hegarty was at scrum-half – he's not the biggest and I thought he was going to be killed that day – while Woody and I sat on a pitch-side bench. Oranges rained down from the spectators every time I got up to move. During the second half, Woody started to warm up and when the crowd noticed, they bayed for blood. The Lions series had neither been forgotten nor forgiven. The first time he got his hands on the ball, not long after his introduction to the game, he headed straight for three of the local players, clustered together. He could have taken a more scenic route, but that wasn't him. I initially feared for his safety but after the collision could only marvel as the three opposition players resembled upturned skittles while Fester continued on his merry way.

He has come to my aid on many an occasion and one for which I was extremely grateful took place after an Ireland–New Zealand game at Lansdowne Road. One of my responsibilities is to bring the presentation case that holds the ties and pins that are gifted to the opposing players. On this occasion, I forgot it. Woody got up to make his speech and took responsibility for the error, apologising to All Black captain Sean Fitzpatrick and his team-mates for an oversight that had been mine.

There are numerous other examples of his thoughtfulness. In Singapore en route to the 2003 World Cup in Australia, I was mulling over the idea of getting a DVD player and some films to fill any downtime. He caught me browsing in the shop and told me that he'd look after 'my education' as he called it. Two days after we arrived in Terrigal, our base camp for the tournament, he strolled into my room, a DVD player in one hand and some films in the other.

The more tournaments and tours we played, the more I learned and the more I honed the list of things that needed to be done. By the time the Five Nations became the Six Nations, I'd got a good routine together.

So what do I do in my role as bagman?

In terms of the primary considerations, there is no difference between being bagman for Terenure or Leinster or Ireland. The jerseys are different colours but the principles are the same. Perhaps I can explain it this way. In Africa, you have the big five animals: lion, leopard, elephant, rhino and water buffalo. In my job, they correspond to the rugby balls, the water, the bibs, the cones and the tackle shields.

The regimen of what I do doesn't alter greatly, the most obvious difference occurs in preparing for a home game and the slightly more challenging circumstances when the team plays outside Ireland. People tell me I have a great job, and I certainly wouldn't argue – but I don't consider it a job. There's work involved, but I enjoy it so much that it's more like a hobby that enables me to travel the world in the company of some great players, meet wonderful people and visit fantastic places. It has provided me with tremendous joy and happiness, but many jobs resemble icebergs and what you see above the waterline is only the tip.

Below is a generic example of what I do in a week when Ireland are playing a test match at home.

SUNDAY BEFORE A SATURDAY MATCH

I pitch up to the team hotel – Carton House – on the Saturday before a test match and the first thing I do is lay out the kit, including clean, fresh training attire (three sets because the players wear one at training, another will require laundering and there is always a spare kit), in the corridor outside my hotel room for collection by the players. I would then start preparing for the training session the next day, cleaning, washing and pumping up the balls for the kicking coach's inspection. I get him to test the pressure.

The players would have their main kitbag with them. I might have one or two in the van from the last camp belonging to players who were flying in and they'd go in the corridor too. That evening I would assist Ger Carmody (Ireland logistics manager) in writing up the itinerary for the next day and getting it signed off by the coach.

When that's done, that A3-sized schedule has to be delivered on the double to every room, players and management, and also the medical and video analysis rooms. It provides the detail to the schedule for the next day, outlining what the players will be doing, where they should be and the correct training kit to wear in terms of colour coding.

Medics and coaches always wear a different colour to the players so they are easily identifiable.

Then I would see Paul, Brian or Arthur from the hotel. I would list our requirements for the next day and the timings involved relating to the hot drinks for the training session like tea, coffee, soup and drinking chocolate. Ruth, the IRFU nutritionist, would have an input into that as she decides on bars and supplement drinks too.

Ger Carmody always tries to give me a bigger than normal room, sometimes two, because it has to house so much stuff. I would pick a corner of the room to devote to pre-preparing match items, six days before a game. I name it after the team we are playing. There'd be oodles of spares – shorts, ties, shoes, belts, cuff-links, jocks, socks – a stud box with three or four different sizes of studs, pliers, laces and spare gum shields. You try and divide things into sections: pre-match and post-match. There'd be twenty-four assorted drinking vessels (chin strap and orthodox) that are cleaned by a machine in the hotel.

I always feel an air of excitement on 'assembly evening' when the players arrive, it's a great time to catch up and listen to the latest yarns. Some are in by six o'clock, some seven, others closer to the deadline (10 p.m.). Assembly night is always 'latish' for me, especially if there are extra chaps coming in, particularly first timers or novices. I'd quietly keep an eye on them and try and help them along, until they've had a chance to settle in after a day or two.

MONDAY

For a training session at 10 a.m., I would be at the pitch by 9 a.m.

My van, which I pick up from the Aviva Stadium on the Saturday, resembles a mini-warehouse. It contains twenty tackle shields, a one-man scrum machine, Mervyn's (Murphy, video analyst) ladder, an ice bucket, water, Powerade, a supplement box, a bag of spare training kit (all colours in case someone is wearing the wrong one), jerseys, shorts and socks, a fruit basket (ripe bananas, mandarin oranges and grapes), eighteen body suits, bibs, six spare subs' coats in case players are standing around or sometimes the management use them when it's freezing, a baby stud box, Rala's emergency box which has another selection of studs, kicking tees, black markers, mouth wash (a favourite of Keith Earls), hand wax (for Jamie Heaslip), banana cake (for Les Kiss), spare whistles, utility poles and white and coloured umbrellas for the management.

Then there is the music, a very important consideration. I have a running battle with Jamie Heaslip and Cian Healy about the music. I would be putting on the Fureys and he'd be trying to put on some techno noise. We play Christy Moore a lot. I love all kinds of music, particularly from the sixties. No one will ever top The Beatles! It'd be blaring out from the van. I would have a few sweets hidden but Rory Best seems to be able to sniff them out at a hundred paces, even when I hide them down the back of a seat in the van. Just as the training is about to start, the music goes off and doesn't go on again until it has finished.

The weather is a big factor in what I can do in terms of putting things out on the pitch. There's no point in leaving tackle suits out if it is lashing rain. I would put out the cones, rugby balls, a soccer ball, a few hurleys, shields, the ladder and get the table – it must have a white linen tablecloth – with the drinks, fruit, tea, coffee, soup, drinking chocolate, cups, saucers, milk and spoons. The tablecloth might be considered inconsequential in the greater scheme of things but to me it is about standards. Irrespective of the number of tables, there will be a cloth for each one. I try and prepare for all eventualities. I'm there to assist the captain and the management team in whatever capacity I can. The boys will arrive at 9.55 a.m. The music goes off at ten. I prepare drinks for the masseurs, Dave Revins and Willie Bennett, because they run on with them when required during the session. As soon as the session finishes – they generally last about an hour and a half – I start the packing up and immediately begin preparing for the next one.

It's back to the hotel to ensure the players' laundry is ready for collection at 2 p.m. In days gone by, there was a code known to a few players. It started with Ronan O'Gara. He would breeze up to me and ask if he'd missed the laundry run. I would tell him to leave it on my bed and that I would 'send it down the yellow brick road'. I passed on that code to a few players by which they could get their laundry in after the deadline. Donncha O'Callaghan cracked it. Brian O'Driscoll was in on it too. I have now changed the reference to the West Quarter Village (Inishbofin) but ROG struggled to remember that one.

I'd oversee the laundry process and make sure it's there for Paul Kershaw to collect, so that we get it back the next day. After lunch, there'd be bits and pieces to be done. I work very closely with Declan Meade, Tony, John and Paddy in the IRFU warehouse in Naas. There would be gear going back and forth as guys change sizes. You always get a bit of that no matter what contingencies you might have put in place. The players must try on everything when they arrive into a camp because there are generally minor fluctuations in terms of sizing.

There'd be time for a mid-afternoon cappuccino with Ger Carmody. There are many traditions that I have enjoyed through the years and one is the Tea Club. I have had to smuggle Barry's Tea all around the world (usually in a sock) as no other brand was acceptable. John Hayes was chairman. He would make contact during the day and decide on a time for us all to meet that night. I would have all the bits ready, kettle, teapot, cups, saucers, spoons, side-plates, knives, sugar and full-fat milk, but he'd make the tea and serve you. As soon as he walked in the door, my job was finished and he took over. Denis Hickie's mum used to send in fruitcake every now and again, so too Eoin Toolan's wife. Gordon D'Arcy drinks chamomile tea while Rory Best, Shane Horgan, Shane Jennings and Denis Leamy were other participants in the ritual. They'd be slagging each other. Then you had to have everything ready for the next evening, but the Bull would normally give you a bit of a warning. When John Hayes retired, that was the end of the Tea Club. I miss John big time, so do all the lads.

One of my last jobs each day is to draw up the itinerary with the following day's schedule, get it signed off by the head coach, print it out and shove it under doors. I'd have also cleaned the balls and got the kicking coach to check them and they'd be back out in the van.

TUESDAY

Tuesday is virtually a carbon copy of Monday in terms of the training, just a little bit sharper because it is media day and there are interviews to be done.

All the while, I'd be adding to the match corner in my room. The match balls, of which there are ten, are introduced at training and they have to be cleaned and marked.

Throughout the week the players are involved in the unholy trinity of darts, table tennis and pool. I tend to let the players off so, if I do play, I get knocked out in the first round of everything. The team room would also contain easy armchairs, a snack table and a fridge. This is where the boys chat, play games and chill out. They'd also watch movies. The preference is to have everything in one room instead of it being split up. I remember the great battles in the board game Risk when we were based in the Glenview Hotel. The Ulster boys were dab hands and premier strategists, people like Paddy Johns, Justin Fitzpatrick, David Humphreys, Tyrone Howe, Ross Nesdale, Kevin Maggs and Kieron Dawson. Nowadays it's poker, Texas Hold 'Em, while all the time retaining the old reliable, Scrabble.

The team room is not a place I hang out in that often. It's the players' den. The medical area would be close by, where strappings and massages are given. Analysts Mervyn Murphy and Eoin Toolan set up their equipment as near as possible to this cocoon of activity. Theirs is usually a pretty quiet area as individual players do their homework ahead of the matches. It's not always possible to incorporate everything in one or two big rooms – for example, the Shelbourne Hotel has a series of smaller rooms.

Declan Meade, who until he retired in August 2013 was in charge of the IRFU warehouses in Naas, would send on the gift cases and the Yellow Box, which contains three flags and a CD of 'Ireland's Call'. You don't need flags in the Aviva Stadium because they are already there but if you were going somewhere like Tonga, you'd give them to the home union. I always have them available. I'd put them in the match corner of my room along with the captain's post-match presentation gifts, such as pins and ties. You are assembling this as you go along.

WEDNESDAY

Wednesday is what the players and management call a 'down day'. Mine would start off assisting the kicking coach with the kickers – Jonathan Sexton, Ian Madigan, Rob Kearney and Fergus McFadden – there are normally four or five players (of course before he retired ROG would have been there, I've great memories of time spent with him). They either do the kicking at Carton House or they might all head off in a people carrier to the Aviva.

I would have to make sure the balls were ready. I'd pack drinks and, if the weather is bad, their showering gear and towels. I'd also bring a few energy bars and a soccer ball – they warm up with the latter. If it is at the Aviva, I might bring some additional match-day stuff and leave it there. The reason I go to the practice is to kick the balls back to the players and to look after the drinks. Practice takes two hours and on our return there is a great tradition, 'the kickers' lunch'. There are usually chips involved.

Wednesday gives me a great chance to work on stuff. I might have gear coming in from the warehouse or if we were playing away, I'd get most of the packing done. I usually go to the cinema on Wednesday evening or go out with the management for dinner. I also try and catch up on sleep. The door to my room is always open, but that's one day when it might be closed for an hour or two.

On the issue of sleep, I have to be very careful not to nod off in the cinema because strange things happen. I have woken up soaking wet, I have woken up covered in popcorn and, on one occasion, I woke to find that I had been left behind. Surprisingly, the lads are never able to help me with my enquiries about what happened when I was asleep.

THURSDAY

Every bagman needs to think ahead, this is especially true on the Thursday before a test match – the day is all about preparation. We train and move hotels. I have to do all the things I'd do on other training days, and then load the van with all the gear from my room and set up shop again in another hotel. At the moment, we move between Carton House and the Shelbourne. One of my little perks at the Shelbourne is being greeted by Paul and Denise as I pull up in my van outside the front door of the hotel, then a member of the staff, though usually it's Denise, comes along, holding a silver salver on which there is a cappuccino and a biscuit. It's something of a tradition now.

The laafterundry arrangements are slightly more complex in that having been collected from one hotel it has to be dropped to another. I simply could not do my job without the help and co-operation of so many people in the IRFU offices, the warehouse, various hotel staff, the lads in the backroom team, the ladies in team services and so many others too numerous to mention. You definitely appreciate you're a small cog in a big wheel. Ger Carmody is brilliant. I would be lost without him.

Various things start to come in for the match. On Thursdays, I would plan to leave several items like shields, balls and cones in the stadium to save me bringing them on match day.

Everything is further complicated if we are travelling to an away match because of air travel, in most cases. The IRFU staff under instruction from Ger would have laid down our requirements and would have visited the hotel in advance, checking bedrooms, team rooms and medical rooms. That would all be in place and I would be given a couple of names to liaise with before we left. You are always slightly apprehensive rocking up to a hotel because no matter what you have been promised, it doesn't always work out. I have been with duty managers, gone through everything that we need on a daily, even hourly, basis for our time in the hotel, and then after spending a couple of hours detailing our requirements with them, they tell me they're off duty for the next three days. Experience has taught me that the second question I now ask after the person's name is, 'When are you off?'

A lot of stuff gets lost in translation. That's why I go through a list with the person, so they know what I need in the lobby at 8 a.m. the following day. Generally, it's forty towels, shampoos, basket of fruit, hot chocolate, coffee, tea, tables. I always build in some leeway. I mightn't be leaving until 9.30 a.m. but I want to see it at 8 a.m. It's a question of establishing a relationship with the staff.

FRIDAY

I get to the stadium about an hour before the players for the Captain's Run, which lasts about half an hour. I'll start getting the changing room ready for the next day and then spend time with the kicking coach and the kickers. When Gary O'Driscoll was the doc, there was a tradition that he and his team would stay behind to kick balls back, but these days I do it. The players bring a rucksack with a change of clothes, keeping what we call the stadium bags for match days.

It's one of my favourite times, the eve of match. The jerseys arrive from Andrew Ellis, and Declan Meade will send in the match shorts and socks. In my spare room, I hang up the match jerseys, the starting set (one to twenty-three), take out the creases and put them on a rail. I put out the shorts and socks (this is in the afternoon) on a bed, neatly. It gets wrecked thereafter. I have a stud-box, laces, black markers, polish, cloths and brushes laid out and would have washed the balls again.

When Ireland are playing at home, I leave two match balls in the stadium after the Captain's Run for the opposing team. I get them back on match day. We have ten match balls and they have to be prepared for a final time. I always pack spares – three or four or more balls, spare shorts and spare socks, spare everything. The players come and collect their match shorts and socks on a Friday night, but the real objective for some is to turn my room upside down.

Donncha O'Callaghan is always first and Brian O'Driscoll the last to pop in. On the itinerary it reads: 'Gentlemen, please collect match shorts and socks at your leisure post dinner.'

I'd be in my room until about 11 p.m. and then crack on with packing for the following morning.

SATURDAY

By 8 a.m. on match day, the jersey rail is in the hotel lobby under guard and the van is packed ready to go. I have a checklist so I'm not wondering if I packed things like the walkie-talkie headsets and chargers required by the coaches and management to communicate from gantry to pitch. After an early breakfast, in the Saddle Room of the Shelbourne, I get to the Aviva at 8.30 a.m. It may be a 3 p.m. kick-off, but I don't like rushing. I prefer to allow scope to chat to people.

I bring a few sandwiches for what I call the A team in Lansdowne – Paddy, Majella, Jimmy and Dessie. They not only help me unload but know where to put the stuff. I have a set routine. The jerseys go up first along with the players' tops for the anthems and from there it centres on how I like to go about things.

Some players, ROG and Donncha O'Callaghan spring to mind, like an extra pair of white socks under their playing socks. I put the programmes out, get the toiletries table ready in the shower area, lay out two towels per player and prepare the drinks for the side of the pitch and the ice bucket. I begin putting the stuff that's going on the pitch – cones, shields, balls, towels, emergency box – outside the door of the dressing room. I won't do that until an hour before the squad arrives.

For about sixty seconds before the players descend, the dressing room is neat and ordered, then bags are thrown down and everything gets moved around.

Utopia is when no one has to ask for anything. I have yet to get ten out of ten, mind you, I'm still striving for that.

It's often something small – I have had a few car crashes like forgetting a tie and pin box for the then New Zealand captain Sean Fitzpatrick or one day climbing on the bus and realising the footies for training were back in my room – but there's always something. The thing is to deal with it with the least amount of fuss.

The final thing I do is put a ball in the centre of the room on a cone. Then I wait outside for the bus to arrive. The boys collect their bags and we get the medical gear inside in the shortest possible time. I try to become invisible while watching everything. The players go out for the photographs and the warm-up. I keep track of the match balls. The players are on a clock. I run around, pick up bits and pieces, go into the dressing room briefly and then back outside the door – I stand close to it in case I hear my name called.

The greatest moment of the week for me is when the captain leads them out. I feel proud and privileged to have made my contribution.

I am in and out to the changing room during the game. When there's a penalty or a conversion, the players are standing still like cattle in the field and I can scan them easily, looking for tears or blood.

About ten minutes before half-time, I stroll into the changing room. I have the iced drinks and supplement drinks ready and hang the second-half jerseys in case anyone wants to change – I might have to help a player in changing a jersey as they are so tight.

From my point of view, the second half is pretty much the same as the first. When I come in after the match has finished, I take my time, unless there is a plane to catch. A bit of food comes in and then I tidy everything up.

The players have laundry bags in which they put their match kit. I take them and they are laundered and returned the next day.

I'd ring Paul in the Shelbourne and tell him to open up my room before I get there. The players know that before I left for the stadium that morning, I'd have put out spare bow-ties, belts, cuff-links, even pairs of shoes of varying sizes on a table.

I enjoy going to the post-match dinners, but I don't always make it. If we are away from home, the demands are even greater because you have to pack up all the gear ready for an early departure the following morning. There is simply no point in adding three or four hours to your night in those circumstances by attending the dinner. The workload will still be there when you get back.

SUNDAY

Time to pack up. There are two vans to be loaded because everything won't fit in one. If there's no match the following week, I'll head home – otherwise it's a case of straight down to Carton House to do it all again.

SHAY 'THE BEAR' RUANE
Terenure team-mate

Rala has time for everyone.

He has a genuine interest in people and one of the best stories by way of illustration is the time that a few of us ended up in Nerja in Spain in 1995. We bumped into a local called Manolo – I suppose you'd describe him as a harmless innocent – on the beach one day and Rala got talking to him. For the two weeks of the holiday, Manolo never left our side, no matter where we went or what time of the day it was. I half expected him to be sitting on the plane going home to Dublin. We were trying to shake him off, but Rala would invite him along wherever we went.

On another occasion, he got up to sing one of his favourite songs – 'Christmas 1915' – in Inishbofin and, out of the blue, this old fisherman started bawling crying. Now Rala can hold a tune so it wasn't his voice that had set your man off, but by the time he'd finished the song, the fisherman was a mess.

Rala was a very good player and is fanatical about his rugby, so you can understand his devastation when we lost a schools cup match to St Mary's College 5–3. He lost the ball against the head in a scrum from which they scored the game-winning try. He was inconsolable. He was very proper in the way he trained and the way he presented himself, so I'm not surprised how successful he's been as a bagman.

He's unique, considerate, funny, great company, a brilliant friend and very loyal. He's very honourable in everything he does – if you told Rala a secret, he'd take it to his grave.

Chapter 3

'Smile – one size fits all.'

In my nearly twenty years as bagman to the Ireland team, I've occasionally been asked which I considered to be the best tour. It's obviously a subjective matter and I know several players who'd disagree, but for me it had to be our visit to the Pacific Islands in 2003 – the Kingdom of Tonga followed by a quick skip across the international dateline to Samoa. The first leg of the tour involved a test match against Australia in Perth after which a number of the marquee players headed home. For the remainder of the group, there was a brief stopover in Auckland before travelling on into the wide, blue yonder, a perfect description of sky and sea.

Palm trees, sun-soaked beaches and breathtaking views of the Pacific Ocean are the obvious visual charms of the islands that make up Tonga, but my memories are of the people I encountered on that tour. They possessed a kindness of spirit that has stayed with me ever since, they had an ability to laugh and derive happiness from so many everyday things that others might consider mundane. They may not have been materially wealthy but they enriched the lives of those of us fortunate enough to spend some time in the Kingdom of Tonga. We were staying in the capital Nuku'alofa, in the International Dateline Hotel to be precise. The pace of life is best exemplified by the fact that the national speed limit is thirty kilometres per hour.

The Ireland touring party, led by head coach Eddie O'Sullivan and manager Brian O'Brien, arrived in the early hours of the morning on a flight from Auckland. It was more of an airstrip than an airport, and I remember that some of the lads who loaded our luggage onto a wooden carousel doubled up when the passports needed to be checked. The sheer volume of equipment left the rudimentary conveyor belt completely knackered by the time the squad had got through.

We weren't the only influx of visitors to Nuku'alofa. The King of Tonga's granddaughter was getting married and, depending on who you spoke to, the wedding celebrations would last between five and seven days. Many of the guests were staying at our hotel, a building that was also undergoing major reconstruction work at the time, but more of that anon.

Forewarned about the nuptials, my desire to bring the King of Tonga a special present from Ireland was to have unforeseen consequences. I'd been walking down Grafton Street before the tour, when I was struck by the idea of buying a Guinness cake I saw in the window of Bewley's. I reckoned it would last the trip, so I went in and bought one. Fast forward to Customs in Auckland airport and the 'Nothing to Declare' line. I was beginning to have doubts about the cake, because they are very strict on foodstuffs. I came up with a solution – give the cake to Alan Quinlan, although he had no idea what he was about to carry.

I hid the cake in an ice bucket and said, 'Quinny, will you bring that ice bucket through?' He said he would.

Quinny was at the top of the queue and I was at the bottom, sweating a bit, when I heard, 'Rala, you f*****!'

They had found the cake.

Quinny called me and I was hauled up in front of the customs officer.

Yer man says, 'What's that?'

I said, 'It's a cake.'

He said, 'Where did you get it?'

I said, 'I got it in Bewley's.'

He wouldn't have known Bewley's from Adam. People think you're being smart when you answer like that.

'Who is it for?' he asked.

'The king,' I said.

'The king of what?'

'The King of Tonga.'

I was pretty sure I was going to be fined but in fairness the customs officer settled for confiscating it.

My last comment to the customs officer was, 'I hope you enjoy it. It's a lovely cake. Don't let it go to waste.'

Quinny was chasing me around for about two days after that.

When I met one of the king's sons by the hotel pool one day, I told him about the cake.

Waiting for us in the airport on arrival in Tonga was Julie, who would be my liaison at the International Dateline Hotel. She was a striking looking woman – diminutive, raven-haired and with sparkling white teeth that were the centre piece of a permanently etched smile.

She asked me my name. I opted for Rala. She misheard and for the next eight days, she called me Lala. As we all bounced up and down on the road from the airport to the hotel, Julie busied herself with telling us about some of the local customs. Pigs have an exalted status on the island – it doesn't prevent the locals from eating them – and are allowed to roam free. Trying to inject some humour into the conversation, I shouted back to the lads that pigs were allowed to run amok, but the boys didn't pick up on my brilliantly witty wordplay on the Irish for a pig (*muc*). Sometimes, you feel that you are in a barren wasteland.

The International Dateline Hotel is separated from the Pacific Ocean by a narrow road and a knee-high wall that leads to the beach. Keith Wood, Brian O'Brien and myself sat and allowed an hour to pass, listening to the lapping water as much as each other. Tired, I returned to Reception only to discover that all the rooms had been allocated.

I was a little concerned because I had the following day's itineraries to compile and deliver, a task that normally took me about three hours, with a bit of fluting around thrown in. I finally finished at six the following morning and managed an hour's sleep on a medical bed in the team room. It was to prove the only air-conditioned, creepy-crawly-free haven on the premises.

As mentioned, the hotel was in the throes of being reconstructed and extended, with the work being carried out by a small army of Chinese men, all seemingly equipped with a hammer and presided over by the general manager, Miss Lee from Beijing. A negotiated settlement prevented them from working before 8 a.m. or after 10 p.m. The idea was to give the players some peace and quiet, but it didn't quite work out that way. Many a morning, we woke to the sound of drilling or the gentle tapping of a hammer. Miss Lee collared me one day and said that if any of the boys wanted to come back after the tour, she'd he happy to offer them a 30 per cent discount – there were no takers.

Now, however bad we felt we had it, the small party of Irish journalists who accompanied the tour – John O'Sullivan (*The Irish Times*), Kieran Rooney (*Irish Independent*), Michael Corcoran (RTÉ), Ciaran Cronin (*Sunday Tribune*) and photographer extraordinaire Billy Stickland (Inpho) – appeared to get the thinner end of the wedge in terms of their accommodation. The Pacific Royale Hotel sounded lovely, but the brochure must have been airbrushed to within an inch of its life. The lads had me in stitches as they recounted their experiences. Things went wrong from the off, when they were stopped for speeding en route from the airport in the courtesy Hiace van – which looked like it was from the seventies – that was sent to collect them. They were doing thirty-eight kilometres an hour. They had to get out of the van, hand over their passports and have them scrutinised in the lashing rain even though none of them was driving.

They arrived at the hotel to find beaded curtains instead of a front door, that the lady behind the desk had no record of their booking – it was 4 a.m. – and that the hotel had full occupancy because the Tongan team was staying there. They were offered the Presidential Suite en route to which they met two cockroaches coming down the stairs, obviously on their way to check out. Many of the fixtures and fittings were missing with just wires sticking out of the walls.

When they arrived at the suite, the security guard couldn't open the door with the key, so he just kicked in the flimsy bolt. Half of the room was open air. There were two double beds and two singles – now, the lads are good friends, but sharing a bed was a step too far. They returned to Reception and other rooms were found, but this necessitated kicking out two of the Tongan players to sleep on mats in a common area that doubled as a team room. When they finally got to their rooms, the chocolate-coloured nylon sheets were still moist and warm from the previous occupants.

A couple of the rooms had no mosquito nets, no hot water, no towels and one of the fourth estate had to time-share with a gecko – it was a dispassionate relationship despite the close proximity. Another of the cadre was given a room with a corrugated iron roof. It rained every night, usually between 3 a.m. and 5 a.m., torrential stuff, so the din was unbelievable.

The media almost got me in trouble with Eddie O'Sullivan. I have a soccer ball that the players use in a warm-up and the lads borrowed it. They decided to have a kick-around, while a training session was taking place in Tupou College, a boys' school just a few miles from the hotel. One particular gentleman suffered a bit of a nightmare moment, as the ball skidded off his shin and rolled twenty yards, slap bang into the middle of a backline movement. Eddie wasn't amused and offered a few suggestions about where to stick the ball.

The food in our hotel wasn't great, so I spent a fair bit of time in Friends Café on the main street – one of two streets in Nuku'alofa. On the flight to Tonga, I had met the new chef, a Canadian, who seemed preoccupied by how he was going to prepare and cook fifty pigs for the wedding feast in what was a rudimentary kitchen set-up. He confided in me at one point that he had a more reliable oven back home than the temperamental contraptions he knew were waiting for him.

On our first morning, I met the liaison officer, a doctor on the island and someone who was to prove both invaluable to me in terms of doing my job but also in offering a friendship. Nothing was too much trouble and no problem was insurmountable. I still have the image of his arrival in his old pick-up truck – T-shirt, Bermuda shorts, sandals and a beaming smile. He had studied medicine in Australia but after qualifying wanted to return home and work with his people, citing the climate, the fishing and a plot of land to grow food as an idyllic backdrop.

A knowledge of the land is prized in Tonga, as is the ability to be self-sufficient in terms of growing food. This was something I noticed at our first training session at Tupou College. We watched as children, carrying garden implements, were led by older boys along pathways that led to mini-allotments. The wooden buildings where the pupils slept were spotlessly clean as was the surrounding environment between dormitories. On one side of the training pitch were some low trees, known locally as shade trees because of their flat canopy, under which the boys and their teachers sat to watch the Ireland team train. They watched quietly, the silence occasionally punctured by a short burst of applause if an Irish player dotted down for an imaginary try.

The interruption to test-match preparations by the odd logistical problem or two didn't take a feather out of the doc. One day, the players were due in the gym at 11 a.m. and I was standing outside the hotel at ten with water, fruit, ice and towels, waiting for the bus to arrive. It never did. So the doc went home, got his truck and ferried the Irish players on the open-top flatbed. On another day, we took a boat to an island owned by a local woman and her Scottish husband – population ten – for a bit of rest and relaxation. The sight of a shipwreck, almost within touching distance of the small bar that I turned into a very pleasant home for whiling away a few hours, was a reminder of the hurricanes that occasionally sweep through the islands.

The squad trained at the Teufaiva Stadium, where the pitch caused one or two concerns. Instead of a top dressing of sand, the groundsmen had used powdered coral. The players and management spent a good forty-five minutes spread across the pitch in a line, picking up jagged pieces and putting them into boxes to try and minimise the risk of cuts and abrasions. The surface was rock hard.

The day of the test against Tonga arrived. I was at the stadium, as normal, ahead of everyone else when my pre-match regime was interrupted by raised voices. Earlier in the week, I had secured two tickets to the match for Julie but she was also trying to gain admission for nine of her friends. The entrance to the changing room was a stone's throw from the main gate where the ruckus was taking place, and my timing – I had nipped out for a lulu – could not have been worse. I was beckoned over and by some miracle managed to get them all into the ground.

My assumption that I wouldn't see them again until we were

leaving the following day was to prove some way wide of the mark. As was custom, I was out pitch-side as the players warmed up. Inclination, sixth sense, call it what you will, sent me back to the dressing room slightly early and the sight that greeted me caused palpitations – Julie and her mates were standing in the middle of the room, each clasping a bowl of fruit that they wanted to give to me and the players.

It was a lovely gesture, but by my reckoning, I had about two minutes before the players would return from their warm-up to prepare for the kick-off and I had to get Julie, her friends and the fruit out of there. Apart from the disruption to the players' mental and physical preparation, there is a fair amount of testosterone in that room when the players are on the cusp of taking the pitch for a test match.

There were two doors in the dressing room and simultaneously as one closed, having ushered the ladies and the fruit outside, the other opened. The players went through their final pre-match preparations blissfully unaware of my panic. The match was a hard-fought, physical encounter, which Ireland won 40–19.

Leaving Tonga was a wrench in terms of the people rather than the facilities. A tour that had started with a test match against Australia in the Subiaco Oval in Perth was set to conclude in Samoa. We flew out the morning after the Tonga test match and had to cross the international dateline.

In 2011, Samoa brought forward their calendar by a day, transferring to the same time zone as Tonga for economic and tourist reasons. They went straight from Thursday, 29 December to Saturday, 31 December – having been the last place in the world to see the sunset, Samoa is now the first to welcome sunrise.

At the time of the 2003 tour, Samoa was still on the western side of the international dateline and provided us with the slightly surreal adventure of experiencing Tuesday, 17 June twice. It happened to be RTÉ radio commentator Michael Corcoran's birthday but, despite his protestations, I don't think his cohorts in the small media party were interested in buying him a birthday drink two nights running.

It was my second time in Samoa, I'd been there in 1997 when the then Ireland coach Brian Ashton had led a development squad to New Zealand and Samoa. Gary Halpin had been captain and the team endured a tough time, having been thumped the length and breadth of the north island of New Zealand before heading on to Samoa where they lost the only test of the tour. I had only been bagman for a little over two years and still had much to learn. I remember the wall of heat when we got off the plane in Apia. The temperature was to prove a formidable handicap to everyone in the party for varying reasons.

In 1997, we'd stayed in a motel about two miles from the airport. A lady called Angelique ran the business on behalf of her father, a member of the local parliament. On arrival we encountered Penny, a Fa'afafine (a group of boys in Samoan society who are raised as girls). Penny was great craic, keeping us all in good spirits and among her duties was to ensure that I had 100 litres of water in my room at all times. It wasn't for my personal consumption — the players would come and take whatever they required.

Penny used to ring on the hour, every hour. 'Rala. How many bottles have you left?'

I used to tell white lies because it was impossible to know. The food was an issue. None of the players were that keen. Meals were served outdoors much to the delight of the squadrons of flying insects. There was a fine line between getting some food in your mouth without letting something else fly in.

It was most obvious one day when only myself and Denise Fanagan, our physiotherapist, arrived for lunch. Eventually, the chef stuck his head through a bamboo curtain demanding to know where everyone else was – he was pretty angry so we decided to make our escape down the back stairs, picking our way past some evil-looking and rather large creepy-crawlies. Things gradually improved – not the food, though – and the preparations for the match gathered pace.

We were due to train in a school up in the hills and on the day in question we woke to the sound of rain cascading down. The din and volume resembled the waterfall at Powerscourt. We squeezed into a little bus with our equipment shoe-horned into an attached trailer. A village elder greeted us on arrival and our hosts were dressed in their traditional attire – it was a very colourful sight.

We were taken to a large thatched building with no walls that ran parallel to the pitch. The squad sat down on benches, surrounded on one side by children and on the other by teachers and some dignitaries from the local village. The speeches began. After half an hour, Brian Ashton turned to me and whispered, 'Rala, is this ever going to end?'

Everything had to be translated. Another half hour went by with no end in sight. At one point, proceedings were interrupted when there was a crash on a small road that ran parallel to the far side of the pitch. This apparently was a very rare occurrence so all the Samoans ran across to see what happens when an ox collides with a donkey!

It started to rain heavily. I had set up a table outside with thirty bottles of water and a couple of baskets of fruit. Each player had his own bottle with his name on it but the ink had started to run in the rain. The doc had told me that infections could be transferred easily by mouth, especially if a player had a cold, which is why each player had his own bottle. There wasn't a Rolls Royce drinking vessel with your name and email address on it in those days.

Just shy of two hours after we had first sat down, the children finished by singing some songs and the formal welcome culminated with the presentation of a pig to the Irish visitors, which we had to take back to the hotel on the coach – it would have been rude not to.

In keeping with the general theme of chaos, it was then that I realised I had no cones, or at least I couldn't find them. Mr Ashton wasn't in great form, so I didn't want to compound his unhappiness. They say that necessity is the mother of invention and we all have to be adaptable and improvise from time to time.

I didn't have an English speaker to hand and my Samoan was limited to about five words. I spotted some coconut trees. Through an elaborate game of charades, I managed to get one of the Samoans to shimmy up a tree and get me a handful of coconuts. I then got him to cut them in half with a machete and I used them as cones. I found the real ones later on during the session.

When training finished, the players asked me where the showers were and for the second time that day, I realised I had erred – I'd forgotten to ask when we arrived. I scurried over to one of the village elders and through an interpreter was directed to a field on the far side of the pitch. There was a big hole in the ground, filled with water, and that served as the shower.

The temperature on match day had blast-furnace intensity. I headed to the ground early complete with five iceboxes – one filled with facecloths, three with water and the fifth a Gatorade mix. By the time I got to the Apia Park Stadium all the ice had melted. The dressing room resembled a sauna. It contained a fan stuck up on the high ceiling that managed to circumnavigate the room about once every five minutes. It went so slowly there were cobwebs on it. I had to go outside every now and again to dream of Atlantic breezes. Whilst I was outside, I looked up into the stand and saw a huge Samoan in national dress and missing most of his teeth using me for a gilly to amuse his mates. I learned afterwards that he'd spent three days drinking on his way down from the hills to the match. I didn't care about becoming the butt of his joke. I just laughed away, as he paraded up and down the stand, pointing to my skin. I was soon to have more pressing problems.

The container of Gatorade, which I had placed in the corner of the room, had attracted some ants. What started as a few stragglers swelled considerably, resembling Roman legions marching in formation. By the time the players arrived, I was in danger of being overwhelmed.

Whilst trying to help the boys in their preparations, my rear-guard action against the ants was reaching a crisis point. Distracted by fixing a stud on a boot, I was alerted by the West Country twang of Kevin Maggs to the fact that the little red devils had formed a film over the top of the Gatorade. I counted to a hundred, walked across to the icebox and with the sleeve of my top wiped away an entire colony. At that point, I had emphatically lost the ice war too and all that was left was warm water.

I thought things couldn't get any worse but a temporary stand collapsed during the game much to the amusement of the local supporters (thankfully no one was hurt) and then an intercept try facilitated a Samoan victory. It was a very tough tour. I had reason to be very grateful to our manager, Pa Whelan, without whose help and direction I wouldn't have survived.

My second trip to Samoa in 2003 had a much happier outcome. For a start, we got to stay in the world famous Aggie Grey's Hotel, arguably the most celebrated lodgings in the South Pacific. Aggie was born to an English chemist, William Grey, and Pele, a local chieftain's daughter. During the Second World War, Aggie traded with the GIs and the proceeds enabled her to build the hotel. The main house is beautifully ornate and surrounded by chalets which are named after some of the cast from the film *Mutiny on the Bounty*, as they stayed there during filming. I can't remember who stayed in the Marlon Brando cabin. The rooms had the most amazing air-conditioning system, ice cold, and were a much sought-after refuge from the 100-degree heat.

Match day arrived, our sixth of the tour, and I waited at the back of the hotel for a Man Friday to help me load up the gear. The fella duly arrived at the appointed time, but he was dressed like a James Bond wannabe. I asked him about his clobber and he told me he had been invited to the post-match dinner. We made an incongruous pair as I looked like a Parisian pickpocket. As the day progressed, though, it became obvious that there was no fear of my erstwhile helper getting sweaty – 007 looked on whilst I carried out my duties.

My memory of the match was one of admiration for how the players handled the extreme heat, particularly the redheads Anthony Horgan and Jonathan Bell.

Towards the end, Hoggy had to come off with sunstroke, and I was told to keep an eye on him. I brought him over to the shade underneath the stand. He was in a bit of a state. He managed to remove, with assistance, his jersey, socks and boots and replace them with a cold towel on the back of his neck and another on his back. It then dawned on me that he was sitting in the same seat that I had sat in six years previously while being pilloried by the Samoan with no teeth.

Ireland won convincingly, a fantastic achievement given the conditions. Players lost between half a stone and a stone (in one or two cases) in weight during the game and some didn't feel well enough to attend the post-match banquet.

It was definitely time to go home.

KEITH WOOD
Hooker for Ireland (1994–2003) and the Lions (1997, 2001)

I remember travelling for what seemed like a lifetime to get to the International Dateline Hotel in Tonga. It was a mess, a building site only partially renovated when we rocked up. I was recovering from serious surgery and was on the tour in an ambassadorial rather than playing role.

Rala rang me the morning after we arrived and asked me to do him a favour and drop down to his room at 2.30 that afternoon. I thought it a strange request because of its formality with a little hint of secrecy. This, after all, was a man I saw about thirty times a day on tour.

When I walked into his room, Rala walked over to a heavy duty, metallic container and produced this bubble-wrapped package, mummified in insulation tape. He gave it to me and told me to open it. When I finally managed to prise free its contents, I discovered three bottles of HP Sauce.

I adore that stuff. To give you an indication, my father, Gordon, had been known as 'thick, brown sauce' on the 1959 Lions tour.

Rala would have packed that case about six weeks earlier. I thought it was magic, a remarkably thoughtful gesture.

The other story that I think about when I think of Rala concerns a particular low time in my life because of a series of family bereavements. I also picked up a neck injury while playing in a World Cup qualifier against Russia in Krasnoyarsk. We returned to Dublin, to the Glenview Hotel, ahead of another qualifier against Romania.

I was in agony. I hadn't slept a wink for about three days at that stage and was walking around like a zombie. The more I lay in bed, the more sore my neck got.

One morning about 5 a.m., I rang Reception and asked them what time Paddy O'Reilly took his breakfast and whether he had it delivered to his room. I was told that he did and liked to eat at 6.30 a.m. I asked them to bring his tray to my room.

I carried the tray down to Rala and knocked on the door. I was greeted by the sight of Rala with a towel round his waist – only Dixie should have to see that vision – then he started to cry, muttering that there was no way the Irish captain should be serving him breakfast.

This was someone who had brought me a thousand cups of tea, and done so much for me, but that is Rala – he always gives and asks for nothing in return.

I genuinely believe that he has been an important man in Irish rugby during his tenure as bagman because of the unbelievably beneficial effect he has had on a couple of generations of players. He's one of my favourite people.

My Great Escapes – Part I
INISHBOFIN

'I will sing of an island, the fairest on earth,
'Tis sweet Inishbofin, sweet isle of mirth,
Where the warm Irish welcome comes straight from
   the heart
Where the stranger who comes, cares never to depart.'
Patrick G. Power

Inishbofin, a little island that lies off the coast of Connemara about seven miles from the fishing village of Cleggan, has become a spiritual home away from my Dublin roots and a place to which I flee whenever the opportunity presents itself. I first came upon the island many years ago when Dixie and I were about to undertake a tour of the west of Ireland. A good friend, Liam Clegg, suggested we pay Inishbofin a visit based on his experiences.

I thought no more of the advice but we loaded up our new blue Mini – I loved that car – and struck out for Connemara. We were entering the town of Clifden when Dix spotted a sign for Inishbofin. I turned the car around and headed for Cleggan where we boarded a boat for the island. It was a sweltering July day in 1976 and, as we rounded the old fort and sought sanctuary in the harbour of Bofin, I thought I had found heaven on earth.

The Island of the White Cow (Inis Bó Finne) has a storied

history that includes tales of a Spanish corsair Alonzo Bosco and Ireland's pirate queen Grainne O'Malley. It was one of the last places to surrender to Oliver Cromwell's forces and during that time was used as a prison for Catholic priests, arrested elsewhere in Ireland.

There is a rock in the centre of the harbour that is submerged at full tide and it was there that Cromwell's forces used to execute priests – manacled to the rock, they drowned. It was a pretty horrible way to go. The barnacle-encrusted remnants of those shackles linger as a ghoulish reminder of man's inhumanity.

It was love at first sight – the island, not that rock – and I haven't been able to, or wanted to, resist its siren call. I'm not alone in that respect. Everyone we have brought there feels a similar enchantment.

On that first visit, we landed at the old harbour and barring our path stood Day's Hotel and Micko's Bar. We encountered the lovely Mrs Day and she regretfully informed us that she had no rooms available but she sent a message up the road to the Doonmore Hotel, where we were able to secure board and lodgings.

We were scheduled to spend one night on the island. As it transpired, that one night meshed into five under the generous care of *bean an tí*, Margaret Murray. Each day, she prepared a packed lunch, and Dixie and I would set off on foot through the West Quarter Village to explore a specific goal or simply saunter along with no fixed destination.

We walked the cliffs, looking out on nearby Inishshark, before carefully plotting a route down to the beach. For five days, I sat with my back against the rocks staring out into the Atlantic Ocean, the musical notes of the tidal wash, a gentle lullaby that soothed body and soul, the on-shore breeze gently mask the true extent of the sweltering temperatures. In the evening, we would return to the hotel, creating a private annex at the bar counter. There, we would drink pints of Guinness and sample the delicious fare. We'd then turn our shoulders towards the harbour, strolling to Micko's for more pints against a backdrop of traditional music. There'd be time for a nightcap or two back at the Doonmore before the sandman beckoned. There was no electricity on Bofin at that time, so night vision was a valuable asset in negotiating darkened corridors. Days rolled into one another, indistinguishable in where one ended and another began.

A highlight was befriending Margaret's husband, Paddy, a great fisherman. One day, Paddy took me out in his boat, passing the cliffs on the west side of the island to haul up his pots. I had never seen or done anything like this before and was overcome with a childlike fascination that took the form of a hundred questions. How many lobsters will you catch? What's a crayfish? Where did you get the currach from? Paddy smiled his way through the third-degree questioning, educating me patiently without a hint of exasperation. I have shared many great days and a few pints since.

We also met Mikey O'Halloran on that first trip and he too had to bear the brunt of my ignorance when it came to fishing matters. He didn't hold it against me and we have become firm friends with the O'Halloran family.

Ann, another O'Halloran, who would marry Turk native Jim Prendergast, is perhaps the focal point of all the friendships because she is always there to greet us at the pier and stands on the same spot, waving as we board the ferry to return to the mainland. Sometimes, I think she's happy to see us – well, me – go. I have known her since she worked as a young girl in the Doonmore Hotel and there's many a battle I've had with her over a fondness for breakfast in bed. If I close my eyes for a split second, I can hear her voice, admonishing, 'Paddy Reilly, you will get up like everybody else and have it in the dining room.'

I have seen her children grow from the cradle, four strong young men, and the first port of call on reaching the island is to visit her house in Dulan. The kettle sings and conversation never draws breath. Her husband, Jim, possesses a dry humour and I'm usually the recipient of a good-natured barb. On a recent visit, Jim and their son, Shane, were busy constructing a house for a neighbour. I walked across to the site and spying a plank that straddled a trench to the foundations of the building, I gingerly stepped onto the wood and, with my arms outstretched like a tightrope walker, negotiated the two and a half paces to the sanctuary of the concrete floor. Jim couldn't resist, 'It's not the Eiffel Tower that you're climbing now, Paddy.'

The O'Hallorans and their kin are a special family. There's Alice (Ann's sister) and Michael Joe (brother) who live on the island, Mary Katherine (sister) and Martin (brother), who live on Jim's birthplace, the neighbouring island of Turk. The musicality of the family can be heard late at night, Ann and Alice's sweet voices accompanied by Michael Joe, occasionally to the backbeat of his bodhrán.

I always wanted to visit Turk and finally got my wish a while back. I was in the Doonmore Hotel one morning when I took a phone call. It was Ann and she said simply, 'The sea will suit you today.' She told me to make my way to the harbour straight away. When I got there, her husband Jim and Neil stood by a currach. It took forty-five minutes harbour to harbour and the sea was a lovely calm. Jim's family house was so close to the sea, you could fish out of the living-room window. We met Delia, her husband Mr Concannon, who, along with his brothers, operates the ferries to Inishbofin, and Mary Jo. There was tea, chats and fruitcake made from an island recipe. Jim and I took off up the mountain road and he showed me the high end of the island where he played as a nipper. He told me that his first job every morning had been to find the horse, which could have wandered off anywhere during the night.

I'd include that afternoon spent on Turk in any collection of my favourite Connemara memories. There is another O'Halloran, Gabriel, now sadly passed to a better place, at whose fireside I whiled away many an hour, drinking tea. I managed to get the odd word in but generally just sat and listened as Gabriel held forth on whatever subject tickled his fancy. One thing I could never work out was that when I'd approach the door to his house, he'd announce that the kettle was already on because he heard I was on the island. Now upon landing, I would make a beeline for his house, and would still face the same proclamation. Ours was a friendship that spanned thirty years, like many I've made on the island.

On one occasion, I was due to go fishing with Willie and his brother Leo. The night before we sank a gallon or two of porter buoyed by the notion of heading off to collect the bounty in the pots that lay just beyond Inishshark. What I didn't realise from the cosy snug of the Doonmore was the wind was whipping up a rainstorm outside. I made my way to bed about 4 a.m. oblivious to the elements, imbued to the gills by Liffey water courage. I woke to a hangover of epic proportions and, against Dixie's advice, prepared to honour my commitment. Willie was waiting at the jetty but there was no sign of Leo, who had literally decided to do a rain check in relation to the arrangements. This left me second-in-command of the ship, well currach to be precise.

The weather wasn't a bother to Willie who had been born into this life, but my bravado disappeared the moment we hit the waves outside the confines of the harbour. I was soon hanging over the side trying to empty the contents of my stomach. By the time I hauled myself semi-upright, we had made good progress towards our destination. I was still green and Willie, understanding my discomfort, charitably offered to return me to the island. It would have cost him at least an hour.

I felt like a right eejit but didn't want him to go all the way back so we compromised in that he left me on a little island called Inishgort. I crawled up the sand, thinking I was some modern-day Robinson Crusoe, and found a patch of grass. I probably looked like a beached whale as I lay on my back, staring up at the blue sky – the weather had improved – and vowing never to touch another drink. It was my last conscious thought as I drifted off to sleep only to be woken shortly afterwards by a high-pitched racket. Disorientated and in something of a tizzy, I got the fright of my life to see a number of sizeable seagulls hovering about four feet above my carcass, helicopter style. It was a photo finish to determine who got the bigger fright.

Willie returned to collect me soon after and, partially revived, I was able to recount my Tippi Hedren moment. This brought a smile to his face but the colour quickly drained from mine when he explained that they were sizing me up for a feed, probably starting with my eyes. That sent a shiver down my spine and taught me a valuable life lesson to boot.

My travails weren't over though. In my haste to get out of the currach when we reached the small beach below the Doonmore,

I foolishly stepped into a dinghy that was moored alongside. I lurched like some crazed tango dancer trying to keep my balance much to the hilarity of Willie and Mikey Jordan, who had come down to the beach to greet the returning seafarers. It was some spectacle, an eighteen-stone landlubber trying not to fall out of a craft the size of a box of matches. I lost my battle to remain upright but somehow managed to land wellies first in about two feet of water.

We adjourned to Murray's bar where I sank a few medicinal brandies that settled my nerves as much as my ailing stomach. Willie has dined out many times on the story. Now, every time I look out on Inishgort, my few hours as a castaway come flooding back, and how I narrowly avoided becoming one-eyed O'Reilly.

Occasionally I'll reminisce about the lure of Inishbofin, trying to establish what it is that draws me to its shores. Is it the ocean? Is it the natural beauty, the beaches, the uncluttered passages of time that replenish life's batteries? A marked contrast to the more rigid regimen of my career as a bagman, where the waking hours of the day are accounted for in black and white.

The answer never changes. I return because of the people. They define my experiences. Inishbofin is about Maria, Pat Coyne, Jackie, the beautiful Ruby Ellen and her love of ice-cream, the brothers Lavelle, John, Francis and family and the pints he'll pull for you while offering a smile and a chat. It's about Alice, Dessie, Michael Joe and Ann singing, a visit to Maria's Heritage Centre and Anne Marie's craft shop. It's about Aileen, Fiona, Andrew, Simon and all the Murray family and about Margaret and her ability to put down a great fire, Mrs Murray's tales of island life and Pat and Dermot Concannon transporting people to the island in his boat.

I have introduced many friends to the island way of life and the characters who enrich the experience of those who make the pilgrimage. I can't conceal a smile when I watch the reaction of visitors to some of the older men of the island, who, having caught the strains of mass on a Sunday from the doorway of the church, celebrate with pints, singing and dancing to the music of the Inishbofin Céilí Band. Everyone has a party piece, even the hotel guests, who are gently coaxed into participation. Inhibition is no match for lubrication.

Many moons ago, the late Dr Mick Smyth, a great friend from my school days, came down with his family for Easter. The weather was gorgeous and Smythy had me destroyed traipsing over bogs and up hills. The highlight of his trip was a visit to Inishshark. I can still feel the heat of the sun from that day as the doc dragged his reluctant travelling companion, 'Sancho O'Reilly' – no donkeys involved, sadly – to the highest point of the island: it was worth the effort. Imagine a Paul Henry painting endowed with the scents of Mother Nature, a lavish banquet for the senses.

Rob Henderson paid a visit and we hatched plans to buy a site and build a cottage. The blueprints were washed away in the bottom of a pint glass. Others followed, some came before: Tommy, the Bear, Goldie, the Prince, Sharon and her two young boys, Robert and my godson Marc, Mu and Ba, Mickey, Letch, Patsy, Helen, Paul and Deirdre, and sisters Liz and Moira.

This camaraderie and bonhomie – my French is improving – is why I once formally invited Princess Diana to Inishbofin. I sent her a letter after watching her interview with Martin Bashir on the *Panorama* programme in 1995, during which she spoke about her bulimia and uttered those famous words about believing there to be three people in her marriage to Prince Charles. She looked so sad, so careworn.

I reckoned she needed cheering up so I asked her to come to Inishbofin and to bring her two boys. I noted one or two small handicaps that we were going to have to overcome, the first of which was that I had no car at the time. However, I offered a solution based on the fact that I saw her driving a big jeep while watching the news. I suggested she drive over on the ferry and I gave her specific instructions on how to negotiate the one-way system that would bring her down Heytesbury Street and the sharp left required to manoeuvre into Arnott Street where she would have to park on the footpath, so as not to block the traffic. I would be standing outside my castle waiting for her. We'd then strike off for Cleggan pier where we'd catch the ferry to Inishbofin. I'd ensure that no one got onto the island, leaning on my friendship with the boatmen. I gave her a guarantee that there would be no media and that she could concentrate on enjoying the music, the craic and that the boys would have a ball out fishing in a currach. I suspect that while reading it she probably checked for a padded cell number and the address of the asylum but my sentiments – there may have been a tiny amount of drink involved when I was composing the invitation – were genuine.

A little to my surprise, I received a response from her private secretary on Kensington Palace headed notepaper. It began 'Dear Mr Ralla' – she misspelled my name but the ability to forgive is one of my virtues – and went on to say that Princess Diana was delighted to receive my letter. It made her smile a bit and while she'd love to go with the boys to Inishbofin, her diary was too cluttered to wangle some free time.

When I met Prince William in the changing room after Ireland won the Grand Slam, I wanted to say to him, 'Look, do you have two minutes to spare? I want to tell you a story about how you nearly came on holiday with me to Inishbofin.' Sadly there were too many people around and there was no way I was going to embarrass the young man or myself by blurting out my anecdote in front of others.

Island life is not for everyone. A summer's day when the harbour resembles a silver millpond, the heat warms the bones and there is little more to trifle with than wondering about the next cup of tea, sandwich or when to chance the first pint of the day is idyllic. Watching the walkers go by or cyclists as they criss-cross Bofin on roads narrower than a blood vessel while perched on a stool or a trestle table, it's tempting to hanker after staying longer. It's a fanciful notion because, as my island friends are fond of reminding me, I wouldn't last a winter.

RORY BEST
Hooker for Ireland (2005–present) and the Lions (2013)

It's great to see Rala finally writing a book. I remember a conversation with him when he told me a well-known book publisher had turned him down. I said that I thought it was very odd because he has so many great rugby stories to tell and that it would make a super read. He stopped me mid-sentence and, in his usual calm way, told me that the book was not rugby related and that instead he had tried to sell the concept of an 'insider's guide to Inishbofin'. I could do nothing but laugh.

I also recall with fond memories the numerous times Rala fell asleep at the cinema, including during the goriest horror film I've ever seen. Probably the best one was the Western where he fell asleep after about five minutes and was only woken by the final scene shootout. He subsequently arrived back to the team hotel to be asked by another player how the film was, and responded that it was one of the best movies he'd ever seen.

Of course, there was the incident when he tied himself up the night before the Grand Slam match in Cardiff, rolled himself to the lift and headed down to the big pre-match function in the lobby – he'll do anything for a bit of attention!

But probably for me the story that sums up Rala was at Killiney Castle Hotel one Six Nations. My wife and son, Ben, who was about eight months old, were down for the day after a game. We'd been trying to walk Ben to sleep for hours but to no avail, so I decided I would use my time wisely and call to Rala for some sweets. Rala welcomed the three of us, including a screaming Ben, into the room and then proceeded to tell all of us a story about Inishbofin.

Within thirty seconds, Ben was fast asleep. It also should be noted that my son is not the first or last male to be put to sleep by one of Rala's long-winded Inishbofin stories. No wonder the book publisher passed on the tourist-guide idea.

Chapter 4

'A smooth sea never made a skilful mariner.'

There are always incidents and accidents doing this job. They're unavoidable and, over the years, I have encountered my fair share. One that still sends shivers down my spine took place in Cardiff on 19 March 2005. Wales were going for a Grand Slam and, under the stewardship of Eddie O'Sullivan, Ireland were looking to retain the Triple Crown.

As usual, we were ensconced in the Hilton Hotel, as central a destination as you could wish with the Millennium Stadium a stone's throw from the lobby. I'm a creature of habit, enveloping myself in routine like a comfy eiderdown. It keeps me focused on the tasks in hand. My role is miniscule in the greater scheme of things but any lapses or forgetfulness can compromise a player's peace of mind. If I forgot to pack new white ankle socks for Donncha O'Callaghan or Ronan O'Gara to go underneath their knee-length Ireland ones, it wouldn't prevent either from taking the field, but it might distract them for a minute or five, and they don't need that – the team certainly doesn't. So, for me, the regimen of what I do is important. I try to prepare for every eventuality as well as the three that I didn't think about.

That particular morning, as is my wont, my alarm clock went off at 7.30 a.m., closely followed by one I set on my mobile phone and then the phone rang with the wake-up call I'd requested from the hotel. I understand that doing something like this in triplicate makes it sound like I have OCD, but until this book came out it was my little secret. My immediate priority after showering and shaving is to assemble all the bits and pieces required for the match that I have stacked ready to go from the previous night.

I rang down to Peter the porter – wouldn't be quite the same if his name was Fred – and asked him to bring up a trolley onto which I could put everything, leaving the match jerseys until the last minute. Generally, I breakfast alone in our own restaurant, as most of the boys would still be asleep at that hour, but this particular morning I shared my toast and porridge with David Humphreys. He's an early riser. I know he's thinking about the game, focusing on something or other, so few words are exchanged. The silence isn't uncomfortable. There are times when players will look to chat, while on other occasions, they'll be preoccupied. I usually wait for them to initiate conversation.

I loaded the van and then returned to my room to collect the match jerseys. Although I have a physical checklist, at this stage, it's more a mental exercise – pre-match warm-up equipment, post-match gear, jerseys and the other paraphernalia. I got to the stadium at 10 a.m. and the lads who were on duty at the players' entrance were very good in helping me unload the van. In the Millennium Stadium, you have to climb a very steep flight of stairs to get to the dressing-room area. Left to my own devices, it would be a decent workout but the extra hands meant that the task was completed in about half an hour.

I slipped outside for a lulu and noticed only a few people around, apart from security staff. I decided to walk out to the centre of the pitch, spinning around in a panoramic sweep of the deserted stadium, imagining what it would be like in a few hours' time, when 75,000 supporters, proudly sporting their colours, would scream and shout themselves hoarse. I knew there would also be at least another 10,000 fans who couldn't get tickets, who'd be shoe-horned into every watering hole in Cardiff. I thought about those at home from Doolin to Dublin, Bloody Foreland to Mizen Head glued to their television sets. The team wasn't due to arrive until 2.15 p.m., so I returned to my 'office', and began to assemble the jigsaw. I'm often ridiculed for striking out for a stadium so early but everyone works to a different rhythm – mine is just a little more leisurely prior to a match.

I put the warm-up equipment outside in the corridor. Then I moved into the dressing room. I hung the jerseys one to twenty-two, as it was at that time. Next was the snack table. Then the toiletries – shampoo, soap, towels – everything in its place, and a place for everything. Cold drinks, chilled facecloths, the spare set of jerseys, stud boxes, tape – nothing was a conscious action.

Routine always takes over. I sneaked out for another lulu and bumped into J.R., the Welsh bagman. I'd known him more than ten years at that stage and we sat down for a chat and a cup of tea. The police and sniffer dogs arrived in and were gone within a couple of minutes. I'm always glad they never find what they're looking for, if that makes sense.

Even in the bowels of a stadium you can sense when the gates have been opened, long before you actually see anything. The last thing to arrive, from my perspective, was the post-match food for the players and management.

The atmosphere began to build and I strolled outside to soak up the occasion. It was 2 p.m. and the Irish team bus was due to arrive. I notice the Welsh arriving being escorted by two mounted police officers. Once through that particular gate into the stadium, there is a noticeable slope that eventually tapers off to a flat surface again. I thought the horses were stepping out a bit lively and, sure enough, one slipped, the policewoman on board went one way and the horse the other. I didn't go either way because I was paralysed with fear – they missed me by a matter of inches. I didn't move for what seemed like an eternity but was probably a couple of seconds before I regathered some composure. That was one photo finish I don't want to see again.

It was to be Wales' day that particular afternoon and they won a Grand Slam. But win, lose or draw, my job doesn't change. The dressing room has to be stripped clean, the equipment and match gear collected and the van reloaded.

That afternoon harboured one more problem. I couldn't get out of the stadium because of the traffic congestion. I was trapped – along with the Welsh team, Peter Stringer and Denis Hickie, both of whom had been drawn randomly to be drug tested. It was two hours before we were allowed to leave but that wasn't the end of the matter, and we had to inch – no exaggeration – our way back to the hotel.

It was about 9 p.m. when we got back and the post-match dinner had already started. I was wrecked and headed straight for my room where I ordered up some food. Some of the boys filtered in for a chat, Brian O'Brien too, but all I wanted was my bed. I didn't dream about flying horses or Grand Slams and Triple Crowns. The final thing I remember thinking about were Dixie's words to me, 'The cares of tomorrow must wait until this day is done.'

The good and bad thing about sport is that you rarely have time to dwell on the past before a new challenge is presented. That summer the Lions, with Drico as captain, headed for New Zealand while Ireland undertook a two-match tour of Japan. We bade farewell to the Irish Lions tourists and our coach Eddie O'Sullivan, who was also headed for the land of the long white cloud as an assistant to Clive Woodward.

Niall O'Donovan was appointed to coach Ireland in Japan, assisted by Michael Bradley and Mark McCall. Joey Miles, a man I knew from his days as an Irish selector, was the manager. We spent the week before we left domiciled in the Castletroy Park Hotel and trained at the University of Limerick.

One of the lighter moments in a hugely enjoyable tour involved our mascot Broc and a documentary shot by Johnny O'Connor. It was moody and atmospheric – and downright seedy as it followed Broc from bar to bar, downing drinks of varying colours, as he engaged some ladies of the night with his repartee. He was also caught sniffing a suspicious white substance and arriving back in the hotel lobby at 6 a.m. in a shocking state. He may have gone off the rails slightly because he sensed that no one appeared to love him. He was Tommy Bowe's responsibility initially but he'd quite a few handlers by the time the tour was over. He's still our mascot to this day.

Broc was not the only one to encounter trouble in Japan. Now many of you will have heard of the Court Sessions conducted by touring rugby teams where players and management are punished for various misdemeanours. Most of the accusations are spurious but the sentencing is unforgiving and penal. Broc's escapades formed part of a double bill one night at the end of tour court session with yours truly the unwitting star of the other main feature.

Throughout the tour, I was filmed secretly on a mini-camera about the size of a packet of smokes. I had no idea. One scene involved Frankie Sheahan and his buddies arriving up to my room. I was quizzed on this and that, nothing too serious, when all of a sudden the line of questioning took on a harder edge.

'If Munster were playing Leinster and Hendo tackled Drico and only one of them got up off the ground, who would you like it to be?'

That was the calibre of questions I faced. I remember another concerned me being stranded on a desert island with Peter Clohessy, Mick Galwey, Marcus Horan and Donncha O'Callaghan. Our little group found a couple of small boats. Claw and Gaillimh were going in one and Donners and Marcus in the other. I had a choice as to my travel companions and the boys wanted to know which boat I'd choose. I stuck to my guns and said that I couldn't possibly make a choice, that I viewed them all as my children, or some blarney like that.

My interrogators spent the whole tour working on the exposé. They showed footage of me having a lulu, a jimmy riddle, falling into the ice cooler and also the time I brought off a great penalty save from Brian Green's shot. Unfortunately, I was wearing sandals on wet grass and ended up doing a particularly unflattering and rather painful version of the splits. Someone whispered that the medical team moved quicker to check on me than they did when a player went down injured. I was hauled before the court and my punishment was to carry weighted kitbags around the room a hundred times. As luck would have it, they couldn't find any bags.

My greatest shame though was an involvement in what was dubbed the 'Sex Scandal'. I was in my room preparing to join a couple of players for a trip to Starbucks. My door was open, as usual. I was shaving, singing a little ditty, having just stepped out of the shower with a towel around my waist to protect my modesty. At first, I didn't hear our liaison officer, the beautiful Asukie-san, arrive at the door, to check one or two arrangements with regard to the following day. A voice cut through my warbling and I shouted that I would be with her in 'two secs'. At that precise moment, Mr Stringer and Mr Sheahan happened to be walking past when they heard a horrified Asukie shout, 'No sex, no sex, La La.'

I don't need to paint any more of the picture to tell you the mileage that the players managed to get out of that one.

The people of Japan were unfailingly polite, to the point where they would not let you carry so much as a box of matches across the lobby. I tested this theory several times, making a beeline from the entrance to the lifts. The most I managed was ten steps before I was surrounded by two or three smiling faces; porcelain figurines, all alabaster skin and jet-black hair. They each wore tags on their uniforms that stated their level of fluency in English. They certainly spoke my language a great deal better than the couple of words of Japanese that I picked up. The language barrier proved to be an occasional handicap when it came to getting provisions for the snack room. I wouldn't be the best of shoppers at home but when confronted with long aisles in a Tokyo supermarket, I was well outside my comfort zone. I couldn't read any of the labels, so establishing whether something was low fat or not was pretty much guesswork.

Kieran Campbell, Trevor Hogan, Bernard Jackman, Matt McCullough, David Quinlan and Roger Wilson made their debuts for their country during a first test victory over Japan in Osaka. Kieran Lewis enjoyed his test start in the second test win at the wonderfully named Prince Chichibu Stadium in Tokyo. Most players would prefer to win a first cap in front of friends and family at Lansdowne Road but it doesn't diminish the experience of pulling on that green jersey for a first time, no matter how many thousands of miles you are from home.

Our two-centre tour could not have offered more contrasting locations. Osaka, while a city with a big population, offered more of a glimpse of Japanese architecture in terms of temples and castles and a slightly gentler pace of life. Tokyo assaulted the senses, a kaleidoscope of flashing neon.

Even though we were bigger physically than most of the locals, it was impossible not to feel dwarfed by the sheer size of the population. At one point, I remember standing on a largely deserted platform down at Metro level in the main Tokyo train station – twenty-six entrances and exits. A train arrived and for about ninety seconds, you could not see a millimetre of the platform.

As a venue it also provided me with one of the most surreal moments of the tour. I had snuck outside for a lulu and was transfixed momentarily by what sounded like the Dubliners performing a gig. Instead, a Japanese ballad group greeted me, giving it holly, and making a decent fist of it too.

Our first home in Japan was a hotel in the shadow of Osaka Castle, a structure situated on the former site of the Ishiyama Honganji temple that dated back to 1583. A daimyo called Toyotomi Hideyoshi, a general who won a series of wars uniting the country under his direction, built Osaka Castle as his base, completing the work on the 16,000-square-foot site in 1590. Hideyoshi, being the consummate general that he was, designed one of the most formidable castles ever built in Japan. A large moat surrounded the sheer outer walls and only two small bridges provided access. These could be easily defended or destroyed if necessary. The grounds inside containing the donjon were built three stories above the moat. Any attacker would have to try and clamber over three sets of high stone walls and three sets of turrets to get to the inner sanctum.

It was in Osaka Castle that the Irish party suffered possibly the most serious injury of the tour when assistant coach Michael Bradley picked up a mild calf strain while on a morning run! You can imagine how sympathetic the boys were to his predicament. Most of the management, including our press officer Karl Richardson, used to get an early-morning run around the grounds. Fortunately it wasn't compulsory. Anyway I was far too busy.

Osaka is Japan's premier port city but a good deal less cosmopolitan than Tokyo. Ground floor real estate is so expensive that many of the bars and restaurants are on the fifth or sixth floor of high-rise tower blocks. It was a little surreal at first to be strolling down the street and seeing very few shop fronts. Your natural gaze remains at eye level but to find places to eat and drink, you had to look at the numbers on doorways. Unlike Tokyo, there is very little signage in English. It was definitely a novel feeling to climb into a lift on the ground floor of a building and when the doors opened again you'd be stepping into a bar or restaurant way above street level. We did manage to stumble upon – not literally, obviously – an Irish pub. In size terms, it was more of a snug but the welcome was typically hospitable.

We also made it to Kyoto, to take in the beautiful temples while others ventured down to Hiroshima and Nagasaki. It was with a certain element of sadness that we left Osaka for Tokyo but many of us were looking forward to our first experience of the bullet train. Our train was due to depart at two minutes past two in the afternoon. We arrived at the station at 1.30 p.m. and just before 2 p.m. took up position in a clearly marked square box that indicated the number of the carriage and listed the seats within. At 2.01 p.m., the train arrived and, at 2.02 p.m., it departed. It was about a three-hour spin, initially quite sedate until we reached the outskirts of the city but then the bullet train hitched her skirts and took off in earnest. For the majority of the journey, all I could see was concrete with mountains in the far distance. The journey passed in jig time.

As I mentioned earlier, Tokyo was the bigger, bolder, brasher sibling, a mecca for any gadget junky. Our hotel was in the shadow of the Tokyo Tower, a radio and television mast with a couple of viewing galleries. It proved a popular destination with the players. We weren't too far from the Roppongi Hills district, the foreign embassy belt, so to speak, and also home to a vibrant nightlife scene – it's where the locals and foreigners come together to party. It had something of a mixed reputation, high-end establishments but also the suggestion that the yakuza had a strong presence in the district. On a personal level, I never found out. My disco-dancing days are from a music era defined by billboards and vinyl. We had to travel a little way to training, but you don't see very much out the window of a bus, though I enjoyed rambling around the shops and temples in the vicinity of the hotel.

I really enjoyed my time in Japan and think that they'll do an excellent job in staging the 2019 Rugby World Cup. Every time a tier-one nation visits, the Japanese learn something to add to how they will host the next team. In terms of organisation and punctuality, they're difficult to fault. I'd like to go back, but at this juncture that's unlikely to be in an official capacity. I'll be as old as Methuselah in 2019.

Back in May 2006, I was in the Castletroy Park Hotel in Limerick, preparing for Ireland's summer tour to New Zealand and Australia. The weather was fantastic. Dixie had come down for the weekend and we watched Rob Henderson play his last game for Munster and marked the occasion with pints in Claw's pub.

According to a historical footnote, I first came across Rob Henderson on Ireland's 1997 Development Tour to New Zealand under the coaching baton of Brian Ashton. I have no recollection to this day of Hendo being on that tour, but Rob and his lovely wife, Angie, have since become great friends of Dixie's and mine. By way of illustration he is only one of two internationals – Johnny O'Connor is the other, although that was an unofficial expedition as he married an island girl – to accompany me to my beloved Inishbofin.

Two playing memories about Hendo involve a hat-trick of tries, the first in Paris in 2000 when he offered Brian O'Driscoll a helping hand in scoring three touchdowns on a day when Ireland recorded their first victory at the Stade de France. In 2001 in Rome, Hendo got his turn to bag the tries – Drico was missing that day – and won the man-of-the-match award. I can still see him happily clutching that wolf, an award commissioned to commemorate the days of Rome's founders Romulus and Remus, in his hotel room.

His heroics that day reminded me of another story from Rome, but this one involved Pope John Paul II. The tale begins on Digger's farm in the Wicklow Hills some months before the 2001 Six Nations match against Italy. The Irish squad and management were told that a meeting with the pontiff had been arranged and, as there were two Polish lads working on the farm, I thought it'd be great to ask them for a Polish greeting that the manager, coach or captain could use when meeting the great man. Even though I would be at the audience, like most of our party, I would be standing at the back. The two boys patiently wrote down the greeting you normally say to someone who visits your house and I conveyed their work phonetically to some of our boys.

The day in question arrived and we took our seats. As luck would have it, I ended up beside the monsignor who had arranged the gig. When it came to our turn, I followed the monsignor halfway to the stage before stopping and turning around to call Woody, the captain, to lead from the front. However, the monsignor decided to reshuffle the pack and I ended up right next to the pope, hemmed in on one side by his throne and the other by two of the biggest messers in the squad, no make that Ireland, Gaillimh and the Claw.

These two bucks kept up a relentless barrage of encouragement, urging me to step forward and greet the pope with the Polish salutation. The pressure mounted and, eventually, I buckled and crossed the space that separated me from the pope. He offered his hand and as I kissed the ring I prepared to speak. Nothing came out. I froze. I stood there like a fish out of water, my mouth moved but nothing came out.

Two cardinals stepped forward, gently squeezing a shoulder each and I was removed to the rear of the group. The lads thought this was hilarious. I was still shaking when I went outside for a lulu only to be confronted by a Sky television crew. The lads frog-marched me in front of the camera to be interviewed. I never did see the footage, thanks be to God, but I was in a minority judging by all the comments I received over the next six months. I'm not likely to forget that first trip to Rome.

In Limerick that week preparing for the tour Down Under took on a familiar rhythm of field sessions, gym and skills work followed by down time. The latter consisted largely of trying to drown one another in a lake. Luckily, no one succeeded – unlike the previous year when our masseur, Willie Bennett, did for me as I was unable to match his nautical sleight-of-hand, so to speak.

Willie was trying to turn our little boat around, but didn't quite communicate his thoughts clearly enough, and I ended up ducking prematurely, which caused the boat to capsize. I lost my favourite hat and my cigarettes and ended up watching the world through a wet sail before the rescue boat arrived and hauled us to safety. All the hours I've clocked up on Inishbofin and in the Pacific Islands have obviously taught me very little.

In quieter moments in the hotel, I'd sit in the team room, looking around me and occasionally spook myself with the ghosts of Ireland sides past. Take David Wallace, for example. I have been with him from day one of his international career, having watched over the exploits of his older brothers, Richard and Paul, in the green jersey. All three played for the British and Irish Lions, an astonishing achievement for one family.

Paul Wallace had been in the Castletroy Park in 1997 when he'd received word that, instead of travelling to Australia with Ireland, he'd be hooking up with the Lions tour to South Africa, his opportunity arising from a back injury to the Claw. In David's case, we were making our way through Copenhagen airport in 2001 en route to Spala in Poland when he was summoned to Australia – injuries threatened the Lions as a breed on that tour.

As I watched him in the team room, David was talking to Ballymena and Ulster prop Bryan 'the Bear' Young. Uncapped before the 2006 tour, Bryan made his debut for Ireland in the first test against New Zealand in Hamilton. Mick O'Driscoll was in the company, a player I first encountered at the 1999 Under-21 World Cup in Argentina, with Leo Cullen beside him. He had been captain of that underage Ireland team, which was coached by Brian McLaughlin and his assistant Mark McDermott. My thoughts were briefly interrupted by memories of the wonderful omelettes served up in the Claridge Hotel in Buenos Aires.

Alan Quinlan was standing nearby. Ask him why he's called

the million-dollar man sometime, he'll be happy to tell you. In 2006, I was training him in to be the next Claw, with some success I might add. He's a great character with a good sense of fun.

In mentioning Peter Clohessy my gaze turns towards Marcus Horan, one time member of the Hole-in-the-Wall Gang before he settled down under the influence of his beautiful wife, Katie. He used to get very upset whenever I spoke about Claw (there was a running joke between Marcus and Donncha O'Callaghan and myself that I preferred Claw and Gaillimh to the two boys in terms of favouritism, I seldom came out on top in those exchanges). John Hayes, the other pillar of this team community, had unfurled his giant frame into an armchair – as mentioned, he was chairman of the Tea Club and someone who I just loved shooting the breeze with as we pored over the latest titbits of gossip.

I couldn't pen this little journal without mentioning more about Peter Clohessy. We were like conjoined twins for his fifty-two caps and no matter how much I refused to acknowledge it, there was a small vacuum when he left. I am not about to chronicle or eulogise his achievements on the pitch, there are more qualified people who have done that with a much better turn of phrase than I possess. What I prefer to dwell on is the Claw as a person and the impact he had on my life. He is also the subject of one of the apocryphal tales that grew gigantic legs.

It revolved around how Woody, Claw and I would spend many a winter's morning in Room 303 of the Glenview Hotel having tea and toast. The passage of time and Chinese whispers meant that I had to answer accusations of bringing the pair a four-course breakfast in bed. It got to the point where, upon arrival at the grounds in Ravenhill on one occasion, a steward asked me if I could confirm the tale that I brought Claw his breakfast every morning. Not that I'm not saying I never did, because that would make me out to be a liar when I recount the story – I can't remember exactly the context – of me arriving to the Claw's room and he was on the phone to his wife, the lovely Anna. He interrupted whatever he was telling her, winked at me and announced loudly into the phone, 'Rala, the porridge is very thick this morning and a little bit cold. It's not up to your usual standard.' I'm not sure what Anna said, but I'll never forget his face as he chuckled away.

During his time as a player, many of those winning a first cap came under his spiritual guidance and would share a room with him to boot. Claw and Hendo were also frequent room-mates and I'm reminded of a story that ties the three of us together. In days past, we occasionally stayed at what was then the only hotel in Dublin airport. It was the starting point for many a long journey in more ways than one.

Once I ventured downstairs to where the bedrooms were situated I invariably struggled to retrace my steps to Reception. It was a maze of corridors. I would joke that there was a skeleton slumped against a wall having tried in vain to find his way back to Reception. On this particular occasion, I was given a room with three beds. My door is always open and I heard footsteps, soon to be greeted by Hendo and Claw. They were sharing together in another room but wanted to know who was sleeping in the other two beds. It was like a scene from *Goldilocks and the Three Bears*. They each decided to take a bed, leaving me with the one in the middle. We were due to leave the following morning at

6 a.m., so I had visions of this being an all-nighter – cigarettes, television, sandwich trail on the hour, every hour – but much to my amazement the pair were asleep inside twenty minutes. I never closed an eye in case it was all a ruse. I wouldn't trust those two buckos in a fit.

Players take turns in assisting me with various duties – Claw was the best 'duty boy' I ever had even though his name never appeared on any list. Whenever I needed something done in a hurry, I would explain the situation to him and he'd arrange everything without batting an eyelid.

In 2002, when he played his final home game for Ireland against Italy in Lansdowne Road, he presented me with his jersey. His final game, a few weeks later, was against France in Paris. I got it laundered, laid it out in my room and asked him to drop by and write something on it. It's a treasured piece of memorabilia. He wrote: 'Thanks, Rala, for all the happy memories.' I can assure you it wasn't a one-sided relationship.

Dixie and I have been guests of Peter and Anna in their Limerick home many times since his retirement and I've got to know his family very well. His son Luke in particular. Claw has been bringing him to Ireland training sessions from the time he was a nipper and I've always kept an eye on him. I don't know where the time has passed but Luke helps me, has done for many years, when we have an Ireland training camp in Limerick. He's a chip off the old block, not in looks but the mannerisms and personality are identical.

The Claw and Gaillimh were great mates and partners in crime when it came to practical jokes. No one was safe and nothing was sacred. It was rare to see one without the other. To reinforce this point, there was one time when Shannon were playing Young

Munster in the all-Ireland league and that evening Ireland were going into camp at the Castletroy Park Hotel. The pair of them walked through the door together that evening, still in their respective playing kits, having spent the afternoon climbing into one another.

The first time that Gaillimh captained Ireland was against Romania in Bucharest in June 2001, a day when Shane Byrne and Mick O'Driscoll made their respective debuts for the national team. To commemorate Gaillimh's achievement, I got my hands on the match ball and inscribed on it: 'To the legend from all the squad.'

In a moment of uncertainty, I thought I had misspelled 'legend' and proceeded to amend it. I then realised that I had been right the first time. I tried to correct the correction with the net result that the ball resembled a felt-pen spaghetti junction given all the scribbles and crossing out. When I handed Mick the ball, he laughed and thanked me for the thought.

The first time I clapped eyes on Paul O'Connell was during a league match between Terenure and Young Munster at Lakelands. The Claw was playing but the dominant figure was a red-headed young tyro, who ruled the roost in the lineout, scored a try and all but hauled his team to victory. Terenure won narrowly.

The second time our paths met was his first week in the Ireland camp, preparing for the Welsh game. It seemed perfectly natural that the Claw, being a proud son of Young Munster, should be asked to look after another son of the Yellow Brick Road. I can still see Paulie sitting at the end of his bed, reading a book, whilst the room around him resembled the last days of Rome. The fug of smoke enshrouded the card players, their discarded sandwich trays, mineral bottles, tea, coffee, cups, saucers and cakes littering the desk and floor. It was like Sodom and Gomorrah minus the women. You could never be in any doubt about whose room you were in.

Donncha O'Callaghan is the architect of most of the 'misfortune' that I have endured in terms of accidents – those unexplained setbacks, the disappearing furniture, unexplainable phenomenon that makes Roswell look like an everyday occurrence. Unfortunately, I've never caught him with the blueprints. I once took him on as a laundry consultant, though it proved a temporary arrangement. His smile is both constant and uplifting, no matter how bleak the circumstances.

Standing nearby in the team room was Denis Leamy, who I once rescued in an airport. He had forgotten to bring his number ones, so I gave him mine and wore my tracksuit instead. The then Ireland coach Eddie O'Sullivan spotted me in my casual attire and came across to give me a bollocking. One of the players piped up that I had given mine to someone else. Eddie wanted to know who but I told him I couldn't divulge that information.

Also in the group were Peter Bracken, someone who brings his own brand of fun to any gathering, and Jerry Flannery, the man who made me laugh more than most. Then there was Anthony Foley. I first came across Axel in 1994, but the family connection pre-dates that encounter as I played against his dad, Brendan, and still have a bruise or two to prove it. Keith Gleeson may be a quiet man around the house but when he laced his boots, there was no doubting the eloquence of his game. Sitting at a table was Rory Best.

He took to calling me O'Reilly, so I responded in kind; he is great craic to be around, full of mischief, and, as trouble usually travels in twos, he would have his great friend Leamy as an accomplice.

Ireland's half-backs, Ronan O'Gara and Peter Stringer, walked through the door. I have stood behind goalposts all over the world watching ROG's metronomic accuracy. I know the hours he put in, his dedication and, most importantly – and what defined him for me – his willingness to share a plate of chips on a Wednesday before a test match. My criteria are simpler than most.

Strings has single-handedly taken me, a child of the sixties, and dragged me kicking and screaming into the twenty-first century, or at least tried to. He's demonstrated great patience in teaching me about computers, phones and iPods and iPads. My music collection would still be on vinyl otherwise.

The two-test tour to New Zealand and Australia that summer was tinged with regret.

We gave the All Blacks two mighty rattles, losing 27–17 in Auckland and 34–23 in Hamilton, before tired minds and limbs eventually succumbed to the Aussies in Perth. The transient nature of sport in terms of winning and losing was reinforced in November that year when we beat Australia (21–6) and South Africa (32–15) before facing into the final test match at the old Lansdowne Road when the Pacific Islanders provided the opposition. It was an appropriate way to bring the curtain down before the old bricks and mortar gave way to a shiny new coliseum because the islanders play with joy and inhibition, trusting their natural athleticism. In some ways, they span both the amateur and the professional eras of rugby union. They are not heavily patterned or structured and are more inclined to follow their instincts.

I was on edge the week before that final match because of the possibility of being caught out by the Hole-in-the-Wall Gang. My nerves got worse with every day that passed because I knew they would get me at some point. When it happened, it was the day before the match – which is usually a relaxing time as I've a lot of my work for the game done. I had been lying on my cot, in my beautiful suite in the Killiney Castle Hotel, when I picked out the telltale sounds of a group trying to tiptoe their way down the corridor. The creak of a floorboard followed by a deafening silence told me that there were people afoot who didn't wish to advertise their presence. I briefly thought of escaping to the balcony but, at four floors up, I didn't want to imprison myself and hand them the keys. I decided to brazen it out but within a matter of seconds, I was bundled out onto the balcony anyway, T-shirt and shorts my only protection against the autumn chill.

They locked me out, turned off the lights and left the room. There was a tiny window and they suspended the key on a hook just inside, tantalisingly out of reach. Scientifically, they have this down to a fine art.

Alone I stood for what seemed like an eternity before I spotted an elderly lady making her way slowly across the car park, huddled against the freshening wind. I shouted down, trying to explain my predicament and pleaded with her to go back into Reception and get Helen to come and rescue me.

Uncertain about whether or not the lady had understood what I'd said, I tried again to get my hand inside the tiny window and reach for the key. At that precise moment, I saw Stringer's face – and only his face mind you, I still don't know how he camouflaged his torso, arms and legs – revealed by the light of the moon. I screamed like a banshee, pitching backwards, towards the balcony rail. My legs buckled as I grabbed a table for support. I don't need to have regular check-ups for my heart, the boys have tested it rigorously down through the years. That night, I was still alert for more skullduggery.

I should say a little more about the Hole-in-the-Wall Gang, who terrorised my days and nights with their shenanigans. If you ever see Marcus Horan, Peter Stringer, Frankie Sheahan, John Hayes, Donncha O'Callaghan, John Kelly and Anthony Horgan walking down a corridor, it's time to be afraid. Now a nicer bunch of individuals you couldn't hope to meet, but corral them in a pack and the mischief-making begins. I'll offer a couple of stories on behalf of the prosecution.

One day I was undertaking a two-hour power nap. My door was ajar, that was my first mistake. Under no circumstances should a person leave their drawbridge down when these knights of mayhem are on a crusade. It was mid-afternoon, the sun was shining and there was a real heat to the day, the equipment was ready to go for the following day's training and the Ireland coach of the time Eddie O'Sullivan had approved the itinerary sheets to be shoved under the players' doors. I'd enjoyed my nap and was feeling good about having everything under control. It was only then I noticed how ominously quiet it was. When you travel with a party of around forty people, there's always some din emanating from one room or another during the day. I was quickly unnerved. I should have smelled a rat. It was then that I could pick out a faint scuffing sound of what proved to be the Hole-in-the-Wall Gang approaching on tiptoes, Red Indian style. I was paralysed and in those few seconds knew that there would be no escape.

In the blink of an eye, they had invaded the room, rolled me in the eiderdown and begun the mummification process, eventually binding me like a spring roll. They taped my hands and feet, put some more over my mouth, then someone wheeled in a porter's trolley and lashed me to it. We were on the eighth floor of the hotel, so they brought me to the lift and pressed all the buttons, right down to the lobby. I scared the living daylights out of one particular lady, who raced to Reception to report the kidnap attempt. The boys removed me from the lift in the lobby and encouraged the gobsmacked audience to take pictures. This wasn't the only time that I ended up bound and gagged – they weren't averse to repeating themselves when it came to their devilment. When I eventually returned to my room, Marcus and Donners had turned it into a crime scene, complete with tape across the door and the chalk outline of a body on the carpet.

They were fond of the toilet trick too, where an innocent party might not notice that the bowl has been covered in cling film, pulled tight and the ensuing jimmy riddle proves a messy business. I'd often return to my bathroom to find 'Rala loves Dixie' written on the mirror using my shaving foam, the contents of which were emptied during the job. I don't know how many cans I have bought at this point.

Then, there were the psychological attacks. During the summer tour to New Zealand in 2006, Strings spread the word that I was prepared to do a reverse bungee, which was set up a short walk from the Crowne Plaza Hotel off Queen Street in Auckland. Word filtered round, and I couldn't go five minutes without someone coming up and asking me when I was going to do the deed. I eventually relented, against my better judgement, but just to get some peace.

It was the worst experience of my life. Our doc, Gary O'Driscoll, the Bull and yours truly were strapped into a cage, affixed to two rubber ropes that were, in turn, attached to a couple of huge cranes. I was petrified. I think the doc was sent with me in case I had a heart attack, but as it transpired his experience was arguably worse than mine. I had the good sense to keep my eyes closed throughout the whole process as we were jettisoned into the air at 100 miles per hour. The gas thing was that Strings wasn't there to see the attempt on my life. I had taken the precaution of writing my last will and testament beforehand and had left it in the safekeeping of Bryan Young.

The gang occasionally went into hiding for a period of time only to resurface when they thought I was least expecting it. Another favourite ploy took place on the eve of a match. This is the time when I lay out the match shorts and socks for each player in orderly fashion on the spare bed in my room, and the players filter in at various points during the evening to collect their kit.

You'd hear the gang coming down the corridor, exclaiming how slippy it was under foot. On arriving in my room, they'd jump in the air and come crashing down on the bed and the kit would be scattered to all four corners. They'd tell me to warn others entering my room about how bad conditions were and would give out that as I'd so little to be getting on with during the day, the least I could do was make some effort with the gear in presenting it nicely. I'd begin to pick things up when the next bunny would arrive and the whole process would start again. Sometimes, I wonder how Jack Kiely and Ian Fleming in Munster survive from one end of the year to the next. They deserve sainthoods.

Unfortunately, sometimes I invite some of their mischief on

myself. The night before the final match at Lansdowne Road against the Pacific Islanders, I was in my room waiting for the players to collect their kit. Some had already been and gone but I was waiting for the final few to appear. Donncha came in and I asked him to ring Marcus and see how he was getting on in Limerick, recovering from injury. It must have triggered a reflex in Donners' mind because, as he jumped all over the bed, he shouted into the phone that I was pushing him onto all the freshly laid out shorts and socks on the spare bed. He then proceeded to mismatch the gear as he picked it up. Two other bunnies, Best and Leamy, would later repeat the act.

The next to arrive was the Golden Triangle – Brian O'Driscoll, Denis Hickie and Shane Horgan – who would generally be among the last to collect their kit. Normally, I'd leave them chatting away but this particular night, I stuck The Kinks' 'Waterloo Sunset' on the iPod and launched into a monologue about the sixties and how good it was. We had the Fab Four, The Swinging Blue Jeans, The Loving Spoonful, Twiggy, free love, hippies, Carnaby Street, Chelsea, the King's Road, George Best, the Great Train Robbery – all the good things. That was the time I told the boys about my emigration to England and how it had been the place to be. Den asked me how long I was there for and when I replied, 'two weeks', well, I don't think I have ever seen a trio laugh so hard or for so long. I was genuinely worried at one point that one of them might suffer a muscle spasm and miss the following day's game.

Luke Fitzgerald, one of three new caps – the others were Stephen Ferris and Jamie Heaslip – walked in on the scene, and while the boys would be well used to my Rala-isms I'm not sure

Luke knew what to make of the whole situation. It's fair to say that he looked a little confused.

The day of the final Lansdowne Road match against the was going to be emotional given the circumstances. Having completed all my pre-match tasks, I went out and sat down in the sin bin area. As my eye wandered, I found my mind drifting to past matches and then specific images. It was a tickertape of faces – Jim Staples, Simon Geoghegan, Paddy Johns, Jeremy Davidson, Gabriel Fulcher, Michael Bradley, Poppy, Woody, Claw, Hendo, Gaillimh, Niall Woods, Justin Fitzpatrick, Denis McBride, Niall Hogan, Eddie Halvey, Mark McCall, Richard and Paul Wallace, Ross Nesdale – and it resembled a Pathé newsreel, snapshots and cameos, individual and collective. The images began to blur and I realised that I had tears in my eyes. I'd had many desks, but Lansdowne Road was head office.

My maudlin moment passed. This was to be a day of celebration. And so it panned out. Ireland won 61–17, scoring eight tries. Paddy Wallace deservedly won the man of the match for his twenty-six-point haul. The scenes at the end of the match will always stay with me – coach Eddie O'Sullivan and captain Brian O'Driscoll leading the players on a lap of the stadium, some throwing various bits of kit into the crowd. It was the perfect way to sign off.

We repaired to the Berkeley Court Hotel for another farewell. It was to be the last official post-match function to be staged there. The players and management gave the staff of the hotel a standing ovation, which was thoroughly merited. We'd been treated like kings there down through the years, getting to know the staff and spending many hours in their company.

At the pre-dinner drinks, I met Barry and Suzanne Coleman.

The timing was uncanny as Barry had been the one to persuade me to take up my first role as bagman. I don't always get to go to the post-match dinner, but I made sure to be at that one with. I'd a bit of a thirst and had no problem in swallowing a bucketful of Guinness.

It had been a day and night of goodbyes that culminated in grabbing a lift back to the Radisson Hotel, our base. I am reliably informed that despite claiming tiredness as I slumped into a chair, I politely accepted several offers of pints. Eventually it was the sandman who wouldn't take no for an answer.

I was woken the following morning at 7 a.m. by Marianne Faithfull singing 'As Tears Go By', something I struggled to appreciate as my head resembled a stomping ground for a herd of wildebeest as they sought out a watering hole. It was my own fault as I'd forgotten to turn off the alarm on the iPod. Dixie and I went for breakfast where we were joined by Cam and Noleen Steele, and Paddy and Tina Wallace.

The last player I saw that morning was Bryan Young, who came to my room to collect a few bits and pieces. We shook hands and I set about doing my chores. I stopped off at Lansdowne Road and the Killiney Castle, collecting and dropping off bits of equipment before returning to Lansdowne to deposit the van and the keys.

I took one last look over my shoulder at the old stadium before I set off on foot in the direction of Baggot Street and a pleasant stroll home. I was blissfully unaware that over the next ten months Irish rugby would experience some wonderful high points but also the crushing disappointment of the World Cup in France. Indeed the French were to prove something of a nemesis for the lads throughout 2007.

PETER CLOHESSY
Prop for Ireland (1993–2002)

Rala – the best butler I ever had! My days in Irish camp would always begin with a gentle knock at the door, 'Claw, Claw, are you awake?'

Then in he would come with my breakfast and a packet of fags on the tray. We would discuss the plans for the day and whether Rala or I would drive the kit van – in the early days, he wasn't too happy driving that van. Two cups of tea and several fags later, we'd have it all sorted.

Rala has the most detailed way of telling a story, which, despite himself, would always be hilarious. Above anyone for me, he took the tediousness out of the many long, boring days we would have to spend in hotel rooms, and on coaches and planes. And on the days when Dixie is with Rala, the craic is more than doubled, she really is the rock behind the man.

Rala was a true professional even before the game was. The logistics of having every item of gear needed for every training session and match for every player in the right place at the right time is not an easy job, but Rala makes it look easy, such is his gentle presence. I can honestly say that I have never heard a bad word said about Rala, who is an institution in his own right.

After a game, Rala would have a little table in the corner of the dressing room with deodorants, aftershave, razors and shaving foam, it was like going into the bathroom in a five-star hotel, the only difference was that we didn't have to leave a tip.

In my day, when new players joined the squad, if they were

inclined to try any pranks on Rala or not show him the respect he truly deserved, I wouldn't be long putting them in their place. I hope that the senior members of today's squads enforce the same respect.

We've become firm friends over the years, and he is a welcome guest at our home, whenever he decides to turn up! Indeed, himself and Dixie are firm favourites of our children, who used to call them Dixie and La La. In fact, any guests to our home sleep in the room known as 'Rala's room'.

Chapter 5

'We cannot direct the wind, but we can adjust the sails.'

By my calculations, 2007 was my thirteenth championship as bagman and definitely one of the most noteworthy. Dave Berry and his film crew captured the essence of the campaign in a celebrated documentary, *Reaching for Glory*. They might have broken a bleep machine if they'd used one, though most sporting dressing rooms would not be mistaken for Sunday school.

The Principality was our first port of call. For me, that meant a 4 a.m. start on a Wednesday morning in the company of our coach driver, my trusted friend, Brendan. On these jaunts, I don't have a clearly defined role but I'd say I'm supposed to be there to keep an eye on the route. It never pans out that way, as I'm usually asleep before we've hit the ferry off-ramp. On arrival at the Hilton Hotel in Cardiff, Peter and his gang helped us unload and, on the Thursday, we headed for the airport to pick up the players and management. After our exploits the previous autumn, with victories over Australia, South Africa and the Pacific Islanders, we were favourites with the bookmakers to win the 2007 Six Nations and we justified that notion with a win against Wales.

We got off to a flying start in the match with a try after just forty-seven seconds from Rory Best. Brian O'Driscoll and Ronan O'Gara also crossed the whitewash on a satisfying day in the Millennium Stadium.

The next morning we dropped the squad at the airport and Brendan and I headed for the boat, arriving at the Killiney Castle about 8 p.m.

We were facing into a very special week, as we were going to play the first game of rugby at Croke Park, the storied headquarters of the GAA, with France providing the opposition. The buzz in the camp was palpable. It was a real privilege and we couldn't wait for a first glimpse of our temporary home. I felt very nervous during that week. I'm not sure why because I wasn't playing and if I looked at things dispassionately, it's not as if my role was going to change appreciably — it was a new venue, but I'd had many around the world.

That said, arriving at Croke Park for the first time was every bit as exciting as I had envisaged. I was fortunate to have one of the masseurs, Mocky, who owned a café in Spala, alongside me. He is a GAA man at heart having worked for many years with Seán Boylan and his beloved Meath. The A-team — Magella, Paddy,

Jimmy, Dessie and Christy – who work on behalf of the IRFU on match days were there as always to help me unload the van and set up shop. They're a godsend and good fun to boot – we know each other's ways.

We were given the Dubs' dressing room. I'd followed the boys in blue down through the years, including their famous four-game saga against Meath in 1991 when the pre- and post-drinking had reached epic proportions as we slipped into the Hill 16 pub and Gills, where Big Larry (may he rest in peace) would produce plates of sandwiches.

One Sunday, Larry had arranged a bus to take the gang to see the Dubs play Wexford in a championship match. That was a long day's night. You'd swear we'd undertaken to go to Timbuktu. At one point, half the lads were trying to finish off their pints and round up the remainder who had wandered off as a form of semi-protest as Larry had promised them they would be home around 9 p.m. It was midnight at this stage and we were still in Wexford.

Heading to the second training session in Croke Park, I took a right turn immediately after the entrance gate and ended up heading in completely the wrong direction. I had to reverse most of the way back, praying that no one had noticed.

Brian O'Driscoll had been ruled out of the match through injury so Paulie led the side and we came to within a whisker of marking the first rugby match in Croke Park with a win. Unfortunately, Vincent Clerc, who has helped himself to a fair few tries against Ireland in his time, popped up in the final throes of the contest to cross the line. But there was no time to dwell on the disappointment because England were due in town.

They were led in coaching terms by my old mate, and one-time

Irish coach, Brian Ashton along with Mike Ford, another who'd swapped the shamrock for the rose. Funnily enough, in contrast to the match against France, I enjoyed the build-up to the England game and anticipated the kick-off like a fisherman awaits a calm sea. Nobody needed a history lesson to understand the symbolic nature of the occasion. When in camp before a match, we operate in something of a bubble in terms of what's going on elsewhere but the excitement and tension managed to seep into the hotel. The surge of goodwill towards the team from the stands was palpable during the singing of 'Amhran na bhFiann' and 'Ireland's Call', as was the respect shown to the visiting anthem. In my experience, the England players, management and supporters are among the nicest people you'll meet, but that wouldn't diminish the desire to beat them one iota. It's a backhanded compliment. Drico returned to lead the team on what proved a stunning day for Irish rugby when we won 43–13.

My immediate post-match concern was to get everything packed up, return the van to the Radisson Hotel and get back to the Shelbourne for the meal at 11 p.m. Mark, Stella and Dixie ensured that I made it in reasonable time.

However, distracted by good company, conversation and food, we missed the bus back to our hotel. In the foyer of the Shelbourne, I noticed that Brian Ashton had suffered a similar fate, so in overtones of times past, we shared a taxi back to his hotel, the Four Seasons, before Dixie and I continued out the Stillorgan dual carriageway.

The next staging post was Edinburgh. On Wednesday, Brendan drove the coach and I fell asleep. We collected the lads from the airport on the Thursday and took them to the Balmoral, one of my favourite hotels. One reason for this is undoubtedly the attention to detail and friendliness of the staff who I have got to know well over the years. Every time I visit, they present me with a gift. There are cartoon strips called 'Oor Wullie' and 'The Broons' in the Scottish *Sunday Post* newspaper, which I love, and they give me annuals containing those characters. Going there is something that I look forward to. In the match, Ireland escaped with a win, thanks to the right boot of Ronan O'Gara.

One week later, on St Patrick's Day to be precise, I was sitting outside a café in Rome, a few doors down from our hotel in the company of Bective Rangers stalwart and IRFU committee member Louis Magee. I was enjoying, in no particular order, the sunshine, a lulu and a cappuccino. Dixie, on her first visit to the Eternal City, was savouring every moment from the shopping to the food, and, of course, the rugby.

Louis was keeping track of events at the Stade de France where the home side was entertaining Scotland. Unfortunately Elvis didn't leave the building and the French number eight Vermeulen scored a try in the dying seconds of the game. There was a brief glimmer of hope when the try was referred to the television match official but after a short hiatus, he confirmed that the grounding was good. France had won the Six Nations Championship from Ireland by a difference of four points.

Earlier that day, Ireland had run in eight tries against the Italians at the Stadio Flaminio, producing a brilliant performance. I'll take that as the memory of the day. There's no doubt that France's late score gave a sense of anticlimax to an afternoon when the Irish squad and management were tantalised by the prospect of winning the championship title. I'm generally a glass-half-full person, so I concentrated on the fact that we didn't suffer any injuries, had won a third Triple Crown in four years and had pushed hard on the final day of the campaign. Maybe my philosophical overview was distorted slightly because I was knackered. It had been a long eight weeks and all I wanted at that point was to go home.

I retraced my steps to the hotel, went to my room and started to get ready for the post-match function. All the gear was stored in the porter's office so it was with a clear mind that I went to join Paulie, Den, Shaggy, Doc and Willie at a table. The company and the craic were equally memorable. By midnight, though, I'd had enough and slipped off quietly to my room to reflect on another campaign. *Tempus fugit* as they might once have said in Rome, from the day we assembled in the Killiney Castle to the morning when the squad would disperse for a final time. My last act was to get up, pack up, get the lads up and leave town.

When I have to rouse tired gentlemen from their slumber on the morning after an away match, vocal exhortations tend not to work, so I have devised a system. I ask a member of staff to let me into the sleepy heads' room, then I walk across to the television and switch it on and change the channel to cartoons or – a personal favourite – mass, turn the volume up full and then walk out of the room clutching the remote control. The air turns blue with the expletives, but it works nicely nine times out of ten to get the gentlemen from under the covers and on their feet.

I scuttled hither and thither on my return to Dublin, rehousing gear and equipment before settling down to enjoy two of my favourite pastimes – the Dublin 6 derby between Terenure and St Mary's and a trip to Inishbofin.

In Dublin 6, it was the final league match. Neither team was in a position to collect any silverware but that didn't mean there was nothing at stake. Bragging rights are important to any rivalry and there is a bespoke intensity to any local spat. I'd played in these matches. I'd relished every lump and bump I'd taken in the process of winning and I'd ached for days, without a scratch on my body, when we'd lost.

Waiting for the match to start that day reminded me of the time when, having swapped my playing days for the role of bagman, we ended up being a man short up in Ballymena. I begged to play, to the extent that I got down on my knees, pointing out that I had my boots and gumshield with me. Thankfully the late Liam O'Dea, an outstanding second row and a man who I'd worshipped when I'd played alongside him, had sensibly ignored my increasingly desperate pleas.

The downtime had recharged my batteries, something I was grateful for when I pitched up to the Radisson Hotel on 7 May and realised quickly how intense the rugby schedule for the next six months was going to be. A potted version would see us travel to Argentina for two tests in Santa Fe and Buenos Aires, go to Spala in Poland, play test matches against Scotland in Edinburgh and Italy in Ravenhill, and also fit in numerous training weeks that included one on Capbreton, which would culminate in a match marred by the fact that Brian O'Driscoll suffered a fractured sinus and damaged eye socket after a disgraceful assault. On a personal level, I was also hoping to squeeze in a holiday to Italy and some time in Bofin.

We were billeted in the Castletroy Park Hotel ahead of the tour to the Pampas and I took the opportunity to go down a few days early and partake in the lavish hospitality that Peter and Anna Clohessy always provide at their ranch. I negotiated a couple of days' work for their eldest son Luke to assist me, while also dropping in on Brian and Olive O'Brien. On the Tuesday night, *Reaching for Glory* was launched in Claw's pub. I must confess to missing most of it as Munster bagman Jack Kiely had spirited me away for a quiet pint but I did see the full version soon after and thoroughly enjoyed it.

Simon Best captained the touring party and there were a few new faces, including a masseur, Dave Revins, and winger Brian Carney – someone who was to become my arch nemesis. Now I believed that, with the Hole-in-the-Wall Gang largely absent, I would be in for a much easier time but that was to prove well wide of the mark. They were replaced by the 5-4-3-2-1 Fellowship, for that was their battle cry. Led by Alan Quinlan, Frankie Sheahan and Mick O'Driscoll, they ensured that every furlong of the tour was a hard one. Brian Carney had a reputation as a practical joker and I found myself zeroed in his crosshairs.

We flew via Brazil to Buenos Aires and holed up in the Panamerico Hotel. It seemed like the entire population passed the front door, day and night, as there was no let-up in the footfall. We played the first test in Santa Fe and this necessitated a coach journey of about six hours with a stop-off in Rosario to take in the Jockey Club, where we enjoyed food and the kickers got in a session. They were amazing hosts and included in their number was former Munster prop Freddie Pucciariello. He took us to the stables and then a training ring where we marvelled at the skill of the riders and the athleticism of their mounts – talk about turning on a sixpence.

A few minutes after we had resumed our coach journey, still a couple of hours from Santa Fe, I heard a cry of 'five, four, three two, one' and the boys descended on me. It was useless to resist. When they had finished, I took out a little black notebook, and listed the names of all the participants and double underlined that of Mr Carney. The Rio Grande was a lovely little hotel with wonderful facilities and I received great assistance from one and all including our liaison officer, who I christened Mr Goodnight, and another chap, Lucas.

The set-up of the hotel meant that I could leave the equipment in a room close to the back entrance and from there it would be transported every day, in the oldest pick-up truck I have ever clapped eyes on, to the training ground, a journey of about ten miles. It never broke down.

Travelling the world, I thought I had seen most things in a rugby context but I had a new experience for the list on the day we travelled for kicking practice to the match stadium – there was a moat around the pitch. I had to improvise with a hastily put together fishing net type of thing to rescue the balls. I'm sure the boys weren't kicking them into the water deliberately!

It was a nice ground with a 26,000 capacity but on match day, it was transformed into a bear pit. I began to understand why there was a moat. Most balls that were kicked into the crowd never came back and every time we had a kick at goal, the home supporters screamed like lunatics. We lost narrowly. We then had to reverse the journey by coach back to Buenos Aires with the same stop in Rosario.

I knew that the 5-4-3-2-1 Fellowship would be back for more so, in preparation, I gave the hotel doorman money to buy the biggest water pistol he could find. My primary target was Mr Carney. He'd done many things but one where he caught me out beautifully occurred soon after we had landed in the country.

He'd disguised his voice and phoned my room. The conversation had gone something like this. 'Hello, this is Mr Murphy. My daughter's dying, my wife's run off with the postman and my son has to have an operation. I'm desperately trying to get some money. If you could just get something signed by the players, I would be most grateful.'

I'd been a bit taken aback as it was midnight and had mumbled something about it being very late and I fumbled for a way to fob him off. There was to be no respite as quick as a flash Mr Murphy had interjected, 'The people told me to go to you. I'm in the lobby, on my way up.'

I'd sat there for about half an hour waiting for Mr Murphy's arrival. The boys had thought this was hilarious but, like the tortoise, I'd been prepared to bide my time.

Along with the water pistol, I got a scrum cap and a bodysuit and put them on before boarding the coach. I passed my intended target; he was sitting in the second row of the downstairs section of the bus.

He looked at me and said, 'Do you think that's going to help, Rala?'

The rest of the gang had taken up seats around me so I knew there was only one course of action left – a pre-emptive strike. I got back off the coach for a few seconds, gathered my courage, re-boarded and squeezed the trigger. I managed to get off one salvo before he grabbed and disarmed me, emptying the remaining contents of the pistol over me. I had the satisfaction, though, of giving him a good soaking.

I wasn't finished with him yet. On returning to Buenos Aires, I enlisted the help of our coach Eddie O'Sullivan. We were training in the Navy Club and the plan was to tell Brian that the RTÉ cameras would be there and for him to arrive at the session in his number ones, as they had asked for an interview. On the itinerary for the day, I had phrased things in such a way that 'the following gentlemen are required to wear their number ones'. His sheet was the only one that contained a name. The following day was like hanging around at the O.K. Corral, waiting for the action to begin. I met him on the way to the coach and innocently enquired as to whether he'd been one of the players requested to wear the formal attire. He pointed to the suit carrier over one arm. I told him I thought he should change right away. Unfortunately, both of us held our nerve. There were no cameras.

We went to a reception at the Irish ambassador's residence, which was a nice break from the regimen of hotel life. I was struggling a little bit with the food until Cameron Steele, our physiotherapist, ordered a lower management night out. I can still taste that fillet steak if I close my eyes, the ice-cream and the liquor camouflaged underneath.

The Harlem Globetrotters were staying in the hotel but we didn't have any interaction with them because they spent most of their time with their heads buried in laptops. My one sporting ambition on that tour – it was my third trip to Argentina – had been to see Boca Juniors play live, but I came up short once again.

The second test was as frustrating as the first. I have taught myself the importance of having a public face for the players and the management. But I was gutted for them and, in the privacy of my own room, shed a few tears.

Routine quickly supersedes everything else though. We were to begin the trek home the following day and there was much to be done. The summer would be dedicated to preparation and fine-tuning ahead of the World Cup in France. There were a couple of trips to Spala, the first of which was for the starting XV from the game in Rome. The second time it involved forty-nine players and fifteen members of management.

In between everything, I managed to shoehorn in a trip with Dixie to Positano on the Amalfi coast in Italy, a glorious odyssey filled with sunshine, relaxation and the best pasta I have ever tasted. But the tranquillity I felt when I returned home was shattered a few months later – there was a rugby storm brewing.

PADDY JOHNS
Lock for Ireland (1990–2000)

In 1998, Rala visited our family in Enfield in London, when I was playing with Saracens. He picked the weekend of a home game in Vicarage Road against London Irish so he could see many friends at one go. We had Richard and Paul Wallace and Irish had Gary Halpin, Mal O'Kelly, Jeremy Davidson, Kieron Dawson, Victor Costello, Justin Bishop, Rob Henderson, Conor O'Shea and David Humphreys — a lot of Rala's boys!

I went to the ground early and Kirsty brought Rala and Dixie in later with our kids, Chris and Emily. When I saw Rala he was wearing his Ireland rugby jersey and on top of his head a Saracens' Fez hat. I heard two elderly London Irish supporters chuckle and say to each other, 'Jesus, would you look at yer man, he hasn't a clue who to be supporting!' But this was typical Rala, everyone's friend and never one to offend anybody.

When we were all gathered in hotels before an Ireland game, Friday evening after dinner was the time we collected our kits. There would be a ritual trek to Rala's room to get what we needed, to polish boots, and have a cup of tea and a chat. Players would drop by in dribs and drabs. You name it, Rala had it — a new pair of laces, a set of studs, a spare pair of socks, toiletries of any description, sweets, energy drinks, bars. Claw spent a long time trying to find something Rala didn't have at hand, but Rala was rarely stumped. If he was, it was only once, as the next time he would be asked, you could be sure he had added the item to 'Rala's list'.

There was a long-running prank with Rala. It happened practically on a daily basis, and Rala fell for it more often than not. The joke was to ask Rala: 'What room are you in?'

He would announce that he was in Room 358, or whatever.

To this, the reply would be: 'No, Rala, you are in the hotel lobby or the bar, or wherever he was standing at the time.'

He would respond with his Homer Simpson impression by cupping his forehead with the palm of his hand and shaking his head in disbelief he had been caught out again.

The 1998 tour to South Africa was a fantastic experience and, as tours go, tough but enjoyable as we had a great set of players and management. Rala had his own crew too. The SARFU had appointed three local black men and given him a truck to transport our gear. The three lads would drive our stuff in their truck between cities and help Rala when they weren't on the road. Before the men would set off on their journey to the next hotel by road (the team flew), Rala would ensure the three lads had loads of bars and drinks for their journey. The lads slept in the truck at night to save their accommodation allowance for their family.

They were great men and always had a big smile on their faces, except for this one morning. I was having breakfast in the hotel, I think in Pretoria, it was near the end of the tour. Rala walked in ushering the lads to our table to have breakfast with us. In the South Africa of a few years earlier, this would have been unheard of and would have landed a black man in serious trouble. The three lads looked very apprehensive, as if they thought they'd been trespassing. It was a real head-turning moment.

Many of the white South African staff and hotel guests couldn't believe what they were seeing. I think Rala was oblivious to the commotion and the fear in the lads' eyes. But that sums him up – everyone put on this planet is equal.

John O'Reilly – what a guy, what a legend, what a servant to Irish rugby, what a friend.

Chapter 6

**'Courage is not how a man stands or falls,
but how he gets back up again.'**

I love Westerns – both films and books – an affair that goes back to my childhood and occasional trips to the pictures. My favourite book is Larry McMurtry's Pulitzer Prize-winning *Lonesome Dove*. Dixie presented me with a copy as a parting gift before my departure for the 2007 World Cup in France and she inscribed on the flyleaf: 'Like this book, the road is long, the way is hard but all that matters is the end.'

McMurtry's tome – it is part of a four-book series, written first, but third in the time chronology of its characters – centres on two

Texas rangers, Augustus McCrae and Woodrow F. Call, and their adventures in journeying from a small town in Texas to the rich plains of Montana. There are twists and turns aplenty in the novel, good, bad and ugly. To me, it echoed Ireland's fortunes prior to and during the World Cup.

Capbreton in France is the starting point for this rugby tale. Our hotel was fabulous and only twenty yards from the most beautiful beach – though my toes never touched the sand. I was too busy 'multi-tasking', a phrase that I adopted for the duration of our stay in France. My room opened out into a little garden where on occasion I entertained visitors and which, the rest of the time, offered a haven from the hustle and bustle of the tour. My nearest neighbours were John Hayes and Marcus Horan. The latter hadn't given up his membership in the Hole-in-the-Wall Gang, so I had to be vigilant, as I found to my cost.

It was late afternoon and I'd all my jobs done, so I lay down for a power nap (I think that's what they call it). My door was open as usual and a lovely breeze was wafting through from the garden. I drifted off happily to the Land of Nod. At one point, I thought I could hear a faint noise but assumed I was dreaming and carried on in my slumber. Slightly disorientated when I woke, I checked to see how long I'd been out – a little over an hour. It was eerily quiet and that unsettled me. I looked over to the door to see if I could hear anyone in the corridor. I couldn't see the door.

I jumped out of the cot. I walked around the room but still couldn't see a doorway. I knew where I thought it should be. My initial concern was that I was hallucinating, losing the plot and the World Cup was still a few weeks away. The euro finally dropped. The sods had constructed a wall with heavy-duty paper over the doorway. In the twilight, it was difficult to spot until I was less than a foot away. They had taken great care – the workmanship was impressive – though I never did find out the builder responsible.

Part of our acclimatisation process for the World Cup was a game against French club Bayonne. It turned out to be quite a counter-productive exercise from the one that everyone had envisaged when the fixture was agreed. There was an awful lot of stuff that went on off the ball, some of which has no place in the sport. The low point from an Irish context was Brian O'Driscoll's fractured cheekbone. He was on the receiving end of a punch as he went to break up a melee. It left a very sour taste. There were concerns about his participation in the World Cup but as he proved countless times in his career, there are few tougher or more resilient players who have laced a boot.

In some ways, it put the tin hat on a difficult preparatory time ahead of the tournament in France. The previous week we had travelled to play Scotland and lost. An injury to Shane Horgan had caused us all some concern, but thanks to the sterling work of the medical team, he'd recovered in time for the tournament. The thirty-man World Cup squad was announced the day after the Scottish match, several days before we headed for Capbreton. I dread the moment a squad is reduced because you get to see, up close, the disappointment of those who didn't make the cut. Words, no matter how well chosen or genuinely expressed, never suffice.

Ireland's final preparatory game had taken place in Ravenhill on 24 August with Italy the visitors. We'd been billeted in the excellent Culloden Hotel, a favourite because, in a different life, I had stayed there on several occasions while playing for Terenure.

I could still see the ghosts of my former team-mates – Wallich, Hebich and Magoo – walking the corridors with their toasted sandwiches, which arrived on the hour, every hour, much to Dave's disgust – he was the man responsible for making sure the bill was paid and he used to go bananas trying to collect the cash when we were checking out.

I'd stayed a night with Ireland prop Simon Best, before moving into the Culloden, lock, stock and barrel the following day, and waited for the players to arrive. When I think back to the time with the Bests, it's tempered by the fact that none of us had an inkling about what was going to befall Simon at the World Cup. I'll never forget the look on Girvan Dempsey's face as he explained that Simon had taken a turn. They diagnosed an irregular heartbeat and he was invalided out of the World Cup and retired shortly afterwards. He's a smashing lad and I was delighted to bump into him recently. He's part of the Banbridge coaching team now and I happened to be in Lakelands when they played Terenure College. It was great to catch up.

After I'd checked in at the Culloden, I went on a quick reccy to my room before getting my head around all the things that needed sorting.

When I turned the key in the door to my room, I suspected there had been some mistake. It was magnificent. I retraced my steps to Reception and tried to point out the error, but the manager assured me that it was indeed my room. As always, it would become a focal point for waifs and strays. The newly formed Tea Club convened here every night. My delight in my surroundings obviously communicated itself to the players because a raiding party was sent there to remove a little of my smugness. The room got a right going over, which took me two days to sort out. One of the violations involved loo paper being entangled in the lighting system. Every time I wanted to use the bathroom, I had to scale new heights, literally. Each day I had to explain to the cleaning staff the latest crisis that had befallen my room. They thought it was hilarious.

We trained at Campbell College, the alma mater of Paddy Wallace. Riding shotgun for me were Dungannon bagman Max, a real trooper who lightened the load considerably, and Brian McLaughlin's son Callum was also a great help. Ireland snuck past the Italians courtesy of what was deemed a controversial, last-minute try by Ronan O'Gara, awarded after consultation with the television match official. Then it was time to decamp to the Killiney Castle and the Radisson in Stillorgan as we conducted final preparations before striking out for Bordeaux.

Hindsight is an exact science. Some choose to major in it. I'm not about to rewrite the history books but I will offer a brief overview of the 2007 tournament and catalogue my own experiences there.

There was no shortfall in dedication or application from players or management. I saw the blood, sweat and tears, the disappointment and the frustration. It's been well documented by others that Ireland came up short in terms of performances and results – and why they did. I was part of the Ireland group. As the campaign stuttered, I didn't think too deeply about why. That's not my bag. My role was to facilitate, to enable others to do what they must and I concentrated on doing what I needed to do to help. There were times when I became aware of the huge criticism directed at the squad. It pissed me off. I didn't care whether it was justified or not, I only saw how it affected everyone. I understand criticism is part of professional sport, but I was too close to this group to sit back dispassionately or objectively and wonder whether or not it was justified.

I felt for the supporters, understood their disappointment and frustration too. We did not achieve what we set out to do. That means we failed. It doesn't mean that sinews weren't strained or guts busted. We got caught in a whirlpool and no matter how much everyone fought, we were sucked down.

It all started so differently, with expectations as high as a Kansas cornfield. My abiding memory of the day before departure is running to stand still. I packed up the truck at the Radisson with the help of Johnny and Titus from the hotel, the gear bound straight for the hold in the plane. Tom Ashe had already transported our scrum machine on a trailer to our training venue in France, which was no mean feat,, but the man from Naas RFC was fantastic. Players and management were limited to one rucksack each. On arriving in Bordeaux, everything was unloaded into another truck, which was then locked with special seals. At the Sofitel Le Lac, I had to witness the seals being broken. It took me about three hours to get to my room and I was anxious to see it because I would be spending the guts of four weeks in the hotel. I wasn't disappointed.

It was at the end of a long corridor and had some interesting neighbours – the Bull and Marcus Horan, Neil Best and Bryan Young, Donners and ROG, Alan Quinlan and Frankie Sheahan, and Girvan Dempsey. I knew I'd have to sleep with one eye open.

We were on the second floor, the team room one below us. It was important to keep up fitness levels, so I walked down and took the lift going up. The staff were excellent but special mention must go to head porter Robert and chef Federico, who travelled with us to Paris. The hotel was situated in a business park across the road from a beautiful lake and about four miles from the city centre. It suited me perfectly well. I can't speak for others.

I didn't get off to the most auspicious start at training. I thought the bibs had been left at our training ground, the Stade Bordelais, only to discover that they were in fact back at the hotel. It was normally a twenty-minute journey on the bus. Claude, my driver, got us there in eight. I was petrified for the entire journey. We switched lanes like we were on a Scalextric track. I was a soggy, if grateful, mess by the time we got back to the stadium. My man Friday, Dominic, and three IRB-stipulated helpers were also present to give me a hand. We turned into quite a little team.

The night before our first match, the Tea Club met and our fare was augmented by Mrs Hickie's cake, which Den expertly carved into wafer-thin slices with the precision of a surgeon. When everyone had left, I couldn't wait to put on a DVD of *Lonesome Dove* that Denis Leamy had kindly sourced (Neil Best had assisted in tuning my laptop).

I was all set when the terrible twins arrived, Quinny and Carney, carrying a document which they forced me to sign. It basically insisted that I was not allowed to watch a Western on my own. Not only that, but they both had to be present before the show could start.

What followed nearly drove me to distraction.

8.30 p.m. in the team room.

Rala: 'Alan, where's Carney?'

Quinny: 'He said he'd be up in the room about nine.'

9.10 p.m. in Rala's room. Carney arrives.

Rala: 'Where's Quinny?'

Carney: 'He's on the phone for two minutes. Let's set up the laptop and be ready to go when he arrives.'

10 p.m. in Rala's room. Carney leaves and a minute later Quinny arrives.

Rala: 'Did you see Brian? He's gone looking for you.'

Quinny: 'No I didn't. I'll go and find him.'

This went on night after night until I could stand no more and tore up the contract. The pair also rarely walked through my door, preferring to walk across the flat roof that separated my room from theirs and drop in via the window. It would put your heart crossways and I never did get used to the Milk Tray moments. They claimed it was to avoid bumping into Eddie O'Sullivan as they were usually laden down with chocolates and bottles of Coke. (I should point out that on such occasions they were not training the following day.)

I was also running the library at the time. It was supposed to be Geordan Murphy's job, based on my original suggestion that it would be nice for every player to bring their favourite book and we would have an instant library from which everyone could borrow. After a day, Geordan came to me and said, 'You and your bloody library. I've got landed with it so you can take it back.' I had the books lined up on my window ledge.

Myself, Quinny and Carney would be there in semi-darkness looking at *Lonesome Dove* on a laptop. The players would filter in and all you'd hear was, 'Rala, when you go to a library, there's normally some light so you can see which book you want.' There was no way we were compromising our viewing of the film. They were told to come back another time.

Sunday, 9 September finally arrived and Ireland played Namibia in their opening match of the 2007 Rugby World Cup at the Stade Chaban-Delmas. Having first taken care to leave three footies behind for the lads to walk through a few moves and practise their lineouts, I headed for the stadium with Dominic in tow four hours before kick-off. The French boys were a bit bemused by my early departure.

There were one or two minor hiccups because of the distances we had to hump the gear, but Dominic sorted that out when he got his hands on a golf buggy. For the record, the tunnel in that stadium from the dressing rooms to the pitch is the longest I have ever come across in my life.

Once there, I slipped into my routine, starting by setting up a couple of fans at either end of a large spacious room. The fridges were well stocked, the facecloths cooling in the icebox, the jerseys were hung, the toiletries table full of the necessary bottles and tubes, and the snack table prepared. On the field, I had laid out the tackle shields, seven bibs for the subs, footballs, cones and three different type of cold drinks. I had the task completed about an hour and a half before the team arrived.

I was slightly perplexed when I saw the Namibian bagman pitch up on the team bus an hour before kick-off. I was having a coffee and sandwich in the courtyard outside the dressing rooms when I spotted him. I'd have a nervous breakdown if I tried that, but each to his own.

Ireland won the match, but the first rumbles of discontent from outside the camp could be heard in the distance. Monday was a down day for the players and some struck out for the city.

Thankfully one of them was Carney, so I got a bit of peace. I joined some of the lads in an Italian restaurant that night, a great success, and we'd return there a few more times during our stay.

Tuesday was quite hectic starting with a training session, followed by the team announcement and then we were guests of honour at a Chamber of Commerce lunch in Bordeaux. The whole affair centred on the wine industry and with our hosts dressed in the local mufti, it was an entertaining couple of hours. On returning to the hotel, the players hit the gym and it was time for me to attend to the laundry.

Since I mention it, I'll offer a brief explanation of the system.

There were forty-five members in our party, multiply that by all the training gear, casual gear and formal wear … well, you get the picture. The IRB in conjunction with a local laundry business devised a superb method of dealing with the issue, the best I have come across in my time. Each room contained two large green cloth bags with the name of the person on them. They would be collected in a cage-style trolley. Every day, the laundry man would arrive at 5 p.m. and, with the help of the liaison officers, he'd empty out every bag, record what was in each and re-pack it. The whole process took about two hours. The players had to make sure their bags were in the cage outside my door in plenty of time for the laundry man's arrival.

Less than twenty-four hours later, the bags would return with everything washed and folded and the dry cleaning on a rail. To my recollection, not one item went missing during our time there.

The last yarn is by way of a preamble to a story that led to my impromptu incarceration. As mentioned, the laundry was taken away in a cage, which was stationed outside my room. One day I got into the cage, wearing shorts and T-shirt but no shoes or socks, to check on a bag whose contents had spilled out. At that moment, I heard Alan Quinlan shout, 'Wait for me, I haven't thrown mine in yet.' He trundled off to get his laundry.

As I was about to crawl out in order to avoid whatever mischief Quinny would make if he came across me in a cage, Frankie Sheahan came out of nowhere and released the hatch clip, which swung the door shut and he locked it. He wheeled me down the corridor, shouting, 'I have Rala. I have Rala.'

That's the sort of message that gathers an immediate audience. He wheeled me to the team room whereupon the cage was completely covered in bandage tape. They started throwing bananas at me. Why bananas? I have no idea.

I was shouting for them to let me out because we had training in a few hours. Then they sort of forgot about me for a while and started playing darts. It was coming up to the team meeting, so they wheeled me down to the appointed room in the hotel.

There were big curtains on one side of the room and they put me behind them. I could hear them chatting away to each other about odds and sods when all of a sudden the room went silent. I couldn't see because of the drapes, but you didn't need to be a nuclear physicist to work out that Eddie O'Sullivan had walked in.

He started off, 'Now, lads, we have a match next Saturday.'

Someone shouted, 'Before you go on, Eddie, Rala is behind the curtains.'

A couple of them wheeled me out. Eddie was standing on a podium; I was in a cage. He was stunned.

I said, 'I can explain this, Eddie.' But he burst out laughing before I got the chance. One of those big, uncontrollable laughs and the rest of the room joined in. I was then rolled outside and they just left me there in the corridor and returned to the meeting. It was about twenty minutes before a member of staff walked by, got a bit of a fright, and then wheeled me up to the team room where I was released from captivity.

The game against Georgia on 15 September followed a similar pattern in terms of the preparation. When you are in the bubble of the team environment, you're inoculated against what's going on outside the camp. It's not a case of placing your hands over your ears and singing to yourself to block out what others are saying. I had enough to be getting on with in terms of the day job. The team beat Georgia 14–10 but the absence of a bonus point meant that qualification from the pool had become appreciably more difficult. At this stage, it was time to head for Paris because the next game was against France at the Stade de France.

The day of the match – it was a night-time kick-off – was to provide me with two of the most bizarre incidents that I have come across in my nineteen years as bagman to the Ireland team.

As you might have gathered as this point, my preference for going to a ground early can at best be regarded as a mild eccentricity, but for those not used to the way I roll, it can be slightly disconcerting.

That was certainly the case for the man assigned to drive my van to the suburb of Saint Denis, which houses the Stade de France. As is customary, I told my new friend that I would like to leave the hotel about five hours before the match was due to begin. He looked at me as if I had three heads. There followed a brief discussion. Well, it was more of a monologue with me doing the talking.

As soon as we clambered into the van, the first thing he did was lean over and switch on a sat-nav. I thought this a little strange. The Stade de France is not difficult to find as it is basically off the motorway that leads from the centre of Paris to Charles de Gaulle airport.

I turned to the driver, pointed at the sat-nav and said, 'What's that?'

He replied, 'Monsieur Rala, it is a sat-nav.'

Me: 'Do you not know your way to the ground?'

Him: 'No, I live 300 kilometres away.'

We got lost. It took us an hour to find Saint Denis, never mind the stadium. People used to laugh at me about going early to a stadium but never in my wildest dreams would I have included getting lost in a list of possible delays, which was generally topped by a puncture. It was amazing that the World Cup organisers would provide a non-Parisian to find his way around the French capital, based exclusively on his ability to use a sat-nav. I expressed my views on the subject, which didn't go down well with my companion, who was more than a little miffed that I questioned his competency.

It wasn't a great start to match day, but it wasn't the only surprise that day. Even though I am never in the hotel lobby when the players make their way through to board the bus, it's pretty standard for a couple of hundred supporters to be milling around and clapping the boys as they head to the game. In Paris, there were gendarmes and security everywhere, hardly a surprise given the tournament. However, despite the official cordon and possibly distracted by the hoopla surrounding the team in the lobby, three people managed to creep into the luggage hold under the bus.

Inishbofin — one of my favourite places in the world

My days playing hooker
for Terenure RFC

Denise bringing me my cappuccino and
a biscuit outside The Shelbourne Hotel

When Dixie and I met
President Mary McAleese
and Martin McAleese
after Ireland won the
Grand Slam in 2009

Visiting 10 Downing
Street after the
British and Irish
Lions tour,
September 2013

Darren, Barry and Scott – three men who have made my life easier through the years

Tommy Bowe in one of my hats

A lot of the lads' mischief takes place in my room – this is Tommy Bowe, Luke Fitzgerald and Rob Kearney during the Lions tour to South Africa in 2009

Parcelled up under the Christmas tree at the Shelbourne

Chief messer
Donncha O'Callaghan

Peter Clohessy –
the best duty boy
I ever had

Rob Henderson
– one of the few
players who have
made the trip to
Renvyle House

Jamie Heaslip was
always a good helper

One of my lists

Ger Carmody and
Willie Bennett

Getting everything
ready

Waiting for
the bus in
Argentina

Packing the van

France 2007 ™

My hotel rooms
tend to get taken
over by lots of kit

The aftermath
of a match

My very own plaque!

After the third test in Australia with Tommy Bowe and Dr Eanna Falvey

My spares table for the Lions

Celebrating with the Lions

The doors would have been open to facilitate the players storing their gear. For the triumvirate, it would be like climbing into a dungeon. They positioned themselves where the bars are, right down at one end of the coach where the bags don't reach.

As happens at every match, I was waiting for the bus to turn up. When the bus stopped inside the stadium, I started shovelling off the bags and medical equipment, as is my wont.

The last person to get off the bus was Willie Bennett, our masseur, and he witnessed what ensued. Having got most of the kitbags, I spied an ice bucket down the far end of the storage area and started muttering to myself about who had been stupid enough to push it all the way down there.

I had to crawl in. I put my hand on the ice bucket, pulled it towards me and suddenly I was nose to cheek with a leprechaun, a female one. I got a terrible fright. 'What the f*** are you doing here?'

There were two other guys behind her and they were giggling. I can't remember my exact words but, with the aid of a few expletives, the gist of it was that they were in serious trouble and that they wouldn't be laughing in about thirty seconds.

The girl turned white. I shouted at them to get out. The gendarmes were only a matter of feet away. Then, as the leprechauns were slowly making their way to where they could climb out, I had an attack of conscience.

I thought, *Now hang on, Rala. If I hand these bunnies over to the gendarmes they will be whisked away to a police station. Their parents would then get a phone call informing them that their pride and joy had been arrested.*

In fairness to the Leprechaun Three, they would have considered it a great laugh at the time as they crawled on board but what they hadn't realised was how dangerous their actions had been. If the bus driver had to jam on his brakes, if the coach had crashed, gone on fire then no one would have known they were there.

I made my decision. I was still annoyed but I told them to stay where they were for a minute – at this stage, they had nearly crawled out.

A short time later, when the last of the gendarmes had left, I got them out and said, 'Back up that road there is the exit. My advice is to run like the wind and straight out the gate. If you have tickets come back in by a conventional route.'

Off they went with me watching the rather bizarre sight of three leprechauns wobbling as fast as they could towards the exit.

In the match, Ireland failed to storm the Bastille and the French held sway.

About two days later, I was in the bar in the team hotel talking to Paul Wallace, Paddy's dad. He turned to me and pointed to a girl sitting about twenty feet away and said, 'Rala, that's your leprechaun, or one of them.' He went and brought her over. She put her arms around me and clung to me, saying over and over again, 'Thanks, Rala. Thanks, Rala. Thanks, Rala.'

Everything that happened in the first three matches – the fitful performance against Namibia, the defeat to France and the failure to get a bonus point against Georgia – conspired to seriously compromise Ireland's chances. As events unfolded it would prove to be an insurmountable obstacle that we couldn't clamber over. France did manage a four-try, bonus-point win against Georgia (we hadn't), which meant the lads had to achieve that exact remit against Argentina to escape the pool.

Ireland ran into an Argentinean roadblock in the final pool match, which confirmed our early departure from the tournament. It was deeply disappointing for all concerned because of the genuine expectation and anticipation going into the tournament.

But the Pumas pulled off one of the surprises of the tournament by trumping the French in their own backyard. The South Americans would go on to prove that it was no fluke by reaching the semi-finals (they lost to eventual champions, South Africa) and beating France for a second time in the bronze medal match.

The Six Nations Championship that followed in the New Year brought the curtain down on Eddie O'Sullivan's reign. I had spent seven years working with him and there's no doubt that under his direction I became a better bagman. I was saddened by the way it ended. When you spend that amount of time with someone, a bond forms, especially a person who has your best interests at heart. I rang him a few days after he stepped down but I doubt my words offered much consolation.

There have been times when I have been glad that fate propelled me in a certain direction. But there aren't many people who realise that I could also have been lost to the position of Ireland bagman five short years into the job. I'm not sure whether the players would have celebrated or commiserated at the time.

It was the 1999 World Cup and we were in France (which was one of the five host nations). Donal Lenihan was manager, Warren Gatland was the coach, and we exited the tournament against Argentina in Lens. It was a horrible night. I have imprisoned most of what happened in the deepest, darkest recess of my mind, hoping never to find the key. Two memories do escape – the thirteen-man lineout and the try by Argentinean winger Diego Albanese.

The mood post-match was funereal. We got back to the little hotel to pack up the stuff, ready to return home the next morning. Once you're out, you're out. I drank a glass of wine with Peter and Anna Clohessy at about 3 a.m.

We arrived back into Dublin in a haze. A lot of our clothing was in the Berkeley Court where we had left our excess baggage. It was a case of get your gear and get out. It was a nice morning as I paused outside the Berkeley Court hotel, bumping into Keith Wood.

Woody had his bags over his shoulders. I asked him where everyone was and he said, 'They're all gone, Rala. It's over.'

That brought it all home to me that the World Cup really was finished.

However, I didn't have time to let the sadness linger because I had been farmed out. That morning, word had filtered back to me that I was to be the bagman for the Argentina team for their quarter-final against France at Lansdowne Road. It came as a shock and sent me into a fug of despair. One of the gentlemen in the IRB had come up with this idea. I won't mention names but I haven't forgotten that I was passed on like the last sandwich on a plate. The Argentinean party was based in the Finnstown House Hotel and I arrived there the next day at the appointed hour. I walked up to Reception and told them who I was and the business I had at the hotel.

The first thing the receptionist told me was that there was no room in my name. I thought, *That suits me fine. Maybe they won't need me after all.* I didn't want to be there and by the look of things, they hadn't made any accommodation for me.

Still I had to be professional, so I set out in search of a man I have always called Fafa. He was a decent fella with good English and I knew that he'd set me straight. He was their usual bagman, despite a heart condition. We had a chat and he informed me that the squad would not train until the following day. I headed home for the night and collected a few bits and pieces ahead of my return to the hotel.

Argentina trained in King's Hospital School. I set up a mini-Rala shop, not the full Monty though. There were no tablecloths and none of the other trappings that I would have had in place if catering for my own boys.

After training, I went back up to the hotel but once again they had no room for me. I took myself off home. I couldn't speak Spanish so, to be honest, I had no idea whether they were annoyed or what they were saying. On the eve of the match against France, I shared Fafa's room.

I was afraid of my life what might happen because of the number of pills, wires and contraptions that he had in his room for his heart condition. I was told by the Argentinean management that I could come along to the post-match function as one of their party. It was pretty much the only communication I had with them during my time with the squad. There was no warmth, no effort at inclusion. I was just a dogsbody, meant to fetch and carry while no one except Fafa felt any compunction to talk to me. I was an outsider in the middle of a camp, spending most of my walking moments cursing the IRB.

I came very close to chucking it in. Fafa was a nice, pleasant lad, but I was tolerated rather than included. Let's just say I didn't peel them any grapes. It was a surreal experience arriving at Lansdowne Road with the Argentinean team, like being on the *Marie Celeste*, or so I'd imagine. France won and when the final whistle went, I packed up my tent and headed off without a backward glance. Well that's not strictly true as I did put their stuff into the team coach. The way I was feeling, it would have been hypocritical of me to attend the dinner. Can you imagine French and Spanish speakers and me in the middle of all that? I said goodbye to Fafa and went on my way.

Most people define Rugby World Cups by the matches, the results and the rugby, but when I think back to those tournaments it is the people and the places that are the first port of call in terms of my memories.

It's not that I'm oblivious to the rugby side of things, far from it. Maybe it is just that my priorities are slightly different. I will do everything I can, in my own area of expertise, to help the team and the management. I want Ireland to win, but what's more important to me is that every Irish player can walk back to the dressing room unassisted. That's what I worry about when they are out on the pitch.

Results come and go. Some days you are the king and on others you feel like a ragamuffin. I love when players retire from rugby at a time of their choosing rather than watching someone go through the trauma of a career cut short by serious injury.

In the 2003 World Cup, Ireland had very nearly beaten their hosts Australia in a pool match – helped by Brian O'Driscoll's soft-shoe shuffle down the touchline – before going out to France in the quarter-final. It was Ger Carmody's first tour. He's become a close, dear friend as we have soldiered together around the world and without him, I would be lost. We even got to enjoy the 2013 Lions tour to Hong Kong and Australia together.

Back in 2003 everything was completely new to him. We struck up a bond and stuck close to one another. The night of the quarter-final defeat to France — a match which the French won convincingly 43–21 after scoring thirty-one early points — signalled Ireland's exit from the competition. Keith Wood had announced his intention to retire if Ireland lost the match. He spoke to the team and management that evening. The place was jammed and I couldn't get into the room where he was making that final speech. I stood beside the great Sonia O'Sullivan at the door. That's as far as we got. All I heard of the speech were the words 'thank you'.

Earlier that day, I'd met the IRFU Chief Executive Philip Browne. Ger was standing beside me. We started to chat and he asked me how Ger was getting on. 'He's getting on great, Philip. Doing a brilliant job. There's only one thing, one weakness. He's fond of the gargle. Most nights, I have had to slip into town and fix up his accounts.'

Philip's mouth opened and his eyes popped out of his head. I continued.

'He goes into all these sleazy old bars. You know, the sort of places where you'd find ladies of easy virtue and ill repute.'

Philip was speechless, until I started laughing. Nothing could have been further from the truth. Ger was the complete opposite. He tells that story, adding that he once had a promising career with the IRFU until he met me.

And then there is the mosquito story. On one particular Ireland tour to Australia, Ger had a lovely room in the hotel in Terrigal boasting an ocean view. I was very jealous because I was down the back of the hotel in a small room, adjacent to where they brought the bottles out at night. All you could hear was bang, crash, wallop into the small hours. I used to head up to Ger's room when it was getting dark. I knew that the flying insect squadrons would be out in force. On the pretext of going outside for a smoke on his balcony, I would open the doors and then the mesh curtains, making sure that all the lights were on in the room to attract the mosquitoes and their pals. I had to duck as these things flew straight past my head. Ger would then spend the whole night battling the plague that had infiltrated his room. I held him personally accountable for my circumstances. Funnily enough, I've always had decent rooms since.

I am privileged to have stayed in some of the best hotels in the world and dined in brilliant restaurants but when it comes to culinary matters, I would be a man of reasonably simple tastes. By way of illustration, I remember extolling the virtues of some seafood restaurant to Shane Horgan. When I eventually finished waxing lyrical about the place, Shane asked what I had to eat. 'Steak,' I replied. He didn't stop laughing for about two hours.

ALAN QUINLAN
Back row for Ireland (1999–2008)

Rala is the only bagman in the world who hasn't lifted a bag! He's a remarkable delegator. I'd equate him to a foreman on a building site, moving people around while keeping the project on track. He'd arrive at a hotel and within ten minutes he'd have five porters lined up and would be issuing instructions. But everything was done for the benefit of the players and the management – they always came first in whatever he did. He took tremendous care of us and we never wanted for anything, major or trivial.

He portrayed this image of an innocent abroad ... couldn't boil an egg, cook a dinner, iron a shirt, but he's sharp as a tack. When I first joined the national squad, I was still quite young and immediately gravitated towards him, possibly because I roomed with Claw for a while and Rala was very friendly with him. I was a bit anxious and hyper but found Rala's company soothing. He was great to chat to, his room is an oasis of calm.

I spent a lot of time with him. He was very witty, told good stories, even if they were a bit long-winded, and bad jokes that were so bad they were funny.

The highlight of the 2007 World Cup for myself and Brian Carney when we were based in Bordeaux was to go to Rala's room every night and watch a couple of episodes of a *Lonesome Dove* box set, drinking Coke and eating chocolate. We'd try to get him going on who was his favourite player or province, but he'd never answer.

In 2008, Ireland were playing the All Blacks and I reiterated to him that I would give him my jersey after my final Irish appearance. I thought I had a year or two left, but Rala, the cheeky sod, asked me if he could have the one I'd be wearing against New Zealand. I pretended to be very annoyed but as things transpired, that was my last cap – I still haven't given him the jersey.

Rala had a way of putting things in perspective for all of us. He's a decent, honest and engaging person to be around, and a close friend to this day.

My Great Escapes – Part II
RENVYLE HOUSE

Another favourite bolt-hole of mine is Renvyle House in Connemara, reputedly built in the seventeenth century, and included in the list of owners is that poet, surgeon, athlete, statesman, classical scholar, aviator, wit and raconteur Oliver St John Gogarty. He came into possession of the 'sea-grey house', as it is affectionately known, in 1917.

In 1953, it was taken over by a triumvirate of Galway businessmen, John Allen, D.D. 'Donny' Coyle and Michael O'Malley. My introduction to Renvyle is an amalgamation of two stories, the first of which rather appropriately had its origins in Terenure College RFC.

In the early 1990s, John Kelly, a talented scrum-half, joined Terenure from Clondalkin RFC. I was bagman for the club at that time. John's initial rugby pathway took him to the third team but he gradually progressed to the firsts where he came into my ambit. He played for a couple of seasons and, when he was leaving, I presented him with the number nine jersey. Now, in case you think I lost the run of myself, we were probably getting a new set for the following season.

A few years later, I was standing alongside Dixie at the bar in the club enjoying a pint of my favourite tipple, when John Kelly walked in. We immediately struck up a conversation. I hadn't seen him in the interim but that was hardly surprising as he pointed out he'd been in Manhattan for the previous five years. In a strange quirk of fate, Dixie and I were due to spend some time there, leaving for New York the following week. He gave me his number and insisted that I ring him, which I did on the Sunday evening of our arrival.

Johnny was working in Smith and Wollensky, a high-end chain of restaurants, under an assumed name. He told me he'd be on duty from 9 p.m. on Monday night and to come down. We walked in about eight. It was a massive place. They had brass nameplates at the bar in recognition of where some of their regulars sat. The fella behind the bar greeted me with the question, 'Are you Rala?' I confirmed that I was and was more than a little intrigued to know how he knew.

The barman volunteered, 'Michael Smith told me.'

I replied, 'I don't know any Michael Smith. Do you mean John Kelly?'

He said, 'Oh we don't call him that round here.'

We enjoyed a couple of drinks. John arrived and insisted we go into the restaurant and have a meal. It was sumptuous by any standards and when I called for the bill around midnight, Johnny told me that he'd taken care of it. He then told me to go to Battery Park on Tuesday evening, where there would be two tickets in my name at the box office for a French-Canadian circus. On the Wednesday, we rendezvoused at La Cite restaurant on Broadway. The circus – no animals – was fantastic and Dixie and I enjoyed our stroll through little Italy on the way home. The houses, restaurants and delicatessens got me daydreaming about *The Godfather*.

We met Johnny in La Cite, had a couple of drinks and were then whisked through to the dining area. I remember distinctly that Dixie had a starter normally shared among four people for her main course. It was the equivalent of a small trawler's catch of seafood peeping out from a mountain of ice on a huge silver platter. Dixie, in devouring the entire contents, drew a crowd from the kitchen to witness how this petite lady was manhandling a four-person entrée. Johnny introduced us to his boss, Mick, another Clondalkin native, who had given him a job. We were brought through to the kitchen to meet the staff and again when I asked for the bill, I was waved away. Johnny invited us to accompany him the following night to farewell drinks in Kate Kearney's pub for Mick's father-in-law, who was returning to Ireland.

We arrived at the bar and were introduced to Mick's wife, Julie and her father, Michael Joe Ruddy, the man in whose honour the bash was being held. At one point, I tried to buy some drinks but was politely told that everything was on a tab that Mick was running. We had a brilliant night – and morning for that matter. At 6 a.m., myself, Dixie, Michael Joe and John Kelly stood outside the pub. The sun was already shining down. We bade farewell to Michael Joe; his parting words were that if we were ever in Renvyle to look him up. As he walked across the road, I turned to Dixie and said, 'That is the last we'll see of him.'

Johnny wanted to grab some breakfast. I told him that the only way that was happening was if I paid for it. The bill came to seventeen dollars and that was the sum total of what we spent over the four nights.

I asked Johnny before he left why he had done all this for me. He replied, 'Well, Rala, when I went down to Terenure and didn't know anybody, you befriended me. You looked after me when I got on the senior team and then to cap it all when I was leaving you gave me my jersey. That's the reason.' I was blown away, humbled by what Johnny had done.

On our return to Ireland, Vincent Flannery, a friend of mine who was the manager of the Connemara Gateway Hotel in Oughterard, where we had spent many happy days and nights, moved to a hotel in Wicklow Street in Dublin. I arranged my niece's wedding to take place there. She moved into our house for a week in the build-up and we shifted to the hotel.

Vincent then informed me he was moving to a place called Renvyle House. We went down during the summer about a year later and Michael Joe Ruddy's name popped into my head. We walked into a pub where two people were sitting at the end of the bar – one of them was Michael Joe. As we walked towards them, Michael Joe looked up and said, 'I don't remember you but I remember her, Bixie or Pixie or Trixie.' We subsequently met his wife, Mary, their other daughters Marian and Debbie and their son Michael. Since then, if I'm down in that neck of the woods on my own I stay in his house.

At that stage Mrs Roche (Dixie's mum) was still working but we felt that she needed to relax more and enjoy the odd treat. We used to have Christmas dinner in her house but then we started going to hotels. When Vincent suggested Renvyle House, we thought it was a great idea. We went down for three days and ended up making it our base for Christmas for ten years in a row. And after our wonderful Christmases, we'd spend New Year's Eve with loads of friends in the Gateway, which was owned at the time by my old school friend, Charlie Sinnott. We had some great times there and were well looked after by Charlie's wife Bridit, Geraldine and Christine.

It provided my introduction to a job that may sustain me into my dotage. During our second Christmas there, Santa Claus failed to show up on the morning in question. Ronnie asked me to step into the breach and I was happy to oblige. I performed the role for nine years. I would go down to the Ruddys' house and Marian would do my makeup. Michael Joe would have arranged my transport back to Renvyle House for a grand entrance: in no particular order I have arrived on a cow, donkey and horse, in a boat and perched atop a cherry picker. One year, we brought twenty-eight people down for Christmas. It was a select crew, handpicked by me.

Whenever I visit Renvyle, I am reminded of Oliver St John Gogarty's words to describe the location.

No easeful meadows or delightful springs,
Nor visionary islands, lure its best,
But far off on the margin of the West,
A sea grey house, whereby the blackbird sings.

There is a tradition that all newcomers feed Ronnie's ducks and the odd interloping swan. He who holds the sliced pan calls the tune, pied-piper style, as the birds surround their benefactor. It's a funny sight, watching someone marooned in the midst of an ever-expanding circle of beaks and feathers.

The tingling sensation that I get steering the car up that long sweeping, tree-lined driveway to the hotel never diminishes. Familiarity merely increases the sense of anticipation – the turf fires ablaze in the lobby, the stairs leading to the old part of the house and plush rooms straight from a Dickens novel or, for younger readers, the sets of *Downton Abbey*. The view from the rooms offers a variety of landscapes and seascapes that pummel the senses. Pebble Beach is the name of the par three, nine-hole golf course on site, just one of several outdoor amenities. It pre-dates its American cousin and is certainly more affordable.

A minor legal kerfuffle arose a few years ago with regard to its name but the American side of the family eventually backed down when a solicitor from a London firm they engaged took the time to travel to Renvyle and look at the 'opposition'.

Then there is the bar, a gluepot from which there is no escape for the late-night revellers. It is our own Abbey Theatre. Pat Trundle, another frequent visitor along with his wife Darina, is one of the best entertainers I have come across and we have shared the stage on occasion, singing 'Christmas 1915', Pat supplementing our voices with his guitar. Other snapshots of times past flood the mind, the carol singers, a Christmas dip in the sea with Rob Henderson for company, the Wren boys and all those who helped make our experiences what they were, including Niall, Sharon, Pat, Muriel, Ave, Tommy, Susan, Eithne, Richard, Fergus.

Ronnie Counihan and his staff do a fantastic job of blending into the background but materialising as you need them. You can have the most expensive furnishings and trappings in a hotel but it is the people, the staff, that make someone's stay memorable.

They say that to come back you must first leave. I think of those words every time I watch the sea-grey house disappear in the rear-view mirror.

It's not only Renvyle House that gave us a treasure trove of Galway memories. We used to travel to the aforementioned Connemara Gateway Hotel to ring in New Year. A dear friend Charlie Sinnott and his wife Bridit owned the hotel at that time. Charlie and I went to Terenure College and for good measure we both lived in Templeogue village.

When Charlie sold the hotel he presented me with the big glass sign, Reception, that I kept in my kitchen at home until it was accidentally knocked over by a workman. Dixie and I have been guests at Charlie and Bridit's magnificent family home where we have spent many a great evening.

He worked extensively in the hotel business before buying the Connemara Gateway and a gang of us would travel down a couple of times a year but would make a point of saying goodbye to the old year in Oughterard, including the millennium when we buried a casket. I cannot for the life of me remember what I contributed to it. I have watched their three boys Darragh, Eoin and Ruairi grow to be fine young men and in naming them it reminds me of an incident when Darragh was a youngster.

Marty Party and I were reclining on a lounger by the pool, grabbing the final rays of the day before heading into dinner when I noticed Darragh jumping into the deep end of the pool. He didn't surface after a second or two and I panicked, ran to the edge and dived in and pulled him from the bottom. At that moment, Charlie was inside serving guests in the dining room and, unaware of the circumstances, caught sight of me hurling myself into the pool fully clothed. He told me later that he thought, *Rala, as mad as ever*.

Charlie currently owns Brooks Hotel in Drury Street, Dublin – where much of this book was written – and the Connemara Coast Hotel in Furbo where the Irish rugby squad stayed once. It had rained for three days solid and Crowley Park, home of Galwegians was completely waterlogged, so much so that a scrum session was conducted on the hotel lawn down by the lake; arguably the most picturesque venue ever.

Oughterard is given added resonance on a personal level because it's where my brother David, and his wife Miriam live. He has a house off the Glann Road beside the lake. I'd often stop in on my way or coming back from Cleggan.

ROB HENDERSON
Centre for Ireland (1996–2003) and the Lions (2001)

There is a picture of Rala and Dixie that sits proudly in my front room. Angie, my wife, and I consider him family. Soon after I had moved over to play with Munster, we were awaiting the birth of our first daughter, Mia, in October. After she was born, we started considering going back to England for Christmas. Rala was having none of it, insisting that we would accompany him, with Dixie and friends, to Renvyle House in Connemara. It's a beautiful place, with its own little community for the festive season. It was absolutely enchanting and we had a brilliant time. I will never forget the sight of Rala, dressed as Santa Claus complete with Wellington boots, riding a donkey across the fields to the hotel.

Rala always addresses people by name. It doesn't matter whether he last met you last week or five years ago. He has a genuine interest in people, nothing shallow or superficial, no matter what their background. It's the mark of the man.

I remember after one Ireland training session a few of us decided to run back from Dr Hickey Park in Greystones to the Glenview Hotel. It's about three or four miles. As we set off, Rala was packing up the van.

When we arrived back there was still no sign of Rala. He did everything at his own pace. He had an uncanny knack of knowing how to bestow just the right amount of responsibility on people when directing them to do things. When he asked you to do something, it was never an imposition. He respected you enough to ask, so you happily obliged.

Rala couldn't do what he does without Dixie's support. She's his rock and they make quite a team. They're great company. The ritual of going to his room before an international to polish boots, have a chat and a cup of tea was always something to look forward to. Rala, Claw and myself enjoyed some great laughs together.

He's had a very positive effect on me, something of a role model and someone who I have always looked up to.

Chapter 7

**'Remember your yesterdays,
dream your tomorrows and live your todays.'**

Declan Kidney's appointment as Ireland coach in May 2008 was accompanied by a new team manager in Paul McNaughton and the introduction of assistant coaches Les Kiss and Gert Smal.

The new regime and forty-four players assembled on 31 July in Jury's Hotel in Cork for a training camp that took us to the Mardyke and also to the grounds of Presentation Brothers College. Cork Constitution and Munster legend Ian Fleming (Flem) – he's never shaken or stirred by what the life of a bagman throws at him – gave me a dig-out with my duties. That extra pair of hands made a massive difference. The sun shone and there was plenty of enthusiasm from young bucks and old as they sought to impress the management team and worked to be included in the squad heading out to New Zealand and Australia. It wasn't all work, though. On the Thursday we had a fabulous meal and night out in Kinsale.

Declan had a little unfinished business with Munster, namely the Heineken Cup final against Toulouse, and so for Ireland's summer tour Down Under, Michael Bradley took the coaching duties, Niall O'Donovan assisted and Joey Miles was manager.

It was a reunion of sorts with a little role reversal. In 2005, when Ireland had toured Japan, Eddie O'Sullivan had been away on Lions duty in New Zealand, so Niall O'Donovan had taken charge, assisted by Michael Bradley. Three years on only Joey Miles kept the same position. Brads had been captain of Ireland when I first started as a bagman for the national team and I was looking forward to working with him again.

That summer tour had a slightly different feel from the off as it effectively began with a match against the Barbarians in Gloucester's home ground, Kingsholm. We were based in the Queen's Hotel in Cheltenham, a beautiful old-style hotel that fits snugly into the affluence of the town itself and, whilst we were there, the care and attention received made us feel like Dresden china.

Leinster had won the Magners League earlier in May and Munster made it a double celebration by beating Toulouse in the Millennium Stadium to win the Heineken Cup. That game took place the Saturday before the Barbarians match and I watched Munster win in the team room with Dave, the bus driver.

That week, I managed to catch up with my old friend Dr Donal O'Shaughnessy, whose party piece was the German clockmaker song, because he was working with the Barbarians. Brian O'Driscoll returned home suddenly because of the death of a friend, but Shane Horgan did a great job in his absence in leading Ireland to victory in some style. The following day, we decamped to the Pennyhill Park and Spa where we were joined by the Munster players. The atmosphere was upbeat but, for me, there was a certain poignancy because Denis Hickie had retired – he'd announced his intentions during the 2007 Rugby World Cup – and Simon Easterby had followed suit. Simon, as a person and a player, has been responsible for some great memories. I'll certainly never forget him or his brother Guy, who I refer to as the 'Easter bunnies'.

On arrival in New Zealand in early June, we were met by an old friend Peter White – ours is a relationship that goes back many years – in his new role as a liaison officer for the New Zealand Rugby Union.

Peter had taken over from John Sturgeon but it was another John (who I knew as 'John the Navy') who captured my attention on that tour. He helped Peter in looking after our every whim. He was in the navy – by that point behind a desk rather than on the high seas. He introduced a few nautical terms, one of which was 'warming the bell'. He told me that when ships are at sea, they'd ring a bell to signify the end of a watch. But when they travelled to colder climes, they'd go up a few minutes before the allotted time and gently strike the ball to warm it up.

If John asked me what time I'd want to go in the morning and I said 8 a.m., he'd respond by saying, 'We'll warm the ball at 7.50

a.m.' So I'd meet him in the lobby then. I learned so much from both John and Peter and was delighted to meet them on the eve of the third Lions' test in Australia in 2013.

As usual, I was assigned two local lads to help me out. These gentlemen proved invaluable, especially when it came to forecasting the weather on the day of the game. They kept referring to an impending storm, which didn't look likely for most of the week. Even though we got a little rain on the night before the game, it seemed that the apocalyptic forecast for match day was going to be an exaggeration. However, the two lads convinced me that the storm would arrive about kick-off time – and but for them I would have been caught out. In preparation, I went to a hardware store and picked up several rolls of tarpaulin and four heavy blankets, and then mustered as many towels as I could find. I arrived at the Westpac Stadium at 3 p.m. and began putting some order on the changing room while singing along to some Christy Moore songs that were blaring from my iPod. Everything was in order – the food and drinks arrived on time, as did the players about seventy-five minutes before kick-off.

On the pretext that a storm of biblical proportions was about to descend on the stadium, I delayed putting out the equipment for the pre-match warm-up.

I was soaking up the atmosphere at pitch-side when a guy came over and informed me that his mate in a helicopter was ten minutes away and a storm was on his coattails. He was right, to the very second. I have never experienced anything like it – sheets of freezing cold rain being propelled by gale-force winds. It was like standing in a power shower with the nozzle turned to the cold setting. I don't know how the players managed.

The replacements bench was on the sideline and more miserable-looking, drenched waifs you'd struggle to find. I used everything I had to try and keep people and things dry, but lost the battle against the elements convincingly. Clearing up after the game was a mammoth task. Everything was soaking wet, including myself. I arrived back in the hotel lobby at midnight with no shoes, no socks and wearing wet tracksuit bottoms and a polo shirt that I'd found discarded on the dressing-room floor. I looked and felt a state. The hotel staff had the good grace not to laugh.

The following morning, we flew to Australia so I had to make sure that the equipment, gear bags and medical paraphernalia – there were 150 bags in total – were ready for 10 a.m. when the truck, which was transporting them to the airport, was due to arrive. Two hours later, I left for the airport myself, where I checked in my luggage (thirty-three pieces) and laid out the lads' gear bags, which they have to check in themselves.

The flight to Melbourne was delayed but the city was worth the wait – it's a beautiful, visitor-friendly place. The staff at the Hyatt Hotel were outstanding, catering for our every need with tremendous efficiency and personality. The only downside was the result of the game. Ireland matched the Wallabies in the try-scoring stakes with two apiece (Denis Leamy and Brian O'Driscoll crossed the Aussie line) but ended up going down narrowly 18–12 at the Telstra Dome.

The day after the match, Sunday 15 June, we flew home and I sought refuge in Inishbofin, where the cares of the season were washed away on the tide. With Dixie by my side and surrounded by friends, the days and nights were filled with laughter and music, untouched by the outside world.

No holiday lasts forever, though, and I was soon back in harness, preparing for the November test series.

Limerick was the first port of call, where Ireland beat Canada in Thomond Park and young debutant Keith Earls scored a try with his first touch of the ball.

It was about this time that the players decided to check out my fitness. I was under the cosh as they were suggesting that I wasn't moving as freely or quickly as I might and felt that I could improve my conditioning – they summarised it as, 'Rala, you're useless.' After some thought, they came up with a novel method to test their theory.

We were in the University of Limerick, in the Bowl, when I was accosted by the boys, who insisted that a GPS tracking unit – the players wore them in training – was fixed to my polo shirt to determine how far I moved and at what speed.

I relented and your man set up his computer, attaching the unit to the neck of my jersey. It's important to think laterally when you find yourself in these predicaments. There was no point resisting and saying no, because God knows where they would have attached the monitor, forcibly I might add. I got behind a rail that runs around the Bowl at UL and stood next to a man with a dog and I got chatting to him (the man, not the dog). I asked him if he would mind doing me a favour. 'Is that dog a good runner?' I asked.

'Jeez he is, Rala. That's why I have him on a lead – he runs all over the place.'

I told him I had this little gizmo that I wanted to attach to the dog's collar. He assured me it would be no problem when I let him in on the details of my plan, chuckling away. The dog ran up the hill, down the hill, over here and there – the reading on the laptop went off the scale. At this point, I was hiding behind the van, well out of sight of the players.

Eventually, the dog came back and I got the tracking unit off his collar and put it back on mine. The guy who was looking after the laptop said, 'Rala, you certainly shift about. I'll be sure to tell the players as much.'

Unfortunately someone twigged what I had done. It was probably based on the distance the tracker said I'd moved and the speed at which I had done it – everyone knew I wasn't exactly Billy Whizz when it came to picking up the cones.

We lost to New Zealand but beat Argentina which, along with the win over Canada, kept us in the top eight ranked teams in the world. This helped with the draw for the 2011 World Cup which was about to take place. Then came the camp in Enfield, made famous by Rob Kearney's rallying call – when the young Leinster and Ireland full-back spoke honestly about the squad needing to become tighter and prioritise Ireland over provincial allegiances and to bring some of that passion and desire when in camp with the national side – before we all headed in our different directions to bide our time over Christmas and prepare for another Six Nations Championship.

PAUL O'CONNELL
Second row for Ireland (2002–present) and the Lions (2005, 2009, 2013)

There are so many stories about Rala to choose from but one of my favourites is the time that David Wallace hurt his ankle and had to use a Compex Stimulator to speed up his recovery and to try and ensure that there was no loss of muscle mass. The stimulator is a pad that you strap to the affected area and it sends out electrical impulses. It gets the muscles to contract and release without you moving. I think at one stage there was an ad on television that promoted it as a way of getting a six-pack stomach without doing any exercise.

Wally was supposed to have it on his ankle but was caught by a few of the lads with it on his stomach. There was a dial with which you could increase the severity of the current. This of course became a challenge amongst the lads to see who could turn it up the most and last the longest. It was quite painful. The boys decided to test it out on Rala. They held him down and attached it to his stomach. He was in his early sixties at the time and I remember thinking that he could have a heart attack and that we should really stop this torture. The boys also attached it to his face. Rala alternated between begging them to stop and laughing his head off.

His speech after the Grand Slam in 2009 had us in stitches. He spoke about what a great day it was for Irish rugby, a great occasion but to remember all those others who had contributed down the years to the evolution of the national team. He said that there were far too many people to mention names and that he wouldn't single out anyone, and then went on to name Claw and had a long list of others. We couldn't stop laughing, thinking he'd forgotten his commitment not to single out anyone. In talking to him afterwards, he knew exactly what he was doing. It was his joke on us.

Rala has a gift for making people feel at ease and special at the same time. When I watch his genuine warmth towards people and his interest in them, he makes me want to be a better person. He remembers small things about you, things that others would forget or dismiss as irrelevant. He sent Emily and me a beautiful wedding present. You could see how much thought he put into it, knowing it would appeal to Emily's taste. He sent a small gift also to Emily's mum and dad, and to my parents too.

He loves everything about Irish culture, history, music and language and reads extensively about it. In an era in which we're giving out about each other, Rala's pride in being Irish is a lesson for all of us. He's an incredible man – patient, caring and genuine.

Chapter 8

'Enjoy all of this, guys, because blink and it will be over.'

It was the eve of the Grand Slam match against Wales in the Millennium Stadium. We were garrisoned in the Hilton Hotel, our usual resting place in Cardiff. I was in my room and a few players were still knocking around, chatting. It was about 11 p.m. That's when the trouble started.

Rory Best was re-enacting his version of the Spanish Inquisition, looking for a confession of sorts. I can still hear him, demanding, 'O'Reilly, where have you hidden those wine gums?'

Beside my bed, on a locker, was some duct tape that I used to cover up logos on scrumcaps and for other minor bits and pieces.

Lying down, I was in a vulnerable position and that seemed to register with the players at the same time as it did with me. They descended on me. Inside two minutes, I was mummified in my duvet, feet bound, arms pinned and duct tape over my mouth.

We not only have our own designated floor in the Hilton, but a security guard, who sits by the lift doors and vets anyone who gets out. The same guy has done the job for a number of years. He might have raised an eyebrow but that's all he did as the players carried me to the lift, positioning me on my back on the floor, and then pressed all the buttons to ensure that it stopped everywhere en route to the lobby. Even at that late hour on a Friday night, there was a substantial crowd milling about in the foyer of the hotel.

I didn't really have time to think about my predicament because the lift doors opened almost immediately one floor down. A man with a walking stick looked on in horror, dropped his cane and ran. On another occasion, an auld one of about ninety looked at me and screamed – it was hardly surprising as the sight of a man bound in a duvet with tape over his mouth is not a common one in most luxury hotels. The players charted my progress and would periodically press the buttons on the lift again. The whole episode lasted about fifteen minutes before they dragged me out and left me on the ground outside the lift on the fifth floor. Our security guard freed me.

I was telling the story to Brian O'Driscoll, pointing out that he wasn't one of the perpetrators – but he smiled and told me that most of the players had watched the events from the balcony, roaring laughing. I suppose that in some way it emphasised the mindset of the players, how relaxed they were facing into the biggest game of their careers. Ireland had only won one previous

Grand Slam, in 1948, and this group were bidding to bridge that sixty-one-year gap. They had come close on a few occasions, so the circumstances weren't unfamiliar.

When you are at the epicentre of events, it can be difficult to sit back and look at the bigger picture. As bagman, I was cocooned in the responsibilities of my job and, in the build-up to the events in Cardiff, I never really sat back and thought about the team winning a Grand Slam. Maybe it's because of previous disappointments – like in 2007 when the team under Eddie O'Sullivan had been on the cusp of winning a Slam – but if I'm honest, it's more likely that my focus doesn't deviate from the immediacy of the next match.

The backdrop to the 2009 Six Nations campaign smacked of a new adventure. Declan Kidney was presiding over his first championship as head coach. France arrived in Croke Park, hoping to recreate their party-pooping exploits in 2007, but the Irish players weren't about to afford them the same latitude. The boys won in convincing fashion, outscoring the French 30–21 with tries from Jamie Heaslip, Brian O'Driscoll and Gordon D'Arcy. After that victory, Ireland sustained that momentum in Rome with a second win.

There is a footnote to that match. The squad learned at the beginning of the week that Dr Gary O'Driscoll had agreed to take up an offer from Arsenal Football Club to become the club's medical officer. It was a great career move for him but, on a personal level, it was sad news. Gary had been an excellent friend for nearly six years. He was a sympathetic listener – a theory I tested during many a breakfast when we discussed all manner of feckology and he had to put up with me prattling on about Inishbofin.

Ireland's third match was against England. They arrived at Croke Park more prepared than they had been two years previously, but the boys managed to edge past them by the narrowest of margins, 14–13. Brian O'Driscoll, not for the first time in his career, defied the laws of physics to squeeze into a gap that didn't exist and burrow his way past two burly English pillars. I've watched the try time and again and still marvel at how he seized that day.

Murrayfield houses many graves to Irish ambition, so the players and management knew that maintaining the winning sequence would be no mere bagatelle and the match echoed that suspicion. Jamie Heaslip's try, following a break by Peter Stringer, might have been the defining moment on the scoreboard but, for me, the best moment in the match was the wonderful, try-saving tackle by Tommy Bowe that helped enable Ireland's victory.

The media's Grand Slam treatises, which had started as a trickle after the England match, turned into a deluge. A small forest was cut down and devoted to Ireland's date with destiny. It would be disingenuous to suggest that the management and squad were oblivious to what was at stake, but it certainly wasn't a focal point of conversation. You can't play a Saturday match on a Monday, Tuesday, Wednesday ... well, you get the idea. It's too mentally wearing, so players welcome distractions – and I'm often on the receiving end.

The week of the Welsh match started off in Dublin on a high note, literally.

Christy Moore, a hero of mine, agreed to come to our hotel in Killiney at short notice and treat us to a gig. He'd done this in the past, but everyone appreciated the vintage show he put on. There was a little audience participation and a few of the players were given the opportunity to sing with him. The hour and a half flew by and everyone was in rare form as they retired for the night.

After such a good start, later in the week there followed what could have been one of the greatest catastrophes in Irish rugby.

It started innocently enough. Following a training session at the RDS, the players organised a race between the various members of the management. It was handicapped, based on age and infirmity rather than ability, so some started on the goal-line with others dotted at irregular intervals. I began on the halfway line, a mere fifty metres from the finishing post.

Geordan Murphy was the official starter and, on his cue, I took off like rain on the wind. That was certainly the image I had in my own head. I was mentally composing my winning speech as I crossed the twenty-two-metre line in a blur, not a soul in sight – then both my legs gave way. The pain was excruciating as I fell, landing on a couple of the match balls that the Welsh Rugby Union had sent across for us to practise with ahead of the game. I was screaming in agony. The players didn't know whether to laugh or be concerned, so they split into two groups.

I had an oxygen mask placed over my face as one or two suspected I'd suffered a heart attack. The only face I could see was ROG's and I'm pretty sure his were tears of laughter. There was a good reason I hadn't run that fast in thirty years.

In the meantime, forwards coach Gert Smal had claimed victory in the management race but unfortunately for him everyone was standing around me, still flat out on the ground. Willie Bennett and Dave Revins, our masseurs, helped me to my feet and from the pitch before driving me back to the team hotel. The boys worked on me for four days to ensure that I didn't miss the trip to Cardiff.

There was no way I was giving that up. To this day, I don't know what made me collapse. The rest of the week was less fraught, the nocturnal, lift-riding events of the Friday notwithstanding.

For some reason, Warren Gatland decided that Wales would occupy the visitors' dressing room for the deciding match. The day before the game, I asked for the Welsh paraphernalia that adorned the walls of the home changing room to be removed.

There had been a quiet focus and resolution in the camp in the build-up to the game. The lads were well aware of what the match meant. It was there in black and white (newspapers) and Technicolor (television). It was impossible to get away from the hype.

Players are different animals when they're in a changing room, different in the sense that some like to sit with their headphones on, others will chat quietly while some like to be alone with their thoughts. You get to know the personality types and their routines. That day everything was in sync. Determination and focus are difficult to measure, but they were almost visible. You sense things and notice body language, you're aware of a slight difference. I'm not saying for one moment that I knew Ireland were going to win – I'd enough to be getting on with in terms of my duties – but maybe it's because I was more aware of what a victory would mean to Irish rugby that I became hypersensitive to my surroundings.

Maybe hindsight has provided me with a greater clarity of what it was like in the dressing room that day. When I remember being in the dressing room before the match, I certainly mix in what players have said since about how they felt – it's not as if I was just sitting on a bench daydreaming about what might be. As I have said a million times, I have a small role to play but if I don't do my job, I'm distracting the team and management from the task in hand, so I keep busy. Obviously I knew what the day meant, but me getting agitated and pumped up by the occasion wasn't really going to help. One, I wasn't playing and, two, you don't need to be Charles Atlas to get the top off a bottle of mouthwash!

I usually stand in the tunnel outside our dressing room as the players run out for the start of a match and watch them go past. For a brief moment, I felt very calm but that feeling certainly didn't last that day and I remember being in a perpetual state of anxiety for most of the game. I forced myself to watch Stephen Jones strike his last-gasp penalty. I like to think that I know a bit about rugby. My initial reaction was that the ball had risen too high, too quickly. I closed my eyes and when I opened them Geordan Murphy was waltzing down the in-goal area.

I found myself screaming at him to kick the ball out of play, which was slightly bizarre on the basis that he couldn't possibly hear me over the deafening din of jubilant Irish supporters. After the match, I offered my theory on the trajectory of Stephen Jones' penalty to Mark Tainton, Ireland's kicking coach – the politer way to phrase his response was to say that I had been mistaken in my analysis.

I sat on a bench pitch-side for a few seconds after the final whistle.

Slightly disorientated by the moment, I returned to the dressing room, stuck a bit of Christy Moore on the sound system and sat there with my head in my hands, trying to comprehend what Drico and the boys had achieved. My good buddy Ger Carmody came to find me and drag me back to the pitch where the celebrations had reached fever pitch. In my fifteenth season as bagman to the Ireland team, I now had the privilege of witnessing a Grand Slam. I was completely aware of how fortunate I was to be standing there.

The celebrations continued in the dressing room but at that point, I also began to realise that there was plenty of work to be done. Ireland might have won a Grand Slam, but the van wouldn't pack itself.

In a way, though, I was too happy to care. A primary source of that joy was remembering Ronan O'Gara's drop goal. I was open-mouthed when it went between the posts. I didn't know what to do with myself, so I did nothing. I stood and stared, probably sporting a silly grin. When I am on my deathbed, I want ROG to come and re-enact that moment. If he smashes a window in the re-creation, I'm hardly going to worry about it.

Everyone pitched in as always and it was soon all ready to go. I turned and looked back at the deserted changing room, the discarded tape, empty bottles, champagne, water and beer, the muck, the bandages, a traditional vista after a rugby international and, just for a second, wondered if it had all been a dream.

That evening, I didn't touch a drop, contenting myself with chatting to various boys and girls in the lobby of our hotel. It reminded me of the time I'd met London-Irish stalwart Kieran McCarthy in Limerick after a match. He introduced me to their bagman, a young lad, who happened to be having a few pints. Kieran asked me if I had any advice for the young fella so I turned to the lad and told him I'd knock the gargle on the head. The following morning, the guy pops out of the lift, looking the worse for wear. Bags were flying round the place.

About 3 a.m. on that Sunday morning in Cardiff, I got a phone call to say that I would be travelling back by plane with the players and management team – ordinarily, I would take the bus home on the ferry with Dave, which affords me a chance to catch up on some sleep. Luke Fitzgerald – I know he won't mind me saying – forgot his number ones, so I lent him mine. This meant I had to do a little bit of ducking and diving because I was the only one on the plane in a tracksuit.

I made a phone call home to Dixie, and with the help of our good friend Mikey Jordan, she smuggled one of my suits, which was similar in colour to the Ireland issued ones, to a prearranged rendezvous point – a laneway at the back of the Mansion House. I nipped back to the coach and changed in time for our civic reception.

There was a big celebration banquet for the players, management, their families and the IRFU staff in Killiney Castle that night. I was still abstemious in terms of alcohol when I was pushed up to the podium to make a speech. I would have written a few words if I had known I was going to be called upon. I spoke about all those players who hadn't won a Grand Slam, pointing out that there were too many to mention and not wishing to single out individuals because I'd be there all night, concluding the sentence with 'people like the Claw'. The whole place dissolved into laughter.

Earlier that afternoon, as we were travelling through Donnybrook on our way out to the team hotel, I heard that Terenure College had won the Junior Cup. It was the perfect end to the weekend.

The next few days are a bit of a blur, although I do remember breaking a bottle of champagne belonging to Jamie Heaslip. He took it well. The squad were invited to Áras an Uachtaráin as guests of President Mary McAleese and her husband Martin. Because of her official duties and regular attendance at rugby internationals, she had already been introduced to most of the players, many of whom would have been in the Áras before too, but this time was special. It's not every day that the national side wins a Grand Slam – twice, to be precise.

I sat at a round table in the far corner of the room alongside some of the management and backroom team – Gert Smal, Brian Green, Les Kiss and Ruth Martin, our nutritionist. At one point, I got up to take Gert, who is South African, out to a corridor to show him the busts of former Presidents of Ireland and explained who they were and how they influenced Irish history. When we got back to the table, I couldn't get to my seat without asking several people to move. As there were two empty chairs nearer to me, I thought it would be easier to sit there. I noticed there was a glass of warm water with a slice of lemon in front of one, so I sat at the other. Suddenly, the president sat down beside me – she moves from table to table and because she has to do a lot of talking she drinks warm water and lemon. I was mortified and quickly tried to introduce everyone else.

She's a lovely lady and we found a common interest in Inishbofin. I had my picture taken and it is one of my most treasured possessions. I couldn't travel to Belfast where the squad met the Queen because I had a prior engagement in London – a meeting with several of my soon-to-be British and Irish Lions colleagues to go through some details for the tour to South Africa which was only a couple of months away.

BRIAN O'DRISCOLL
Centre for Ireland (1999–present) and the Lions (2001, 2005, 2009, 2013)

One of my favourite stories about Ral (that's what I call him) pre-dates my time in the Ireland squad. It goes back to a tour to South Africa in 1998. Denise Fanagan was the physio and, after one of the matches, discovered she had a ladder in her tights. Ral was appalled that he didn't have a spare pair because he prided himself on being able to deal with most contingencies. From that point on, he has carried a spare pair of tights even though we haven't had a female physio since Denise. I'd like to think that none of the players have requested them!

In the early years, I would be one of the last in to camp on a Sunday night, and one thing I really looked forward to was the large bar of chocolate and can of Coke he'd discreetly tuck away in my room. At some point, I realised that it wasn't really the sort of snack our nutritionist would approve of and the tradition stopped.

Even when I stopped being captain, I'd find my bags in my room when I arrived at a hotel and my laundry hanging on the back of my door. He didn't have to do that, but then there's so much that he didn't have to do, but still did.

I still try to be the last person who nips down to his room on the night before an international, arriving about 11 p.m. It's a chance to chat to him about something and nothing, listen to a story or nibble away on a piece of chocolate. That time in his company is very dear to me.

He's as sharp as a tack, but plays the innocent. I remember eating a toasted ham and cheese sandwich in the team room when he wandered in. The conversation went as follows.

Ral: 'What's that?'

Me: 'It's a toasted ham and cheese sandwich.'

Ral: 'How'd you make one of those?'

Me: 'You get some ham, cheese, two slices of bread … do you want me to make you one?'

Ral: 'Would you mind?'

He's the only common denominator in the Irish squad at weddings. Not every player would go to every wedding for obvious reasons, but Ral would be pretty much at them all. That's a measure of the esteem in which he is held.

In a popularity contest in the squad, he'd win by a mile, and there'd be no argument from anyone.

Chapter 9

'There is greatness all around you – use it.'

When the joy of winning the Grand Slam had died down a little, Dixie and I took a quick trip to Inishbofin and then headed for Claw's ranch, catching up with Woody and his family while we were there. Dix returned to Dublin, courtesy of the Claw, who was driving his son to the airport. In the meantime, I moved lock and stock to the Castletroy Park Hotel, our base for an Ireland training camp. The national side was heading to the USA and Canada that summer while the Lions were heading to South Africa. We had a sumptuous dinner on the first night after which the team, management and backroom staff were presented with watches by the IRFU to commemorate the Grand Slam.

The Castletroy Park is one of my favourite hotels, not primarily for the bricks and mortar, although it's a nice looking place at that, but for Fiona O'Shea and her team. They cater superbly to our every whim.

Several months later, and at Fiona's behest, myself and Dixie paid a visit to her father, Mike O'Shea, on a visit to Dingle. We arrived on the Friday of the weekend of the All-Ireland Football final between Kerry and Cork and booked into the Dingle Bay Hotel. You couldn't get a more central location to explore the delights of the town and there was the added bonus of being able to look out the bedroom window at the marina across the street. We stuck our head around a few bar doors, eventually settling down in McCarthy's, where Tom, our host, not only gave us directions to Mike's house but reinforced what a truly small world we live in by pointing out he was Fiona's second cousin.

Our journey in actual travel-time might only have taken an hour for the round trip, but it was nine hours later when we walked back through the door of the hotel. I'm a great believer that if you have time, take it, especially when you're in a place of such outstanding beauty. There's no point in rushing around with your hair on fire.

Those of you familiar with Slea Head will know of the mountain stream that crosses the road at one point. That spot was the cornerstone of our directions but given that my navigation gene has been long dormant, a local man called Bobby came to our aid. He not only directed us to the gate of the property but rang Mike to see if he was at home.

While we waited for him to make contact, I gazed out at the Blasket Islands, having once visited An Blascaod Mór when playing rugby for Terenure College. While on the island, I got it into my head to go for a run on Trá Bán, which, as its name suggests, was a beach of stunning beauty with its white-gold sand. The islanders used to play hurling there, tweaked to their own rules, for a special contest on Christmas morning. My run was less aesthetically pleasing to the eye and culminated in a pulled calf muscle, which hindered my rugby career for a long time. But it was a small price paid for the memories I took away.

My reverie was interrupted by the directions we were given – we were told to seek out the gate decked out in the Kerry colours. I nudged the 4x4 up a small boreen and started to worry immediately as the climb got appreciably steeper.

When we hit a bit of level ground, I stopped. And, very opportunely, Mike O'Shea arrived to meet us on his quad bike, taking Dixie as a passenger while I opted for Shank's pony. The views from his cottage were breathtaking, the ocean glistening in the sunlight, boats and cars reduced by our elevation to tiny Matchbox models. I got a spin around the farmland and listened with great interest about the difficulties of mountain farming. Mike was a generous host in every respect and we left a few hours later with two bags filled with the freshest potatoes and carrots.

We stopped for a bite to eat and met a man who knew former Ireland manager Brian O'Brien. We gave him some of our newly acquired vegetables and then continued to Ballydavid, stopping off in a pub recommended by a friend of Dixie's. They too took a few spuds. On arriving back in Dingle, we repaired to McCarthy's to share porter and stories.

A couple of days later, we meandered our way back to Limerick, stopping for a night in the gorgeous Dunraven Arms Hotel before making our way to the Castletroy Park. Declan Kidney was being conferred with a doctorate from the University of Limerick and we had been invited to attend.

Between the Grand Slam win and our trip to Dingle there was the small matter of the Lions tour to South Africa. I still marvel at the experience. I was going to be part of something that had captivated me as a boy. The stories about the old tours, the Pathé newsreel footage of matches and then in the 1970s and 1980s eagerly gobbling up the television pictures of those red jerseys and the match reports on the winning series in 1971 in New Zealand and South Africa three years later. It had been twelve years since Ian McGeechan had led the Lions to a test series win against the Springboks, and now I was going to be travelling with the great Scot.

The logistics of moving the Lions players, management, coaches, physiotherapists, masseurs, analysts, communications, commercial and sundry other personnel was quite a feat of organisation, and was managed brilliantly by Louise Ramsay, Head of Operations, and Guy Richardson. Added to that, at each stop of the tour, hotels provided me with designated assistants, something I appreciated. The amount of kit and the distances being travelled all added to the potential for things to go awry.

Guy and I used to engage in a little verbal tango when it came to preparing for each match. He asked me what time I wanted to leave for the ground. I'd respond by double-checking the kick-off time. For a 5 p.m. start, I'd head to the ground at 10 a.m.

I certainly didn't lack for company. Neville, whose firm transported the Lions' gear around South Africa, was always on hand, so too Guy, who would always head back for his breakfast when things were sorted. Neville, Guy, myself and the local liaison man would travel from the hotel to the stadium in our separate groups, but we'd arrive at the stadium at pretty much the same time. Then there was Charlie McEwen and his commercial team, who were responsible for erecting the backdrops, posters and for putting up and taking down the personalised plaques in the changing room. The plaques showed the players' number and name, then there was a second one that went underneath, with the names of some of the outstanding players to have worn that number in the past – so underneath Paul O'Connell's plaque, there would be another with names like Willie John McBride and Martin Johnson. They would go up before games and be taken down immediately afterwards. I even had one of my own, which I found slightly disconcerting.

My job is fundamentally the same no matter what the match is, sometimes the scale is just a little bigger. On this tour, there were six or seven of us attending to various jobs in the changing room before the matches. I'd stay. This was my environment. I would stick on some music and go about my business. Of course, over the course of the morning and the early afternoon, some familiar faces would pop in for a chat and to take the odd photo. It was like a who's who of former Lions – Keith Wood, Ieuan Evans, Scott Quinnell, Paul Wallace, Dewi Morris, Will Greenwood and Ian 'Mighty Mouse' McLauchlan would all call in for a chat and a cup of tea or coffee. There is a fantastic sense of community: once a Lion, always a Lion.

I'd be up at 7 a.m. – traditionally on that tour I woke to Fleetwood Mac's 'Albatross' – and would then breakfast alone. I'm not being antisocial, it's just a habit. Anyway you wouldn't get too many takers at that hour of the morning.

As always, my van was loaded the night before. A typical

inventory for a match day was ten shields, a pack of cones, seven bibs, eight stadium coats, fifteen rugby balls, water, ice, protein shakes, Viper belts, stud box, seven blankets, sixty towels, thirty lots of shampoo and soap, a case containing toiletries, spare scrum caps, cycling shorts, shoulder pads, shin guards, gum shields, table, clocks, sweets and chocolate.

After I'd had my breakfast, I'd load the rest of the kit, match jerseys, a spare set, match shorts, a spare set, my own attire and the plaques, before setting out for the stadium.

By the time we played the third test – the final match of the tour – no verbal communication was required to complete the unloading and loading routine. Neville would set up the toiletries table and also Craig White's drinks table, Guy would help Charlie and Hannah with the posters and plaques while Bert would tend to the water and hang the jerseys on the hooks. Two hours from start to finish with a break for the odd lulu.

The Lions received a fantastic welcome wherever they went in South Africa. Most of the time, we trained in local schools where the facilities were absolutely superb. The rapport and camaraderie within the squad was striking and it was manager Gerald Davies and head coach Ian McGeechan who set the tone that fostered that harmony. If there was work to be done, then it was a case of all Indians, no chiefs. It was commonplace for players and coaches to collect cones or bibs after a training session. But no matter how much you know about the scale of a Lions tour, nothing prepares you for that moment when you emerge from the dressing room and out onto the pitch pre-game to be greeted by an ocean of red – the colour, the noise and fervour of the Lions' supporters serenading their team is an abiding memory that will never fade.

No matter how often I was greeted by that scene, it still made me catch my breath.

After every match, I was assigned 'duty boys', two players who would help me clear up, pack up and get everything into the van. The post-match dressing-room area can be pretty manic for a while but, as players leave, it becomes a more manageable environment. On one occasion, the duty boys were Wales out-half Stephen Jones and the England winger Ugo Monye.

The two lads started collecting all the discarded towels and then began to dismantle the toiletries table at which point I stopped them, thanked them and told them they'd done enough. They refused to go, pointing out that it was their responsibility to stay with me until every task was completed and they could see that there was still a lot to do. Having that assistance made a massive difference to my job. I always pack up neatly and in a certain order because it simplifies things for the next day and saves a lot of time – it also provides a mental checklist.

During that tour we visited Rustenburg, Bloemfontein, Durban (twice), Cape Town (twice), Port Elizabeth, Pretoria and Johannesburg (twice). The transport was executed with a military precision that was a sight to behold. Whenever we had to fly, British Airways crew would arrive at the hotel to check-in all the luggage and equipment and we would then board a coach that would take us straight to the plane. Louise Ramsay was an absolute whizz.

Guy was equally efficient. He'd often shoot on to the next location to ensure that the luggage – and when you consider the numbers involved, it was a sizeable collection of bags – was in the allocated rooms with the rest of the equipment and kit stationed in the requisite storage area. This simplified my job hugely.

The door to my room is always open with Ireland and it was no different with the Lions. Players and coaches would stop by my room for a chat, and have some of the tea, biscuits and sweets that I always kept on hand. It became a place for players to congregate, listen to music or just to meet and talk. England prop Andrew Sheridan would bring his guitar and play a few songs. He was shy about playing in company, but I was privileged to hear him sing a few of his own songs. He was a big Christy Moore fan, which only cemented our bond further.

If I close my eyes, the memories come flooding back. Proud Welshmen Adam Jones and Shane Williams taking to the hurley and sliotar with great dexterity, Phil Vickery for his ability to catch me out with a squirt from a water bottle at the most inopportune times, and the owner of the game reserve who brought me into a lion cage and stood in front of me – I was petrified. There was the time spent with Warren Gatland and Craig White, invariably laughing – I knew both well because of their time with Ireland. It took me a while to break down Shaun Edwards, he wasn't a man of many words but that isn't a hanging offence, and I enjoyed his company.

One of the great characters on tour was Paul 'Bobby' Stridgeon, the England fitness coach, who was an assistant in that particular area of expertise with the Lions. He resembled the 'Duracell Bunny', on the go from seven in the morning until midnight and beyond. He never flagged and had no off switch. He was genuinely very funny with a finely honed sense of devilment. It was he who instigated the 'Bobby Cup', a trophy made out of tin foil and awarded to the person who did the best practical joke. It's changed hands several times but to the best of my knowledge it currently resides on Jamie Heaslip's mantelpiece. I was the victim of a sketch he conjured up, where he did a piece to camera saying that I was down to one cigarette a day, and then produced this four-foot-long cigarette made primarily from surgical neck collars.

It is not unknown for me to single out an individual, either with Ireland or the Lions, and, unwittingly for the victim, bend him to my will, a 'Rala-slave' if you like. It is usually a slow, gentle process. I decided that our Bobby fitted the bill nicely, a decision that owed much to his heritage. I love pies and given that Bobby is from Wigan, which is noted for the excellence of and devotion to the humble pie, he was just the man. I charged him with sniffing out some decent pies as we travelled the length and breadth of South Africa. It was a brilliant choice on my part. Still is, because he continues to bamboozle me with the quality of pies he brings to the table. Whenever England plays Ireland at the Aviva Stadium, he produces one. I have no idea of his sources but the quality is first class.

Then there was our first port of call on the tour, Rustenburg, where we stayed in the Wigwam Hotel. Our rooms were like little chalets with stable-style doors that opened top and bottom. I was informed by one of the players that a frog had been let loose in my room and that it was venomous. I spent four hours scouring the place in David Attenborough mode and slept with one eye open. There were plenty of monkeys though, an active troop as they raced across the fairways of the on-site golf course. There was also a parrot – 'Paddy' – who used to launch the most foul-mouthed tirades as people walked past.

On another occasion in Bloemfontein, I think, Tommy Bowe

approached me and said that he had to interview me by a pool for a video diary. He manoeuvred me into position and just as I was about to answer the first question, Donncha O'Callaghan poured a bucket of water over my head.

I wasn't the only one who had to endure the odd practical joke or five. Prior to the arrival of Leigh Halfpenny – he came out late because of injury – Keith Earls, as the youngest member in the squad, was charged with the safe-keeping of the mascot, Lenny the Lion. But, true to form, the other players kept nicking it and hiding it. Keith spent more time than is healthy trying to find Lenny and his face wore a haunted expression constantly. He was thrilled when Leigh arrived and he could pass over the duties.

Lenny did lead a charmed existence at times. Five minutes before the team was due to take the field for one match, no one could find him. I discovered him with seconds to spare beneath a couple of bags that had been plonked in the corner.

It wasn't the only time that things were misplaced. There was one particular after-match function when a number of the players had forgotten their formal dress shoes. As is my wont, I had a number of spare pairs, which I gave out to various gentlemen. Unfortunately, by the time I was approached by Brian O'Driscoll and England hooker Lee Mears, I was down to a pair of black shoes and a pair of brown shoes.

I will never forget the two of them playing Rock, Paper, Scissors to decide who'd get the black ones. To compound their problems, neither pair fitted particularly well so the two of them ended up walking around like Charlie Chaplin for the night.

The night before the third test – the final match of the tour in Johannesburg – a group of players, including Paul O'Connell, Jamie Heaslip, John Hayes, Luke Fitzgerald, Rob Kearney, Alun Wyn Jones and head coach Ian McGeechan, dropped into my room in search of tea, studs and a chat, then several more joined the cluster. The plan was that everyone would head off to the team room at about 9.30 p.m. to watch the Western, *Unforgiven*. This suited me fine because I was going to have to be up early in the morning. The craic was good, everyone relaxed and the appointed time came and went without anyone budging.

Someone suggested to Paulie that he read out a page or two from the notes I was keeping for this book. The laughter could be heard the length of the corridor and drew a few more to the room. A singsong began and Luke offered a tuneful rendition of 'The Flickering Light'.

For some reason, I put on the East 17 song 'Stay Another Day' and everyone joined in. The inadvertent choice of music lent certain poignancy to the night as everyone realised that the tour was drawing to a close. It was after 11 p.m. when the last person left and the following day, the Lions went on to win the third test, having lost the first two in heart-breaking fashion.

Getting to know everyone had taken time but by that final week, we were a pretty tight-knit group. I was even forgiven the odd aberration. Kicking coach Neil Jenkins overlooked the time I sent him off to a practice session with underinflated rugby balls. He never said a word. I did indulge in a little bribery. I knew that Stephen Jones liked wine gums, so I used to leave a little tub on his towel in the dressing room. I also think I managed to convert Ian McGeechan and Gerald Davies to Barry's Tea, Graham Rowntree too.

The players had a system of fines and Welsh hooker Matthew Rees and Tommy Bowe were two of the honchos in charge of doling them out.

When I am with Ireland, I will always bring spare jerseys, shorts and socks of the correct colour for that particular day on the basis that players have been known to turn up in the wrong gear. I continued doing this with the Lions but, after a week, I received a tap on the shoulder from Rees telling me not to – it seemed my baling out players who'd turned up with the wrong gear was stopping a main source of income for the fines committee.

Not long after Rees had put me straight, he had his first victim. Ireland's number eight Jamie Heaslip mooched over to me and asked me for the correct coloured jersey. I told him I didn't have one. I can still see the look of bewilderment on his face. A line in the sand had been drawn – the fines would have to be paid.

Little did I know that I would become a principal beneficiary of the money raised from those fines. During the tour, players and coaches spoke about what they intended to do when it finished. Some were off to Las Vegas, others to more exotic destinations dominated by sand and sea. I said that I was hoping to take Dixie to the Pennyhill Park and Spa for a few days. It was a throwaway remark.

I first expressed the notion to the general manager of the hotel, Julian, while we were there pre-tour. When I returned with Dixie in August we were treated royally. The suites are named after famous rugby grounds and it seemed apposite that we ended up in Newlands. It was a magnificent room. On the day we were leaving, I went to Sandra on Reception to settle up the bill. I was speechless when told that the Lions had already taken care of it.

I immediately thought of Ian McGeechan and Gerald Davies and bought some thank you cards. To this day, I don't know if they ever got them.

However, when I arrived to an Ireland camp in Limerick later that month, I sought out Paul O'Connell to tell him of the amazing gesture. He stopped me before I'd got the first sentence finished. 'I know, Rala. The players did that.'

Apparently they raised about £5,000 in fines and distributed most of it to local charities in South Africa with a sum reserved to pay for our stay in Bagshot. It was out with the cards again – I sent them to Phil Vickery, Ross Ford, Stephen Jones and Paulie as representatives of the four nations.

It wasn't the only kindness shown to me on the tour. My great friends Tommy D'Arcy, Michael Jordan and Elizabeth Long brought Dixie to South Africa for the final two test matches. As a thank you, I resolved to try and get them in to watch a training session for the final test. I went to Paul O'Connell and he arranged permission to bring them to the Captain's Run on the eve of the test. They were thrilled and managed to have photographs taken with Ian McGeechan. In the wake of the tour, a book was commissioned for the Lions and those who'd taken part and, in it, there is a picture of Dixie, Michael, Tommy and Liz.

The 2009 Lions were a mini-community devoid of cliques where the players and management mixed easily. The wonderful spirit in the group survived the most galling defeats in the first two tests. The margin between success and failure was wafer thin but the players refused to bow the knee and got what they deserved in the final match. It wasn't just losing that they had to bear with fortitude but the injuries that saw players invalided out.

I had a farewell drink with Adam Jones and Brian O'Driscoll, who left the tour early through injury – they're two of my favourite people, but I was spoiled for choice in that respect. There's no doubt that on this tour, my saddest moments were losing the first two tests – that was shattering – and the pinnacle was winning the third one. We were so close to winning that series – I think that's what irks me most. It would have been great to emulate what Keith Wood and his gang had achieved in 1997. That 2009 tour reinforced the small margins that can determine winners and losers in sport, how injuries or just the bounce of a ball can influence how teams are remembered.

On my return to Ireland, the November tests consumed my focus with Australia, Fiji and world champions South Africa paying their respects to the Irish public. Cian Healy made his debut against the Wallabies and a draw was salvaged when Brian O'Driscoll – who else? – crossed for a try with pretty much the last play of the game. Brian received many honours that year but the one he should have got, the IRB World Player of the Year, rested on someone else's mantelpiece. It was a travesty.

Jonathan Sexton took his bow in a green jersey against Fiji at the RDS, scoring sixteen points, while Keith Earls scored a brace of tries. The boys saved the best until last with their 15–10 victory over the Springboks at Croke Park. It was a case of here's Johnny, as he kicked five penalties.

My rugby travels in 2009 took me to Cork, Dublin, Belfast,

Limerick, Edinburgh, Rome, Cardiff, Capetown, Port Elizabeth, Rustenburg, Johannesburg, Durban, Pretoria and London – eighteen matches, fourteen victories, two defeats, two draws, many miles, training sessions, hotels, wine gums and people. As the song says, 'Those were the days, my friend, I thought they'd never end.' I didn't want them to.

But the days do end. Some days you are fated to be the statue rather than the pigeon.

DONNCHA O'CALLAGHAN
Lock for Ireland (2003–present) and the Lions (2005, 2009)

If Rala gets twenty minutes into a story, I'd go over and close the door to his room. I couldn't bear the thought of anyone walking in, because we'd have to start again – at that point, we'd probably only have been a third of the way through it.

I absolutely love his story of the time he emigrated to England. If there is a new player in the squad, I'll round up a posse, head for Rala's room and get him to tell that one. I never tire of hearing it and it never fails to have everyone roaring laughing.

We affectionately refer to him as 'the slug' because he moves as slow as a snail but is too lazy to carry a house on his back. I could tell you so many stories poking fun at him, but I'd hate to upset him. That'd be like getting a bollocking from Santa Claus.

He is so important to the dynamic of the squad. One of the great things in walking back in after winning a test match is to see his face, and how proud and happy he is – it's like a window into how the nation feels.

We once played a World Cup qualifier against Russia in Krasnoyarsk. I was the subbing cover – the twenty-third man, in a squad of twenty-two – only there in case someone went down, because we were so far from home. No one did and I became Rala's little helper. He gave me one job, to go and get ice. We were in Siberia so this would be a doddle. Two hours later, I came back without so much as a cube. He managed to secure some in time for the match.

You're so pumped up in the week of an international, you

need a little down time. That happens in Rala's room, a safe haven from coaches and management. The rule is no rugby talk. It's like going to your granny's where you can be yourself instead of a professional rugby player.

Rala is fiercely loyal. On one occasion he was stopped, not for speeding I can assure you, on the way to a training session in Greystones. The garda asked me where he was going. Rala replied, 'I am going to help prepare your national side for a test match this Saturday.'

The garda apologised for stopping him and offered to escort him the rest of the way.

Rala treats everyone the same and he sums it up best himself when he says, 'Even a cat can look at a king.'

Another time I remember, Denis Leamy brought his black-tie gear instead of number ones for travelling so Rala gave him his. Eddie O'Sullivan saw Rala wearing his tracksuit and came over to talk to him about it. One of the players piped up that it wasn't Rala's fault, that he had given his to someone who had brought the wrong gear. Eddie asked Rala, who shrugged and said, 'I can't tell you that.'

All the while Leamy was standing ten yards away with an ill-fitting suit that made him look like Tom Hanks' character in the film *Big*.

Rala, though, is like Switzerland in those situations.

Chapter 10

**'Always keep your face to the sun,
and the shadows will fall behind you.'**

Dixie and I strolled down Wexford Street and turned into George's
Street as we made our way to Temple Bar and then the Button
Factory where we had a date with Luka Bloom and a support
act called Band on an Island. The night of 26 March 2010 was
an excellent one. The city was alive, people singing, dancing,
laughing and smiling on the streets. Restaurants were full, as were
the pubs. My fifteenth Five/Six Nations Championship campaign
had ended (albeit on a disappointing note when Scotland not only
beat us in our final game at Croke Park but also denied us a Triple

Crown). We had beaten Italy, Wales and England but lost to France in Paris. I'm not one for dwelling on what might have been, I've always been ruthlessly focused on enjoying the here and now or wondering what delights the future may hold.

On one weekend in early April, I watched five rugby matches, four in the flesh – Heineken Cup wins for Leinster and Munster, Terenure's victory over Thomond and also the club's under-20s triumphing against arch rivals St Mary's – and the final one, Stade Francais and Toulouse on the television. I can assure you I don't normally watch that amount of rugby.

Ireland rounded off the 2010 season with a trip to New Zealand and Australia in June – my twentieth tour and, to my knowledge, Drico and I were the only survivors from the 1999 trip to Australia when he won his first cap. It's hard to say which of us has had the greater influence over Irish rugby since then – though I think he's missed a few more games!

Sean Dempsey, the head chef in the Killiney Castle Hotel, accompanied us on tour and this meant that I was able to put in several requests for my own personalised steak and kidney pies. Just before we left, we went to the opening of the brand-spanking new Aviva Stadium and I was mightily impressed. I investigated all the nooks and crannies in my theatre of operations and must confess to being blown away by the state-of-the-art facilities. I was looking forward to working at our new home, but there were more pressing matters.

I'll start at the end of the tour and work my way back. I received a lovely letter in the aftermath of that summer tour from Mary, the wife of the then President of the NZRFU, John Sturgeon, who I knew well from all our tours to the southern hemisphere. It was my first time to meet Mary, a lovely woman. Anyway the gist of the letter was to say thank you for a box of jelly babies and to say his much she enjoyed the 'mouse story'.

The 'mouse story' happened many moons ago in Dixie's mum's house in Meath Street. In those days, it was customary for Shay 'the Bear' Ruane and I to visit Dixie and her mum in the heart of the Liberties on a Thursday night after training with Terenure. Now we didn't pick Thursday out of a hat. You see Mrs Roche, who owned a famous fruit and vegetable shop, used to take a half day on the Wednesday and head farther afield to do some shopping and the Bear and I were the principal beneficiaries of her excursions. On those cold winter nights, we made a beeline for the house to be greeted like a couple of forgotten explorers returning from the South Pole. We were offered two rocking chairs in front of a roaring fire.

There followed a meal fit for royalty, huge steaks from Larkin's, a butcher's up the road, Golden Wonder potatoes, fried onions and to round it off custard slices fresh from a Dawson Street bakery. Between mouthfuls, there would be snippets of conversation. The cumulative effects of training, fine food and the roaring fire invariably guaranteed heavy eyelids and forty winks.

One evening, Shay and I woke simultaneously to be greeted by a mouse sauntering across in front of the fireplace, brazen as you like. Confronted by the monster, we two brave buckos jumped out of the chairs, as if propelled from a gun, collided and hugged each other for safety. I'll never forget the look on the faces of Dixie and Mrs Roche. It wasn't our finest hour.

Before departing for New Zealand, Ireland had a fixture in Limerick against the Barbarians, whose number included Malcolm

O'Kelly and Alan Quinlan – they finished on the winning side and it was difficult to begrudge them their moment.

We arrived in Auckland, where I met friends from home, their sons and daughters and various in-laws and outlaws. We lost the test match and then decamped to Rotorua for a clash with the New Zealand Maoris, who were celebrating 150 years of rugby.

One incident confirmed that a place on the *X Factor* is probably beyond me. We were invited to enjoy Maori culture and heritage of an evening.

Brian O'Driscoll led us to the reception, whereupon a Maori warrior in full regalia greeted us. There was some singing and dancing, before we were ushered into a hall and waited for the elders to greet us formally. One thing that I have learned from my travels around the world is that players get restless on these occasions, so it's best to make yourself scarce or risk becoming the focal point of their amusement.

I found a nice little spot down the back and soon the voices began to sound a little distant. I fell asleep. Suddenly I felt a hand on my shoulder. I opened my eyes, disorientated – I'd no idea where I was.

It was Ger Carmody looking for the gift for the Maoris. I duly handed over the plaque. My resolve to stay awake didn't last long and soon I was back in the Land of Nod. For a second time, I woke with a start, this time after hearing my name. John Callaghan, the IRFU President, was calling on me to sing a song for our Maori hosts. To buy some time, I explained the Irish custom about singing sad songs and told the background story to the boxer Jack Doyle before launching into the song 'The Contender'.

Christy Moore does that when he's performing, although I

think the comparison ends there. The night finished with a young Maori lad singing 'Danny Boy'. Beautiful it was too.

The Heritage Hotel proved to be a gem from the staff to the facilities. Rotorua attracts a huge number of visitors from those interested in the Maori culture to the mud baths and geysers. The only downside is trying to get used to the smell of sulphur. It's fair to say that there had been a touch of it in the atmosphere the previous weekend when Ireland had gone down 66–28 to New Zealand – a red mist had descended early in the game and, when it lifted, the visitors were down to fourteen players.

The final leg of the tour was in Brisbane but, by that stage, the touring party had been whittled down. Jamie Heaslip had gone home, so too David Wallace (his wife was expecting a baby), John Muldoon and chef Sean Dempsey, while Jerry Flannery never made it onto the field of play. Lonnie, the son of a man for whom I had the utmost regard, the late Anton Toia, was our liaison officer in Australia. It was good to catch up and relive some memories. Ireland lost 22–15, the Aussies scoring two tries to none, through a Luke Burgess intercept and another from Quade Cooper. Johnny Sexton kicked five penalties. It marked the end of a long and at times frustrating season on the pitch.

I love the anticipation of coming back from a tour, the tingle I get in my stomach at the prospect of heading for Inishbofin and Renvyle.

The locations provide backdrops, and stunning ones at that, but I look forward to meeting my friends again – there is always something or someone new to see or to meet. On that trip, it was Amelia, who I nicknamed the Queen of Connemara. Her knowledge of Connemara resembled a treasure trove as she provided flesh to the bone of place-names and people. I simply sat and listened.

In September 2010, we were in the Vanilla nightclub at the behest of Stephanie O'Kelly and Anne Marie Dempsey to celebrate the careers of Malcolm and Girvan, recently retired. The neighbouring rugby villages of St Mary's and Terenure came to honour their sons, co-celebrants alongside current international and provincial team-mates and those of an older vintage. I met Rainbow's son, Peter Smyth – it had been Rainbow (Jimmy Smyth) and Dave Gargan (Old Wesley) who had nudged me on the road to being a bagman and given me the instruction to survive the journey.

The November tests heralded the arrival of world champions South Africa, Samoa, New Zealand and Argentina to Dublin. Defeats to the Springboks and the All Blacks and a victory over Samoa provided the preamble to the week of the Argentina game.

It was then that I received an unexpected honour. Liam Doyle, the general manager of the Shelbourne Hotel, told me that I had been chosen to turn on the Christmas lights, a tradition of some 190 years' standing I'm told. My moment in the fairy lights was to take place on Friday, 26 November – the match was on the Sunday – and it was included in the players' daily itinerary. I knew they wouldn't let me escape unscathed, so about 4 p.m., two hours before I was due to flick the switch, I made myself scarce. I was going to dress up in the number ones and Dixie would be there to witness my fifteen minutes of fame. I was up on the fifth floor, hiding. The phone rang and Ger Carmody's name came up.

'Ger, I am up on the fifth floor hiding from those bunnies.'

The phone went dead. The feckers had got the phone from Ger.

My blunder had been not giving them enough credit for their trickery.

Minutes later, a posse descended on my room. I was mummified in bandages, a living King Tut, gaffer taped into a wheelchair and deposited beside the huge Christmas tree in the lobby, slightly out of sight. Staff, visitors and the choir were assembling at this point and I was still imprisoned in my surgical casket. Hotel security arrived and freed me but not before Dixie – she was bemused to find me like an unmade bed – informed me that several Americans had been taking photographs. The boys were laughing their heads off. I didn't have time to go back to my room to change into my number ones so I performed my official duty in a sweaty T-shirt, tracksuit bottoms and flip-flops. Liam said a few words and, in response, I sang a verse or two. It seemed to go down well as I flicked the switch on a big brass plate to turn on the lights. I haven't forgotten those responsible and the names of Tony Buckley, Geordan Murphy, Donncha O'Callaghan, Mick O'Driscoll and Tommy Bowe have made their way into my little black book.

There are plenty of others in there too. It was about that time that the Rala–Jamie war began. It's an ongoing saga. I also took something of a busman's holiday following a phone call from Girvan Dempsey asking me to recommend someone to act as bagman for a Leinster A fixture against the Cornish Pirates. I volunteered and thoroughly enjoyed the trip, despite the cold, catching up with Collie McEntee, Girvan and team manager Mal O'Kelly. I even managed to eat the odd Cornish pastie or three.

As we started into the 2011 Six Nations Championship, we knew nothing of the challenges that lay ahead. In some respects that's both the beauty and the downside of sport. One day you're cock of the walk, the next you're a feather duster. In the first match of the championship, we were a little lucky to escape from Rome with a win but then Lady Luck turned her back, as did a lot of other people, when it came to the wrong ball that was used in the quick throw that allowed Welsh scrum-half Mike Phillips to scamper down the touchline and score in the corner at the Millennium Stadium. We all make mistakes in life – it just happens that some are more public than others. The lads outscored France by three tries to one yet narrowly lost the game, while England came to the Aviva looking for a Grand Slam and left without the dust catcher for the trophy cabinet.

Mentioning England reminds me of one of my favourite stories. It centres on a former English player who I grew to be very fond of, despite that friendship placing an undue strain on my liver. Jason 'Fun Bus' Leonard, to give him his full title, was a marvellous character who gave everything on and off the pitch. He had a great sense of humour and epitomised old-school values in the professional era. The story relates to a post-match dressing room scene after Ireland had beaten England at the old Lansdowne Road. Keith Wood, who played with Leonard at Harlequins, asked me if I'd mind bringing in a cup of tea to the English prop. I got a cup, saucer, milk, sugar, teapot, strainer and biscuits, put them on a tray and knocked on the English dressing room door. It was a dead zone, full of battered bodies and disappointment. Clive Woodward, the then England coach, was sitting in a corner. I couldn't see Jason initially, so I asked about his whereabouts and was directed to an alcove. He greeted me with a 'Howya, Rala? Thanks for the tea. See you for a pint in the Berkeley before dinner.' Several of his team-mates sat there with mouths open. I made the mistake of taking Jason up on his offer of a pint before dinner.

Everyone left to go to the function, except for the two of us who ate it at the bar while supping pints. I was a lightweight in his company and excused myself at about 10 p.m. Fortunately, the only things I bumped into were walls and doors as I beat an unsteady retreat back to my room.

In general, I would be pretty abstemious after a match. It's not as if I am some paragon of virtue, it's just that I have plenty of work to do in packing up and making sure that everything is shipshape and Bristol fashion. If you factor alcohol into that equation, it's a recipe for mistakes. There are times when you celebrate with a pint or two but it's generally been a long day and I'm happy enough when the sandman comes calling.

The last piece of business for 2011 was the World Cup in New Zealand, potentially a six-week odyssey to the southern hemisphere. Four years earlier, Ireland hadn't managed to escape their pool – Eddie O'Sullivan would be trying to plot Ireland's downfall this time as he was coaching the USA team that Ireland faced in their opening match – but that disappointment would not have to be endured this time. The preparation hadn't quite gone to plan with four defeats in as many warm-up matches while the knee injury that David Wallace sustained in the England match was particularly unfortunate. Shane Jennings got the call to replace him. In theatrical circles, they say that a bad dress rehearsal foretells a good opening night. Ireland just had a few of them but made up for it when the tournament proper started.

I particularly enjoyed my time in Queenstown, a great town

for outdoor pursuits and home to a phenomenal hamburger place called Fergburger.

To the best of my knowledge, Fergus McFadden has no vested interest in the place. It was a gourmet joint, selling hamburgers, chicken burgers, lamb burgers, cod burgers … well, you get the picture. The Ireland squad had a tab there. The place opened at 11 a.m. in the morning and there were queues outside. Breakfast burgers were also on the menu. If you opened one in Dublin, you'd make a fortune.

While in Queenstown, we had a day off. The players and management were offered a number of non-rugby distractions like the Shotover Jet, a speedboat ride down a river, bungee jumping and various other activities. They were up on a board in the lobby of the hotel and people would put their names down for whatever they wanted to do. I had conducted a little research into the area and decided that Rala Tours would organise a visit to Arrowtown, an old gold-mining town from 1862 at the height of the Otago gold rush, restored to faithfully represent that period in history. It was about twelve miles away. There was a museum with the mining instruments and shops were in the old livery. I thought I would be travelling on my own but to my surprise I noted that Geordan Murphy, Shane Jennings, Ronan O'Gara and a few alicadoos had signed up. It must have been the way I sold it on the board. My notice read:

Those wishing to visit Arrowtown, a tranquil, easy-as-you-go place, please meet in lobby for noon minibus. Rala will lead the expedition.

There was a travelling show of Anne Frank's story, an unexpected bonus — well, for me it was because ROG and the boys went straight for the coffee house, picking up some gold nugget liquorice to boot. I loved the old place and took my time in exploring. On the way back, we stopped at a winery. I bought a bottle. Geordie bought a case and had it shipped back to the restaurant he owns with Martin Castrogiovanni in Leicester.

When we got to Auckland for the game against Australia, the lads went into a local delicatessen and told them not to serve me because I was a 'pie-aholic'. They told the staff that if I came in looking for a pie of any kind to send me on my way. Sure enough, when I stuck my head in, one of the girls said, 'Are you, Rala? We can't serve you. Get out!'

The lads got great value out of that one.

An abiding memory of that tournament apart from a brilliant victory over Australia is the warm-up before the quarter-final against Wales. I was heading to the changing room when I bumped into Warren Gatland.

All he said to me was, 'How's Dixie?'

'She's great. Thanks for asking,' I replied.

It was slightly surreal given our friendship but it was ten minutes to kick-off and, in fairness, there wasn't time to have a chat. There was no point in offering a shallow good luck. It would have seemed slightly weird in the context of the upcoming match.

World Cups haven't been kind to Ireland, sometimes it's small margins, but the tournaments have been frustrating for one reason or another.

While I really want to see the boys achieve everything they want, I am invariably preoccupied by my own role.

They can't ask for an elephant in a pink frock and expect me to produce it on the spot. I may be able to get one, but may need a little bit of time, so the more warning I get, the better. While I have shared the good times and bad when it comes to a succession of World Cups, the daily regimen helps to keep me grounded. Win or lose, I have a job to do that requires my full attention.

I empathise and share in the disappointment but the immediacy of my work after a match and my responsibilities thereafter means I can't afford to dwell on it for too long. In some respects, it keeps me sane.

After we exited the tournament, there was a chance for the players to get back on the horse, so to speak, with their provinces, but I would have to wait until the 2012 Six Nations.

GER CARMODY
Logistics manager for the Irish team (2003–present) and the Lions (2013)

It was 26 November 2010 and we were staying in the Shelbourne Hotel in Dublin.

Rala loves the hotel. He describes it as his favourite in the world – I'm sure one of the reasons is because he's greeted at the front door of the hotel by Denise with a cappuccino and biscuit – and he was asked to switch on the Christmas lights. This was big news in Irish camp and word spread quickly. Rala was hugely honoured to be asked.

He was preparing for the task ahead when some of the players hatched a plan to kidnap him as a joke. He got wind of the plan and decided he was going to go into hiding prior to his big moment. As his loyal friend and colleague, I knew Rala's whereabouts and, of course, would not tell a soul.

Well that's not strictly true. After all these years, I have a confession to make – I aided and abetted the players in finding Rala's location. I hit the call button and handed the phone to Mick O'Driscoll.

Rala, thinking it was yours truly, gave up his hiding place. I have been walking around with all this guilt since so if feels good to finally come clean.

He was quickly bundled into a bedroom, tied to a hotel luggage trolley and wrapped up like a Christmas present. The boys proceeded to wheel him down to the foyer through all the hotel guests gathered for the special occasion and placed him under the tree like you would any Christmas present.

People looked shocked at this and, of course, Rala took it in his stride and carried out his function with dignity and pride after he had been cut free with the boys cheering him on. It was certainly the first time in the history of the hotel that the person arriving to switch on the lights was wrapped up like a Christmas present and placed under the tree.

Chapter 11

**'Life is not about waiting for the storm to pass,
it's about learning to dance in the rain.'**

Sport and injury are synonymous, at least for the participants, irrespective of standard. However, when you are the bagman, it doesn't quite carry the same gravitas. Mind you, much like a player, you do find yourself asking the medical team the same questions – like, 'How long will I be out for?'

It's a predicament I suffered in the summer of 2012. Ireland were due to tour New Zealand for three tests but, in the build-up to travelling, would take a short hop across the water to play the Barbarians at Kingsholm in Gloucester. It was the renewal of a fixture and a venue from a few years backs and I was looking forward to again experiencing the delights of Queen's Hotel in Cheltenham.

About two weeks before we left, I gave my back a bit of a jolt. I struggled through a few training sessions in Carton House but had Darren riding shotgun. He was fantastic. John Moran was also there as my aide-de-camp in all matters including driving the van. He did a splendid job. There was a lot of packing required. I tried to do some of this lying on my back, which was quite cumbersome and time-consuming for the simplest of tasks. I didn't help. I was determined to go to New Zealand, but my first commitment was to the gaime against the Barbarians. When we arrived at the beautiful Queen's Hotel, Gail and Claire were there to greet me.

I carefully picked my way to Room 109 with a shuffling gait and rigidity of frame that would have looked very peculiar to anyone watching my progress. As a bagman, lifting and carrying is part of the job spec, so a back injury is a pretty fundamental problem. There was a lovely mini garden out the back where I'd go for the occasional lulu. The match against the Barbarians provided me with a chance to catch up once again with my old friend, Doc O'Shaughnessy. On match day, I received some valuable assistance from the photographer extraordinaire Billy Stickland who helped to position the cones for the pre-match warm-up. I'm not sure how enamoured he was with my precise instructions about the specific way that the various colours had to be laid out. He didn't complain though … much!

My old mucker Mick O'Driscoll had just announced his retirement from rugby and he was sporting the Barbarians colours.

This is the same Corkman who always addressed me by my correct, as it transpires, name – John. His favourite refrain when I was the victim of player shenanigans was to shrug and say, 'It wasn't me, John. I was trying to stop them.'

The Barbarians came out on top thanks to a late intervention from Dr Felipe Contepomi. Little did I know from a personal perspective how much matters medical were going to dominate the next twenty-four hours.

Dr Tadhg O'Sullivan arranged for me to go to a clinic in Bristol for a scan at 7 a.m. the next morning. I returned to finish packing the van – well, in truth, John Moran did most of it. We drove straight to the Sofitel at Heathrow airport in preparation for the flight to New Zealand. At this point, I was in a lot of pain and my condition had worsened.

The entire touring party went out for a meal to Gaucho's restaurant in Richmond. The setting and food were fabulous. I had a couple of glasses of wine, which was unusual for me in that context. I enjoyed the grub, but it felt like the last supper. During that meal, Paul O'Connell joined us. He was injured and rated as touch-and-go to travel to New Zealand. The banter at the table was great but, every now and then in a quiet moment, I found it hard to shake the feeling that the tour was slipping away from me.

It was about 11.30 p.m. when I got a tap on my shoulder. It was Declan Kidney. He said, 'Are you right? We're going back to the hotel.'

Paul O'Connell came too, the three of us in a taxi, an unusual triumvirate for the late-night jaunt.

We arrived back in the hotel to hear the pips of midnight. Declan said that we would reconvene in my room in ten minutes.

The Ireland team doctor Eanna Falvey was waiting for us. He had been at a conference in Oslo and so had missed the Barbarians game. Declan and Eanna took turns in explaining to Paulie why he wouldn't be going to New Zealand.

Looking at things entirely from my perspective, which I admit is very selfish, it was like being in the dentist's waiting room. I could hear the drilling and knew it would be my fate too. It took them about ten or fifteen minutes to tell Paulie. Doc then moved to the bottom of the bed. He turned to me and said, 'You won't be going to New Zealand either.'

Luckily enough I was lying down so I hadn't anywhere to fall. Declan, being the diplomat, shook my hand and expressed his condolences. I met Declan in the IRFU offices a short time after the tour and he said, 'I'm sorry I had to do that to you.'

I told him I understood that he was doing what was best for the team.

It had taken me a while to reconcile things in my own head, but I now knew it had been a crazy idea of mine to even string it out to the Barbarians game. As the saying goes, 'The graveyard is full of indispensable people.'

Returning to the night in question, the players returned from the restaurant. Word had already filtered through that neither myself nor Paul would be travelling. They came over straightaway to commiserate.

Although I appreciated the sentiment, I found the whole thing slightly surreal – after all Paulie, who was a huge loss, was standing just twenty feet away across the lobby.

I don't know why, maybe it was travelling to the other side of the world, but it got me thinking about a story involving the legendary explorer Sir Ranulph Fiennes. It dated back to an evening in Citywest when Eddie O'Sullivan was Ireland coach. I tracked down Eddie after a lengthy search to approve an itinerary for the following day. There was this man sitting beside him at the bar.

I said, 'Eddie, how are ye?'

I turned to the man beside him to apologise for butting in and continued, asking Eddie, 'What time are we training at tomorrow and what colour jerseys will we be wearing?'

The man was Ranulph Fiennes. If I had known it was him, I would have got down on my knees and kissed his ankles.

Eddie liked to bring in the occasional motivational person and my favourite was the great American middleweight boxer 'Marvellous' Marvin Hagler. Whispers had gone around during the day that there was a famous boxer coming to talk to the lads. When everyone hit the room, they saw BBC commentator Jim Neilly up at the top end. No disrespect to Jim but, initially, there was a feeling of anticlimax until he introduced Hagler. I remember the beautiful suit that he wore – Marvin that is, not Jim.

I was fit and well and back in situ with Ireland in time for the November test series having undertaken rehabilitation for my back under the care of my good friend Ailbe McCormack. The lads had beaten Fiji in a non-cap match in Limerick, and won impressively against Argentina, having lost narrowly to South Africa. I had two wishes for the New Year of 2013, that Ireland would win the Six Nations Championship and that the British and Irish Lions would be victorious in the test series against Australia.

People generally view routine in one of two ways, a millstone of tedium or something that provides a welcome structure to their lives. I'd be in the latter camp.

On 7 January 2013, I set about preparing for another Six Nations, starting with a familiar trip to Naas, where Tony and Declan helped me to sort out some of the items on the agenda, beginning with transporting the weights, footies and medical equipment to our base at Carton House. I met our head of fitness, Jason Cowman, there, and then unloaded James Allen's medical equipment.

I'm a people person so bumping into Gearoid Hayes, Gordon D'Arcy's school-mate and an artist with a studio on Baggot Street, was a real pleasure as was catching up with my niece Nicola and Dixie's mate Liz for a coffee. I'd earlier received a text from Ger Carmody in Australia, he was Down Under to fine-tune some of the logistics for the Lions tour. I was as happy as Larry – I'd love to meet him whoever he is, some day, he must have a great life.

I went to a management meeting later that week in the Clyde Hotel, chaired by Declan Kidney who ran through a schedule that included the Ireland Wolfhounds game against the England Saxons, which was due to take place in Galway on 26 January. After all my efforts to try and get the senior team to have a camp in Connemara, now I was going to miss the next best thing. The reason for that was the Terenure RFC club dinner, where I was to be the guest speaker. After the meeting, we adjourned to Searson's and then decamped to a Chinese restaurant. The craic was mighty, the days ahead framed by hopes and ambitions.

When I talk about Inishbofin or Renvyle being a second home, they would have a rival in Naas, purely on the basis that I have worn out the road to the IRFU warehouses. Having collected all the match paraphernalia for the Six Nations, on the Friday I hooked up with Ger Carmody to discuss what promised to be a hectic next seven days – what with the senior team, Wolfhounds and the fitting for Lions gear all taking place at Carton House. Lions coach Warren Gatland also came over to watch a couple of the Irish training sessions.

I was invited to the pre-match lunch for Terenure's league game against Banbridge and bumped into former Ulster and Ireland prop Simon Best, who was helping out with coaching the visitors. It was nice to catch up. It was then back to Carton House where I met Paul Maloney and Nikki from Adidas and then spent some time with the Lions operations manager Guy Richardson. There was just enough time to squeeze in a bite to eat with Stephen Ferris in the Lemon Tree that night. I finally got to bed at 1 a.m. and was up again six hours later to be greeted by snow flurries blanketing the estate. It was very picturesque, but not conducive to my line of work.

The Wolfhounds trained in the morning and the senior squad in the afternoon so it was a double pitch session for me. I was waiting for Martin Joyce, the Connacht bagman, to arrive as he would fulfil that duty for the Wolfhounds that Saturday. We trained on pitch number two because the other one was covered in snow. John, Mark and the rest of the ground staff worked hard to clear the pitches for the following day. Word came through that Richardt Strauss would be sidelined for seven weeks because of injury, which put a bit of a dampener on things.

On the Tuesday, forty players trained outside on a bitterly cold day. It's fair to say that there was a bit of a run on the soup and hot drinks. I also had to empty the van ahead of a DOE test in Naas the following day. It was both messy and inopportune, to borrow a word I heard used that morning.

As always, my room was a halfway house for chats and Cian Healy, Simon Zebo, Andrew Trimble and team manager Michael Kearney all dropped by at various times. Michael kindly ran through my speech for the Terenure dinner that Friday night. Being guest speaker was a notion that left me petrified, so I needed all the moral support I could drum up.

Taints and Axel were also forced to listen, so too Rory Best. They copped on quite quickly that taking the mickey out of me wasn't really on the agenda unless they were prepared to see a grown man break down in tears. The squad went for dinner in The Avenue restaurant in Maynooth that night. The next couple of days were spent preparing for the two matches and then waving off Martin Joyce as the van departed for Galway.

The day of my date with a rostrum in Terenure College RFC – Friday, 25 January – dawned. It was cold and wet but I'm not sure that it was the weather that had me shivering. Following a pitch session with the senior squad, I showered, climbed into my Lions number ones, and fidgeted in the lobby while waiting to be collected by Adrian Long, who was charged with getting me to Terenure. I did think, briefly, about baling out. When I got there, I met loads of people who I hadn't seen for ages. I didn't let a drop of porter touch my lips, suspecting that alcohol wouldn't be performance enhancing. Fergus Thornberry was there as my guest for his first rugby dinner. Arthur Fitzpatrick, Ian Morgan, Donal our president, Louis Magee, vice-president of the IRFU and Fr Eanna from the school spoke – with me last. I'm told the speech went down well but then again the audience was pretty receptive. They'd all be afraid of Dixie anyway.

The following day, I was back in Carton House, watching the

Wolfhounds go down narrowly 14–10 to the Saxons. I collected Dixie for an overnight in the hotel, had dinner in The Avenue followed by a few pints in O'Neill's. On the Sunday morning, we had breakfast and I dropped Dixie back to the auction rooms where she works. It was fine arts viewing day.

The players were due in that night to prepare for the game against Wales in the Millennium Stadium the following Saturday. On my to do list was to get the Welsh footies – in the Six Nations all the countries send their opponents balls that are going to be used on match day – back from Johnny Sexton. He'd borrowed them to practise his kicking.

The week didn't get off to an auspicious start when gales blew down the parasol that I use to shield the tables from the elements, breaking several flasks in the process. We had a visit from the head honcho of Google Ireland, a very interesting man, albeit that a lot of what he said went over my head.

The 2013 Six Nations campaign carried a certain resonance for me. Theoretically, it was to be my last as I would celebrate my sixty-fifth birthday in April and that automatically meant I had to step down as a full-time employee of the IRFU. However, thanks to the intervention of Michael Kearney, the union kindly agreed to let me to keep my position on a contract basis. That confirmation ddin't come through until after the Six Nations had finished. It was brilliant news. Quite simply I love my job. Boy, do I realise my good fortune.

At 5 a.m. on the Tuesday morning, I was down in the lobby of the hotel. I'd got a wake-up call at 3.45 a.m. to allow for some coffee and toast. All the gear – mine, the medical boys and our nutritionist Ruth's – was lugged to the bus, a job for myself, Dave

Revins and Willie Bennett. We'd left everything in the hotel lobby the night before to make things easier. Our masseur Willie was travelling with the bus. Once everything was loaded, they were off to Rosslare and the ferry crossing. The bus left at 5.10 a.m., after which I hit the sheets again until 8.30 a.m. That morning Doc Eanna fixed my ailments, which from memory included a toe, eye and finger.

I was travelling to Wales with the kickers – ROG, Johnny and Ian Madigan – but had to make a little detour. Sean O'Brien wanted to use a Canterbury scrumcap and I hadn't got one, so I rang Leinster's bagman Johnny O'Hagan and he dropped two into the IRFU's offices. Players have a habit of losing or mislaying things. The logistics of travelling are made much easier by other people, in this case Nicola and Jane from the IRFU office and the wonderful people of Aer Arann.

By the time I arrived at Cardiff airport, my truck for the weekend was there to meet me, and I headed for our traditional base, the Hilton Hotel. Dave, Willie and Ruth had all the equipment set up in the team room and, along with the porters, helped me to unload the truck. I was given my usual abode, Room 515. The Friday centred on the Captain's Run. I use it as an opportunity to bring most of my match-day stuff to the ground. Terry, who looks after the changing rooms at the Millennium Stadium, was there to help me manhandle it up three steep flights of stairs. Others pitched in. I ended up walking back to the hotel with Dan Sheridan, a photographer from Inpho – later, he would act as the official snapper for the British and Irish Lions for the second tour running. I have christened him Dan-de-lion. I'm pretty proud of that one.

That night, I encountered a little trouble with my bed. I left our young flanker-cum-second-row Iain Henderson in charge of my room because I had to nip downstairs. On my return, my bed was gone and so was he. Apparently it had been taken apart and put in a storage closet down the corridor. The culprits were never apprehended.

On a match day, I'm always up early and this was no exception. I had breakfast with our media manager Karl Richardson and at one point he asked me if I'd any polish. He had the whole week or even last night to ask me. So why wait until breakfast? I emptied my pockets and told him I didn't have any on me but there was plenty in my room. It's all in the timing.

My memory of the match was a stunning first-half performance from the boys, a great victory, a wonderful atmosphere and brilliant sunshine.

Little did I realise it was to be a high point in the campaign. Jane Kilkelly, who makes all the transport arrangements for the squad, treated me to a Costa coffee before we loaded the truck, headed for the airport and waited for the boys to arrive for their flight home.

When they got off the bus, I got on and prepared for the journey to the ferry. We were in Pembroke at 12.30 a.m. for a 2 a.m. sailing. The mattress in my cabin bunk never felt so soft. We arrived back to Carton House at 9 a.m. and I managed a couple of hours' kip between 11 a.m. and 1 p.m. England were due in town for the following weekend and for the early days of the week, we had the company in Carton House of the Polish soccer team, who were playing the Republic of Ireland in a friendly match.

It was bitterly cold that week with a light dusting of snow and it brought to mind another story. I have a cache of Rala hats.

They're just ordinary beanies with 'Rala' on them. The players all have their own official Puma hats but they are forever losing them. Any time it's cold there is always a big run on the Rala hats. It got me into trouble with Puma when we were in Italy. We had asked them for hats but were told that they didn't have any in stock. I had about twelve of mine and they were snatched from the table in seconds. That night's television news showed footage of the players training and the Rala hats were pretty prominent. Puma were not pleased and we had a new consignment within twenty-four hours.

The weather was awful. At the kickers' practice at the Aviva, there was a slight delay when some of the ground staff joined in a kickabout with a soccer ball. When we got back to Carton House, the Coffee Club slipped away to the Tesco car park in Maynooth, where there is an O'Brien's outlet. It's a select vestry – Declan Kidney, Mark Tainton, Ger Carmody, Eoin Toolan, Dave Revins and my good self.

The England game was the first time that the O_2 Jersey Guardians were used. We had to ring the twenty-three lucky competition winners and tell them whose jersey they would be carrying to the Aviva Stadium on the Sunday. It was a great success, unlike the actual match. The day offered mixed emotions – the great joy with the news that Brian and Amy O'Driscoll became parents on the arrival of little Sadie, offset against a disappointing 12–6 defeat, exacerbated by injuries.

I met up with Dixie and friends in the Shelbourne bar to talk about anything but the rugby. There was a gap to the next match, so I squeezed in a few pints in the pub called The Bar With No Name and a bite to eat in Fade Street Social over the next few days. The backroom team and the players who'd started against England spent a couple of nights in Dunboyne Castle, one highlight of which was a game of table tennis against Sean O'Brien. At one point, he hit a ball up against the ceiling and it dropped back onto the table. He claimed it was perfectly legal and so on the very next point, I lammed it up against the ceiling. Unfortunately it got caught in some drapes. We only had the one ball. His language was unparliamentary.

The rest of the Six Nations passed in a fug of thwarted ambitions. The draw against France was a brief respite from defeats to Scotland and Italy, the latter for the first time in the Six Nations. I leave it to others to sift through the ashes of defeat. From my perspective, I saw the dedication and energy that the players and the management brought to each match. That never waned. During that part of the rugby calendar, you can't afford to dwell on the games that have finished because the next challenge is just around the corner. It's good and bad. Sport is by nature unpredictable, otherwise it would have limited appeal. Injuries were definitely a factor in the games that were lost.

That's not apportioning any blame on the players introduced; to a man they were magnificent in embracing the challenge. They gave everything but experience is earned and the lumps and bumps in acquiring that development are part of that process. The spirit was terrific. Iain Henderson celebrated his twenty-first birthday during the championship, a landmark we celebrated in The Avenue in Maynooth, and while in the midst of the celebrations and craic, I wondered if it was time to sling my hook. All the lads were getting younger, while I'll soon be eligible for free travel. Maybe it was the notion that I might be put out to pasture that left me so maudlin. I thought about it for a minute or two and realised that I didn't feel any different physically and also didn't believe I was losing my faculties.

Life unfolds whether you're watching closely or not. Sometimes, when you're at the epicentre of something, you're unaware of what's taking place farther away from the action. Maybe I'm inclined to bury my head in the sand like an emu (yeah, I know it's an ostrich but having made the mistake once the boys won't let me change). I've a whole lot more where that came from.

Before April was out, Declan Kidney and Mark Tainton had disembarked from the good ship Ireland, and their departure was a blow. Our media man Karl Richardson also left, so too my good mate and Ireland's forwards coach Gert Smal, after the summer tour to North America in June. They are confidants, people in whose company I have spent many years, months, days, weeks and hours from here to Timbuktu. We had enjoyed the good times and negotiated a passage through the bad ones, all the while trying to steer an even keel. When you become attached to people, it's hard to let go. It's a weakness of mine, has been from the first day I picked up a bag. I see players as people. I see coaches as people. I don't care what they have achieved in the sense of treating people differently; although the players insist I have my favourites. Pauper or prince, it makes no odds to me.

On my return from a short trip to Inishbofin, I was encouraged to attend a retirement course by the IRFU held on Harcourt Street, a stone's throw from my house. On the day of my birthday, I repaired to Davitt's pub with Dixie for a pint or three, and was gobsmacked when my good friend Stephen Murray, the owner of the events company Modern Green, and his crew pitched up with a present. I nearly lost my life when I saw it was a Roberts Radio, which can get stations from around the world. I had wanted one for ages. Jamie Heaslip also dropped by. I finished the course the next day in great spirits. I absorbed the news from out west that Eric Elwood would be stepping down as Connacht coach, while Johnny O'Concrete (O'Connor) and Adrian Flavin were retiring. It got me reminiscing about the old days when China (Elwood), then Ireland's out-half, would greet me on his arrival in camp with the words, 'Anything for me to sign, china?'

My last few days in Dublin before leaving on my second Lions tour as bagman were spent in a few of my favourite places. I had the privilege and pleasure of presenting an award at Terenure's end-of-season bash. As I have already mentioned, the powers that be have seen fit to make me third in line — junior vice-president — to the Lakelands throne. Roughly 500 people sat down to dinner in the marquee and then got up to bop the night away to sixties music. That's my kind of heaven. It was the culmination of a very successful year for Terenure on the pitch.

There was a family christening in Skerries, a brunch with Leslie and Steve and also a trip to the Stag's Head pub in the company of Liz, Adrian, Tommy and Susan. After a few pints we moved on to the tapas in Fade Street, where we bumped into former Terenure scrum-half Derek Hegarty and his missus and Steve McIvor, an old face from an Ireland Development tour to New Zealand. The night ended with me falling asleep after a documentary on the great American country singer Glen Campbell. It was to be my last weekend at home for quite a while, and I doubt that I could have enjoyed it any more. On the Monday morning, I set off for

Naas where eleven boxes were waiting to be transported to the Vale of Glamorgan, the Lions base in Wales, on the Thursday.

Shay Ruane, my one-time flat-mate, dropped down to collect my car, which he'd said he'd hold on to for safe keeping until my return from Australia.

People occasionally ask me about the frequency of travelling and the duration of my time away from home. I do get slightly homesick and I definitely miss Dixie and my friends, but when you are immersed in routine, you don't dwell on those things for too long – there's always something to do. Sometimes, in a quiet moment, you might wonder what people are doing back home but it's not as if I have suddenly adopted the life of a hermit. I only have to walk less than six feet from my bedroom door for company. The carpet is worn from the trail of players that drop by for chats, sweets, tea, coffee, a book, a movie or simply picking up their kit on the night before a match. I also like meeting new people and experiencing the local culture. In many respects, I am with my extended family. And family look out for one another.

I was about to be fostered out to another family, the Lions one. There were nine Irish boys in the original selection, and more would follow on because of injuries to others. They knew my ways and foibles, as did some of the players who I had journeyed to South Africa with in 2009, but there were plenty of players who would be meeting me for the first time, and I worried about how they'd cope. I'm pretty sure I'm an acquired taste in terms of the way I do things.

JAMIE HEASLIP
Number eight for Ireland (2006–present) and the Lions (2009, 2013)

My introduction to Rala was the same as any other Irish camp rookie, a bit of a blur. A moment that was full of apprehension and excitement calmed for an instant by this random man wearing an Inishbofin jumper.

It was January 2006 in the Citywest Hotel. I had just hurt my shoulder playing for Leinster and had arrived in Irish camp, struggling to carry the new bag of gear that I was refusing to let go of. However, this elderly gent approached me and introduced himself as Rala, explaining that he was the bagman (not baggage master) and that if there was anything I needed, to come to him. He then proceeded to help me with the bags that I was so obviously struggling with. However, he did it in the only way he knew how, by great delegation, and it gave me a glimpse of how he operates! In minutes, two members of staff from Citywest arrived, took my bags and brought them down to the room.

Over the years, though, I've bonded closely with Rala. He's a gent, a role model, a serious operator who never forgets anything twice! (Yes, I've caught him out with a few things that haven't been on his famous pre-game checklist.) But, more importantly, he's a great friend who I meet quite regularly for coffee in Green 19 on Camden Street. Our table has to be outside, though, so he can have a lulu. He's the type of friend that you can go to when you've been away from family and friends for six weeks and he knows exactly what to say, knows how you're feeling.

He's a very positive man with great ethics that gives off such a great aura … that could be the combined smells of the lulus, coffee, tea and biscuits.

I could tell you many stories about Rala, but then again he could probably tell you more about me, or any player who has had the honour to wear the green of Ireland over the past twenty-five years. But that would compromise the phrase 'what goes on tour, stays on tour'.

The best story I know though is not my own. It's from the time when Rala was interviewed for the Lions bagman job, and it sums him up. At the end of the interview, the Lions' representative asked if he had any questions. 'No,' he said.

The representative, baffled, said, 'Rala, we've been talking for the past fifteen minutes about the job, and not once have you asked about the wage.'

Rala replied, 'Oh, I thought I was doing it for free!'

I make him tell me that at least once every time we're with Ireland. It makes me proud to know the man and puts things in perspective. It makes me remember what representing and being involved with Ireland is all about. The honour, the privilege and the love of it all.

Chapter 12

'Sticks in a bundle are unbreakable.'

It's my nature not to make assumptions. I knew that I would be in contention for the role of bagman to the British and Irish Lions team for the 2013 tour to Australia as I had fulfilled that remit for the 2009 series in South Africa. There were many repeat tourists amongst the backroom team, and I desperately wanted to go – but the choice would ultimately be Warren Gatland's. I had been bagman to the Ireland team when he'd been in charge and I would consider him a friend, but that didn't mean I was a shoo-in. I thought I had as good a chance as anybody but no more than that. Until I received a call telling me one way or the other, I tried to manage my anxiety.

Mentally, I prepared myself for disappointment. In all the years I've been the bagman to the Ireland team, I honestly never believed I had a divine right to the job. I had to pinch myself from time to time at my good fortune. I suppose in some respects I tried to live in the moment, without looking back or looking forward.

The call came on 8 December 2012, an early Christmas present. Terenure College were travelling to Cork to play Highfield in a league match and I was on the boogie bus with the rest of the Lakelands Ultras. We had stopped in Cahir when my phone rang; it was Ger Carmody. He said it looked like I had the job and that the official confirmation should come early the following week. It was great to share that moment with him. We had soldiered together with Ireland and now we would do the same with the Lions. It would be his first tour. I wanted to jump up and punch the ceiling but couldn't let anyone know the news at that point, so even thought the bus was noisy, I sat calmly. I caught Dixie's eye and made a small gesture. She understood and smiled.

On the Monday, I got a phone call from the Lions chief executive John Feehan. Joxer might have gone to Stuttgart, but I was suddenly able to wax lyrical about Rala going to Australia.

I looked on as the squad, under the captaincy of Sam Warburton, was announced. There was a playing party of fifteen Welshmen, ten Englishmen, nine Irishmen and three Scots – crucially though they came together as one team. The nature of a Lions tour demands an accelerated bonding process. That can be difficult for some people, those who are a little more quiet or reserved, but I can say with my hand on heart that this touring party clicked from day one. They were an unbelievable bunch and a joy to be around, players, management and backroom staff.

I remember some advice that Dixie offered before I left. She'd said that I wasn't going to win these guys over on the first day. I was going to have to do it slowly. That's exactly the way it panned out.

It would take some a little while to get used to me and my ways. I gave them a little insight when I was asked to address the entire travelling party. Thankfully I didn't have too much time to think about things, so I was just plain petrified. I wasn't expecting Warren Gatland to call on me to speak. Now just in case you think I was singled out for special attention. I wasn't. Everyone had to stand there and tell the rest of the party a little about themselves. It was just like 2009 but, this time, I didn't leave it to someone else to speak for me and managed to say a few words.

I concluded the initial part of my speech by stating that 'my door is always open … except when it is closed'. The Irish boys knew what I meant, but I think it took about five minutes before the laughter subsided. I also let them into my non-verbal lines of communication, where I squeeze my hand-grenade style red whistle (which is hung around my neck at all times). These went along the lines of: 1 x squeeze = yes, 2 x squeeze = no, 3 x squeeze = I'm going for a lulu and 4 x squeeze = I want someone to buy me a pie. I can't remember who was supposed to speak next, but he had to wait a few more minutes for the laughter to stop.

My first official commitment had taken place a month earlier when I travelled to the Vale of Glamorgan in Wales on 12 April for an orientation day. We then decamped to London the following day for what is known as 'Messy Monday', or more formally the day of the Lions kit issue which covered all clothing, playing and training gear, and also formal wear. There was a barrage of tailors on hand to adjust, well, anything that had to be adjusted. Players had to try on every last stitch.

The tour began in earnest for me on 10 May. I woke at 6 a.m. and arrived at the airport by taxi at 7.45 a.m. for a 10 a.m. flight to Cardiff.

It was delayed by two hours, hardly the most auspicious start. Ger Carmody and I were meeting up with some of the backroom team at our base, the Vale of Glamorgan (Welsh rugby's equivalent of Carton House).

It's a magnificent facility, rugby and hotel, with super staff, led by Claire. The first task for me and Ger was to drive several Land Rovers up to the hotel from the main road because the truck delivering them couldn't get up the driveway. Then with the help of Neville, who I had first met in South Africa four years earlier – he did such a brilliant job that the Lions invited him on the Australian gig – and Ger, I set about transferring some of the gear into the special travelling cases, labelling them and taking a complete inventory. This was done for all the equipment we had at that point.

The following morning the Adidas truck, guided by Paul, arrived with fourteen pallets of kit. This had to be sorted, counted and redirected. Some would remain in the Vale, some would go to London, to Carton House, while a percentage was bound for Australia. The players arrived, or at least those not involved in cup finals, which reduced the number to about twenty. The very first training session was Tuesday, 14 May. In the morning, they trained in the Barn and after lunch it was out on the pitch. I stayed behind with the kickers, Owen Farrell, Leigh Halfpenny and Stuart Hogg, and kicking coach Neil Jenkins, getting a right soaking in the process.

Our next stop was Carton House. I headed there on the Friday with the players given the weekend off and not due in until the following week.

On the Tuesday night, the touring party hit Jamie Heaslip's Bear restaurant – he is a part owner – and were treated royally. Some of the players then mooched along to Kehoe's in South Anne Street to soak up culture as well as the odd drop of Liffey water. I headed back with Sexto to pick up some of his kit. He certainly had plenty of distractions at that point; two finals with Leinster, a Lions tour, getting married and then preparing to move to Paris to hook up with his new club, Racing Metro 92.

Like the Comanche taking to the Great Plains of America, it was time to move again, following the rugby to London. We'd have a few days there before heading for Hong Kong. Before leaving Dublin, I managed a couple of nights at home and took the chance to catch up with friends. I took a stroll over to Modern Green to meet up with the gang. They have a balcony that overlooks Camden Street. If you could spy round corners, you'd be able to see my house. It was a little snapshot of Dublin to store in my mind's eye, to sustain me for my seven-week sabbatical to Hong Kong and Australia and tide me over until I saw a couple of familiar faces in Dixie and Liz Long who were coming out for the test series.

Ger Carmody and I met at Dublin airport once again and talked about what the future might hold. He was bound for Hong Kong, while I had a short hop to London and the Royal Garden Hotel in Kensington. It was a quiet enough day but the following morning, the trucks arrived with the Lions gear at 5.30 a.m. Myself, Nev,

James Robson (the Lions' team doctor who was on his sixth tour) and six hotel staff finished unloading the gear by 8 a.m. The Lions trained at 2 p.m. in the Latymer School, a beautiful setting, and then there was a quick turnaround for an official dinner at the magnificent Royal Courts of Justice. At that juncture, we had the entire squad in situ, but one of the first things that I would see the following morning was Rory Best's smiling face. He'd been a late call-up for Dylan Hartley, the Northampton Saints hooker who had copped a suspension for remarks he'd made during the Aviva Premiership final against the Leicester Tigers.

The touring party flew to Hong Kong in two batches. Our base there was the Grand Hyatt Hotel. Man, what a place to hang your hat. I've been fortunate to stay in some decent hotels but this was sensational. The views from Room 1817 were breathtaking.

Sleeping for eight hours on the flight exacted a pretty severe tariff as I woke at 4 a.m., bright eyed if not bushy tailed. I rambled down to the garden and pool area on the eleventh floor, which is open 24/7.

At midday, I left the hotel in the first of two vans. Nothing prepared me for the heat. The humidity was off the scale too. I was wearing shades, sun cream and a hat but I still suffered badly. I don't know how the players managed to train. I was a bit more clued in to the requirements that the weather demanded the following day. I had cold water, iced facecloths, cold suits and a fan that sprayed cold water. After a couple of days, my open-door policy was starting to attract visitors. It was thirty-two degrees that day; thirty-five degrees the next, which was also the Captain's Run, a short training session or more of a run through for the team.

Paulie had the honour of leading the Lions against the Barbarians. I went off to the match venue with one of my local helpers, Jackie. His English was perfect, which is great, because my Chinese isn't.

In preparing the gear for the match the following day, I came across a bit of kit that I had never encountered before – ice vests, a jacket that's frozen on the day and helps the players cool down their body temperatures very quickly. These, along with the fans that spray a haze of water, were the main things I had to help the players cope with the conditions. And ice and more ice. There are about fourteen items of gear for each player, multiplied by twenty-three players – two pairs of socks, two shorts, two jerseys, pre-match warm-up top, pre-match warm-up wet top, skin-tight top, red-crested Lions towel, sub coats, Lions blankets, gloves, hand warmers, players' plaques, subs' bibs, shields, cones, footies and toiletries (Dixie had given me a Chanel balm for the players).

I transported some of the kit on two handrails. At this point, the security men that accompany us on the tour had given up trying to track my whereabouts. At the beginning, they had wanted to know where I was and what I was doing for what seemed like every minute of the day. They'd ring me on the night before a game and ask me what time I was leaving at the following morning. I think their concern was based on the fact that I rarely answered the Lions phone that I had been given. When I'm working I tend not to have a phone to hand and I don't pay much attention to it as a result.

Match day arrived, 1 June, and it was 30 degrees with 82 per cent humidity. The kick-off for the Barbarians game was at 8 p.m., but my preparations began at 9 a.m. when the truck arrived. With the help of Nev, Chris and Sunny (and the hotel's helpers James and Ivan Ho), we loaded up and I left for the ground at eleven. I had a sneaky snooze on the medical bed in the changing room at one point, drifting off to the dulcet tones of Leonard Cohen. The lads won well that night, but there would be tougher days ahead. Win or lose, my job doesn't change. I packed up the changing room with the help of many people including players, got back to the hotel at 1 a.m. and after a quick snack was in bed an hour later. We were up again early to fly to Perth. I'm good at sleeping on planes and logged about seven hours.

The Bobby Cup had also made it to a second Lions tour. It had been devised by Paul Stridgeon, whose party piece in 2009, which reappeared in Australia, was to grab a lamppost with two hands and support himself horizontally, ramrod straight. He called it the flag. He must have stomach muscles of high-tensile steel.

However, the criteria for winning the trophy had changed – it was now to be awarded to the player of the week for excellence in training, matches or a combination of both. Mako Vunipola and Leigh Halfpenny were recipients, so too Paul O'Connell. Paulie had been invalided out of the tour through injury when he was given the Bobby Cup. The players had snapped a picture of him studying opposition lineouts at midnight in the team room. It emphasised his selflessness and that attitude was by no means uncommon in the touring party.

I had been asked to speak at the inaugural presentation of the Bobby Cup on that tour. I noticed that whatever way the camera guys who were filming the official DVD had set up the lighting it cast a shadow on the far wall. I did a shadow puppet of a dog, complete with 'woof, woof' sound effects. It brought the house down. In fairness to the Lions video analyst team, led by Rhys

Long and assisted by Rhodri Bown and Michael Hughes, they worked unbelievably long hours. Given that all the games had 8 p.m. kick-offs, they wouldn't get back to the hotel until after midnight and they'd still be working when we came down for breakfast the following day. It wasn't as if they could just slope off to bed then. They had to video the training sessions, catching up on sleep when they could find some down time.

The players had got to know my little foibles and I theirs. One of my favourite characters was Welsh wing George North. He was great craic and probably my most frequent visitor. George was very fond of jelly snakes. The most popular brand in Australia is Pythons. I had to battle for them. The first match, they gave me three packets of mini snakes. I said to the guy who handed them over that there was about sixty of us, enquiring as to how I was going to divide the snakes up without a tweezers and a scalpel. I made an overture to the match-management team – Lisa and Wayne were in charge for all our matches in Australia and anything we needed was requested through them. They facilitated us brilliantly. I asked for fifteen mince pies and three big bags of the Pythons for each game. I would leave George his own stash in a cup on top of his gear in the changing room.

English prop Matt Stevens was fond of a bit of chocolate. He'd asked me for some after the first game in which he played. Thereafter when he was on active service, I'd put a little sleeve of Ferrero Rocher in his corner. He wasn't the only one with a sweet tooth. One day one of the fitness guys came to me and said, 'We're trying to get the weight off them and you're giving them Ferrero Rocher.'

I told him I didn't think it would do any harm.

Generally speaking, I get a bit apprehensive when a tour starts, wondering whether all the pieces of the jigsaw will be in the box. These thoughts career around my brain. Some would suggest that there is a lot of room for them to build up speed.

As normal, when we arrived in a town or city, I'd have one or two designated local officials – LOs as we referred to them – to help me with my chores. In any walk of life, there are often teething problems and I had a bit of a battle to secure the right size van in the early days of the tour. In the end, I was given a small truck. It was badly needed because I had to transport so much stuff, including items belonging to other departments, like marketing and commercial.

The LOs were mostly superb, led by Tony and in particular Timmy, Stephen, Brendan, Sydney and Quincy, who used to be bagman for the Brumbies. I would have been floundering when I got to the training ground without their assistance because there is so much stuff to be unloaded, set up and then, when everyone's done and dusted, disassembled and put back in the truck.

By way of illustration, for every training session on this tour, four trestle tables were required, more than in South Africa four years earlier. Brian Cunniffe, our sports scientist from Roscommon, needed two tables for his GPS unit and laptops, Paul Stridgeon had another for his protein drinks and recovery shakes and then there was mine, laden down with tea, coffee, hot chocolate, biscuits, water, sugar, milk, Coca-Cola, sweets, an iPod and speakers and various other bits and bobs of gear that included spare jerseys, socks, shorts and a stud box.

We trained in some marvellous venues – one in particular, the North Sydney Oval Cricket and Rugby Club, named a stand, the O'Reilly Stand, in my honour. Well, not really. Apparently it was dedicated to a famous cricketer, Bill 'Tiger' O'Reilly, a contemporary of the legendary Don Bradman.

In the build-up to training, the music blared out but, as usual, it was switched off when the last player had taken the pitch. I estimated that there were thirty-one training sessions in total and only once was there no music, in the Barn in the Vale of Glamorgan. The acoustics made it just too noisy. It's amazing how many of the younger generation dig the sixties. But there was a more eclectic mix. I had two iPods, containing 10,000 songs each, which Johnny Boyle from Modern Green had made up specifically for the Lions. He's a DJ in The Village on Saturday nights. I even played my Christmas songs.

In the build-up to our first game in Perth, I was sitting outside a local coffee shop enjoying a brew, as the lads like to call it, when this clapped out old banger came to an unceremonious halt beside me much to the embarrassment of the man who owned it. I started to smile, not at his misfortune, but because it took me back to a story from my youth, and in particular a dear departed friend, Bill Doyle.

I first came across Bill in O'Byrne's pub in Rathmines as we sat cheek by jowl at the bar, strangers at that point. My sister Pauline worked there at the time. I gazed down at my empty packet of fags, picked up the box and tossed it towards a bin on the other side of the counter.

Suddenly twenty Rothmans were slipped under my nose with an invitation to take one. Coincidentally, Pauline arrived on cue to introduce me to my fellow 'stoolie'. 'Paddy, this is Bill Doyle. Bill, this is my brother.' A friendship was born and lasted until he died.

What an effect he was to have on the lives of our gang: me, Shay Ruane, Mikey Jordan, Dixie, Adrian Long and all our kith and kin. Some of the yarns concerning this man cannot be recounted, as some are still way short of the statute of limitations. He was a very funny man.

One very hot day, many summers ago, Bill and I decided to sample the delights of Bel-Air in Ashford, County Wicklow, for a picnic. We were frequent visitors as we both indulged in a little horse-riding. (No laughing down the back, please.) At the time, he was driving a black Austin Princess, a bit of a beast, size-wise. Unfortunately, the floor was a bit wonky; well in truth it was largely non-existent. Think Fred Flintstone and Barney Rubble but there was nothing 'Yabba, Dabba, Do' about it. You had to carefully place your feet on either side of gaping holes, as you watched the road race by underneath. We were young and foolish, reckless to a fault. We didn't overthink things, as you can probably gather. We left our house in Limekiln, which we shared with Mikey Jordan and the Bear, with the intention of making the short journey to Meath Street to pick up Dixie. Her mum was responsible for putting together a truly magnificent picnic: turkey, ham, stuffing, smoked salmon, coleslaw, thick slices of crusty bread, butter, milk, custard slices, jam tarts, tomatoes, scallions and fruit … and that was only the half of it.

It was a lovely, sunny, Sunday morning. The bells of Christchurch and St Patrick's Cathedral broke the sleepy silence as we watched some of the locals standing outside pub doors waiting to get in, chasing a cure for the previous night's overindulgence. As we floated past Engine Alley, we paused briefly to speak to an old friend, Frank. He used to stable his horses there, a team that drew his carts to and from the markets.

On reaching Meath Street, we took hold of the massive picnic basket and put it in the boot as Dixie gingerly climbed aboard, choosing her footing carefully – there was virtually no floor in the back either.

Bill kick-started the Princess, which responded by belching out black plumes in a very unladylike manner. You didn't need to be a mechanic to realise that she was on her last legs. Wicklow seemed a long way off. There were four pubs at a junction on Clanbrassil Street, one that was joined by Patrick Street, Dean Street, New Street and Kevin Street. These hostelries were known locally as the 'Four Corners of Hell'. Scraps were commonplace. One had a public toilet outside and, as we passed it, the car died, engine, lights, windows, the whole shooting match.

We were literally outside the pub door as it opened for custom and decided to seek shade from the hot sun inside. Our journey had taken us less than a mile. We called three pints as we pondered what to do.

One round led to another and another. We gave up on Bel-Air, instead wandering out to the Princess to eat our picnic in the car. We left three half pints but I told the barman we'd be back as our taste for the Wicklow adventure was eclipsed by that for porter. Having lined our stomachs royally, there was only one item on the agenda. Drinkers left to be replaced by new crews. The first inkling we got that we had been there for quite a while was when the morning tipplers came back for their evening pints. As I watched the car being towed away, I turned to Bill and said, 'You and your bleedin' Princess.' Dixie left to go home and Bill and I took a taxi out of town. Thus ended our day out in Wicklow; the two of us ossified, carless, broke and less than two minutes down the road from where we set off.

The Lions beat Western Force but victory exacted a heavy toll. Cian Healy's injury overshadowed what should have been a great day. He's becoming a favourite of mine and to see him leave for home was tough.

Gethin Jenkins would follow him, but I can only marvel at the work of the medical team led by James Robson and that included our own Eanna Falvey. Every one of them performed miracles, to fast-track the rehabilitation of several players who would go on to play pivotal roles in winning the series. The players' dedication must be acknowledged too but the medical staff did unbelievable work.

We welcomed some new faces on tour including Simon Zebo, from the USA and Tom Court, who'd had a slightly shorter commute from Brisbane, and a blast from the past in Shane Williams. I was once again in the middle of the bubble, preoccupied by my own duties, establishing a rapport with hotel staff and others who would have a direct impact on my ability to do my job. I was determined to be perfect in everything that I undertook. I didn't achieve it, but that tour was probably the closest I've ever come. It was far from a relentless grind, and I really enjoyed the company of the boys who would drift in and out of my room. The one exception was Dan-de-Lion, as I prefer to call him, because he scared the living jaysus out of me one particular night in Newcastle with his ghost stories. I woke the following morning after finally nodding off to a sight that reminded me of Inishbofin, four ships sailing out to sea, although these were a great deal bigger, laden with coal and bound for China.

Dixie came out for the test series and the boys delighted in winding me up on her arrival, suggesting that they hadn't seen me for days and asking her if she knew whether or not I'd be coming back on tour at any point. It was great to have her out in Australia and she and Liz were the recipients of a wonderful gesture from Lions manager Andy Irvine. Between the second and third tests, the Lions spent a few days in the beautiful bolthole of Noosa. I bumped into Andy on the morning we were leaving Brisbane for Noosa and in the course of a brief chat, he asked me when Dixie and Liz were arriving at the resort. I told them that they weren't and would instead make their own way to Sydney. He looked at me and said, 'Rala, they are coming to Noosa with the rest of us.'

They couldn't travel with us that day but Andy arranged for them to get on a flight the following day and stay in our hotel, all courtesy of the Lions. It was incredibly thoughtful. Warren Gatland's wife, Trudi, did a fantastic job in ensuring that the players' wives and girlfriends were made to feel part of the expedition when they arrived later in the tour. Noosa was stunning, the perfect place to unwind.

From my perspective, my nerves were shot to pieces after the first two tests and the way they panned out. I didn't know where to look half the time and didn't know how I'd make it through the final test.

But maybe things are different for the players. I remember the night before the second test. Normally on the night before a game, I'd have eight to ten players come to the room looking for studs and a chat. Some preferred to do them on the day of a game, Adam Jones springs to mind, because it killed the time. That night, my room seemed a little more crowded.

Alun Wyn Jones (who led the team the following week in the

absence of the injured tour captain Sam Warburton), George North, Richard Hibbard, Sexto, Leigh Halfpenny and half a dozen others were scattered around. Drico was there, Jamie too. I went down for a lulu and when I came back the players kept making references to my bed. I asked them what they had done.

Earlier in the tour, they'd taken to throwing boxes of TicTacs and M&Ms under the duvet and sheets. I was crawling round looking for them. Next thing, the Irish boys hit me like an avalanche. I was bound, gagged, put on a trolley, and brought down in the lift to the main lobby.

They pushed the trolley across the lobby. The bar was full of people watching this trolley hurtling past at a fair old lick across the bar. People whipped their phones out to take photographs. The hotel staff weren't impressed. It took them about twenty minutes to get me out. The boys are very handy with the medical tape. It's fair to say it lightened the mood – funnily enough, it echoed the night before Ireland's Grand Slam victory against Wales – and if my being rolled up and around helps relax the players and take their minds off the game ahead, I don't mind one bit.

Everyone knew what was at stake in that final week – a shot at, if not quite immortality, then achieving what only a select few had managed in a Lions jersey. Warren Gatland's decision to drop Brian O'Driscoll pretty much overshadowed everything else as far as the media and supporters were concerned. When I returned home to Ireland, it was the first – and in some cases only – thing that people wanted to know about. Warren made his decision and while Brian was gutted to miss out, the way he reacted shows the character of the man. It didn't surprise me – nothing does as far as he's concerned. He did everything he could to be of assistance that week – Jamie Heaslip too – to the team, remaining supportive and positive.

In the final test, the Aussies were mauled, and the Lions, for the first time since 1997, had the victory they craved.

After the match, Daniel Craig, aka James Bond, came in to say hello – I think the only person that wasn't pictured with him was our mascot BIL, although come to think of it, I think even he has his own personal photo. The boys hummed the James Bond theme when Daniel walked into the dressing room. I'm sure that wasn't a first for him, but he took it all in good humour even when I grabbed him for a few words and told him that we'd met before. We had at Twickenham but I'm convinced he thought I was hallucinating and probably a bit doo-lally.

To stretch an analogy, from the moment the players and management came together, a bond – geddit? – was formed. I understand that people are sceptical when they hear that everything in a squad was sunshine and light, because they naturally think that in a competitive, sporting environment professional sportsmen are not going to accept being considered second best. But for a tour like the Lions to work, there has to be selflessness on the part of the players. There are only fifteen starting places, twenty-three in the match squad. So disappointment follows as surely as the sun rises.

The lads, to a man, refused to be an emotional millstone if they were passed over for selection. Warren Gatland and his fellow coaches made some tough decisions but because of the players' attitude, there was no question that it would poison the environment.

The Lions won the series for the first time in sixteen years but there were many more layers, especially on a human level, that fleshed out that success. Winning was brilliant but the people in the party made it a special tour.

I was sitting outside at a party in a house in Oughterard with David, Miriam and friends, overlooking the Corrib shortly after my return to Ireland, watching a beautiful sailboat glide across the surface with barely a ripple. In moments of tranquillity, I often indulge in a little introspection.

The IRFU had agreed to give me a one-year contract with options, which will keep me on as bagman for the national team. I met Joe Schmidt, the former Leinster and new Ireland coach, briefly and was very taken with the man. My goal remains to fulfil my role to the best of my ability. After nearly twenty years with Ireland, my enthusiasm hasn't waned – if anything, having reached a certain age, I've a far greater appreciation about how much this all means to me.

I don't want to think about the future too much or how long I'll carry on being a bagman because that means I don't savour the present – and maybe the choice won't be mine to make. It reminds me of one of former Ireland coach Declan Kidney's favourite sayings. 'If you want to make God laugh, tell him what you're doing tomorrow.'

TOMMY BOWE
Wing/Centre for Ireland (2004–present) and the Lions (2009, 2013)

There is no one quite like Rala. Something that's very noticeable in the reaction he received from the English, Welsh and Scottish players on two Lions tours – to South Africa in 2009 and Australia in 2013. The other countries don't have anyone like him.

On the night before the second test against the Wallabies, we called down to Reception and asked for a luggage trolley to be sent up to his room. We tied him up in a duvet and strapped him with tape to the trolley. He was lying on his back, immobile. We did take some care … putting aloe vera in his hair so that the body lotion wouldn't stick to it. The boys from the other countries could not believe we were doing this to a man of his age.

We brought him down in the lift and so as not to be seen shoved him across the lobby, filled with hundreds of spectators, at a rate of knots. People had their camera phones out, taking pictures, and the receptionist's face was a picture of disbelief. The staff raced to cut him free with scissors. When he managed to free himself and come back upstairs, the other lads thought he'd be livid, but he was just laughing.

I remember at the first official meeting, Andy Irvine and Warren Gatland spoke passionately about the tour and it went around every head of department to say a few words. It finally came to Rala and he stood up to say the few words he'd scrawled on what looked like the back of a napkin. Facing the squad, he began, 'Ladies and gentlemen', which started the laughter, and he finished with his now famous line of 'my door is always open except when it's closed'. He was the only one who got a clap.

As those from other countries got to know him, the number of visitors to his room rose appreciably. By the end, there were fifteen or so squashed in, polishing boots, eating sweets, having a chat and listening to music. Alun Wyn Jones downloaded a Christy Moore album when he got back from the tour.

From my first day in the squad, he has been nothing but brilliant.

And, joking aside, he does his job at a level that no one else can match. When he does retire, I think the Irish team might fall apart. We all get the same welcome, whether we're winning our first cap or our hundredth. He's a legend of a man.

My guardian angels –
a cast of thousands

Tours, tournaments or matches don't define my rugby memories – people do. I recall a conversation with actress Jade Yourell on a visit to the Gate Theatre. During a brief chat, she pointed out how actors come together to rehearse a number of weeks or months before opening night, see out the run and then disperse, knowing that they might not see some of the cast again. Others will be reunited for the next play where they'll renew friendships and enjoy the craic. Rugby is exactly the same – the coming and going, the nip and tuck in personnel as your journey from match to match and season to season unfolds. It's an emotional rollercoaster where peaks and troughs predominate.

It's the nature of sport, uplifting in one instance and distressing a heartbeat later. You try and pedal your bike down the middle of the road in embracing victory and defeat. You acquire a thick skin but it's never thick enough. Disappointment has a way of seeping through what appears at surface level to be the most watertight of barriers.

For me, winning or losing has a context – injuries don't. When an Ireland team takes the field, I want those involved to walk back through the dressing room door under their own steam. It's probably a mother-hen syndrome. I get to know the players as people first and foremost, their likes, dislikes, superstitions and all the little things that make them who they are. The squad and backroom team is like a family, although traditionally with less squabbling. There are new additions and others who fly the nest – either at their own behest through retirement or at that of others through selection.

In chronicling my years as a bagman, I want to mention all those people who have helped – and continue to help – make it possible for me to do my job. I may well be charged with the sin of omission because I can't name-check everyone, but I'd like to plea bargain in advance – to all those who don't make the final cut, I'm sorry.

Firstly, those in the management and backroom team whose names have been frequent interlopers in the chapters of this book. Since taking on the job as bagman, I have had the pleasure of working with eight Ireland team managers – Noel Murphy, Pa Whelan, Donal Lenihan, Brian O'Brien, Joey Miles, Ger Carmody, Paul McNaughton and the present incumbent Michael Kearney, who I almost played against in the black-and-white days of my career.

There's a reason why people say that comparisons are odious. I found every one of those gentlemen to be kind, generous and helpful. They provided me with great leeway and assistance in doing my job and they also gave me the enjoyment of their company. They brought personality to the job and a skillset that enriched the environment in which they operated.

The man of Shannon, Brian O'Brien, resembled a second father. I have fished off the west coast of Clare with him, I have walked the roads of Inishbofin with him, and I have travelled the highways and byways of world rugby listening to his counsel. You don't do all those things, go to all those places and remain unaffected by those whose company you keep. As I mentioned, I first met Pa on a wet, windy day in Lakelands. He educated me in the ways of the job and, but for him, my career as bagman would have been very short-lived.

Noel Murphy was my first manager and he'll always have a special place in my affections. My very first gig was an IRFU President's XV versus a Munster President's XV in Cork. We stayed in Silver Springs. Back then, Mars bars were considered nutrition, as were Jaffa Cakes. I remember the first day I met the then IRFU's new fitness guru Liam Hennessy, a man who I hold in the highest esteem and who I spent a great deal of time with in travelling across the globe, particularly when we went to Spala.

I was with Leinster at the time and Liam, in his new role, dropped in ahead of a training session one morning. The sun was shining and I was at peace with the world as I awaited the arrival of the players. I'll never forget the look on his face as he cast an eye on what must have looked to him like a buffet. I had set up a table, covered it with a white linen tablecloth, arranged several chairs around it and it was laden with food – cornflakes, sugar, milk, toast from Kiely's, sausages and rashers. Victor Costello and one or two others would come down early ahead of training for breakfast. Liam came over and introduced himself. No sooner had we exchanged a pleasantry or two than Victor arrives in his car, parking almost on top of the table, jumps out, pulls up a chair and starts buttering his toast. There was steam coming out of Liam's ears. He turned to me and said, 'What's happening here, Rala? The players can't be doing this.' Let's say it was a turning point in the dietary preparations of the players.

I worked with Donal Lenihan for a number of years when he was first a selector and then manager until he took the manager's position with Graham Henry's Lions that toured Australia in 2001. A few of my friends were annoyed that I didn't get the bagman's gig on that tour. I can't deny that I would have given my right arm to be chosen, but I tried to explain to them that it was a minor consideration and that I respected Donal's right to choose.

Joey Miles, like Donal, was a selector first and then took over as manager for Ireland's tour to Japan in 2005. Perpetually smiling, the man from the Malone club was great company. Paul McNaughton was someone who I have huge admiration for, a brilliant man. He knew me down to a tee, and often spoke on my behalf if occasionally I was asked to report at a management meeting. He would condense my scattered thoughts into a couple of sentences, a nice concise briefing, knowing full well that if I was left to my own devices and allowed to ramble, many present would have grown a beard by the time I'd finished. The current manager Mick Kearney, a man of Lansdowne, is a playing contemporary and he too is someone whose friendship I value.

Finally there is Ger Carmody, last to be mentioned but not least, far from it. I could not do my job without Ger's steady guidance and assistance. He has fulfilled a variety of roles within the backroom team and excelled at them all. He is a friend, confidant, sounding board and teacher, someone who helps me to help myself.

Frank Sowman, a former national team selector, is another to provide important guidance at a time when I wore my naiveté on my sleeve. He was the first to call a management meeting (in the lobby of the Berkeley Court Hotel) before a training session. I wonder what he'd make of the current set-up.

I owe a great deal to Gerry Murphy and not just because he allowed me to become bagman to the Ireland team in 1994 when he was coaching the national side. He is one of the funniest people I have come across with a great turn of phrase. His after-dinner-speaking prowess is legendary. It didn't hurt my opinion of him either that he went on to coach my beloved Terenure College.

New Zealander Murray Kidd was my next boss as Irish coach and when I think back to those times, the two things that immediately spring to mind are warm weather training and an international against the USA in January 1996. I was really looking forward to the trip, conjuring visions of *Gone With the Wind*, tours of the film set and old Southern mansions, conducted in brilliant sunshine that would warm the bones and a perfect antidote to the harsh northern-European winter that we would be leaving behind.

The wind chill factor as we deplaned would have made a snowman blanche. I thought we'd landed in the wrong city. There was snow everywhere. As a starting point it was devastating but much to my disgust this was only the tip of the iceberg. The weather deteriorated further over the next few days. Turning the kit around twice a day had become a nightmare within forty-eight hours as the laundry people refused point blank to handle it because the mud was clogging up their machines, leading to breakdowns of a different nature to the ones on the pitch. Each day brought further misery as freezing temperatures and awful training conditions made everyone cranky. The day of the game arrived – the test match took place in Life University – and we faced a major stumbling block because it was a huge campus and the pitch was roughly a mile away from the changing rooms.

The plan was that a minibus would take the players to the pitch in two or three groups and that I would grab the last horse out of Dodge, so to speak. I was pretty sceptical about the arrangements and with good cause as it transpired. As kick-off time approached, there was no sign of a minibus and I was left in not so splendid isolation. Salvation arrived in a peculiar fashion. I spotted several lads clambering over a wall, obviously looking to bunk into the match for nothing. I brokered an agreement with them to each carry a couple of bags and, in return, I wouldn't pass any comment on their access point to the stadium. They hoisted spare gear, towels, blankets and footballs plus my usual accoutrements and we began our forced march in the torrential rain and mud to the pitch. By the time we arrived, the game had already started. It got to the stage that I had to hide my rapidly dwindling stock of spare gear or else those who lasted to the final whistle would have had nothing to change into for the journey back to the hotel.

The game was a bizarre spectacle, not least the moment when a ball was kicked towards Ireland full-back Jim Staples. It landed in a massive pool of water and started to drift away from him as if caught by the tide. Ireland won the match, but there wasn't a hint of celebration as the only thing on people's minds was getting back to the hotel, having a hot shower and hitting the airport for the flight home.

The sense of urgency was ramped up a hundredfold when word

filtered through that all the airports were closing down. Team manager Pa Whelan managed to secure our passage on the last flight out of Atlanta. The fact it was heading for Copenhagen didn't matter a jot. The plan was to fly to the Danish capital and then home to Dublin, via Manchester. One member of the squad, scrum-half Christian Saverimutto, decided to give me a little grief because he lived in Manchester and pointed out that he'd be home eating some lovely grub while I was still in the air on the way home to Dublin. I laughed myself silly when, on landing in Dublin, I spotted his luggage keeping fit by doing laps of the carousel. As an aside, the bold Savy was the first rugby player I ever came across using a mobile phone by the side of a pitch.

My first major overseas tour was conducted under the baton of Ireland coach Brian Ashton. It was a development tour in name but in playing terms it couldn't have been more arduous as Ireland were beaten the length and breadth of New Zealand. On a personal level, the highlight was an opportunity to meet All Black legend Colin Meads. But it was another chance encounter that was to introduce a little hardship into my life. I bumped into Paddy Flynn, who I had played with in the 1970s and who subsequently emigrated to New Zealand. The chat was good. I had already moved the gear, lock, stock and barrel, to the departure point but when I got there, the bus was gone and it had started to lash rain. I took shelter under a big tree, positioned the gear around me and lit up a lulu. I was pretty philosophical about my lot at that stage. I reckoned that someone would eventually remember that I was nowhere to be found and the bus would be sent back.

That's exactly what happened but not before a few well-oiled locals thought they might have a bit of fun at my expense. I quickly set them straight to such an extent that they helped me load the gear on the bus when it arrived – in return, I brought them to the post-match function at a nearby golf club.

I found Brian Ashton to be a great character and good company. My last contact with him as Ireland coach was after he stepped down and the IRFU sent me over to Bristol to collect the car they had given to him for the duration of his tenure. Brian met me at the airport and handed it over. I don't have the greatest sense of direction and I'm pretty sure that it took me almost as long to get out of Bristol as it did to reach Holyhead in north Wales. He had a dry sense of humour. One night when we were staying in the Castletroy Park Hotel I was allocated the Presidential Suite. He arrived in carrying about ten bags, took one look around and said, 'Bloody hell', and then struggled to his room that was about one tenth the size.

It was fated that I would get on with Ireland's next coach, Warren Gatland. We shared a love of the west of Ireland and our better halves got on famously. Warren would wander down to me for a chat and a laugh – the players would have a slightly different relationship, as you would expect. There was one particular time in the early days when I thought I would get a right bollocking. I sent out his blazer for dry cleaning and it came back about half its original size. I was mortified, shaking when the moment arrived to confess the sin. He just laughed. I did give him mine though to try and atone slightly.

Eddie O'Sullivan dragged me out of my comfort zone and I found him to be a good boss. I had become a little stale, lacklustre, maybe taking too many things for granted but he re-energised my career. He set exacting standards for himself and expected the same from those around him. I'd like to think that I took up the challenge to his satisfaction. I always tried to include him if some of the backroom team were going out for a bite to eat.

Declan Kidney was a joy to be with. He'd hardly ask you for the time of day, like Ian McGeechan. It makes you more determined not to let him down.

When I started this gig the backroom team was relatively small, something that can be gleaned from the fact that I used to run onto the pitch with the kicking tee. One of my abiding memories in fulfilling this duty was Ireland's famous Six Nations win over France in Paris in 2000 when a young whippersnapper called O'Driscoll grabbed a hat-trick. David Humphreys was preparing to take what turned out to be the match-winning penalty in a 27–25 victory and he noticed as I handed the tee over that my hand was shaking like a leaf. He smiled and said, 'Don't look so worried, Rala. I'm going to kick it.' He wrote me a lovely letter after his first season, a classy person on and off the pitch.

On my introduction to the Ireland set-up, Stillorgan's finest, Joe Doran, did the 'rubs'. In modern parlance, he would be referred to as the masseur. He had hands like a vice and there was nothing gentle about the way he set about removing lactic acid from tired limbs. A lovely man, he kept a bottomless supply of sweets on his person. In this particular part of the backroom team I forged a deep friendship with a successor, 'Willie Boy' Bennett, a man of Garryowen. We have soldiered together across the length and breadth of the globe. I have never heard him utter a bad word about anyone. He's always in a good mood and if there's a bit of devilment afoot, he won't be too far from the source of the action. He's partial to a glass of beer when the day's work is finished, a euphemism that's pre-empted a sore head or three on my part. Willie starts work early in the morning and doesn't stop until late at night, looking after the boys in the best manner.

I, more than anyone, have reason to appreciate Willie's help. He would make a superb bagman. He's got me out of several difficult moments. For example, if a game was due to finish at four o'clock and the bus had to be loaded by six, he would be my priceless aide-de-camp. He would already have done his own work before turning to me and announcing that he would start with the towels, move onto the warm-up equipment, the stud box, other bags and then take charge of the Ireland captain's post-match presentation gifts, making sure that Drico, or whoever, received them in good time. Willie is invaluable to me. He has a sidekick, Mocky, another renowned masseur, who lives in the country with his wife and two daughters, affectionately known as two sleeps and three sleeps respectively. He's a bit of a businessman too, what with his café (Mocky's) in Spala and he also runs a wee bar, Brady's.

On the physiotherapy side of affairs, Ballymena man Cameron Steele, or Cam as I know him, made it something of a crusade to improve my lifestyle choices – especially when we were in Spala. He would refuse to let me out of the pool until I had completed fifty lengths. It's many a morning I tried to avoid him, but his network of spies and snitches made it impossible. He had an uncanny knack of pinpointing my whereabouts. A saving grace from his relentless harassment in terms of my exercise regime was the bars of dark chocolate he managed to procure – this donkey needed the occasional carrot.

Cam's predecessor was Ailbe McCormack. It took me about two years to be able to spell his Christian name and I must belatedly apologise for the phonetical offerings that I produced in the interim. He was a great character, good company and possessed some wonderful one-liners with his sharp sense of humour. When Ailbe departed, he left me with two cushions from his cottage in Tipperary, a pair of Aran Island trousers, which I hope to wear some day, and the honour that he christened his son Patrick.

Denise Fanagan, daughter of Joe 'Banana' Fanagan – he called everyone banana – and sister of Walker Cup golfer Jody, is someone very close to my heart. We gigged together, initially with Terenure College, before joining forces at Ireland, where she spent three years as physiotherapist to the national side. We enjoyed the good times and endured the bad days as we travelled many miles, a journey lightened by her sunny demeanour. I remember the first time we met. Terenure were travelling to play Young Munster and I made my way down the bus for an introduction and a chat. I still drop in chez Denise for a cup of tea.

Continuing on the medical theme, I have had the privilege of spending time with a succession of Ireland's finest sawbones, who brought not only their skills as doctors but differing personalities that enriched the hotchpotch already there. Rathfriarland's Donal O'Shaughnessy – his party piece was to stand on a stool and sing about a German clock maker – remains to this day the doctor to the Barbarians but in his time with Ireland he was a senior member of the Eight-O'Clock Club, that met for over two years when the squad was billeted in the Glenview Hotel. We would sit in the restaurant overlooking the N11 and watch the long line of cars heading to Dublin as we gathered to discuss the topics of the day. Sometimes we would invite a guest or two to offer their tuppence worth.

Limerick's Mick Griffin was a poet and marathon runner. He was capable of penning a few verses – not sure about the iambic pentameter – at a moment's notice, irrespective of subject matter. He boasted a pretty impressive classical music collection and I spent many an hour relaxing to the strains of Mozart, Beethoven, Brahms and Schubert. Gary O'Driscoll, now of Arsenal FC, is a cousin of Brian, and son of Barry, an Ireland full-back from the 1970s. His selfless nature can be gleaned from offering to accompany me on the reverse bungee jump in Auckland, something for which he is still not the better.

He used to keep all my vital statistics alongside those of the players in a laptop that he appeared to carry with him at all times. Quite why he had mine, I have no idea. Maybe he needed a laugh every now and again. He couldn't pronounce Inishbofin so he insisted on calling it 'Itchy Bottom Island'. I'll forgive him that one. He'd be the first person that I saw in the mornings, walking down the corridors of a hotel, clutching his notes and gadgets, and looking for the first signs of life. Dr Jim McShane is still involved and even though he's from St Mary's and it puts us immediately at loggerheads given my allegiance to the premier club in Dublin 6, we formed a great friendship.

It's not a coincidence that the players frequently pay tribute to our analyst Mervyn Murphy and the work he does in dissecting opposing teams, players and referees. He hides away in his technology-stacked bunker, splicing and dicing footage, before uploading it on a server for the players to pore over. That glossary of technical terms I had to run by someone else. The only thing I use my laptop for is to watch my beloved Westerns.

Merv and I are locked in an unceasing battle of subterfuge,

where winning and losing is based on an ice-cold nerve and the ability to stay secreted for a long period of time. I am of course referring to the ancient art of sneaking up and frightening the living daylights out of each other. I have hidden behind curtains, walls and hedges but my speciality, and it's a tough skill to acquire, is an ability to sit motionless under a dinner table for long periods and await his arrival. He has learned to check under any low-hanging tablecloth but occasionally forgets – to his cost. There is also psychological warfare whereby I would float his name on the wind and watch him whirl around to identify the source. When we're not involved in this game of wits, I'll be the one handing him a cup of tea, as he sits perched on a ladder, videoing a training session, come wind, rain or shine.

Craig White, who hailed from Wigan, was Ireland's strength and conditioning coach for about three years and he proved a great friend. I once persuaded him to come to Renvyle House at a time when Connemara was picture-postcard beautiful, covered in a blanket of snow. He endeared himself to the locals during his three-day stay. It was on that trip that a deal was struck whereby I would accompany him in my van to Wigan to bring back some furniture and he in return offered to take me to Liverpool, to enjoy the Beatles tour, and then on to visit the Lake District. The sea journey turned into a nightmare because of a bowl of Guinness stew but thereafter it was a joy. I had to correct the tour guide on a few matters in relation to the Fab Four but the highlight was a trip with his mum and dad to the local bingo hall where we partook of a Wigan delicacy, ham and pea soup and a few pints of mild bitter.

Fermanagh's Mike McGurn followed Craig in the role – though the two could have been brothers in a previous life, given how alike they were. I plagued Mike in my quest for music and enjoyed dropping into his room for a chat. Niall O'Donovan was another with whom it was easy to strike a rapport, a consummate professional. I think that in the dim and distant past I might have played against him but that's where the similarity ended in terms of our rugby careers!

Brian Green, a quiet American, helped hundreds of players through post-injury rehab. He's returned to the land of his birth but his contribution won't be forgotten. In the realms of defence, Mike Ford and Graham Steadman helped make Ireland more difficult to break down while Mark Tainton worked with the place-kickers down through the seasons. This son of Bristol was a sharpshooter during his playing days before overseeing the proficiency of others in that department. Sadly, on a personal note, he is no longer with the Ireland team. I miss his company and his friendship. I tag along to the stadium or wherever with the place-kickers on the team's down day from training to retrieve the balls, and my reward comes in the form of a plate of chips.

The lowest turnover, personnel wise, has been in the media relations and communications department. My first recollection of John Redmond was on the 'Lucky Man' tour to South Africa. Every time I think of his name, it makes me smile. He was great craic. On that tour, he was fined every day because he wasn't wearing the correct training jersey, even though he didn't possess one. He paid up without a grumble.

Karl Richardson took over that role before moving on in 2013 to become head of communications for Rehab. I didn't see much of him either. Maybe it's because he was away on some tiny island or up in the Urals writing my profile details for match programmes.

I used to joke that if anyone came across him would they send him home because I was happy to make do with the one sentence he'd managed to scribble out. Stephen McNamara has taken over as head of communications. I wonder what he'll make of my way of conversing. I hope he has plenty of patience.

I've had Luke Clohessy since he was about ten years of age and during that time written more letters to his school saying that Ireland needs him. Andrew Ellis' son, Scott, is a joy to behold and a great bagman, as are Darren and Barry from Terenure. Lar, another Limerick man and the UL Bohemian bagman, was brilliant too.

Along with all the backroom staff who have made my job – and my life – so much easier, there are many from around the world who have helped me immeasurably along the way. Wherever we've travelled, I have been indebted to people from all walks of life who allow me to do my job just that little bit better. These are people I hold dear for a variety of reasons.

The first person to make a serious impact on the way I performed my role was Anton Toia, who I met in 1999 when Ireland toured Australia. He was assisting the liaison officer and doubled as a bagman and a 'rub' man, a common jobbing trait in southern-hemisphere rugby circles. As each day passed, he increased my knowledge of the role of bagman tenfold just by listening and watching. As an indication of his excellence, Scotland brought him over from Australia for the World Cup that same year.

He made quite an impression from the get-go. On the first day when the laundry came back, some of the Irish players had not marked their kit for identification purposes. He threw the said kit over his shoulder where it landed in a heap on the floor. I choked and spluttered in amazement before finding my voice. 'Anton, you can't leave the kit lying round like that for collection.'

I'll never forget his response.

'Yes you can, Rala. If the boys are not bothered to mark their kit, I am not going to collect it and stack it in neat bundles.'

When he had left the room, I picked up the gear, folded it and matched the items as best I could. I could not be Anton, but I understood the point he made. When it came to the last post-match dinner on the tour, Ireland team manager Donal Lenihan presented Anton with a piece of Waterford Crystal, thanked him for his assistance and expressed the wish that Ireland's bagman – me – had been paying close attention so that I could learn from a master.

On that tour, I briefly met Anton's son, Lonnie, who would go on to uphold the family tradition. Lonnie would accompany us at the 2003 World Cup in Australia, fulfilling the same role as his father. When Donal Lenihan was appointed as manager to the British and Irish Lions in 2001, he asked Anton to be bagman for the tour. While Anton was with the Lions, I found myself in Spala, Poland, with an Ireland squad. We journeyed as far as Warsaw to catch the test matches. I awoke one night to a vivid dream that Anton had died of a heart attack and was stunned to be told later on that day that he had. He suffered a heart attack while out swimming with some of the Lions players. He taught me so much and not just about being a bagman. He'd be proud of his son, Lonnie.

On the east coast of Australia, just outside Perth, Burswood to be precise, I was indebted to Ash and his crew when we stayed there in 2006. It's a holiday resort containing the Intercontinental Hotel, casino, restaurants and an Irish pub. The food and the craic were mighty. Ireland were based in Terrigal for the 2003 World Cup and that is where I bumped into Peter, a hotel porter from Cornwall in England. He knew what I needed before I did. We had a little ritual upon my return from daily training where I'd emit a low Harpo-like whistle and before I arrived to my room, there would be a cappuccino and a small plate of biscuits on a table on the balcony – I don't know how he did it and he never let me in on the secret.

In New Zealand, I had the good fortune to have my education shaped by John Sturgeon, a former manager of the All Blacks and a past president and honorary life member of the NZRFU, and Peter White. There was nothing that these two gentlemen couldn't do or fix.

When we toured South Africa in 1998, I came under the guidance of Bernard Adams, our liaison officer from the SARFU. He arranged for two guys to drive our truck, full or equipment, along the highways and byways – their names were Mr Okay and Mr Avel. The two lads didn't speak much English but between the three of us, we mastered the art of charades and so the communication channels remained open and accurate on both sides. On that tour we travelled quite a bit and the boys would be forced to strike out for a new destination at some ungodly hour. It was occasionally a twelve-to-fourteen-hour drive. The last thing I did was to seal a big lock on the back of the truck and this would not be opened until I arrived at our new base. I'd stress that these two lads were honesty personified but they were happy to go along with the system because if anything was missing, it couldn't be their fault. Bernard also reminded me gently not to refer to the lads as 'boys' because it had an insulting connotation in their eyes.

On one occasion in Bloemfontein I was gathering up the equipment in the dressing room when I got a message to get to the truck as quickly as possible. I ran outside to find a drunken mob surrounding our truck in search of some free gear. The two lads were petrified, so I insinuated myself into the middle of the set-to. My presence didn't really have a calming effect and it was only when I managed to attract the attention of two security guards, who up to that point had been largely uninterested in what was going on, that the situation was resolved. They came over and dispersed the mob.

In Pretoria, I had occasion to check the truck very early one morning and discovered the two lads asleep in its cab, which was parked in the hotel car park. To save a few Rand, they would sleep in the truck rather than a guesthouse. From that point on, I insisted on bringing them into whatever hotel we were in for breakfast. They were reluctant and the language barrier didn't help but I managed to drag them inside. In undertaking those long journeys, I made sure they had enough food and water to keep them going. When the tour finished, the players showed their appreciation in a generous manner.

After the final test, Denise Fanagan and I were shattered on reaching the lobby of the hotel, for different reasons obviously, and could go no further, so we sat like bookends on a sofa. Bernard Adams spotted us and insisted that we accompany him to Barristers restaurant for steak, chips and a bottle of wine. It was one of the best meals I've ever enjoyed – the food, the company and the craic.

On another tour to South Africa, I came across a guy called Freddy in Port Elizabeth, who was an assistant to the liaison officer. He was a great character who always made me laugh. Despite posting an itinerary each evening, Freddy would ring me at 7.45

a.m. with the same question: 'What time are we going training?' That included match days! Now Freddy spoke very slowly so by the time he got round to finishing the sentence, I could have my teeth brushed or my shoelaces tied.

My most surreal experience took place when Ireland travelled to Krasnoyarsk in Russia for a World Cup qualifying match in September 2002. The team won handsomely, 35–3, but my anxiety levels went through the roof even before we'd left Dublin. My main concern was the playing kit and whether it would arrive. It's not as if it would be straightforward to replace if anything untoward happened. I did suggest to the IRFU's Martin Murphy – he's now the commander-in-chief at the Aviva Stadium – who was leading the trip from a logistical perspective that the players might wear their match kit on the flight but that idea was shot down.

Along the way I encountered unusual characters and situations. The first speed bump was at Moscow airport where we had to unload all our kit and check it in again. It took a fair amount of time and effort in the cold Moscow air. Goodness knows what it is like in winter. While we were indulging in the toing and froing, I got quite peckish and remembered that I had a secret stash of Curly Wurlys. As I tried to sneak them quietly out of an icebox, I was rumbled by one of the players and was promptly forced to share my rations. On the basis that Moscow wasn't even halfway to our final destination, I went in search of more food. It was a fruitless crusade. I did come across a tea stall. Getting a cup proved to be quite a convoluted process given the language barrier and the range of choices that had to be made. The tea was scalding hot, so balancing it while looking around to make sure that the rest of the Ireland touring party didn't leave without me was a dangerous process. I gave up on the tea and turned my attention to secretly scoffing my emergency Curly Wurly away from prying eyes.

We eventually made it to Krasnoyarsk, through about five time zones, although that might be a bit of an exaggeration. It was black and cold when we arrived and there was a camera crew there to record the moment for posterity. I decided that a cigarette was more important than standing round and trying to smile through gritted teeth.

When we arrived at the hotel, the players made their way up to the rooms and I was left in the lobby with the rest of the equipment. My room was on the fourteenth floor so I assembled all the bags in front of the lift, pressed the button and waited for what seemed like an eternity. Eventually the doors opened and just as I was about to start loading, the receptionist told me not to take the lift. I asked him why and his response sent a chill far deeper than the weather outside. 'It might get stuck halfway with that load.' I asked him if I could store the equipment in the room behind the check-in desk, but he told me that probably wouldn't be a good idea as he could not guarantee that it would be all there in the morning. I decided to take my chances with the lift and fortunately survived the experience.

The next morning at breakfast, I was accosted by the most striking waitress I have ever seen. She was about six foot two inches, thin as a lath, and sporting makeup as if she was preparing to strut her stuff down a catwalk in Milan. She also wore the shortest mini-skirt I have ever seen. Each morning, I would attempt the same conversation, which was to try and order an omelette and every time I would fail dismally. She brought me many things from the kitchen, but never an omelette.

After breakfast I'd have my constitutional lulu, not daring to stray too far. I watched the world go by on a lovely tree-lined street. It was strange to consider that a matter of three weeks later, the Siberian winter would bring temperatures of under minus 30 degrees Celsius and that the place could be cut off for up to three months. I like to be ordered and in control – so Krasnoyarsk was my worst nightmare.

I also had a nagging feeling that I was missing something. I couldn't put my finger on it at first. That changed the following day. Ice. I wanted to fill the ice bins to store the drinks, but when I made my request the porter came back with a glass containing three ice cubes. I tried to explain, mostly by hand gestures, that I needed a great deal more. He eventually managed to communicate two things – that the machine was on the blink and if I hung around for a few weeks I could have all the ice I wanted when winter arrived. Fortunately we managed to negotiate a supply and were sorted by match day. When anyone suggests that I should call myself a bag master I tell him or her about the time I went to Siberia and couldn't initially muster up more than a cup of ice.

On my travels, one place that I did not form an initial bond with was Spala in Poland. It is a Spartan existence in this self-enclosed training camp, isolated in a forest, where there is little distraction from the daily regime of sleeping, eating and training for the players. It's a mini community of elite athletes from a variety of different sports. They travelled there from all over the world. It allowed the fast-tracking of conditioning and the benefits for the lads were obvious but there was definitely a mental challenge to being there too because there is nowhere to go during my down-time.

There is no doubt that the occasion of my first visit, a three-week camp with the Ireland squad, coloured my view of the place. The heat, the mosquitos, the food that I struggled to stomach all contributed to my discomfort. The road from Warsaw to Spala is etched on my brain. My perspective changed, no doubt facilitated by reducing the time spent there to just under a week. Familiarity softened any misgivings or perhaps everyone was just better able to cope when it came to filling in the down time. Going there was the brainchild of Dr Liam Hennessy, who knew about the place from his athletics background. Liam planned every moment down to the tiniest detail. There are no pitch sessions, no matches and no drills.

The traditional role I fulfil is tweaked to adjust to the environment. I'd wake to a 7 a.m. alarm call and then head for the balcony of my room to see if I could locate Marek. He worked in the grounds as a handyman but when the Ireland squad were there, he became my right-hand man. I would usually spot him loading the 'Molly Malone' as I called it – a hand cart that transported cooler boxes full of ice, water, Powerade and fruit. My early-morning ablutions included a swim, a toasted cheese sandwich, several coffees and a chat with Marek, outside the team room, wedged into a couple of comfy chairs. I say chat but it was really a series of gestures and smiles, as Marek only knew one word of English – 'No.'

The players would be ensconced in their pre-training preparation and my priority during those mornings would be to ensure that I kept track of the training locations and that the players had access to fruit and drinks at all times. I would slip off every now and again, occasionally catching up with Marek's daughter, Martha, who worked in the administration office. She spoke very good English. I'd also seek out Ziggy, our liaison officer, an amazing man, passionate about his homeland and a fund of tales. An hour or two could slip by quite easily.

After the morning training, I collected T-shirts and shorts from the players and brought them round to Renata in the laundry. She spoke no English, nor me Polish – fortunately I am fluent in the language of Harpo Marx, so we understood one another.

Lunch consisted of potato soup, sprinkled with strawberries and an egg batter on top. By that time, I would already have re-loaded the cart for the afternoon session. That didn't start until mid-afternoon so most people in the Irish party, particularly the players, took time out for a nap.

The players would go into the cryotherapy unit at about 6 p.m. – three minutes at about 140 degrees – and I would use this time to load 'Molly' again for the following day. When dinner had been eaten, the rest of the evening was free. I used to listen to music and catch up on some reading, and usually some of the lads would drift down to my room to watch a movie on the laptop.

The rules of the house would be written up on the door for all those who sought entry. No mobile phones were allowed, there was a compulsory lulu break for me at 10 p.m., one person was designated to provide the Coca-Cola for the audience and we would take it in turns to decide on the film.

Wednesday was designated a half day and the 'Pizza Eight', as I liked to call them, would make their way to a pizza parlour, which the boys christened Frankie and Hendo's, in the local village. The ritual, well eating pizzas to be more precise, took about an hour and a half. There was a strict time limit because the boys had to be back to rest up.

In the summer, the heat and mosquitos were fierce, and there's no air-conditioning. There was a little tuck shop on the campus that shut each evening at 9 p.m. They had a Coke machine and ice-creams apart from the usual health foods and dried biscuits. Hendo and Anthony Horgan were sharing a room in an attic, which was even hotter. They have built a hotel since our time and the Welsh boys stay in it. Every night, the boys faced the usual conundrum of who would go down and get the Coca-Cola and the Magnums. I used to look forward to that every day, the opportunity to sneak up to the attic and enjoy a private party. This was in the days before you had the in-house movies. We could only watch Eurosport or the occasional cartoon. In fact you looked forward to the ads for a bit of light relief.

Anyway, one night we drank the Cokes, ate the ice-creams and then the smokes came out. My Coke bottle was beside me and I was using it as an ashtray. There were a couple of butts and the dregs of the Coke. Hoggy picked it up and necked it. Next thing, between coughing and spluttering, he screamed, 'Jesus, Rala, I'll kill you.' He was spitting debris everywhere for about five minutes – to the best of my recollection I don't think he was a smoker and after that experience will never be.

Actually in mentioning Hoggy and as an aside I have to tell a story against myself, one in which he played an unwitting part. I was travelling down to Cork for the launch of Donncha O'Callaghan's autobiography. I had mentioned this to some of the lads a few weeks beforehand and they suggested that I should make contact with Hoggy because he had a car company and would be happy to collect me from the train station. I thought this a capital idea so I rang Hoggy, leaving a voicemail when he failed to answer.

When I didn't hear anything back I believed everything to be hunky dory and so boarded the Cork train at Heuston Station. Now in my voicemail I asked Hoggy not to make a fuss, no stretch limousines, just an ordinary car would suffice, while also providing him with the time of my arrival. When I arrived at Kent station, I looked around initially and didn't see anyone who looked like they were waiting for someone. I went out to the taxi rank and again there wasn't anyone hovering around. I rang Hoggy but got no reply. I thought my lift could have been delayed in traffic so I hung around for about twenty minutes and waited. Time was getting a bit tight, so I eventually jumped in a taxi to get to the launch.

On arrival, I bumped into some of the boys and proceeded to give them chapter and verse on my travel problems. I was a little bit miffed that there had been no explanation. The lads sympathised with my plight, and there was a lot of head shaking and grimacing. Hoggy arrived a couple of minutes later and I sidled over, sure that he'd be feeling bad about the collapse in the arrangements and to tell him not to worry about it. I knew by the expression on his face that something was amiss and this was confirmed when I heard gales of laughter from behind me. Hoggy doesn't and never did have a car firm or a taxi company. He confessed that he thought I might have been drunk when I left the original voicemail, so he didn't bother ringing back. The boys had set me up in spectacular fashion and I had swallowed the bait, hook, line and sinker. I was flushed to the gills with embarrassment.

On those visits to Poland, we have seen many beautiful places and some sinister ones. Spala had been where the Russian Tsars had a hunting lodge in the forest but after an incident in 1912 they never returned. Alexei, the son of the then Tsar, Nicholas, had one of his worst bouts of haemophilia there. He almost died and to expunge the memory the family never returned because Spala reminded them of Alexei's cries, when apparently no one could help him except Rasputin. We travelled to the picturesque medieval city of Krakow, where the late Pope, John Paul II, grew up and at the other end of the scale to Auschwitz, a terrible reminder of the depravity to which some will stoop.

On the way home, we always stopped in Warsaw, heading for a slap-up meal at the Westin Hotel and then on to Kevin's pub for a pint or two and a bit of craic. On one occasion, the lads thought it would be hilarious to get my arm tattooed and on the strength of the alcohol consumed I relented. It was a tattoo of a girl. The lads said they'd explain to Dixie that I'd had a few drinks and it wasn't really my fault. There was a crowd of Hell's Angels nearby and a couple of the players, led by Hendo, approached them. They introduced me saying that I wanted to get a photograph taken with them sporting my new tattoo. I was afraid of my life. The next morning I woke, saw the tattoo and was horrified. The boys eventually told me that it was a henna tattoo and it would wash off.

The camps generally finished on a Saturday after lunch. Marek and co. used to come by to see us off and I would have a sneaky look back as we were leaving. It is something I have always done on my travels because you're never sure you'll be going back.

Fiona O'Shea, who hails from the Dingle peninsula, and her team at the Castletroy Park ensure that our stays there run smoothly. However, left to my own devices things can get a little rocky. It was during Pa Whelan's time as Ireland manager and we were staying there. Professionalism had taken hold and the players had strict dietary controls. It sometimes meant that the food wasn't that appetising. There are only so many ways that you can serve pasta or chicken. This particular day, the dining room was full and I was last in. I had a quick look at the menu and whispered to one of the waitresses that I didn't want anything on it but could she instead bring me steak and chips. I pleaded with her not to do so until everyone else was filing out of the restaurant. There was only one vacant seat – it happened to be beside Pa.

I nursed my soup, taking tiny amounts to stall the process, but to my horror on glancing towards the door, I spotted the waitress making a beeline for me carrying a plate piled high with steak and chips. All the knives, forks and spoons were set down and forty pairs of eyes focused on the plate being carried towards me. I tried to hide but she found me to a chorus of 'Oh, that's just great, Rala. You eat the steak and we'll make do with what we have.'

Shamefaced, I looked at my plate for about five minutes before Pa eventually turned to me, and said, 'You'd better eat it, as we're paying for it.'

When I arrive at a hotel, it's vital that we set up a link with the manager and designated staff. When I request things to be done it is not for me. My responsibility is to ensure that the players and management are catered for on and off the pitch. I really appreciate the consistent hands-on help I get from the Ireland lads and the backroom team, as I wouldn't be able to fulfil my role without it. But if I were handing out bouquets, it would be to all the people in hotels around the world who have helped me in a million different ways.

I establish a system, food for training sessions, the laundry, which is usually sent out, and various other requirements. Our office (IRFU), through Ger Carmody, would have laid down the requirements of the Ireland party and would have visited the hotel in advance, checking on bedrooms, team rooms, medical rooms. That would all have been put in place. I would be given a couple of names to liaise with prior to arriving.

I generally get a bigger room or sometimes a couple of rooms because I have got to store so much kit and this occasionally inspires a little of the green-eyed monster from the players. They really start to whinge when I'm given a suite. On one occasion, at the Culloden in Belfast, the previous occupant was none other than Tom Jones. It's not unusual for me to move in such exalted company. Now these are the very same players who spend a fair bit of time in my room so they should be grateful that we are not all squeezed into a phone box, listening to music or watching a Western.

Sometimes, you have to build a little clairvoyance into your routine. Around 2005, following an Ireland training session on a freezing cold day, made worse by sleet, at St Gerard's School, a number of the players decided that they were going to have a shower then and there. It wasn't part of the itinerary. They normally clambered aboard the bus, returned to the team hotel and took a shower there. So even though no one told me that they were going to have a shower in Gerard's, I had packed forty towels and shampoos to cover the contingency. You have to be prepared – but you'll never cover everything.

I have learned that through experience and it's why I will be forever a bagman and never a bag master. When the day arrives where everything is perfect, it'll be the time to retire. I suspect that day might only happen when I'm dreaming.

Rala's Caps

DATE	OPPOSITION	VENUE	SCORE	TOURNAMENT

Where no tournament is listed, the match was a stand-alone international.

DATE	OPPOSITION	VENUE	SCORE	TOURNAMENT
05.11.1994	USA	Lansdowne Road	W 26–15	
21.01.1995	England	Lansdowne Road	L 8–20	Five Nations Championship
04.02.1995	Scotland	Murrayfield	L 13–26	Five Nations Championship
04.03.1995	France	Lansdowne Road	L 7–25	Five Nations Championship
18.03.1995	Wales	Cardiff Arms Park	W 16–12	Five Nations Championship
06.05.1995	Italy	Treviso	L 12–22	
18.11.1995	Fiji	Lansdowne Road	W 44–18	
06.01.1996	USA	Life College, Atlanta	W 25–18	
28.01.1996	Scotland	Lansdowne Road	L 10–16	Five Nations Championship
17.02.1996	France	Parc des Princes	L 10–45	Five Nations Championship
02.03.1996	Wales	Lansdowne Road	W 30–17	Five Nations Championship
16.03.1996	England	Twickenham	L 15–28	Five Nations Championship
18.05.1996	Barbarians	Lansdowne Road	L 38–70	Peace International
12.11.1996	Western Samoa	Lansdowne Road	L 25–40	Autumn games
23.11.1996	Australia	Lansdowne Road	L 12–22	Autumn games
04.01.1997	Italy	Lansdowne Road	L 29–37	
28.01.1997	France	Lansdowne Road	L 15–32	Five Nations Championship
01.02.1997	Wales	Cardiff Arms Park	W 26–25	Five Nations Championship
15.02.1997	England	Lansdowne Road	L 6–46	Five Nations Championship
01.03.1997	Scotland	Murrayfield	L 10–38	Five Nations Championship
22.05.1997	Northland	Walker Stadium	L 16–69	Irish 'A' Developmental tour
26.05.1997	NZ Rugby Academy	North Harbour	L 15–74	Irish 'A' Developmental tour
29.05.1997	Bay of Plenty	Rotorua	L 39–52	Irish 'A' Developmental tour
01.06.1997	Thames Valley	Paeroa Domain	W 38–12	Irish 'A' Developmental tour
06.06.1997	King Country	Owen Delaney Park	L 26–32	Irish 'A' Developmental tour
10.06.1997	New Zealand Maoris	Palmerston North	L 10–41	Irish 'A' Developmental tour
14.06.1997	Manu Samoa	Apia Park	L 25–57	Irish 'A' Developmental tour

15.11.1997	New Zealand	Lansdowne Road	L 15–63	
30.11.1997	Canada	Lansdowne Road	W 33–11	
20.12.1997	Italy	Bologna	L 22–37	
07.02.1998	Scotland	Lansdowne Road	L 16–17	Five Nations Championship
07.03.1998	France	Stade de France	L 16–18	Five Nations Championship
21.03.1998	Wales	Lansdowne Road	L 21–30	Five Nations Championship
04.04.1998	England	Twickenham	L 17–35	Five Nations Championship
30.05.1998	Boland	Wellington	W 48–35	South Africa tour
03.06.1998	SW Districts	George	L 20–27	South Africa tour
06.06.1998	Western Province	Cape Town	L 6–12	South Africa tour
09.06.1998	Griqualand W	Kimberly	L 13–52	South Africa tour
13.06.1998	South Africa	Bloemfontein	L 13–37	South Africa tour
16.06.1998	North West	Potchefstroom	W 26–18	South Africa tour
20.06.1998	South Africa	Loftus V, Pretoria	L 0–33	South Africa tour
14.11.1998	Georgia	Lansdowne Road	W 70–0	1999 RWC qualifier
21.11.1998	Romania	Lansdowne Road	W 53–35	1999 RWC qualifier
06.02.1999	France	Lansdowne Road	L 9–10	Five Nations Championship
20.02.1999	Wales	Wembley	W 29–23	Five Nations Championship
06.03.1999	England	Lansdowne Road	L 15–27	Five Nations Championship
20.03.1999	Scotland	Murrayfield	L 13–30	Five Nations Championship
10.04.1999	Italy	Lansdowne Road	W 39–30	
31.05.1999	NSW Country	Woy Woy	W 43–6	Australia tour
05.06.1999	New South Wales	Sydney	L 24–39	Australia tour
10.06.1999	Australia	Ballymore Stadium	L 10–46	Australia tour
19.06.1999	Australia	Subiaco Stadium	L 26–32	Australia tour
28.08.1999	Argentina	Lansdowne Road	L 24–39	
02.10.1999	USA	Lansdowne Road	W 53–8	1999 RWC
10.10.1999	Australia	Lansdowne Road	L 3–23	1999 RWC
15.10.1999	Romania	Lansdowne Road	W 44–14	1999 RWC
20.10.1999	Argentina	Stade Félix Bollaert	L 24–28	1999 RWC
27.10.1999	Argentina v. France	Lansdowne Road	26–47	1999 RWC
05.02.2000	England	Twickenham	L 18–50	Six Nations
09.02.2000	Scotland	Lansdowne Road	W 44–22	Six Nations
04.03.2000	Italy	Lansdowne Road	W 60–13	Six Nations
19.03.2000	France	Stade de France	W 27–25	Six Nations
01.04.2000	Wales	Lansdowne Road	L 19–23	Six Nations

28.05.2000	Barbarians	Lansdowne Road	L 30–31	125th Anniversary Game
03.06.2000	Argentina	Ferro Carril Oeste	L 23–34	Summer tour
10.06.2000	USA	Singer Family Park	W 83–3	Summer tour
17.06.2000	Canada	Fletchers Field	D 27–27	Summer tour
11.11.2000	Japan	Lansdowne Road	W 78–9	Autumn games
19.11.2000	South Africa	Lansdowne Road	L 18–28	Autumn games
03.02.2001	Italy	Flaminio Stadium	W 41–22	Six Nations Championship
17.02.2001	France	Lansdowne Road	W 22–15	Six Nations Championship
02.06.2001	Romania	Stadionul Dinamo	W 37–3	
22.09.2001	Scotland	Murrayfield	L 10–32	Six Nations Championship
13.10.2001	Wales	Millennium Stadium	W 36–6	Six Nations Championship
20.10.2001	England	Lansdowne Road	W 20–14	Six Nations Championship
11.11.2001	Samoa	Lansdowne Road	W 35–8	
17.11.2001	New Zealand	Lansdowne Road	L 29–40	
03.02.2002	Wales	Lansdowne Road	W 54–10	Six Nations Championship
06.02.2002	England	Twickenham	L 11–45	Six Nations Championship
02.03.2002	Scotland	Lansdowne Road	W 43–22	Six Nations Championship
23.03.2002	Italy	Lansdowne Road	W 32–17	Six Nations Championship
06.04.2002	France	Stade de France	L 5–44	Six Nations Championship
08.06.2002	New Zealand Div XV	Alpine Energy Stadium	W 56–3	New Zealand tour
15.06.2002	New Zealand	Carisbrook Stadium	L 6–15	New Zealand tour
22.06.2002	New Zealand	Eden Park Stadium	L 8–40	New Zealand tour
07.09.2002	Romania	Thomond Park	W 39–8	2003 RWC warm-up
21.09.2002	Russia	Krasnoyarsk	W 35–3	2003 RWC qualifier
28.09.2002	Georgia	Lansdowne Road	W 63–14	2003 RWC qualifier
09.11.2002	Australia	Lansdowne Road	W 18–9	2003 RWC qualifier
17.11.2002	Fiji	Lansdowne Road	W 64–17	2003 RWC qualifier
23.11.2002	Argentina	Lansdowne Road	W 16–7	2003 RWC qualifier
06.02.2003	Scotland	Murrayfield	W 36–6	Six Nations Championship
22.02.2003	Italy	Stadio Flaminio	W 37–13	Six Nations Championship
08.03.2003	France	Lansdowne Road	W 15–12	Six Nations Championship
22.03.2003	Wales	Lansdowne Road	W 25–24	Six Nations Championship
30.03.2003	England	Lansdowne Road	L 6–42	Six Nations Championship
07.06.2003	Australia	Subiaco Oval	L 16–45	
14.06.2003	Tonga	Nuku'alofa	W 40–19	
21.06.2003	Samoa	Apia Park	W 40–14	

16.08.2003	Wales	Lansdowne Road	W 35–12	2003 RWC warm-up
30.08.2003	Italy	Thomond Park	W 61–6	2003 RWC warm-up
06.09.2003	Scotland	Murrayfield	W 29–10	2003 RWC warm-up
11.10.2003	Romania	Central Coast Stadium	W 45–17	2003 RWC
19.10.2003	Namibia	Sydney FS	W 64–7	2003 RWC
26.10.2003	Argentina	Adelaide	W 16–15	2003 RWC
01.11.2003	Australia	Melbourne	L 16–17	2003 RWC
09.11.2003	France	Colonial Stadium	L 21–43	2003 RWC
14.02.2004	France	Stade de France	L 17–35	Six Nations Championship
22.02.2004	Wales	Lansdowne Road	W 36–15	Six Nations Championship
06.03.2004	England	Twickenham	W 19–13	Six Nations Championship
20.03.2004	Italy	Lansdowne Road	W 19–3	Six Nations Championship
27.04.2004	Scotland	Lansdowne Road	W 37–16	Six Nations Championship
12.06.2004	South Africa	Vodacom Park	L 17–31	
19.06.2004	South Africa	Newlands	L 17–26	
13.11.2004	South Africa	Lansdowne Road	W 17–12	
20.11.2004	USA	Lansdowne Road	W 55–6	
27.11.2004	Argentina	Lansdowne Road	W 21–19	
06.02.2005	Italy	Stadio Flaminio	W 28–17	Six Nations Championship
12.02.2005	Scotland	Murrayfield	W 40–13	Six Nations Championship
27.02.2005	England	Lansdowne Road	L 13–19	Six Nations Championship
12.03.2005	France	Lansdowne Road	L 19–26	Six Nations Championship
19.03.2005	Wales	Millennium Stadium	L 20–32	Six Nations Championship
12.06.2005	Japan	Nagai Soccer Stadium	W 44–12	Summer tour
19.06.2005	Japan	Prince Chichibu St.	W 47–18	Summer tour
09.11.2005	New Zealand	Lansdowne Road	L 7–45	Autumn series
19.11.2005	Australia	Lansdowne Road	L 14–30	Autumn series
26.11.2005	Romania	Lansdowne Road	W 43–12	Autumn series
04.02.2006	Italy	Lansdowne Road	W 26–16	Six Nations Championship
11.02.2006	France	Stade de France	L 31–43	Six Nations Championship
26.02.2006	Wales	Lansdowne Road	W 31–5	Six Nations Championship
11.03.2006	Scotland	Lansdowne Road	W 15–9	Six Nations Championship
18.03.2006	England	Twickenham	W 28–24	Six Nations Championship
10.06.2006	New Zealand	Waikato Stadium	L 23–33	Summer tour
17.06.2006	New Zealand	Eden Park Stadium	L 17–27	Summer tour
24.06.2006	Australia	Subiaco Oval	L 15–37	Summer tour

11.11.2006	South Africa	Lansdowne Road	W 32–15	Autumn series
19.11.2006	Australia	Lansdowne Road	W 21–6	Autumn series
28.11.2006	Pacific Islanders	Lansdowne Road	W 61–17	Autumn series
04.02.2007	Wales	Millennium Stadium	W 19–9	Six Nations Championship
11.02.2007	France	Croke Park	L 17–20	Six Nations Championship
24.02.2007	England	Croke Park	W 43–13	Six Nations Championship
10.03.2007	Scotland	Murrayfield	W 19–18	Six Nations Championship
17.03.2007	Italy	Stadio Flaminio	W 51–24	Six Nations Championship
26.05.2007	Argentina	Santa Fe	L 20–22	Summer tour
02.06.2007	Argentina	Buenos Aires	L 0–16	Summer tour
11.08.2007	Scotland	Murrayfield	L 21–31	2007 RWC warm-up
16.08.2007	Bayonne	Stade Jean Dauger	W 42–6	2007 RWC warm-up
24.08.2007	Italy	Ravenhill	W 23–20	2007 RWC warm-up
09.09.2007	Namibia	Bordeaux	W 32–17	2007 RWC
15.09.2007	Georgia	Bordeaux	W 14–10	2007 RWC
21.09.2007	France	Stade de France	L 3–25	2007 RWC
30.09.2007	Argentina	Parc des Princes	L 15–30	2007 RWC
02.02.2008	Italy	Croke Park	W 16–11	Six Nations Championship
09.02.2008	France	Stade de France	L 21–26	Six Nations Championship
23.02.2008	Scotland	Croke Park	W 34–13	Six Nations Championship
08.03.2008	Wales	Croke Park	L 12–16	Six Nations Championship
15.03.2008	England	Twickenham	L 10–33	Six Nations Championship
27.05.2008	Barbarians	Kingsholm	W 39–14	Summer tour
07.06.2008	New Zealand	Wellington	L 11–20	Summer tour
14.06.2008	Australia	Melbourne	L 12–18	Summer tour
08.11.2008	Canada	Thomond Park	W 55–0	Autumn series
15.11.2008	New Zealand	Croke Park	L 3–22	Autumn series
22.11.2008	Argentina	Croke Park	W 17–3	Autumn series
07.02.2009	France	Croke Park	W 30–21	Six Nations Championship
15.02.2009	Italy	Stadio Flaminio	W 38–9	Six Nations Championship
28.02.2009	England	Croke Park	W 14–13	Six Nations Championship
14.03.2009	Scotland	Murrayfield	W 22–15	Six Nations Championship
21.03.2009	Wales	Millennium Stadium	W 17–15	Six Nations Championship
30.05.2009	Royal XV	Royal Bafokeng	W 37–25	2009 Lions tour match
03.06.2009	Xerox Lions	Coca-Cola Park	W 74–10	2009 Lions tour match
06.06.2009	Free State Cheetahs	Vodacom Park	W 26–24	2009 Lions tour match

10.06.2009	The Sharks	The Absa Stadium	W 39–3	2009 Lions tour match
13.06.2009	Western Province	Newlands	W 26–23	2009 Lions tour match
16.06.2009	Southern Kings	Nelson Mandela St.	W 20–8	2009 Lions tour match
20.06.2009	South Africa	The Absa Stadium	L 21–26	2009 Lions first test
23.06.2009	Emerging S'boks	Newlands	D 13–13	2009 Lions tour match
27.06.2009	South Africa	Loftus Versfield	L 25–28	2009 Lions second test
04.07.2009	South Africa	Coca-Cola Park	W 28–9	2009 Lions third test
15.11.2009	Australia	Croke Park	D 20–20	Autumn series
21.11.2009	Fiji	RDS Grounds	W 41–6	Autumn series
28.11.2009	South Africa	Croke Park	W 15–10	Autumn series
06.02.2010	Italy	Croke Park	W 29–11	Six Nations Championship
13.02.2010	France	Stade de France	L 10–33	Six Nations Championship
27.03.2010	England	Twickenham	W 20–16	Six Nations Championship
13.03.2010	Wales	Croke Park	W 27–12	Six Nations Championship
20.03.2010	Scotland	Croke Park	L 20–23	Six Nations Championship
04.06.2010	Barbarians	Thomond Park	L 23–29	Summer tour
12.06.2010	New Zealand	Yarrow Stadium	L 28–66	Summer tour
18.08.2010	New Zealand Maoris	Rotorua	L 28–31	Summer tour
26.08.2010	Australia	Suncorp Stadium	L 15–22	Summer tour
06.11.2010	South Africa	Aviva Stadium	L 21–23	Autumn series
13.11.2010	Samoa	Aviva Stadium	W 20–10	Autumn series
20.11.2010	New Zealand	Aviva Stadium	L 18–38	Autumn series
28.11.2010	Argentina	Aviva Stadium	W 29–9	Autumn series
05.02.2011	Italy	Stadio Flaminio	W 13–11	Six Nations Championship
13.02.2011	France	Aviva Stadium	L 22–25	Six Nations Championship
27.02.2011	Scotland	Murrayfield	W 21–18	Six Nations Championship
12.03.2011	Wales	Millennium Stadium	L 13–19	Six Nations Championship
19.03.2011	England	Aviva Stadium	W 24–8	Six Nations Championship
06.08.2011	Scotland	Murrayfield	L 6–10	2011 RWC warm-up
13.08.2011	France	Stade Chalban-Delmas	L 12–19	2011 RWC warm-up
20.08.2011	France	Aviva Stadium	L 22–26	2011 RWC warm-up
27.08.2011	Scotland	Aviva Stadium	L 9–20	2011 RWC warm-up
11.09.2011	USA	Stadium Taranaki	W 22–10	2011 RWC
17.09.2011	Australia	Eden Park	W 15–6	2011 RWC
25.09.2011	Russia	International Stadium	W 62–12	2011 RWC
02.10.2011	Italy	Otago Stadium	W 36–6	2011 RWC
08.10.2011	Wales	Regional Stadium	W 10–22	2011 RWC

05.02.2012	Wales	Aviva Stadium	L 21–23	Six Nations Championship
11.02.2012	France	Stade de France	Match abandoned	
25.02.2012	Italy	Aviva Stadium	W 42–10	Six Nations Championship
04.03.2012	France	Stade de France	D 17–17	Six Nations Championship
10.03.2012	Scotland	Aviva Stadium	W 32–14	Six Nations Championship
17.03.2012	England	Twickenham	L 9–30	Six Nations Championship
10.10.2012	South Africa	Lansdowne Road	L 12–16	Autumn series
18.10.2012	Fiji	Thomond Park	W 53–0	non-cap
24.10.2012	Argentina	Lansdowne Road	W 46–24	Autumn series
02.02.2013	Wales	Millennium Stadium	W 30–22	Six Nations Championship
10.02.2013	England	Lansdowne Road	L 6–12	Six Nations Championship
24.02.2013	Scotland	Murrayfield	L 8–12	Six Nations Championship
09.03.2013	France	Lansdowne Road	D 13–13	Six Nations Championship
16.03.2013	Italy	Stadio Olimpico	L 15–22	Six Nations Championship
01.06.2013	Barbarians	Hong Kong Stadium	W 59–8	2013 Lions tour match
05.06.2013	Western Force	Paterson Stadium	W 69–17	2013 Lions tour match
08.06.2013	Queensland Reds	Suncorp Stadium	W 22–12	2013 Lions tour match
11.06.2013	Combined Q'land/NSW	Hunter Stadium	W 64–0	2013 Lions tour match
15.06.2013	NSW Waratahs	Allianz Stadium	W 47–17	2013 Lions tour match
18.06.2013	ACT Brumbies	Canberra Stadium	L 12–22	2013 Lions tour match
22.06.2013	Australia	Suncorp Stadium	W 23–21	2013 Lions first test
25.06.2013	Melbourne Rebels	AAMI Park	W 35–0	2013 Lions tour match
29.06.2013	Australia	Etihad Stadium	L 15–16	2013 Lions second test
06.07.2013	Australia	ANZ Stadium	W 41–16	2013 Lions third test

Acknowledgements

I would like to thank the following people without whom this book would not have been written. In no particular order, they are as follows: Ciara Doorley, Breda Purdue and all the staff at Hachette Books Ireland; Stephen Murray and all the staff at Modern Green, and Green 19 for the coffee; the CEO of the IRFU Philip Browne and all his staff; John Feehan CEO of British and Irish Lions, and staff; Sandra Kennedy-Doorley; Charlie and Bridit and the staff at the Brooks Hotel, Drury Street; and Billy Stickland and Dan Sheridan at Inpho Photography.

Huge thanks to all the contributors for their stories and memories; all Irish players and management past and present; Terenure College RFC; and all the fans and supporters at home and abroad.

Thanks to the people of Connemara and all my friends everywhere.

And most especially a huge thanks for his patience and the many hours spent listening to my stories in the Brooks Hotel during the writing of this book, my good friend John O'Sullivan.

Photo permissions:
All photos courtesy of Inpho Photography or author's own.

Index

5-4-3-2-1 Fellowship, 127, 128–130

Adams, Bernard, 275, 276
Aggie Gray's Hotel, 75
Albanese, Diego, 149
'Albatross', 191
Allen, John, 157
'Amhran na bhFiann', 123
Áras an Uachtaráin, 183, 184
Arsenal FC, 1, 177
Ashton, Brian, 71, 72, 73, 101, 123,
    265–266
Ashe, Tom, 139
'A Song for John Hayes', viii
'As Tears Go By', 117
Attenborough, David, 195

Band on an Island, 204
Barbarians, 167–168, 206, 218–221,
    242, 269
Balmoral Hotel, 123Barrett, Mike
    (Flower Power), 21, 23
Bashir, Martin, 86
Bell, Jonathan, 75
Bennett, Willie, 51, 103, 125, 147,
    179, 227, 267–268
Berkeley Court Hotel, 116, 211, 263
Berry, Dave, 120
Best, George, 115
Best, Neil, 139, 140
Best, Rory, 45, 50, 52, 89–90, 109,
    115, 121, 225, 241
Best, Simon, 127, 137, 224
Big, 202
Bishop, Justin, 132
Bloom, Luka, viii, 204
Boca Juniors, 130
Bosco, Alonzo, 80
Bowe, Tommy, 45, 96, 178, 195, 198,
    210, 254–255
Bowen, Jimmy, 38
Bown, Rhodri, 244

Boylan, Seán, 121
Boyle, Johnny, 246
Bracken, Peter, 109
Bradley, Michael, 95, 99, 116, 167
Bradman, Don, 246
Brando, Marlon, 75
Brennan, Trevor, vii
Brewer, Mike, 10
British and Irish Lions, 1
    1959, 77
    1971, 25, 190
    1974, 190
    1997, 46, 104, 190, 200, 252
    2001, 104, 262, 274
    2005, 95
    2009, ix, 1–7, 187, 190–198, 200,
        233, 235, 236, 239, 243, 245, 254
    2013, ix, xi, 152, 169, 184, 222, 224,
        227, 232, 233, 236–246, 249–253,
        254
Brooks Hotel, 163
Browne, Philip, 153
Browne, Ronan (My Left Foot), 21
Buckley, Tony, 210
Burgess, Luke, 208
Burke, Peadar, 28
Burlington Hotel, 41
Byrne, Shane (Munch), 38, 108

Callaghan, John, 207
Campbell, Ciaran, 98
Campbell, Glen, 232
Canniffe, Donal, 24
Carmody, Ger, 48, 49, 52, 56, 152–
    154, 181, 207, 209, 216–217, 223,
    229, 237, 239, 240, 260, 262, 285
Carney, Brian, 127, 128–130, 140–
    141, 142, 155
Carton House, 48, 54, 55, 60, 219,
    224, 225, 227, 228, 229, 239, 240
Castletroy Park Hotel, 95, 101, 104,
    108, 126, 187, 188, 190, 266, 284

'Christmas 1915', 61, 162
Churchill Cup (2009), 3
Citywest Hotel, viii, 222, 234
'Clare to Here', vii
Claridge Hotel, 104
Clarke, Ciaran, 26
Clegg, Liam, 79
Clerc, Vincent, 122
Clohessy, Anna, 2, 106, 107, 126, 150
Clohessy, Harry, 2
Clohessy, Jane, 2
Clohessy, Luke, 2, 107, 126, 273
Clohessy, Peter (Claw), vii, 2, 45, 96,
    101, 103, 104, 105–107, 108, 116,
    118–119, 126, 132, 150, 155, 164,
    174, 183, 187
club teams
  Ballymena, 126
  Banbridge, 137, 224
  Bayonne, 136
  Bective Rangers, viii, 124
  Blackrock College, 16, 19, 21, 36, 37
  Capbreton, 126, 135
  Cashel, viii
  Castleknock College, 16
  Clondalkin, 157
  Cornish Pirates, 210
  Edenderry, 20
  Edinburgh, 40
  Galwegians, 163
  Garryowen, 267
  Griqualand West, 46
  Harlequins, 211
  Highfield, 237
  Lansdowne, 24, 262
  Leicester Tigers, 241
  London Irish, 132, 182
  Malone, 262
  Newbridge College, 16
  Northampton Saints, 241
  Old Wesley RFC, 25, 36, 38, 39
  Racing Metro 92, 240
  Saint Jean-de-Luz, 40
  Saracens, 132
  Shannon, 107

  Stade Francais, 205
  St Mary's, 3, 16, 23, 25, 40, 61, 125,
    209, 270
  Toulouse, 167, 205
  Terenure, x, 3, 11, 18–29, 31–33,
    36, 37–39, 43, 108, 125, 136–137,
    157, 159, 162, 183, 189, 205, 209,
    223, 224, 225, 232, 237, 262
  UCD, 25
  Wanderers RFC, 11, 24
  Young Munster, 38, 108, 269
Clyde Hotel, 223
Coffee Club, 229
Cohen, Leonard, 243
Coleman, Barry, 36, 116–117
Coleman, Suzanne, 116
Coleman, Eddie, 40
Colet Products, 18, 34, 44
Concannon, Delia, 83
Concannon, Pat, 83, 85
Connacht Rugby, 232
Connemara Coastal Hotel, 163
Connemara Gateway Hotel, 160, 162
Connolly, Billy, 44
Connolly, Christine, 4
Connolly, John, 20
Contepomi, Dr Felipe, 220
Conrad Hotel, 44
Cooper, Quade, 208
Corcoran, Michael, 66, 71
Corkery, David, 26
Corrigan, Reggie, viii, 46
Costello, Michael, 26
Costello, Victor, 40, 132, 261–262
Counihan, Ronnie, 161, 162
country teams
  Argentina, 104, 126, 127–130,
    148–151, 172, 209, 222
  Australia, 40, 62, 70, 101, 104, 110,
    152, 153, 167, 200, 205, 208, 213,
    222, 236, 273, 274
  Canada, 171, 172, 187
  England, 26, 42–43, 122, 123, 178,
    205, 211, 212, 227, 229 England
    Saxons, 223, 226

Fiji, 200, 222
France, 42, 45, 102, 107, 121, 122, 123, 124, 144, 148, 149, 150, 152, 177, 211, 230, 267
Georgia, 145, 148
Ireland A, 3, 40
Irish Wolfhounds, 223, 224, 226
Italy, 102, 124, 126, 136, 177, 205, 211, 230
Japan, 95–101, 167, 262
Namibia, 142, 148
New Zealand, 57, 71, 101, 104, 110, 113, 155, 167, 172, 205, 208, 209, 218, 219, 265–266, 275
New Zealand Maoris, 207
Pacific Islanders, 110, 115
Romania, 77, 108
Russia, 77, 200, 277–279
Samoa, 70–76, 77, 209
Scotland, 2, 23, 123–124, 126, 136, 178, 205, 230, 273
South Africa, 45, 46, 110, 133, 149; 185, 200, 209, 222, 236, 272, 275–277
Tonga, 54, 62, 69
USA, 187, 212, 231, 262–265
Wales, viii, 42, 89, 91–95, 120, 121, 175, 204, 213, 226, 251
Court, Tom, 249
Coyle, D.D., 157
Coyne, Pat, 85
Craig, Daniel, 252
Cranitch, Lorcan, 13
Cranwell, Ben, 22
Cromwell, Oliver, 80
Cronin, Ciaran, 66
Crossan, Frankie, 20, 21, 25
Crossan, Sean, 21
Cullen, Leo, 104
Culloden Hotel, 136, 137, 286
Cunniffe, Brian, 245

'Danny Boy', 208
D'Arcy, Gordon, 52, 177, 223
D'Arcy, Matt, 26

D'Arcy, Tommy, 199
Davies, Gerald, 192, 197, 199
Davidson, Jeremy, 116, 132
Dawson, Kieron, 53, 132
Day's Hotel, 80
Dean, Paul, 39
Deering, Shay, 16
Dempsey, Anne Marie, 209
Dempsey, Girvan, 13, 23, 26, 137, 139, 209
Dempsey, Sean, 205, 208
Devlin, Paddy, 14
Dickens, Charles, 161
Dingle Bay Hotel, 188
Doonmore Hotel, 80, 81, 82, 84
Doran, Joe, 267
Downton Abbey, 161
Doyle, Benny, 28–29, 30
Doyle, Bill, 246–248
Doyle, Dennis, 28–29
Doyle, Jack, 207
Doyle, Liam, 209
Doyle, Marty (Party), 23, 28–29, 30–31, 163
Doyle, Terry, 21
Duggan, Alan (Dixie), 40
Duggan, Willie, 19
Dunne, Ben, 44
Dunboyne Castle, 230
Dunraven Arms Hotel, 189

Earls, Keith, 50, 196, 200
Easterby, Guy, 168
Easterby, Simon, 168
Edwards, Shaun, 194
Eight-O'Clock Club, 269
Einstein, Albert, xiii
Electric Light Orchestra, 1
Ellis, Andrew, 57, 273
Ellis, Scott, 273
Elwood, Eric, 232
Emmerdale Farm, 22
Evans, Ieuan, 191

Falvey, Dr Eanna, 221, 226. 249

Fanagan, Denise, 72, 185, 269, 276
Fanagan, Jody, 269
Fanagan, Joe (Banana), 269
Farrell, Owen, 239
Feehan, John, 4, 237
Ferrari, Enzo, 32
Ferris, Stephen, 115, 224
Field, Maurice, 45
Fiennes, Sir Ranulph, 222
Finnstown House, 150
Fitzgerald, Luke, viii, 115, 183, 197
Fitzpatrick, Arthur, 225
Fitzpatrick, Justin, 53, 116
Fitzpatrick, Sean, 47, 59
Five Nations Championship
   1985, 21
   1998, 42
Flannery, Jerry, 7, 109, 208
Flannery, Vincent, 160
Flavin, Adrian, 232
Flavin, Paul (Fla), 38
Fleming, Ian, 114, 166
Flutey, Riki, 5
Flynn, Kevin, 26
Flynn, Paddy, 265
Flynn, Willie, 21, 25
Foley, Anthony (Axel), 109, 225
Foley, Brendan, 109
Ford, Mike, 123, 272
Ford, Ross, 199
Four Seasons, 123
Francis, Neil, 39
Fulcher, Gabriel, 116
Fusco, Dominic, 14, 15

GAA
   All-Ireland football final (2009), 188
   Dublin v Meath (1991), 121
Galwey, Mick (Gaillimh), 96, 103, 105,
   107–108, 116
Gargan, David (Guggs), 36, 39
Gatland, Trudi, 250
Gatland, Warren, 149, 180, 194, 214,
   224, 236, 238, 250, 251, 252, 254,
   266

Geoghegan, Simon, 45, 116
Gleeson, John, 14
Glennon, Jim, 39
Glenview Hotel, 53, 77, 105, 164, 269
Gone with the Wind, 263
Governey, Michael, 44, 45
Grace, Tom, 16
Grand Hyatt Hotel, 241
Grand Slam,
   1948, 8, 177
   2009, xi, 3, 89, 173, 175–178,
      180–184, 187, 190, 251
Green, Brian, 97, 184, 272
Green 19, 234
Greenwood, Will, 191
Griffin, Mick, 270

Hagler, Marvin, 222
Halfpenny, Leigh, 196, 239, 251
Halpin, Gary, 71, 132
Halvey, Eddie, 116
Hanks, Tom, 202
Harbison, Harry, 25
Harlem Globetrotters, 130
Hartley, Dylan, 241
Haycock, Paul, 26
Hayes, Gearoid, 223
Hayes, John, x, 52, 105, 112, 114, 135,
   139, 197
Healy, Cian, 50, 200, 225
Heaslip, Jamie, 45, 50, 115, 177, 178,
   183, 195, 197, 198, 208, 210, 232,
   234–235, 240, 251, 252
Hedren, Tippi, 84
Hegarty, Derek, 46, 232
Hegarty, Fr, 14
Heineken Cup
   2008, 167
   2009, 3
   2010, 205
Henderson, Angie, 102, 165
Henderson, Ian, 228, 230
Henderson, Rob, 86, 96, 101–102,
   106, 116, 132, 162, 164–165, 282,
   284

Henry, Graham, 262
Henry, Paul, 86
Hennebry, Paul, 26
Hennessey, Christy, 44
Hennessey, Dr Liam, 261–262, 280
Heritage Hotel, 208
Hibbard, Richard, 251
Hickie, Denis, 17, 52, 94, 115, 125, 140, 168
Hideyoshi, Toyotomi, 99
Hilton Hotel, 91, 121, 175, 227
Hipwell, Mick, 25
Ho, Ivan, 243
Hogan, Niall, 13, 26, 39, 116
Hogan, Trevor, 98
Hogg, Stuart, 240
'Hold on Tight to Your Dreams, 1
Hole-in-the-Wall Gang, 105, 111–115, 127, 135–136
Holt, Ted, 18
Horan, Marcus, 3, 96, 105, 112, 113, 115, 135, 139
Horgan, Anthony, 75, 76, 112, 282–283
Horgan, Shane, 17, 45, 52, 115, 125, 136, 154, 168
Howe, Tyrone, 53
Hughes, Michael, 244
Humphreys, David, viii, 45, 53, 92, 267
Hyatt Hotel, 170

Inishgort, 84
Inishshark, 80, 86
Inishbofin, 51, 61, 79–88, 89–90, 125, 126, 170, 177, 184, 187, 208, 223, 231, 261, 270
Inpho Photography, 66, 227
Intercontinental Hotel, 274
International Dateline Hotel, 63, 65, 77
Ireland, George, 226
'Ireland's Call', 54, 123
Irish Independent, 66
IRB, 143, 150, 151

IRFU, 21, 43, 122, 124, 153, 183, 187, 223, 226, 231, 253, 261, 266, 285
Irvine, Andy, 250, 254

Jackman, Bernard, 98
Jennings, Shane, 52, 212
Jenkins, Gethin, 249
Jenkins, Neil, 197, 240
Jenkinson, Colm, 14
Johns, Christopher, 45
Johns, Kirsty, 45
Johns, Paddy, 45, 46, 53, 116, 132–133
Johns, Kirsty, 45
Johnson, Martin, 191
Jones, Adam, 194, 200, 250
Jones, Alun Wyn, 197, 250, 255
Jones, Felix, viii
Jones, Stephen, x, 181, 193, 197, 199
Jones, Tom, 286
Jordan, Mikey, 34–35, 183, 199, 246–248
'Joxer Goes to Stuttgart', vii
Joyce, Martin, 224, 225
Joyce, Paul, 36, 37
Jury's Hotel, 166

Kearney, Michael, viii, 225, 226, 260, 262
Kearney, Rob, 54, 172, 197
Kelly, Alan, 39
Kelly, John, 112, 157–159
Kennedy, Frank, 25
Kennedy, Ken, 19
Kershaw, Paul, 52
Kidd, Murray, 263
Kidney, Declan, viii, 3, 166, 167, 177, 190, 220–221, 223, 229, 231, 253, 267
Kiely, Jack, 114, 127
Killiney Castle Hotel, viii, 23, 89, 111, 121, 125, 138, 183, 205
Killkelly, Jane, 228
Kiss, Les, 50, 166, 184

Lamborghini, Ferruccio, 32
Lavelle, Francis, 85
Lavelle, John, 85
Leamy, Denis, vii, 52, 109, 115, 140, 170, 202
Leinster Rugby
  A, 210
  senior, xi, 3, 38, 39, 40, 44, 167, 205, 234, 253
  under-20s, xi, 38
Leinster Senior Cup (1978), 24
Leinster Senior League (1978), 24
Lenihan, Donal, 149, 260, 262, 274
Leonard, Jason, 211
Lloyd, Micky, 39
Lonesome Dove, 134, 140, 141, 155
Long, Adrian, 225, 246
Long, Liz, 199, 240
Long, Rhys, 244
Loughborough University, 39
Love, Robbie, 39
'Lucky Man', 45, 46
Lyons, John, 44
Lyons, Paddy, 18

Madigan, Ian, 54, 227
Magee, Louis, 124, 225
Maggs, Kevin, 53, 74
Magners League, 3, 167
Mahony, Michael, 14
Maloney, Paul, 224
Marsh, Ronnie, 18
Martin, Ruth, 184
Martina, Gerry, 22
McAleese, Martin, 183
McAleese, Mary, 183
McBride, Denis, 45, 116
McBride, Willie John, 191
McCall, Mark, 95, 116
McCann, Donal, 13, 16
McCarthy, Kieran, 182
McCormack, Ailbe, 222, 268–269
McCuaig, Fr, 16
McCullough, Matt, 98
McDermott, Mark, 104

McEntee, Collie, 210
McFadden, Fergus, viii, 54, 213
McGeechan, Ian, 190, 192, 197, 199, 267
McGowan, Alan, 39
McGrath, Paul, viii
McGurn, Mike, 271–272
McIvor, Steve, 232
McKenna, Mick, 23
McLauchlan, Ian (Mighty Mouse), 191
McLaughlin, Brian, 104, 138
McLaughlin, Callum, 138
McMurtry, Larry, 134
McNaughton, Paul, 166, 260, 262
McShane, Dr Jim, 270
Meade, Declan, 54, 57
Meads, Colin, 265
Mears, Lee, 196
Miles, Joey, 95, 167, 260, 262
Milroy, Joe, 18, 20
Modern Green, 232, 246
Moore, Christy, vii–viii, 50, 178, 181, 194, 207, 255
Moore, Nicky, 21
Monye, Ugo, 193
Moran, John, 219, 220
Morgan, Ian, 225
Morris, Dewi, 191
Morrissey, Niall (Flash), 21
Morrissey, T.P., 38
Muldoon, John, 208
Mullins, Mike, 46
Munster Rugby, 3, 38, 101, 164, 167, 167, 205
  Munster President's XV, 41, 261
Murphy, Brendan, 18
Murphy, Geordan, 34, 141, 179, 181, 210, 213
Murphy, Gerry, 40, 43, 263
Murphy, John (Spud), 39
Murphy, Martin, 279
Murphy, Mervyn, 50, 53, 270–271
Murphy, Mike, 13
Murphy, Noel, 41, 260, 261
Murphy, Paddy, 18, 20

Murray, Margaret, 80
Murray, Paddy, 81
Murray, Stephen, 231
Murray, Willow, 39
Mutiny on the Bounty, 75

Neill, Aidan (7–6), 21
Neilly, Jim, 222
Nesdale, Ross, 53, 116
North, George, x, 244, 251
NZRFU, 168, 205, 275

O₂ jersey Guardians, 229
O'Brien, Brian, vii, 63, 65, 95, 127,
    189, 260, 261
O'Brien, John, 26
O'Brien, Olive, 127
O'Brien, Paddy, 9
O'Brien, Sean, 230
O'Callaghan, Donncha, xiii, 51, 58,
    92, 96, 105, 109, 112, 113, 115,
    139, 196, 202–203, 210, 282
O'Carroll, Mick, 21
O'Connell, Paul, viii, 108–109, 122,
    125, 173–174, 191, 197, 199,
    220–221, 242
O'Connor, Johnny, 95, 102, 232
O'Dea, Liam, 22–23, 126
O'Donovan, Gimper, 20
O'Donovan, Niall, 95, 167, 272
O'Driscoll, Amy, 229
O'Driscoll, Barry, 270
O'Driscoll, Brian, viii, 17, 23, 51, 58,
    95, 96, 102, 115, 116, 121, 122,
    123, 152, 168, 170, 176, 178, 181,
    185–186, 196, 200, 205, 207, 229,
    251, 267, 268, 270
O'Driscoll, Gary, 1, 57, 114, 125, 177,
    270
O'Driscoll, Mick, 104, 108, 127, 210,
    216, 219
O'Gara, Ronan, vii, 51, 54, 58, 92,
    110, 121, 124, 138, 139, 179, 182,
    213, 214, 227
O'Hagan, Johnny, 39, 45, 227

O'Halloran, Ann, 81–82
O'Halloran, Gabriel, 83
O'Halloran, Mikey, 81
O'Kelly, Malcolm, vii, 132, 207, 209,
    210
O'Kelly, Stephanie, 209
O'Leary, Tomás, 6
O'Malley, Grainne, 80
O'Malley, Michael, 157
'Ordinary Man', vii
O'Reilly Auction Rooms, 40
O'Reilly, Bill (Tiger), 246
O'Reilly, Brendan, 9
O'Reilly, Brian, 9
O'Reilly, Christopher, 9
O'Reilly, David, 9, 163
O'Reilly, Helen, 8, 10
O'Reilly, Geraldine, 9
O'Reilly, Granny, 9
O'Reilly, Jeanette, 9
O'Reilly, June, 8
O'Reilly, Paddy, 8, 9, 10, 15, 24
O'Reilly, Pauline, 8, 12, 246
O'Shaughnessy, Dr Donal, 168, 219,
    269
O'Shea, Conor (Caesar), 38, 39, 132
O'Shea, Fiona, 188, 284
O'Shea, Mike, 188–189
O'Sullivan, Declan, 18
O'Sullivan, Eddie, 63, 67, 91, 95, 109,
    112, 116, 129, 141, 144, 149, 167,
    177, 202, 212, 222, 266–267
O'Sullivan, John, 66
O'Sullivan, Knick Knack, 18–19
O'Sullivan, McFriendly, 20
O'Sullivan, Sonia, 153
O'Sullivan, Dr Tadhg, 220

Pacific Royal Hotel, 66
Panamerico Hotel, 127
Panorama, 86
Pennyhill Park and Spa Hotel, 4–6,
    168, 198
Phillips, Mike, 211
Pim, Chris, 39

Pope John Paul II, 102, 284
Popplewell, Nick (Poppy), 41–43, 116
Power, Patrick G., 79
Prendergast, Jim, 81, 82
Prendergast, Shane, 82
Prince Charles, 86
Princess Diana, 86
Prince William, 87
Pucciariello, Freddie, 128

Queen Elizabeth II, 184
Queen's Hotel, 167, 219
Quinlan, Alan, 7, 64, 104–105, 127,
    139, 140–141, 144, 155–156, 207
Quinlan, David, 98
Quinnell, Scott, 191

Radisson Hotel, 117, 123, 126, 138,
    139
Ramsey, Louise, 190, 193
Rasputin, 284
Reaching for Glory, 120, 127
Redmond, John, 272
Rees, Matthew, 198
Renvyle House, 157–163, 164, 208,
    223, 271
Revins, Dave, 51, 127, 179, 227, 229
Richardson, Guy, 2, 3, 6, 190, 192,
    193, 224, 231
Richardson, Karl, 99, 228, 272–273
'Ride On', vii
Ridge, Martin, 38
Rio Grande Hotel, 128
Robson, James, 241, 249
Roche, Barry (Rover), 21–22
Roche, Dixie, 2, 3, 24, 29–31, 40, 43,
    78, 79, 80, 83, 95, 101, 107, 117,
    118, 119, 123, 131, 132, 157–159,
    164, 170, 183, 187–189, 198, 204,
    206, 209, 214, 225, 226, 229, 231,
    233, 237, 238, 240, 246–248,
    249–250, 284
Roche, Jack, 37
Roche, Mick, 21
Roche, Mrs, 37, 160, 206

Rooney, Kieran, 66
Rowntree, Graham, 197
Royal Garden Hotel, 240
RTÉ, 66, 129, 130
Ruane, Noel, 18
Ruane, Shay (The Bear), 14, 18, 21,
    28–29, 30, 43, 61–62, 86, 206,
    233, 246–248
Ruddy, Michael Joe, 159–161
Rugby World Cup
  1995, 43
  1999, 149–152, 273
  2003, 47, 77, 152–155, 202, 274,
    275, 277
  2007, 117, 130, 134–148, 155, 168,
    212
  2011, 212–215
  2019, 101
Rugby World Cup (under-21)
  1999, 104

SARFU, 133, 275
Saverimutto, Christian, 265
Schmidt, Joe, 253
Sexton, Jonathan, 54, 200, 208, 226,
    227, 240, 251
Sheahan, Frankie, viii, 96, 97, 112,
    127, 139, 144
Sheen, Martin, 44
Shelbourne Hotel, 54, 55, 58, 60,
    209–210, 216–217, 229
Sheridan, Andrew, 194
Sheridan, Dan, 227, 249
Sherry, Brendan, 25
Shudel, Maureen, 31
Silver Springs, 261
Sinnott, Bridit, 160, 162
Sinnott, Charlie, 160, 162
Sinnott, Darragh, 163
Sinnott, Declan, viii
Sinnott, Eoin, 163
Sinnott, Ruairi, 163
Six Nations Championship
  2000, 102, 267

2001, 102
2002, viii, 107
2004, 26
2005, 91–95
2007, 120–125, 177
2008, 149
2009, xi, 3, 4, 89, 172, 173, 175–183, 190, 251
2010, 204
2011, 210
2012, 215
2013, 222–223, 226–231
Smal, Gert, viii, 166, 179, 184, 231
Smyth, Dr Michael, 14, 24–25, 86
Smyth, Jimmy (Rainbow), 36
Smyth, Peter, 36
soccer teams
  Poland, 228
  Republic of Ireland, 228
Sofitel Heathrow, 220
Sofitel Le Lac, 139
Sowman, Frank, 263
Spala, 104, 126, 131, 261, 279–284
Sparks, Pat (Pop), 25
Sparks, Robbie, 25
stadia and grounds
  Aviva Stadium, 50, 54, 58, 195, 205, 211, 229, 279
  Campbell College, 138
  Croke Park, 121, 122, 177, 178, 200, 204
  Crowley Park, 163
  Donnybrook, 21
  Dr Hickey Park, 164, 203
  Killing Fields, 38
  Kingsholm, 167, 218
  King's Hospital, 151
  Lakelands, 18, 20, 27, 108, 137, 232, 261
  Lansdowne Road, 47, 110, 115, 116, 150, 151, 211
  Life University, 264
  Mardyke, 166
  Millennium Stadium, 91, 93, 21, 175, 211, 226
  Murrayfield, 2, 123, 126, 178
  North Sydney Oval Cricket and Rugby Ground, 245
  Ravenhill, 106, 126, 136
  Stradbrook, 37
  Stade Bordelais, 140
  Stade Chablan-Delmas, 142
  Stade de France, 42, 102, 124, 145–146
  Stadio Flaminio, 124
  St Gerard's School, 286
  Subiaco Oval, 70
  Telstra Dome, 170
  Templeville Road, 11
  Teufaiva Stadium, 69
  Thomond Park, 38
  Tupou College, 67, 68
  Twickenham, 26, 42, 252
  Westpac Stadium, 169
Staples, Jim, 116, 264
'Stay Another Day', 197
Steadman, Graham, 272
St John Gogarty, Oliver, 157, 161
Steele, Cameron, 117, 130, 268
Steele, Noleen, 117
Stevens, Matt, 244
Stickland, Billy, 66, 219
Strauss, Richardt, 224
Stridgeon, Paul (Bobby), 194, 243, 245
Stringer, Peter, viii, 94, 97, 110, 112, 113, 114
Sturgeon, John, 168, 205, 275
Sturgeon, Mary, 205
Sunday Post, 124
Sunday Tribune, 66
Sweeney, Niall, 18, 44

Tainton, Mark, xiii, 181, 225, 229, 231, 272
Tea Club, 52, 105, 137, 140
Terenure College, 13, 14, 15–17
'The Contender', vii, 207
'The Flickering Light', 197
The Godfather, 158
The Irish Times, 66

Thornberry, Fergus, 225
Thornton, Des, 25
Thornton, Eddie, 20
Thornton, Johnny, 21
Three Lakes Hotel, 31
Toia, Anton, 208, 273–274
Toia, Lonnie, 208, 274
Toolan, Eoin, 52, 53, 229
Tormey, Gerry, 25
Tormey, Pat, 14
Trimble, Andrew, 45, 225
Triple Crown
  1985, 21
  2004, 26
  2007, 125
Trundle, Darina, 162
Trundle, Pat, 162
Twiggy, 115

Ulster Rugby, 45
Unforgiven, 197
University of Limerick, 95, 171, 190

Varley, Damien, viii
Vermeulen, Elvis, 123
Vickery, Phil, 194, 199

Wallace, David, 104, 173, 208, 212
Wallace, George, 38
Wallace, Paddy, 45, 116, 138

Wallace, Paul, 104, 116, 132, 191
Wallace, Richard, 104, 116, 132
Walsh, Peter, 26, 43
Warburton, Sam, 237, 251
Ward, Greg, 36
'Waterloo Sunset', 115
Whelan, Pa, 18, 20, 76, 260, 261, 265,
  284–284
White, Craig, 192, 194, 271
White, Peter, 168, 275
Wigwam Hotel, 195
Williams, Shane, 194, 249
Williamson, Niall, 36
Wilson, Roger, 98
Winters Cup (1968), 23
Wood, Gordon, 77
Wood, Keith (Fester), vii, 6, 39, 46–47,
  65, 77–78, 103, 105, 116, 150,
  153, 187, 191, 211
Woodward, Clive, 95, 211
Woods, Niall (Crow), 37, 38, 116
WRFU, 179

X Factor, 207

Young Bryan (the Bear), 104, 114, 139
Yourell, Jade, 259

Zebo, Simon, 225, 249

Helping and Supporting Students

Helping and Supporting Students

Rethinking the Issues

John Earwaker

The Society for Research into Higher Education
& Open University Press

Published by SRHE and
Open University Press
Celtic Court
22 Ballmoor
Buckingham
MK18 1XW

and
1900 Frost Road, Suite 101
Bristol, PA 19007, USA

First published 1992

A catalogue record of this book is available
from the British Library

Library of Congress Cataloging-in-Publication Data

Earwaker, John, 1936–
    Helping and supporting students /John Earwaker.
        p.   cm.
    Includes index.
    ISBN 0–335–15666–5. — ISBN 0–335–15665–7 (pbk.)
    1. Counselling in higher education — Great Britain.   2. Academic
advisors — Great Britain.   I. Title.
    LB2343.E26   1992
    378.1'94'0941—dc20   91–43033
                                                                      CIP

Typeset by Graphicraft Typesetters Limited, Hong Kong
Printed in Great Britain by St Edmundsbury Press,
Bury St Edmunds, Suffolk

Contents

Preface   vii
Acknowledgements   xi

Part 1: The Student Experience   1

1 The Experience of Problems   3
   Four case studies   3
   Unravelling problems   6
   Problems in the early stages   8
   Typical student problems   9

2 The Experience of Development   12
   Development as a person   13
   Development as a student   15
   Development in relation to specific occupations   17
   Complex pathways of development   19

3 The Experience of Transition   22
   Metaphors of change   23
   Adjustment   24
   Socialization   26
   Transition   29

4 The Changing Student Experience   33
   Past and present   33
   Representation and reality   37
   Explaining change   38
   Solidarity and diversity   39

Part 2: Tutorial Support   43

5 The Tutor's Point of View   45
   The tutoring experience: an investigation   46
   The contribution of tutors to student support   47

Tutors' feelings about their support role   49
Sources of role strain   51

6 The Tutorial Relationship   55
   Interviewing, counselling and tutoring   56
   The tutorial: its agenda and its management   58
   The use and abuse of power   61
   The paradox of helping   65

7 Confidentiality   68
   Dealing with sensitive information   68
   Privacy, secrecy and confidentiality   71
   Confidentiality: a five-dimensional model   73
   Professional responsibility   74

8 The Tutor's Role   78
   Front-line support   78
   Roles and relationships   79
   Setting boundaries   81
   Referral   83

Part 3: Institutional Policy   89

9 Patterns of Provision   91
   Examples of institutional provision   91
   Discussion   94
   Improving current provision   98

10 'Pastoral Care' and 'Counselling'   101
    The British tradition of higher education   102
    The idea of pastoral care   106
    The counselling model   108

11 Alternative Models of Support Provision   113
    Support provision via the curriculum   115
    Workplace welfare   119
    Peer support and group-building   120

12 Rethinking Student Support   124
    Students' need for support   124
    The institution's responsibility for provision   127
    Rethinking institutional provision   130

References   135
Index   137
The Society for Research in Higher Education   142

Preface

I should like to explain how this book came to be written. The matters discussed here are issues I have lived with in my own working life as I have tried, over many years, to offer students appropriate help and support. Although I make reference, throughout the book, to a number of writers whose ideas have helped me to make sense of my work, what is written here comes directly from my own situation and my reflection upon it. I am writing out of experience, not out of other books.

Within my own institution I fulfil a double role. As a member of an academic department I play a full part in teaching, course planning, course leadership and administration, and in giving my students the tutorial support they need within that context. At the same time, as Polytechnic Chaplain, I belong to a team of people specifically designated to provide a back-up support service throughout the institution. I thereby attempt to straddle a most interesting divide. To move repeatedly across this boundary, perhaps several times in a day, is to gain practice in looking at the institution through two eyes. Yet the two roles are very different and any attempt to combine them is necessarily fraught with contradictions. For example, academic credibility does not sit easily with counselling accessibility; the one may easily be sacrificed for or achieved at the expense of the other.

Of course, every lecturer experiences tensions between teaching, examining and supporting students. There is a long tradition, too, of college chaplains having a teaching role. Why then do I feel my role to be so special? To answer that question is to anticipate some of the arguments of this book. Briefly, it has to do with the institutional context and the ideological framework within which I work. The clergyman-scholar in an Oxford college can, even now, take for granted certain assumptions about pastoral care which offer a coherent, if somewhat anachronistic framework within which to work. However, to work in a thoroughly modern, secular, bureaucratic, specialized and managerially-run institution, which is used to separating out distinct functions, dividing up responsibilities and assigning specific roles, and to have a foot in each of two very different camps, is a quite different experience.

It is from this experience that I write, confident that what from one point of view might be seen as a predicament, or as a difficult balancing act, may also be seen positively as a uniquely privileged position from which to consider the task of helping and supporting students.

The fact that I have worked in the same institution for over 20 years is misleading. It is not the same institution. What I joined as a College of Education with rather more than a thousand students has become one of the largest higher education institutions in Great Britain. My initial role in teacher training was followed by a period of teaching social studies to a much wider range of students. At the same time, my chaplaincy role brought me into contact with a cross-section of the whole institution. I began to discover just how sheltered my previous experience had been.

Like many teaching staff, I imagined that many students must find such a large institution daunting and perhaps alienating; that they might be lonely, anxious and afraid; and that they would appreciate it if someone was willing to befriend them, offer practical help and possibly some advice as well. That, of course, is all true, but it is not the whole truth. As part of the student support services I have found myself caught up in problems more severe and more complicated than I had experienced in my parish ministry. Drug addiction I had read about, but not encountered first hand. I knew about alcoholism, but I did not expect to be visiting in hospital members of staff who were 'drying out'. In four years of parish experience I had never had to visit a prison and only once faced someone who threatened suicide. Yet within months of undertaking chaplaincy work in higher education I had come up against almost every problem imaginable. I was startled and shocked. It was as if I was seeing below the surface of the institution, discovering all the things usually kept hidden.

The idea for this book began to take shape during a short period of secondment when I conducted an investigation into tutorial support within the institution. There was widespread concern that the previous arrangements could not be sustained and that students were not getting the help and support they needed. My suspicion was that a small number of staff (particularly First Year Tutors, of whom I was one) were, in fact, ensuring that this did not happen, but at considerable personal cost to themselves. An account of this investigation appears in Chapter 5. The point to notice here is that this raised questions about the role of the tutor in student support, which has become a major theme of this book.

I began to provide opportunities for colleagues to come together to discuss these issues, and these consultations later developed into a year-long course for interested staff. This was, in turn, incorporated into a wider programme of in-house staff development which has since become part of a Masters programme. In all this I have found surprisingly little help from published literature. While there are many books which give practical guidance on how to give help to others in a quasi-counselling context, there are very few attempts to deal with the underlying issues as they confront a lecturer who is concerned to be helpful to his or her students; and there are none, so far as I know, which challenge the prevailing conception of student support as ancillary to the main task of higher education.

It will now be clear why I had to sketch something of the background in order to explain how this book came to be written. After a great deal of discussion with colleagues in my own and other institutions it has gradually become clear to me that this whole area of work requires much more radical rethinking than it has so far received. It is not, as is commonly supposed, just a matter of resourcing; we need to be much clearer about what we need the resourcing for.

My ideas have gradually taken shape around the headings of 'students', 'tutors' and 'institutions', and this three-fold framework is reflected in the structure of the book.

Part 1 of the book, Chapters 1–4, may be seen as a series of widening circles. It seems obvious that one should start by looking at students and their problems; yet further reflection suggests that this may not be such a good starting-point, in that it implies that our concerns are remedial only. We then look at students and their development, and discover that, while this approach is refreshingly positive, it still focuses too much on the individual and is liable to ignore the interpersonal and social dimensions of experience. The third chapter considers the way in which people make the transition into (and out of) the student state, finding it necessary here to take an explicitly psycho-social approach. Finally, we look at wider social changes which have affected the character of student life, trying to set current concerns in a broader historical context.

Part 2, Chapters 5–8, tackles the issues from the perspective of the tutor. Here I have evidence to offer, drawn from interviews with some of my colleagues; this forms the starting-point of this section. In the light of this I then go on to discuss the tutorial relationship (and in particular, ways in which it may go wrong, so that efforts at helping turn out to be counter-productive), the thorny problem of confidentiality and the limits of the tutor's role. Throughout this section I take for granted what elsewhere might be much more problematic: the tutors' commitment to helping and supporting students in this way.

In Part 3, Chapters 9–12, I look at the question of how institutions can best provide support for students. Here, I develop the thesis that two powerful sets of ideas have been at work and have had the effect of distorting a great deal of our effort in this area. I try to open up a number of other possible approaches, while at the same time insisting that student support should be seen as a whole, that it belongs within the educational task and that the role of the tutor is crucial.

Throughout the book I use a variety of strategies to link the ideas with actual experience. I offer case studies, cameos and vignettes as well as referring to real life stories, to exemplify specific issues. I am aware, of course, that stereotypes can be dangerous; they can also be extremely useful in throwing into relief the implications of our beliefs and attitudes. The purpose in each case is to illustrate a particular point, no more.

I am conscious that the book rests on a great deal of personal experience as a chaplain, a teacher and a tutor with administrative responsibilities. It also rests in a rather special way on my research into the work of some particularly conscientious tutors in my own institution; on the staff training courses for which I have been responsible; and on my input into my own institution's developing policies in this area. This doubtless gives it a particular slant. I am very aware, for instance, that while I have undertaken some first-hand investigation of the perceptions of staff involved in student support, this book does not rely on any comparable direct investigation of student perceptions of their own experience. Thus, it is very much a personal statement, written from a particular point of view.

What runs through the book is, I hope, a strong line of my own. To a large extent it is coloured by my double role in combining an academic teaching appointment with my chaplaincy work. I am, therefore, able to see, in a way which is open to very few colleagues, the necessity to hold together these two aspects of our work. The theme to which I keep returning is that helping and supporting students is not some kind of 'extra' which may be tacked on as supplementary to the educational experience, but an integral element in the educational process.

Acknowledgements

More than anything else, my continuing contact with students is what has made this book possible. I am grateful to them for the way in which they have let me into their lives and allowed me to share some of their practical, intellectual and personal struggles.

More directly, I am indebted to colleagues, too numerous to mention, with whom I have discussed these ideas on many occasions. In particular, those involved with my course on Student Support have helped me to think through these issues. Special thanks are due to the University of South Carolina and, in particular, to Professor John Gardner and his team for their gracious hospitality in the Spring of 1989.

Four people read the whole book through in draft form before publication: Peter Ashworth and David Clark of Sheffield City Polytechnic, Elaine Graham of Manchester University and Mark Greengrass of Sheffield University. They are all friends whose opinions I value and whose judgement I trust. Their comments have been extremely valuable in the closing stages of putting the book together.

Lastly, and most of all, thanks to my wife Janet for the way she has given help and support to me.

Part 1

The Student Experience

1

The Experience of Problems

As the proportion of students in the population rises and institutions of higher education grow in size, there is a real risk that the individuals with particular needs and difficulties will disappear from view. Students have always had problems, but current trends mean that they may now be more acute, harder to alleviate and perhaps more difficult to identify. There are more mature students returning to study after substantial experience of employment, often bringing with them various personal and domestic difficulties. There are more students from overseas, whose diverse cultures and different expectations may clash quite sharply with what is offered here. Home-based students, on the other hand, are finding it ever harder to establish their own independence. Thus our higher education institutions, under growing pressure to be cost-effective, have to respond to a widening range of student needs.

These current strains only serve to exacerbate what is at any time a rather stressful existence. Even at the best of times students confront difficulties which they may be unable to handle alone. These problems will be of many different kinds, ranging from the ordinary troubles of daily living (e.g. physical health, accommodation, finance, relationships) to major crises (e.g. accidents, injuries, bereavement, mental breakdown, suicide), plus a further set of problems more specifically associated with student life (e.g. academic difficulties, study problems, course choice, career decisions).

Suppose we begin by looking closely at some of the actual problems students experience? The following case studies outline the predicaments faced by four fairly ordinary full-time students. We may call them Adrian, Barry, Christine and Denise.

Four case studies

Adrian, aged 19, is in his first term reading Business Studies. His father is a solicitor and his mother a doctor in general practice. He has two younger sisters. His parents have recently separated and are intending to get divorced as soon as possible. Adrian is anxious about his course. He now recognizes that he chose it more because he was determined to strike out on his own than because he knew or cared much about business. An able student, he is not finding it as interesting or as intellectually challenging as the work he did for his A-levels at school. He wonders whether he is on the right course. However, he is uncertain about how he would negotiate any change in the financing of his course. With two professional parents each with a substantial income, he is not entitled to any grant from his local education authority. He is, therefore, entirely dependent upon his father and/or mother for financial support. Neither of his parents was keen that he should study business and each of them would have preferred him to go in for something more like their own professional career. He fears that to reopen discussion about his future at this point will be divisive; he is also very much afraid that either or both his parents could withdraw financial support if he were to change course. Although he has got on reasonably well with his fellow students, he has found them disappointingly dull, mostly having interests very different from his own. He has not yet acquired any close friends with whom he can discuss his family situation. Somewhat to his surprise, he finds himself longing to talk to his two sisters. He feels very responsible for them, now that the family is breaking up, and is conscious that they are still involved in the tensions between their parents whereas he is now out of it. His immediate concern is how and where to spend the Christmas vacation.

Barry, 26, is studying Construction Studies after completing an Access course. He worked on a building site for a number of years, and is a skilled brick-layer and plasterer. He would like to get a qualification in surveying. His hobby is football which he follows with great interest, regularly supporting his local club. Partly due to the Access course which introduced him to wider social issues to do with housing policy, he is beginning to become more polit-ically active. He lives with his girlfriend who works as a state-enrolled nurse. Both of them are members of the campaign for nuclear disarmament through which they come into contact with a wide circle of friends. They have little money and Barry gets no back-up from his family who cannot understand why he wants to go to college. Barry feels that the other members of the course, who are mostly straight from school, know very little about the realities of the building trade or about life. By contrast, he feels he has a great deal of relevant experience and he is surprised to find how little this is appreciated on the course. Barry has real difficulty in judging how well he is getting on, since he has little idea of the standard required. Naturally, he is anxious to do well, but he has no tradition of higher education in his family to fall back on. His girlfriend has told him she thinks she may be pregnant and this has thrown him into a panic. At present he receives a grant which is barely adequate, so his girlfriend supports him financially when necessary, but their joint finances are precarious and depend crucially on his girlfriend's modest income as a nurse. He feels that his long-awaited chance of higher education could now be jeopardized. His girlfriend, on the contrary, wants to have a baby and thinks he is overestimating the difficulties.

Christine is 38. She left school aged 18 with one A-level pass and has worked for many years as a secretary. Married with teenage children, she is now studying English Literature. Her husband has strongly encouraged and supported her to embark on a degree. She eventually enrolled on an Open University Foundation course which led to her acceptance onto a full-time course at her local university. She appears a confident and capable woman who has brought up a family, held down a job and still looks after her elderly parents. Yet her domestic problems are beginning to mount up to a point where she is having difficulty in meeting course deadlines. The problems now include: her son is truanting from school; her husband's work has suddenly become insecure; her elderly mother has had a fall; and her teenage daughter has started going out with a boyfriend whom she and her husband regard as unsuitable. Christine is reluctant to ask for extra time to complete coursework, and repeatedly insists that she does not want favoured treatment.

Denise is 20 and is studying Electronic Engineering. She is well-qualified in comparison with the rest of the group, where she is one of only three women among 32 men. Her schooling was in a single-sex Roman Catholic school where she was encouraged to take up science subjects and was very well taught by a series of excellent women teachers. She is appalled both by what she sees as the loutish behaviour of the young men on her course and by the quality of the teaching which seems to her very casual. Her lecturers are all men and she is particularly wary of approaching them outside the classroom. She now feels, having been somewhat spoon-fed at school, that she is very much on her own. Throughout her first term she travelled home most weekends to see her boyfriend, despite the cost of doing so and the effect it had on her work. It is now January and it has become clear to her during the Christmas vacation that her boyfriend didn't really want her to come home so frequently, and also her parents are urging her to make new friends and develop more social life at university. Her personal tutor has now discussed her work with her and encouraged her to think of herself as a potential high-flier. Far from being pleased, she feels this simply puts more pressure on her to do well. She is also feeling very insecure about her relationship with her boyfriend. She feels that perhaps her parents are right and that she should have mixed more with the other students, but it seems too late now to start relating differently within the student group. She wonders whether to change course. Her personal tutor is totally mystified as to why she would want to do that, and says so.

These four students may serve as a focus for the rest of this chapter. They are not meant to be fully representative (for one thing, all four students are studying full-time, for another, they are all white), but their stories are typical of student life as it is actually experienced. Together they provide a close-up view of some common student problems and suggest some issues which need to be explored.

Unravelling problems

My first observation is that problems are rarely simple or straightforward; several problems may be bound up together. Adrian's decisions about his future are locked into his family situation and questions of financial support; Barry may feel obliged to leave his course and get a job because of his view of how an adequate husband and father should behave; Denise needs to sort out the social side of her life before she will be able to settle down to work properly. Clearly, human problems do not lend themselves to neat classification, and anyone who sets out to help and support other people in coping with their problems (which is not the same as solving their problems for them) is likely to be drawn into dealing with the whole person and their situation seen as a whole.

Thus, problems will often have to be unravelled before they can be dealt with. The problem initially identified may turn out to be, on further investigation, not the central problem at all. Denise, for instance, suggests to her personal tutor that perhaps she should leave the course. This might, indeed, be a possible way forward for her, but from the evidence available it does not seem to be the best starting-point for a discussion of her problem, which is much more to do with her own commitment and maturity. By contrast, one might imagine that Adrian, perhaps reluctant to reveal too much of his family's upheaval, might mention to his tutor that he had not yet decided where to spend Christmas. It would require a good deal of sensitive questioning to discover the facts of the situation and what he felt about it. It might then be appropriate to explore with him some of the options open to him, and to provide the kind of support that would enable him to reconsider his future plans without being unduly influenced by either of his parents or by his adviser.

It is clear that problems are not just hard to solve; they are hard to identify. Not only is there a real danger of jumping to conclusions too soon, but possibly there will be no neat 'solution' to be had. It should be noted that none of these cases is susceptible to 'a quick fix', but requires instead the provision of steady and continuous support. Adrian needs to reconsider the direction he is taking, but this will take time. His situation is complicated and he needs an opportunity to sort out where he is emotionally as well as making career decisions. Barry is in danger of being panicked into a decision he may later regret; whatever he decides will require some thoughtful adjustment on his part. Christine is hoping to find a way of being a student that will enable her to continue to cope with the ups and downs of family life, and it remains to be seen whether this is reasonable or not. It would be relatively easy to 'solve' her problems at a stroke by encouraging her to fall behind with her work or even to withdraw temporarily from the course, but that would probably not be helpful to her, nor is it what she is asking for. Denise needs to be encouraged if possible to work through her problems rather than to run away from them, always supposing that she is serious about leaving the course. It is quite likely, however, that this suggestion is little more than a cry for help, intended to indicate to her personal tutor just how awkward she feels her position to be.

This may partly explain why the provision of help is not always experienced as helpful. As the case of Denise shows, a tutor's well-intentioned concern may actually make the problem worse if the complexity of the problem is not recognized. Her tutor expresses surprise at her suggestion that she should leave the course when she has made such a promising start. However, by reacting in this way the tutor has effectively raised the stakes as far as Denise is concerned. The last thing she wants to hear is that her tutors have great hopes for her. Far from relieving her anxiety, the tutor may have contributed to it by putting her under further pressure. Something similar could arise in the case of Christine. Her tutor will have to make a judgement as to whether it is actually going to help her if she is allowed extra time to complete her work. Will it perhaps add to the pressure she is under? It is certainly possible that, from Christine's point of view, it may seem like that.

Of course, what is a problem for one student may not be a problem for another. Christine takes major difficulties in her stride while Denise seems to be getting 'stuck' over what appears to be something of a side issue. Barry and Denise would probably regard Adrian as extremely fortunate and privileged, and might have difficulty in understanding his scruples about precisely where his financial support was coming from. People differ both in their perception of problems as well as in their ability to cope with them.

People do not always understand their own motives either. The reason why Denise visited her boyfriend so frequently might not have been that the relationship was a close one, but only that she wished it was. She could have been treating it unconsciously as a kind of anchor offering security at a time when she was facing major change in other areas of her life. Or perhaps it was rather that, finding herself in what seemed to her a very vulnerable position in a class consisting almost entirely of male students, she had a practical need to be able to refer to a settled and established relationship as a way of signalling her non-availability. Yet she may have done this quite unconsciously. Again, Adrian may not realize that his opinion of the academic content of his course is likely to be coloured by the fact that he feels a fish out of water in the student group. Barry, too, may be unwittingly motivated by a feeling that he should not be living parasitically on his girlfriend's earnings, but should take full parental responsibility.

In all these cases, a conversation with someone not emotionally involved would probably help them see their problems more objectively, and clarify their own feelings and motivations. Clearly, our concern has to be with the unravelling of problems, not simply with their solution. Indeed, as we shall see in Chapter 2, we may wish to resist the idea that our concern is primarily with 'problems' as such.

Problems in the early stages

My second observation is that students appear to be especially vulnerable at the start of their courses. Most experienced counsellors and student advisers agree that it is in the first year that students need most support. Some would say that the first few days are crucial. Why is this?

There is plenty of evidence (e.g. of military units) that unpleasant conditions can be tolerated given that people can see some point to it, know there's an end to it, and have a sense of 'all being in it together'. A course of higher education is often experienced as demanding, but it is voluntarily undertaken and it does not last for ever. Even very unhappy students sometimes manage to persist once the end comes into view. However, in the initial stages the end is often not clearly seen, the value only dimly grasped, and there may be very little sense of being involved in a joint undertaking. It takes time to establish one's own networks of support, and many new students are literally (or feel themselves to be effectively) cut off from previous sources of help. Also, it is of the nature of higher education that its benefits are often better appreciated with hindsight. Doubts about its worth, therefore, can very easily be entertained before one has got very far.

Many students have to cope with sharp discontinuities of teaching methods and styles. For Denise this discontinuity was experienced as a severe handicap; after years of clear guidance she felt she was left to fend for herself. Adrian too had previous experiences which were a less than ideal preparation for the higher education he embarked upon, for in his case he had been encouraged to develop lines of enquiry of his own in a way which could not be accommodated in his Business Studies course, with the result that he experienced it as a strait-jacket. Problems of this sort could become more common in future as school-leavers, whose experience of schooling may latterly have been of small-group teaching, encounter a higher education system operating with relatively high staff–student ratios and making more use of open learning systems. Increasing numbers of students from abroad, too, may find it necessary not only to adjust to British weather and food, but to acclimatize themselves to a different style of teaching and to different ideas of how learners should behave.

Like any other social role, being a student is to some extent a matter of 'knowing the ropes', and today large numbers of students, like Barry, enter higher education with no very clear idea of what to expect or what will be expected of them. It takes time to settle into a new environment, find one's feet and establish a web of relationships within which support and help can be both given and received. The difficulties of coping with change loom large in most students' experience. Chapter 3 will explore this issue further and will suggest some alternative ways of conceptualizing it.

Typical student problems

My third initial observation is that the difficulties students face no longer seem to fit into the category of 'student problems'. There are certain kinds of problem, such as 'examination stress' or 'homesickness', that have traditionally been seen as part of student life. Until quite recently it was reasonable to assume that student advisers were largely concerned with matters of this sort (see Bramley 1977). Today, however, students' problems are significantly different. This is partly because the student body now includes a large proportion of mature students. Indeed, on many courses students aged 18 or 19 may well find themselves to be a minority group. This means both that their problems are likely to be rather different and that they may need a rather different kind of support from that provided a generation ago. Yet it is not just older students who have different kinds of problems. The nature of student life has been significantly altered, not least by the changed pattern of recruitment, so that the experience of all students has a different character.

This can be illustrated by reference to the case of Adrian and Denise, the two younger students. Clearly, there are problems of transition into higher education which, even for students who come straight from school, are not exactly cases of 'homesickness' as traditionally conceived (i.e. missing your home, your parents, your mother's cooking, your dog), but involve a more complex set of possibly conflicting emotions. There might be, in Adrian's case, some relief at being away from home, mixed with feelings of guilt that, had he stayed at home, he might have been able to hold his parents together, and a strong urge to cling fiercely to such family relationships as remain intact. Many students, like Denise, travel home frequently not to see their parents, but on account of someone else with whom they have an intense emotional and possibly sexual relationship. Thus, the notion of 'home-sickness' has to be radically redefined.

Older students may bring with them into higher education a range of problems not previously associated with student life. These include parental responsibilities, and problems with childcare and travel arrangements. Their relationship problems, too, may be of quite a different order. For instance, whereas in Adrian's case he had to cope with the upset of his parents splitting up, some mature students try to continue with a course of study while experiencing the breakdown of their own marriages.

This shift in student problems is evident in other ways. Financial worries now loom much larger than they did for many students, partly because of the decline in the value of the grant, but partly also because students cannot help being aware of inequalities between one student and another. As Adrian's case illustrates, it is not always simply a matter of having enough money, but of who provides it and on what terms. Parents and partners, as well as industrial sponsors, can offer financial support 'with strings attached', thereby creating an uneasy or uncomfortable dependency. Funding policies which in practice require greater parental contributions not only put equal opportunities at risk, but prolong students' dependence on their families and extend their indebtedness to them.

Another issue arises from greater awareness of gender inequality. As one of three female students enrolled on an almost entirely male course, Denise faces a problem quite different from that of a few years ago when women were effectively excluded. Many young women find they have exchanged the frustration of being academically thwarted for the spotlight of being pioneers in a man's world. In their experience it may be only marginally preferable.

Anxiety about academic potential, too, is much more of an issue than it was. A student like Barry enters higher education with very little idea of where he stands in relation to the rest of the group; he may be unnecessarily over-anxious, or he may be unwarrantably cocksure. Nor is it just lack of ability that causes problems. Part of Adrian's problem may be that he perceives himself, rightly or wrongly, to be capable of following a course that is more academically demanding than the one for which he has enrolled. What seems to be happening is that whereas once it was largely a matter of avoiding distractions and doing enough work, today many students genuinely wonder whether they have the ability to meet the required standards. This may be partly due to the general expansion of higher education, reaching sections of the population who have no tradition of educational success and, more specifically, to the deliberate recruitment of less well-prepared students. However, it is also due to a more highly-pressured social environment which encourages the single-minded pursuit of examination success. The student who dabbles in a wide range of activities, whether sport, amateur dramatics or producing a student newspaper, is no longer widely admired. Today, most students work quite hard and what distinguishes the most successful is not so much their motivation, but their ability. They are, therefore, susceptible to fears that their performance will turn out to be disappointing, especially if told, like Denise, that their early work is promising.

So it is not just that students in general present a different profile of problems from those of a generation ago; in many contexts the whole experience of student life has altered, become less insulated, in a way that affects every student. Wider access is only one expression of this changed approach characterized by greater openness. It follows that students' problems are less of a special category and much more like everyone else's problems. Higher education is much less of an enclosed world in that students' lives tend to be intertwined with those of other people external to the academic institution. Barry, Christine and, in a different way, Adrian, all have domestic or family responsibilities that actually or potentially impinge on their work as students, while Denise is failing to do her best work because of an unsatisfactory personal relationship.

Of course, it has always been the case that there was more to students' lives than being a student. However, there have been some far-reaching changes to the higher education experience, both in the way that parents are excluded from it and in the other commitments that students bring to it. Students' problems are not just student-type problems, but reflect quite accurately the sort of problems which are faced by almost anyone. In Chapter 4 we shall look more closely at the broad social changes which have made such a difference to the student experience.

This chapter has started from the assumption that student support is all about dealing with and responding to students' *problems*. However, to focus on problems may not be the most appropriate way to think about the help these students need. Given the complex nature of quite commonplace problems, the language of 'finding a solution' is liable to mislead us by providing the wrong kind of frame. The aim in providing support is not simply to enable students to survive, but to ensure that they derive maximum benefit from their course and, indeed, from their whole experience of student life. Adrian, Barry, Christine and Denise all need a clearer sense of who they are, what they want, where they are going and why – benefits which the very experience of higher education is often supposed to provide. Already, then, it is possible to see how the task of helping and supporting students might be conceived as much more central to the higher education experience. This will be a recurring theme throughout this book.

We began straightforwardly by looking at students' problems. It is now possible to see that this may have been something of a false start. All students, whether they appear to have problems or not, need help and support through their student careers, and this help needs to be seen not simply as enabling them to surmount obstacles, but more positively, as encouraging in them the development of their full potential. Our next step, then, will be to challenge the emphasis on problems by introducing a broader, developmental perspective.

2

The Experience of Development

Because of the emphasis on dealing with students' problems, student support tends to be seen as a back-up service, in principle available to all but in practice needed only by those who are overwhelmed by difficulties. To suggest that student support has a wider role than that of an ambulance service, and indeed that it should be integral to the higher education experience, is to offer a sharp challenge to this approach. The objective, it is argued, is to contribute positively to the ongoing development of all students whether they have problems or not. The aim of this chapter is to explore this developmental perspective and to consider what it might mean to encourage and promote students' development.

In what way, then, do students develop and how can this process be fostered? This question highlights two key points. First, while we may say that it is part of higher education's task to bring about the academic and personal development of students, we have to acknowledge that growth towards maturity occurs spontaneously and takes place independently of higher education. Development figures in any account of the student experience, both as a process which goes on concurrently and as an essential element within higher education itself. However, second, we have to recognize, now that there are so many more mature students and now that, in any case, 18 not 21 has been declared to be the age of majority as far as the law is concerned, that the developmental process is often considered to be nearing completion, if not actually completed, at the point when students enter higher education. So long as mature students were a tiny minority it was possible to think of students as typically going through late adolescence, i.e. in the process of completing the final stage of their journey to adulthood. This is clearly no longer an appropriate way of thinking about student life. Institutions of higher education do not teach students who are on their way towards adulthood; they teach people who are already adult.

However, while physical maturity and legal adulthood may be attained by the age of 18, a person's psychological development continues into adult life. Human development may be seen as extending throughout the life course, as a lifelong process. Furthermore, in so far as educational processes help towards improved self-understanding, they clearly foster psychological development.

It is true that the extension of educational opportunity to allow more and more young people to remain longer in the educational system has sometimes seemed to be an extension of the period of adolescence, delaying entry to the adult world of work. Yet higher education institutions do not have to be seen as places where young people are kept in tutelage; they might be better described as agencies offering people of any age a particular kind of service, namely the possibility of self-development consciously pursued and deliberately fostered. Thus, it is not just for 18-year-olds that the experience of being a student is intertwined with, and perhaps even indistinguishable from, the experience of being a developing person. All students, whatever their chronological age and degree of maturity, can experience higher education as a process of personal development.

To suggest, then, that student support is not primarily a matter of dealing with students' difficulties, but of providing on-going support to enable them to develop through their courses is to do more than to redefine student support; it is to raise questions about those developmental processes which precede, coexist with, and are inseparable from the educational process. How are we to understand this development? How can students be supported as they go through this developmental process? And how, if at all, is it possible to help the process along?

Within the student's experience it is possible to distinguish three dimensions along which change may be taking place: development as a person; development as a student; and development in relation to some specific career. We need to discuss each of these in turn before considering how they may be interrelated.

Development as a person

First, then, what sort of personal and psychological development might we expect to see typically taking place in students? Notwithstanding the recruitment of many more older entrants, students are still mostly young, often very young adults. Are there developmental processes which they would be going through in any case, whether they were students or not? Does the concept of development through the life course mean that the experiences of older, more mature students are also to be understood developmentally?

There is a sense in which it is relatively easy to answer these questions. Any standard textbook will give a description of adult development which accords with commonsense observations such as, for example, that someone young and relatively inexperienced in life is likely to flounder in circumstances which an older person would probably take in their stride. Yet there is a major difficulty with this approach; to describe personal development as a lifelong process is to redefine what one is talking about.

As is well-known, developmental processes were first studied in children. Founded on the work of paediatricians, the discipline of child development was initially concerned with tracing the progress of physical growth. It seemed obvious that in childhood some major developments such as the ability to walk or talk might have an immediate and dramatic impact on other aspects of development (social, cognitive, emotional, etc.) and that all aspects of the developing child (even, less plausibly, moral and linguistic development) were to be understood as parallel and interlocking developmental processes.

Of course, the further one moves from purely physical development the harder it is to find a common pattern. Nonetheless, developmental psychologists have tried to identify stages of development from infancy to adolescence, so as to provide a comprehensive psychological account of how younger members of society *gradually* (step by step) find their way towards adulthood. Young people in society have been portrayed as having to learn how to relate to others, how to form relationships, so that they may then proceed through courtship to marriage and parenthood. Likewise they have been portrayed as needing to acquire knowledge and skills which they then practise, at first clumsily, later more proficiently, so that eventually they are able to make a smooth progression into adult working life.

However, such an account of adolescence, relying on a simple extension of developmental processes, is bound to be inadequate. The simple idea that physical development triggers other kinds of development cannot be sustained beyond childhood, even supposing it is valid there. Once past childhood, there are very few physical changes which are universally shared. Physical development, which for certain kinds of strength and stamina reaches its peak around age 19 or 20 or even earlier, can hardly serve as a model for all aspects of personal development. In any case, how plausible is it to suggest that adult life be conceived as a series of stages through which the individual passes? What is lacking in this kind of account is adequate recognition of the social dimension of personal experience.

In order to appreciate this, let us consider a down-to-earth example: a student who becomes unexpectedly and unintentionally pregnant. It does not take much imagination to see that the psychological effects depend to a large extent on the surrounding circumstances. What is good news for one may be disastrous for another. The person may experience it as being trapped or as being released, as a disgrace or as an honour. For one student it may provide a welcome way out of a course of study which is proving too demanding. For another it may threaten carefully-laid and long-cherished career plans. It may be seen as a kind of rite of passage to unequivocal adult status, where this has previously only grudgingly been granted. It may forge close links with one's parents, or it may finally foreclose the possibility of ever speaking to them again. It follows that those who offer students help and support need not only a wide repertoire of responses, but the sensitivity to recognize what is actually being experienced in each case.

That example may help us to see that, for our purposes, a more helpful kind of developmental theory will be that which focuses on common elements of human experience: the kinds of things that occur at some time in nearly everyone's life and which are almost bound to have some effect upon their self-understanding. The interesting questions then become the way in which these experiences may combine, coincide or overlap in an individual's personal biography.

It is clearly necessary to reject both the idea that growing up is a once-and-for-all process which for our students will inevitably lie in the past, and the idea of adult development as a steady or uniform process. There are indeed processes of growth, but they are not so much processes of growing up or even growing older. They are better thought of as growing *through* all one's life experiences. Just as there will be various levels and types of maturity evident among our students, not always related to chronological age, so the processes of growing in and towards maturity will be taking place through and alongside their higher education experience.

Put like that, it is clear that the experience of higher education, while not one that is universally shared, is nonetheless one with common features and which will exert a strong formative influence on the lives of most students. That is not to say that it will always have the same effect, of course. It belongs in the same class as, say, 'parenthood' or 'unemployment', in that while people experience these things differently and some people may miss them altogether, for those who do experience them it is likely that they will impact upon their lives quite powerfully and may indeed, by the pressures they exert and by the responses they evoke, set up patterns which shape the subsequent course of their lives.

Once this is clearly recognized it becomes easier to see how students and others undergoing such potentially formative experiences can be encouraged to use them creatively and grow through them. For experiences do not come with their meaning written on their face; their meaning has to be constructed, and they have the potential to develop or to diminish the person. The task, therefore, is to help students to construct positive meanings out of the new materials available, which include the student's own past as well as current experiences.

It is worth noticing how different this is from the traditional view of adolescent development as a kind of apprenticeship to adulthood with the early stages seen as a kind of rehearsal or preparation for the later stages. Once it is recognized that *the life-cycle itself* is subject to change, it is no longer possible to use the model of growth towards maturity in this simple way. People grow apart as well as grow closer. Careers no longer have the smooth trajectory or the defined destination that were once presumed. As the course and direction of an adult life becomes harder to predict with any confidence the idea of somehow being prepared for it no longer fits. Increasingly, student life needs to be seen not as a preparation for what is to come afterwards, but for what it is in itself. It is not an introduction to adult life, it is part of adult life.

Development as a student

We now need to ask whether there are particular kinds of development that may be seen specifically among students. Can we identify ways in which there is development in 'studenthood' as well as development towards 'adult-hood' (see, for example, Perry, 1970; Chickering, 1972; Astin, 1984)?

Clearly, there are likely to be some common patterns of development for students who move through a sequence of shared experiences. For instance, we might expect some cyclic process to be visible as students go through the three years of full-time study on a single subject honours degree course, year 1 being characterized by the problems of settling in, finding one's feet, getting one's bearings, and year 3 by the job-search, interviews, the need to distance oneself somewhat from student life, and the stresses of final examinations. What, then, of year 2? Often it constitutes something of a trough between the year of arriving and year of leaving. In the traditional folk-lore of student advisers, it has often been thought of as the year in which there is typically a good deal of agonizing about whether one is following the right course, studying the most appropriate subject, making the right friends, making best use of one's higher education, working hard enough, etc. In the USA the term 'sophomore slump' (Lemons and Richmond, 1987) has been used for this phenomenon, which is considered common enough and serious enough to require some theoretical explanation.

There are, certainly, a number of problems which may surface around mid-point in a full-time course, such as: Why am I studying this? Is it *really* what I want to do? It is perfectly understandable if, as the work gets harder and progress becomes more of a struggle, some students voice their concern at how hard it is getting and how long it is taking. There may also be motivational problems in the second year of a three-year course. Once into the second year of a traditional straight-through course, one's options appear considerably narrowed. The novelty of student life has worn off, and the anxiety of the final year has not yet loomed large. Yet if the work load continues to feel heavy it is sometimes the student with broad abilities and lively interests who is most aware of the sacrifices having to be made, and who wonders whether it is worth it.

That said, it is obvious that it is more complicated than this. Courses have their own ups and downs (Olesen and Whittaker, 1968) which correspond to a wide range of factors: the pattern of terms and vacations; the timing of assessments; and perhaps the length of work-based placements where they are included.[1] Nonetheless can student development be positively facilitated and enhanced? Many would argue that it can, and that there are common qualities and skills which can be identified and deliberately fostered in students.[2] There are interesting questions as to precisely how this occurs, but undoubtedly teaching strategies involving personal portfolios and learning records can have the effect of raising students' awareness of their own learning processes, which in turn may enhance their performance.

It now appears that what the employers of graduates want and what adults in our society need are much the same. Thus, educational programmes which successfully develop key personal skills and qualities in students may serve three purposes at once: they may help students towards a more mature and fulfilling adult life; help them towards a more skilful and sophisticated student learning experience in higher education; and enhance their prospects in the job market. Such skills and qualities are conceived as general and transferable. However, there are also many more specific skills and qualities developed within particular courses, especially where the student's studies are 'applied' and have a clear vocational relevance. So our next question is: Can vocational or professional learning be conceived developmentally?

Development in relation to specific occupations

Alongside a student's personal growth to maturity and his or her development through the student career we may look for a third set of processes by which the student is transformed into the member of a particular occupational group or profession. Does the following of a particular course, or the pursuit of a particular career or profession offer a distinctive kind of development? Vocational courses, and those which carry some professional qualification or recognition, clearly have built into them, explicitly or implicitly, elements of occupational socialization. Even courses which are strictly speaking non-vocational may, nonetheless, convey to students a sense of being drawn into the profession of, say, historian or artist, of being in some way initiated into a way of looking at the world. So at one and the same time a young person may be learning how to be a student, discovering how to be a more adult person and beginning to acquire an academic or professional identity.

It seems likely that professional or vocational development may be experienced not as a steady progression, but as a series of steps, each prompted by some significant event. Just as it is sometimes suggested that events such as becoming a parent or one's children leaving home act as triggers for developmental stages through the life course, so it is possible that specific events within a college course might mark a significant movement towards the desired professional role. It is possible, for instance, that for a medical student the first injection given, or the first patient who died, might be experienced as a 'significant event' in this sense, i.e. a step on the road to becoming a fully-fledged practitioner.

Three rather different patterns of occupational socialization might be distinguished (Earwaker, 1986) simply on the basis of how different courses are structured. Some courses of professional training are orientated towards the profession right from the start. Students enrolled on such courses might reasonably expect that they would be immediately plunged into professional concerns and that all their theoretical studies would be made relevant to professional practice. In some cases students might know that their acceptance on the course virtually guaranteed them a job on graduation. The transition from trainee to practitioner would, therefore, normally be very smooth indeed. One might call that pattern 'instant professionalization'. Almost from the first, students on such a course can count themselves as new members of the professional group.

At the other extreme is the type of training pattern which defers direct contact with the professionals until certain purely academic requirements have been met. The first part of the course consists of 'foundation' studies, and successful completion of this first stage is a pre-requisite for admission to the second stage of explicit training. Yet this training is still broad and generic, is issue-based rather than problem-based, and is, perhaps, undertaken alongside students preparing for a variety of professional roles. Much of it is carried out in college rather than on the job. Placements cannot allow the job to be carried out unsupervised, so they consist of more observation than practice. Typically, students following courses such as these have major adjustments to make on entry to their first job. They do not feel they really belong in the profession until some time after graduation and beginning work. One might call this pattern 'deferred professionalization'.

In between these two extremes is another pattern which can be observed, in which students begin as novices who initially have no right to be taken seriously as members of the profession, but are progressively led through a series of practical experiences and theoretical studies so that they gradually come to see themselves, and to be accepted as, members of the professional group. This acceptance more or less coincides with graduation, since the course requirements embody the professional requirements. Throughout, there is the sense of the process being a gradual and incremental one, and that it would be as wrong to accelerate the process by treating students as fellow-professionals too early as it would be to withhold recognition from final year students as they approach graduation.

In so far as these models correspond to the felt experience of students preparing for specific professional roles, they suggest ways in which it would be appropriate to offer help and support in each case. There is no implication that any one pattern is better than the others; it suits some students to defer commitment, whereas others are keen to identify with the profession as soon as possible. Yet it is easy to see how students might experience a mismatch between the pace of professional development presupposed by their course and their own sense of growing into the professional role. Yet both frustration and trepidation might be turned to positive effect with appropriate help and support.

Some experiments (Earwaker, 1987) in which students were invited to plot the shape of their professional development on a graph, while broadly validating the three-fold distinction suggested above, yielded some surprisingly diverse patterns. Some saw their development step-wise, others as a straight line moving steadily upwards, but many drew shapes which indicated one or more major crises, often indicated by a downward dip followed by an upward surge, as if to suggest that crises can also be learning experiences and that surmounting problems can lead to growth. This strongly suggests that the notion of development is inherently problematic. Far from implying steady progress or the systematic build-up of expertise or confidence in successive stages, the most significant advances are often experienced as great leaps forward following a period of sterility or difficulty, rapid recovery from a crisis, or the sudden removal of a blockage. Patterns of development there may be; but individuals often make progress by fits and starts, sometimes with the most spectacular breakthroughs consequent upon the most testing challenges.

Complex pathways of development

Three sets of developmental processes have been distinguished. It is likely that the experience of many students will include development along all three of these dimensions, in that they are simultaneously becoming adults, becoming students and becoming whatever it is that their course is preparing them for.

First, there is the general developmental process of growing up and growing older which affects everyone in some way or other, together with whatever processes are specific to their own particular age-group. These are processes that would be going on in any case, whether they were students or not. Second, there is the student career. Third, there is the process by which the student is introduced to, learns the routines of, acquires the standards of and is socialized into the norms of a particular profession. We are used to thinking of this as a social process of learning a new role, which indeed it is. So is becoming a student. However, in both cases the processes can be construed as developmental, analogous to the process by which one grows towards and through adulthood.

These three sets of processes overlap with each other. More than that, they are actually interrelated; they have mutual influence on each other. For instance, a male student who immerses himself in his work may be trying to get free from what he experiences as undue parental influence in the only way he knows, and hopes to do so by establishing himself in due course as a respected professional person. So his professional development offers a route to adult status. Similarly, a female student who experiences severe examination stress may actually have quite low aspirations for herself, but feel that her parents' expectations are impossibly high and tied to career aspirations which she does not share. Her own personal development is, therefore, tangled up with her status within the family and a projected career path to which she feels uncommitted. Both these examples show clearly the way in which personal development has to be negotiated in the face of conflicting pressures, both positive and negative, from a variety of sources. Students are often confused about their own identity, feeling under pressure to conform to expectations from their teachers, their family and their peers, and wanting to reconcile these different sets of expectations with their own sense of themselves as developing persons.

It should now be clear that the notion of student development is a useful correction to the idea that student support is simply a matter of helping people cope with problems. Equally, however, its weaknesses and limitations are now rather apparent. To extrapolate developmental processes into adulthood while continuing to think of them as individual growth is not, after all, such a radical step. What transforms the understanding of development is the recognition that these processes are prompted by and shaped in interaction with external influences.

The point being made here is not that there is a mismatch between models derived from infant development and the reality of adult development, but that development, at every point, has to be seen as an interactive process. Even development in babyhood is now seen as inherently social (Kaye, 1984). Thus, the kinds of processes outlined in this chapter are not very adequately described as processes of 'development' if that term is taken to suggest elements of the personality gradually unfolding from within. Development beyond childhood is commonly brought about by a certain quality of interpersonal engagement, such as might be found in a teaching–learning encounter, rather than by simply growing up or growing older. Much of the personal development of students in higher education will occur as a result of external influence, often in response to some sort of challenge or pressure. Indeed, the problems which students face may be seen positively, not just as pressures to be withstood, but as circumstances to be coped with, ordeals to grow through or challenges to be responded to. Student development, like any other developmental process, occurs in interaction with the physical and social environment.

This exposes a fundamental weakness of this theoretical framework. To become an adult, or for that matter to become a student or an accountant, is not simply a process of individual development. It is a social process by which one is progressively granted, by others, a certain social status. It is governed not simply by one's own rate of developmental progress, but by other people's assessments of it and, more subtly still, by one's own internalization of those assessments. To some extent it may depend upon opportunities being available and circumstances being favourable. For instance, broad social changes giving wider access to higher education may have in some ways accelerated and in other ways slowed the process by which one becomes adult in our society.

This chapter will have succeeded in its purpose if it has brought out the unsatisfactoriness of a purely developmental account of student life. The student experience may of course, be described as an experience of development. Higher education's task is then seen more clearly to be one of continuously optimizing this experience rather than simply removing difficulties for the student or helping the student to surmount obstacles. However, a more rounded understanding of the student experience will place it in a broader framework of social relationships and will respond to it accordingly. The student experience is not fully or adequately described in purely psychological terms as an individual experience of change or growth or development. The next chapter necessarily moves towards a broader, psycho-social perspective.

Notes

1. Olesen and Whittaker (1968) followed a group of student nurses and tried to chart their group psychology as they surmounted obstacles and endured the plateaus of their course.
2. Under the recent 'enterprise' initiatives a number of higher education institutions have launched programmes involving elements of student-centred learning designed to develop students' personal skills and qualities.

3

The Experience of Transition

Nearly every student experiences the beginning of a course of study as some sort of disruption. Even for a part-time student whose domestic and social arrangements remain more or less intact there is likely to be some sense of entering upon a new phase of life, embarking upon a new enterprise. For full-time students it may involve a sudden change of circumstances with profound effects on social life, vocational aspirations and self-understanding. While these effects are often positive they do not come without cost. The process has to be described not just as change, but exchange: a relatively comfortable, settled existence may be traded for an uncertain future, a gamble in which the risks are great and the stakes high. There is often an element of sacrifice, if not in paying substantial fees or in postponed earnings, then in time given up or status lost.

Before discussing possible difficulties involved in what is a potentially stressful experience, it must at once be admitted that transition to a different kind of life is not bound to be fraught with problems; in fact, it may often be a welcome change. It may be experienced as release rather than as a threat or a burden. Mature students especially may experience student life as, initially, one of enormous freedom from domestic responsibilities. Yet to note this is not to concede that the transition occurs completely without stress. New students face major challenges which loom so large in the individual's consciousness that everything else is suspended and the normal pressures of life temporarily fade into the background. The situation is not unlike that of new recruits in the forces; minor aches and pains tend to be forgotten as one large worry eclipses all the rest. Something similar may sometimes be experienced at the approach of examinations. So a student's entry to higher education may be experienced as a kind of release, not because the transition occurs without stress, but because of the way stress works on individuals. Many, probably most, incoming students are in a state of high arousal in which all the resources of the person are fully stretched. Entry to higher education may be accompanied by excitement and even euphoria as well as by panic and despair.

It also needs to be pointed out that the transition to student life may be much less of a change for some students. Older students who continue to live at home may not only be better at adjusting; they may have less adjust-ment to make. It may be that much of their lives can continue as though nothing had happened. Of course, the more one is locked into domestic routines, family networks, neighbourhood contacts and regular leisure pursuits, the more supports one has available. The domestic responsibilities which from one point of view seem to create difficulties for many mature women students can from another point of view be seen as supports which many younger students simply do not have. Problems arise when, say, a spouse is unsympathetic or unco-operative, and family life can absorb a great deal of energy. However, young students living away from home for the first time often have to begin their social life all over again. They start with nothing, knowing nobody. In this respect mature students living at home have a huge advantage; at worst, their support systems have not been totally disrupted, and at best they may remain firmly intact. Moreover, belonging to a group, whether of family, neighbourhood or community, not only gives direct support by providing companionship or a listening ear when required, but it helps indirectly as well. The circle of friends which most people estab-lish around them over time helps to create a continuing sense of identity which can sustain them through minor difficulties. The value of this should not be underestimated.

In anyone's life course it is possible to identify key events or turning-points. In some lives these may be changes of a quite drastic and dramatic sort, such as a sudden religious conversion, or 'coming out' as gay. We might identify going to college as another event of this sort, an experience so power-ful and transforming that nothing could ever be the same again.

Yet entry to higher education may be experienced in very different ways. It may offer risks or it may provide security; it may involve financial sacrifices or it may constitute a prudent investment; it may in some cases offer a fast route to success, so justifying the risks taken and the sacrifices made, yet in other cases it appears, in career terms, to be leading nowhere, justifying itself, if at all, in intrinsic satisfactions and rewarding experiences. Becoming a student may be either a step up or a step down the social ladder. What determines its significance will be not so much the student's chronological age as his or her personal circumstances.

Metaphors of change

So how do people cope with change as they go through life? In what ways are people able to sustain themselves through a difficult transition? It is helpful to consider some of the most common metaphors for change. Some have already been mentioned, such as adjustment and transition. One could add a long list of such terms, which would include socialization, learning, being accepted, getting used to it, finding ways of coping, devising appropriate strategies, getting 'slotted in', fitting in, square pegs in round holes and so on. There are clearly many different ways of conceiving the process, some of which may be better than others.

Unfortunately, many of the words and phrases commonly used to describe a student's initial experience of higher education commit us prematurely to some quite specific frame of reference. To speak of 'homesickness', for instance, is at once to imply a medical model in which the student is a patient suffering from a quasi-clinical condition. 'Transition' is a rather imprecise term, but it may, for this reason, be preferred to metaphors which in some way restrict our understanding of the processes of change. It may be used to refer to a wide range of events, processes and experiences. It allows us to consider together, for example, both the student whose initial experience of higher education is of entering a world of undreamed-of cultural richness and the student for whom it means above all focusing attention on quite a narrow area of experience; both the student who has come away to college after years of being looked after at home with the rest of the family and the student who in order to return to study has had to surrender an independent and perhaps relatively prosperous lifestyle. Transitions may be of many sorts and by using this umbrella word it may be possible to keep this broad frame of reference.

Why is transition experienced as a problem in human life? It appears that any radical discontinuity can pose a threat to our sense of who we are. It is as if the thread running through our lives has been, or is just about to be broken. Thus, in moving into new circumstances we are not just having to recover from the shock of the new, but we may actually have to repair damage to the self, to reconstruct our sense of who we are when our previous self is apparently no longer appropriate or viable. In considering the problems associated with transition, therefore, we are forced to consider what provides the continuity. Is it a relatively straightforward matter of regularity of behaviour which is now disrupted and has yet to settle into a new pattern? Or is it an altogether more profound continuity related to a sense of personal identity which formerly rendered life meaningful and which has now been lost? The process may, indeed, be conceived as a matter of surface behaviour only, or in terms of underlying motives and cognitive schemes. However, consistency in an individual's conduct may depend more on coherence of purpose than on continuity in patterns of behaviour. The underlying question here, then, can be put like this. Is the thread running through our lives a thread of habit or a thread of meaning? (Danziger, 1971:27). Different answers to this question will lead to different accounts of why transition can be a problem, what damage it can do, and what can be done to help.

Adjustment

Personality theories have generally presupposed a model in which the individual remains constant while situations change. That is to say, life consists of a series of adjustments to new situations. The person has to accommodate him or herself to changes, but remains fundamentally intact so that questions can be asked in the form 'What impact did this (the event) have on you (the person)?' or 'How did you (the person) manage to adjust to this (the event)?'

Peter Marris (1986) in his book *Loss and Change* claimed that every situation of change could be thought of as an experience of loss and understood on the analogy of a bereavement. This is a helpful idea in that it enables us to appreciate that any change is a shock to the system, and it is likely that the stages of recovery from the shock are likely to look similar whether the event impacting upon the personality is loss of a loved one, loss of a home, loss of a job or loss of a lifestyle. Marris claimed to find common threads running through experiences as diverse as the failure of a business, going away to college and slum-clearance in Nigeria. Clearly, people react to change – of any sort – in fairly predictable ways. Exactly how people adjust to a new situation will doubtless depend to some extent on the personality of the individual, his or her previous experiences, and perhaps crucially on the strategies that have worked successfully for that individual in the past. However, this insight relates mainly to the stages of recovery from the impact of a single shocking event, whereas the transition to student life, like most changes in life, has to be seen not just as a single event, but as an ongoing experience requiring a series of adjustments over time. Marris is surely right to draw attention to the common features of the experience of different kinds of change, but there does not seem to be any reason why we should identify the common features with the negative aspects of the experience. Change in human life means saying hello to the new as well as goodbye to the old; if loss and bereavement are discernible in almost every kind of upheaval, then so are elements of challenge and opportunities for fresh beginnings.

The question seems to be about how people adapt to change. Yet by putting the question in that form we may already be making certain assumptions about the process of change or transition. Do we have the right model? Is it a matter of seeing how fully-formed and stable personalities manage to make the necessary adjustments, or is that to rely too heavily on a perspective drawn from individual psychology?

Whereas early personality theory worked on the assumption that people behaved in a fairly consistent manner across different situations and over time, more recent research questions both these assumptions with evidence that, for example, there can be enormous personality changes following marriage. People change and are changed by each other. The kind of explanation of personal change that starts from personality theory and relies entirely on a purely psychological approach is likely to pay insufficient attention to the social dimension of experience.

A good example of this may be seen in the work of Vincent Tinto (1988) who has explored the process by which students leave college at the end of their course. Leaving higher education is, of course, another process of transition which may be understood in much the same way as entry to it, or for that matter any minor personal transitions which occur in between. Although Tinto acknowledges his debt to the Dutch anthropologist Van Gennep, and specifically echoes Van Gennep's 'rite of passage' terminology, Tinto's frame of reference remains obstinately psychological. He offers a stage theory of student departure, according to which the student progressively withdraws commitment from one community and moves towards engagement with another. What is striking here is the persistence of the developmental stage model and its application to what is clearly a social process, explicitly acknowledged to be such. The dominance of developmental psychology in interpretations of personal experience through the lifespan has repeatedly resulted in experiences which are manifestly social processes being interpreted as stages of personal growth, and student development is no exception.

It is, of course, not too difficult to discern some sort of regular pattern in any gradual or progressive change, but that frame of reference can easily dominate our thinking to the extent that we focus simply on tracing an individual's personal pathway through the life course with an eye only for continuities and discontinuities, regularities and stages. We may not then notice that gradual separation from one community and progressive incorporation into another are, crucially, social processes. Adjustment is not just a personal matter; other people are involved. Parents have to relinquish control of their offspring if the young person's bid for independence is to succeed. The new entrant to higher education can only make the transition to 'being a student' in the fullest sense if the relevant academic and social communities are open to this possibility, and facilitate participation and belonging.

Socialization

Sociological accounts of transition focus much more on the changed circumstances and use concepts like role to suggest ways in which individuals might acquire new ways of behaving to meet new expectations. From this perspective, the questions to ask new students will not be 'How well have you managed to adjust?' or 'What stage have you reached in your settling-in process?', but rather 'How are you getting on in your new role?' or 'Are you managing to work out what is expected of you?' Entry to higher education, for instance, will not be interpreted as a personal ordeal so much as an unfamiliar game where the rules have to be learned and the skills practised in order to join in fully.

Every transition may be interpreted in this way as a social experience, and the concept of socialization throws into relief the way that in any new situation there are rules and routines to be learned and practised, and expectations to be met. This is true even of very personal and apparently private experiences like becoming ill (Robinson, 1971). The onset of illness is not a purely private matter, but is dependent upon shared frameworks of meaning that have been socially-constructed; becoming a patient is not simply a matter of possessing physical symptoms, but involves new ways of behaving according to sets of expectations that are commonly understood and accepted. The same is true of becoming a student. There are shared ideas of what it is to be a student, of how a student will behave, even of what a student will look like, and part of the transition to student life is falling in with these role-expectations to some degree or other.

Thus, the transitions of an individual's life are not the relatively private life-events sometimes supposed, but moves in a social game. More than that, the points of transition may themselves be socially specified. However idiosyncratic the individual's life story, it is likely to fall into a familiar shape, structured around certain common markers that constitute turning-points in everyone's life. While norms of physical development, so important in infancy, are hard to establish beyond childhood, common patterns of social experience are relatively easily identified. Every society has rites of passage and growing up may be conceived as largely consisting of passing through these predetermined gateways, often at a predetermined rate. In our society as in all others there is a standard pattern; we have set ages for starting school, for leaving school and for making the transition from one form of education to another. There may be only limited scope for experiencing this differently, with the result that, with a few exceptions, each individual's personal biography assumes roughly the same shape.

This is not, of course, to underestimate the impact of these transitions. Change may still be experienced as traumatic while being, nonetheless, utterly predictable and normal. The point to emphasize here, though, is that transitions are partly given by the social structure. The individual's educational experience for instance, cannot be seen in isolation from the way the educational system is constructed, the kinds of institutions that have been established and the points of transition that have been predetermined (and which doubtless suit some individuals better than others). Blyth and Derricott (1977) in their book *The Social Significance of Middle Schools* have shown clearly and graphically how change in the age of transfer from one school to another can re-shape pupils' experience not just of schooling, but of growing up. A change in the age of transition meant that pupils who would once have been the youngest group within a school for older pupils now found themselves the oldest group within a school designed for younger pupils. Clearly, a reorganization on that scale has a major impact upon children's experience, and is a powerful influence upon their perception of what it is to be 'junior' or 'senior', and of the growing up process as a whole.

A similar point might be made about higher education in the 1990s: its structural shape goes a long way to determine the experience of its students. A binary system both reflects and reinforces a divided experience of higher education. To end it is to recognize and to re-establish higher education as inherently unified. Changes in the internal structure of institutions may have similar effects. Altering the composition of the student body by, say, increasing the numbers of mature students has an effect on the students' experience. As the number of mature students grows, they have less reason to feel exceptional or odd either within the student group or in society at large. Thus, the very meaning of the word 'student' gradually shifts, so as to put less emphasis on youth or immaturity and more on the activity of studying which is the remaining common feature of student life. So to 'become a student' gradually loses the connotations of 'going back to school', as if this were something inappropriate for an adult to do, and begins to acquire the status of an activity undertaken with due seriousness with an eye to preparing oneself for some specific (though not necessarily life-long) role in society. The transition may still be a difficult one to make, but it is a different kind of transition. It is in this kind of way that public institutional arrangements contribute substantially to the texture and pattern of people's private lives.

This is a fairly obvious point to make in relation to legal and institutional arrangements such as the age when children start going to school and the social composition of the student body. It is less obvious, but important to note, that the freely chosen actions of individuals may, nonetheless, fit into a coherent pattern in conformity with social norms which have no legal or institutional force whatsoever. It has often been noted that while the average age at which couples get married has altered considerably in recent years, the age-difference between the partners in a first marriage has remained remarkably constant, husbands being on average about two years older than their wives. We see here evidence of social conformity in an area of life which on the face of it one would expect to be purely a matter of individual preference. As with Durkheim's pioneering work on suicide (1952), which produced definitive evidence of national differences in suicide rates, even in something which commonsense regards as a matter of free choice and where there are no formal constraints at all, we can see startling regularities which suggest the operation of powerful social norms.

Hammersley and Turner (1980) looked at the ways in which pupils adapt to secondary school, basing their ideas on Merton's (1957) analysis of types of social adaptation. They identified five characteristic modes of adaptation which they termed retreatism, ingratiation, compliance/ritualism, opportunism and rebellion. What is valuable here for our purposes is not the list as such, though clearly it is suggestive for modes of adaptation which might be characteristic of students entering higher education, but rather the point that these processes are always social processes, never simply a matter of individual adaptation. What we are looking at when we observe transition into (or for that matter out of) student life is a shared experience which goes on within a sub-culture, and which to a greater or lesser degree is helped or hindered by the group of which the student is (again to a greater or lesser degree) a part.

Thus, the obvious fact that many students feel lonely at first should not mislead us into considering their situation as belonging to them alone. The student experience is, crucially, a psycho-social experience; it is understood, experienced and coped with by groups of students who are constantly looking over their shoulders to compare with how others are getting on, and who are capable of making matters either very much better or very much worse for each other. We misconceive the process of adjustment if we treat it as a matter of individual psychology only, a process in which the tensions are simply between continuity with our own personal past and the demands of the present. There are also tensions between the kinds of conformity required by the group and the strength of one's own personal commitments, convictions and habits. These tensions are tempered by the extent to which group approval or disapproval is felt to matter, and by the help and support that may be available to sustain or modify personal beliefs and behaviours in the face of challenge.

Transition

A more interactionist account, therefore, pays attention to these features of interpersonal and group life. In trying to understand how people go through changes in their lives it is necessary not simply to trace the continuity and/or disruption of their own life course, nor simply to examine the structural constraints which determine the pattern of most people's lives, but to appreciate how people interact with one another and with their different environments. People do not merely pass through change, but are actually affected by it. Life changes are not just things that *happen* to you, but things that *alter* you; they are, as Anselm Strauss (1962) says, 'transformations of identity'.

From this perspective the questions to ask students would not be about personal adjustment or about meeting role expectations; rather, they would be of this sort: 'what difference is it making to you'? 'how is it affecting you?' This approach appears to offer a more subtle account of transition, in that it is possible to see the process not simply as a relatively stable personality being confronted with a situation in which extensions to the repertoire of behaviour are required, nor simply as a fairly rigid set of social expectations into which an extremely pliable person has to be fitted, but as a process of negotiation in which there is a gradual matching of what the individual brings and what the new situation demands. The person gradually develops, consciously or unconsciously, a new identity, not merely to meet a set of externally imposed requirements, but to make them his or her own. At the same time as the situation impacts upon the individual, the individual impacts upon the situation so as to fill out, rather than to fit into, the new role. The self is not chameleon-like, infinitely variable, nor is the self as coherent and consistent as personality theorists have sometimes implied. Similarly, roles such as that of student are neither as rigid nor as elastic as some have suggested. The process by which square pegs fit into round holes is one of *mutual* adjustment.

Although we are inevitably caught up in change as we go through life, on the whole we experience new things by somehow fitting them within the pattern we have previously established. As human beings we feel it necessary to establish some meanings which give stability; coping with life means being able to do this. Whether we say the process is one of adjustment or socialization or identity-construction matters little so long as we are clear that it is an interactive process. It is also a cumulative process; it snowballs. Anyone undergoing a new experience seeks to make sense of what is going on in terms that are already familiar; then, in so far as the person is successful in doing this, these meanings themselves become part of the given framework, a context within which to make sense of everything else. Once students have committed themselves to higher education, to a particular institution, to a specific course, and to a particular way of behaving as a student, then these commitments contribute to the character of their student experience and act as constraints on further choice.

H. S. Becker (1964:59) coined the term 'situational adjustment' to describe the process by which

> the person, as he (sic) moves in and out of a variety of social situations, learns the requirements of continuing in each situation and of success in it. If he has a strong desire to continue, the ability to assess accurately what is required, and can deliver the required performance, *the individual turns himself into the kind of person the situation demands*. (emphasis added)

This draws attention to the way in which the adjustment may be voluntarily undertaken. Unlike some accounts of the socialization process which appear to leave very little room for the individual to negotiate the role, emphasizing only the extent to which the role is shaped and determined by structural constraints, this account suggests that to a large extent individuals, having once perceived what the existing role-expectations are, often have considerable scope to develop the role to suit themselves.

The process is a complex one in which the person is continually seeking to match perceived requirements of the role with his or her personal resources and to bring about a satisfactory fit between the two. For this reason it may be helpful to introduce Erving Goffman's (1968) term 'career' at this point, since these negotiations are never sorted out once and for all, but are continually under review. It is a matter of on-going negotiation within which the person can progressively develop ways of behaving that are as continuous as possible with previous behaviour, thus gradually bringing self and role into line.

Of course, it may be a relatively simple matter of appropriate behaviour if the role is one that requires little more than an external performance. On the other hand, it may often involve a large element of changed perception, of seeing meaning, purpose and significance in what is going on. Student life is like this. It is not merely a matter of performing certain tasks or performing them to a certain standard, but coming to understand what is expected and viewing oneself afresh in relation to these (often implicit) demands. In so far as students grow in self-understanding, one may say that the continuity in their lives springs not so much from the constant repetition of similar behaviours, but from the steady renewal of purpose through the discovery of some fairly consistent meanings (Bannister and Fransella, 1971). Thus, to answer Kurt Danziger's question, the thread which runs through our lives may, indeed, be seen in different circumstances *either* as a thread of habit *or* a thread of meaning. Often we shall be able to see that lives are held together by threads of *both* kinds. However, if the line of argument set out here is correct, it is the thread of meaning which is stronger, less easily broken and more easily repaired.

The argument here has been that, in seeking to understand the process by which anyone comes to terms with a new environment we need a psycho-social, rather than a purely psychological or sociological perspective. It should be noted that similar considerations apply *a fortiori* in respect of any kind of helping relationship. If we need a psycho-social perspective to adequately interpret the process of transition to a new environment, how much more indispensable will such a perspective be for understanding inter-personal help and support. Social psychologists are at one in telling us that it is from interaction with others that we derive our sense of personal identity, though they differ as to precisely how this works. Some have suggested that people are helped interpersonally by being better able to derive a *coherent* sense of self (see Laing, 1971), which is why receiving conflicting messages can be so damaging. Others have emphasized not so much the need for coherence but the need for *positive* feedback about the self as the way to build a satisfactory self-image (see Rogers, 1973). What is not in doubt is that interpersonal relationships are a major source of support to the individual in any situation and especially in a situation of stress such as transition to a new environment. One aspect of the experience of stress is feeling confused and inadequate, unable to form a satisfactory view of oneself in an unfamiliar context. It is for this reason that a relationship which offers an opportunity to build a more optimistic (or even just a less uncertain) view of self will be experienced as helpful.

In this chapter it has been suggested that there may be three rather different approaches to 'transition'. First, it may be treated in relation to the concept of personality. On this view, it is seen as a change of circumstances requir-ing some sort of adjustment or adaptation on the part of the individual. Second, it may be treated in relation to the concept of role. On this view, it is seen as a process of socialization requiring the learning of a new role. Third, and I suggest preferably, it may be treated in relation to the concept of career. On this view, the process is seen as developing a secure sense of personal identity which can accommodate a variety of life-situations and a good deal of discontinuity between them.

What is wrong with the image of pegs in holes is that it suggests that the transition to student life is simply a matter of predetermined fit. First year students who encounter problems early on are quite likely to think of it like this, and to suggest that the obvious solution is for them to withdraw from the course. The considerations set out here might encourage anyone advising them to be a little more cautious in jumping to that conclusion. There may be a real lack of fit, of course, but neither the individual student nor the role they are trying to fit into are static entities. Both are capable of some adjust-ment. The student who says 'I will never make it as a student' may be think-ing of 'a student' in some stereotyped way, and the appropriate response might be to suggest that there is no need for him or her to conform to that model. The student has to find his or her own way of 'being a student' which is within the bounds of what the peer group, the course, the institution and society at large will tolerate, but which, nonetheless, represents some sort of continuity with the student's past sense of personal identity. This gives a good deal of scope for mutual adjustment and negotiation.

Working with this model it is possible to see that for an institution to discard a potential student because he or she doesn't fit in, or for a student to withdraw from a course because it doesn't perfectly match up to expectations, may sometimes be unnecessarily drastic. There is often a measure of influence upon, or choice within, a course that the student can exercise. Increasingly, institutions are recognizing the extent to which effective higher education relies on the development of processes of negotiation with students not just about peripheral matters like social events, but about the nature of the course being followed. The process of transition, far from being a cut-and-dried process of checking to see whether you fit, is actually an ongoing process in which both the student and the institution come to terms with each other.

Institutions which seek to recruit non-traditional students, be they mature students, women on engineering courses, ethnic minorities or students from overseas, know they have to make adjustments to provide a more receptive and less hostile environment. Equally, students have to cope with the fact that student life will probably be in some respects very different from what they imagined, and that their course will almost certainly include elements they could not possibly have foreseen. These are both active processes which may need to be undertaken quite consciously. Students who simply wait to see whether the course will suit them, and institutions which simply wait to see whether students will meet their requirements, have each got to do more to accommodate the other.

4

The Changing Student Experience

In exploring the student experience we have already unravelled a number of distinct strands and looked at it from a number of complementary perspectives. It has been shown that, while students often experience problems of one sort or another, the help they need is much more than dealing with problems and extends to continuous support in their development through the whole of their student experience. Consideration of the idea of student development exposed the fact that, while it is true that students experience change on a number of fronts and may be expected to grow psychologically along a number of different dimensions, there are aspects of the student's development that are social and interpersonal rather then simply personal. This idea has been further explored by examining the kinds of personal disruption which characterize the student experience and, in particular, the difficulties associated with transition into student life. On closer inspection the experience of transition has turned out to be neither a set of private difficulties nor an individual developmental experience, but rather a psycho-social process of step-by-step assimilation in which individual and institution come to terms with each other.

The student experience may, however, be seen in a broader perspective altogether, as the corporate, social experience of a segment of the population. There are important sociological considerations about the place of young people in society, their economic status, their political significance, their own self-understanding within the culture and how all these have been subject to historical change. This chapter, therefore, will look at the student experience within a rapidly changing culture, drawing out its socio-economic and politico-cultural significance and, in particular, how it has changed over time.

Past and present

How then can we begin to get a feel for contemporary student life as it is actually lived? It may be necessary to consciously put aside certain items of mental furniture, the images and pictures that are readily conjured up by a word like 'student'. Here is a male lecturer in his fifties describing his own higher education at Oxford in the late 1950s:

I suppose my student experience was coloured by the fact that we were all together in a college, and the college was small enough for everyone to know each other at least by sight. The college was where we lived; it was the centre of everything for those years. That meant living on the premises, close to each other, and pretty close to some of the lecturers too. But it meant more than that. Looking back, I can see that the college was invested with a kind of symbolic significance – it became a focus of loyalty. There was a lot of intercollegiate rivalry, especially in sport. We wore our college scarves all the time, to show *where* we belonged and to show *that* we belonged. That was it really. It was a matter of belonging to the college. Not just living in it, and certainly not just attending it, but belonging.

Of course, we never used the word 'student' in those days, not at Oxford anyway. We were 'undergraduates'. And 'members' of the College – junior members, but still members. The college servants – yes, they were called that – called us 'Mister X', even though they were old enough to be our fathers! They used to wake us up every morning and bring us hot water for shaving because we didn't have running water in our rooms. And of course we had to wear those black gowns to go to lectures, and for dinner in Hall, and in Chapel. In some ways it was almost a kind of monastic existence – all male and with a strong religious ethos because it was a Christian foundation. The tutors were pretty awesome figures to most of us. We knew them all by sight, even those who taught subjects other than our own, but although we knew their names we didn't really know them as people at all.

Of course, in some ways the atmosphere was quite lax. I had a weekly meeting, on my own, with my particular tutor, and he gave me work to do. Apart from that, I just did what everyone else did – pursued my interests, tried to take advantage of being in a lively cultural centre where things were always happening, and relied on working systematically and hard right through the vacations. The problems? Well, I didn't have enough money for one thing, so I couldn't buy many books. That was a real handicap compared with some other people. Also, there were clubs and societies I would have liked to join but I couldn't afford the subscription. The other problem was time. I simply couldn't get everything in. I never got a job in the vacations – I needed that time for work. My parents understood that. The way we thought of it, it was a privilege to be given a university education, and it involved you in making some sacrifices. Studying hard through the vacations was the only way I could ever have coped. But during term time it seemed better to take advantage of everything that was going on. I never went home in term time.

From the start it was impressed on us that we were not at university to learn anything useful or to acquire training or skills; we were there to engage in a discipline, to explore for ourselves a bit of knowledge that was already well worked-over and which we were told was worthwhile for its own sake. We were encouraged to develop wide interests, and to take part in lots of social occasions, many of them quite formal, such as dinners and balls where you had to wear the right clothes and to observe the right etiquette. What did I get out of all that? I think there was a strong sense of being absorbed by a tradition, gradually learning to be at home in it, whether it was a matter of social etiquette or of intellectual discipline. It felt like being given a grounding in your cultural heritage, encouraged to stand on this ground, and yet at the same time to stretch yourself within the given frame. It wasn't a matter of being stretched, rather of stretching ourselves. We were helped by the collegiate experience because that meant some of your best friends were doing different subjects. I learnt a lot that way. In a sense you could say that it was not the dons who educated us, but rather that the college made it possible for us to be educated by ourselves, by each other.

It is immediately obvious that the student experience in the 1990s is very different from this. The increased size of modern institutions of higher education probably means that, for many, the experience of student life is one of anonymity. 'Community', therefore, while not necessarily a thing of the past, has radically changed. Students form themselves into friendship groups which remain remarkably static. Shared residence, often male and female students together, is popular, not least because self-catering can be cheaper than living in a hall of residence. In many institutions it is only a minority of students who ever live in college accommodation; in any case, to live in a hall of residence is often quite different from a 'collegiate' experience. Halls of residence may instil little sense of community, none of loyalty, but simply serve the functional purpose of facilitating the initial stage of friendship-making. So, typically, today's student moves into hall in order to find friends with whom to move out as soon as possible.

The idea of 'belonging' no longer seems to fit in this new environment. The larger the institution, the smaller the proportion of students, it seems, who are willing to participate in clubs and societies. Even sports fail to attract more than a minority. Many students travel home very frequently, some nearly every weekend. Convenient rail travel now begins to emerge as a major factor determining a student's choice of institution. Few students are without a student railcard and most travel a great deal. Much the same could be said of lecturers. Few lecturers live 'on the job', and some actually choose to commute 30 miles or more every day. Even when they live nearby they are likely to draw fairly firm lines between their work lives and their private, domestic or family concerns, not encouraging any encroachment of the one into the other. Yet contact between students and staff is relaxed and informal; the element of 'social distance' seems to have largely disappeared. Students are known by their first names as a matter of course and so, as a rule, are their lecturers.

While relationships are fairly relaxed, teaching is often expected to be quite formal. Attempts on the part of lecturers to launch out into less formal methods of teaching are sometimes greeted with disconcerted dismay. Tutors may regretfully apologize that they cannot provide the individual tuition they would like, but students may find the prospect of such close scrutiny somewhat alarming, and frequently fail to take full advantage of such tutorial opportunities as are offered. So although outwardly relationships seem very informal and there is even a good deal of personal intimacy, the character of higher education institutions is increasingly that of a large bureaucracy, the tone of which is initially set by tedious enrolment procedures involving long queues and the completion of endless forms, a mode of welcome for new students which comes in for surprisingly little criticism.

Higher education now takes place, for the most part, in secular institutions from which all trace of religious influence has gone. Many of the old ideals have gone too. Today's students have to be practical and careful if they are to get by, as many of them do, on a very tight budget. Few manage without a substantial parental subsidy, or a bank loan, or by getting a job right through the summer months. They don't buy books unless it is absolutely necessary, and are quick to dispose of them afterwards. This illustrates the down-to-earth instrumentality of the modern student. Higher education is something to avail yourself of for a purpose. Students mostly know why they are there, and expect the institution to serve their purposes. They are inclined to regard as a 'cop out' any suggestion that students should be encouraged to educate each other; it is felt that it is the tutors' job to provide what they are paying for. This has the merit of straightforwardness, but is seriously flawed as a view of higher education. It is perhaps significant that the Students' Unions, once great debating societies, continue into the 1990s as institutions whose chief function appears to be the provision of entertainment (see Barnett, 1990a).[1] Students look to their Union for respite from study, not for a deepening or broadening of it.

These remarkable and far-reaching changes may be attributed, in part, to demography. The student experience, once the prerogative of a fortunate few, has become much more widely available. The supply of 18-year-olds in the population has diminished at the same time as higher education provision has been expanded, so that entry to the higher education experience is less competitive. Given that admission to higher education is in any case skewed towards social classes I and II, many families might quite rightly predict that for their offspring a university or polytechnic place is a virtual certainty. For them, entry to student life may be experienced almost as a natural progression; while there may be some disappointment at failing to secure a place in a specific subject in a given institution at a particular time, as far as many of higher education's clients are concerned there is hardly any competition at all for entry into higher education *in some form or other*. Higher education has never been so available as it is now. So if student life is experienced less as a privilege and more as an entitlement, this simply reflects the fact that now, at any rate within certain social classes, almost everyone who wants a higher education experience is able to have one.

This is not, of course, to suggest that higher education in Britain has lost its elite character, or that it has yet become an open or a mass system of higher education. It may be more available, but that does not mean it is more accessible. Its clients remain a privileged minority, whether they feel themselves to be so or not. Their selection has effectively taken place further back, well away from higher education itself. The crucial division occurs at age 16 rather than 18; access to higher education now depends more than anything else on staying on in the education system beyond the minimum school-leaving age (Corbett, 1990).[2] After that, it becomes more a matter of motivation and confidence than of selectivity and exclusion. For most of those who have continued in education to the age of 18 and who seek admission to advanced courses the question is not so much *whether* they will get into higher education, but *where*, *what* they will study and perhaps *when*.

Representation and reality

There is no doubt that, in the past, the student's family has often served as a useful source of advance information about higher education. The child of graduate parents, and perhaps graduate grandparents too, was able to set out on a career in higher education with an inbuilt advantage. While much has been done to widen access to higher education, at least in the sense of opening the doors of higher education institutions to non-traditional students, it remains true that such students are disadvantaged in that they lack access to traditions of behaviour which higher education has in the past presupposed. However, without denying that such inequalities persist, it needs to be recognized that the nature of student life has now changed to an extent which may paradoxically render this kind of traditional background, at least in some contexts, a source of misinformation. While this group may be in demographic terms still a significant proportion – indeed, a barely diminished proportion overall – yet in cultural terms they no longer represent the centre of gravity of student life. With the possible exception of Oxbridge, the tone is no longer set by those who by background and upbringing are rooted in the traditions and the values of a higher education experience understood as part of a cultural heritage. Rather, in many institutions it is the privileged who are more likely to feel out of place; certainly, it is they who have most to learn about the realities of student life.

It is understandable if graduate parents feel they can be of rather little help to their student offspring in preparing them for student life. As we have seen, even teaching staff in higher education are quite likely to misread the student experience. Today's lecturers are yesterday's students; despite being professionally in touch with student life they often have little direct contact with it and are liable to view it through the spectacles of their own student experience. While academics know very well the extent to which their subject has been transformed during the course of their own professional lifetime, they do not always appreciate how much the extra-curricular student experience has changed during the same period, perhaps more than the curriculum itself. Given the rapid overall growth of post-school education through recent decades, norms of student behaviour inevitably reflect the values of students with no family tradition of advanced study, and with little to guide them except the cultural images publicly available to all.

Yet the student experience is not only different from that of an earlier generation; it contrasts quite sharply with the view of student life that is current in the popular imagination. Incoming students are often unprepared for the reality of student life. Or perhaps it would be better to say wrongly prepared. The media offer representations of student life which, if not downright misleading, are seriously distorted. Just as policemen and nurses distance themselves from the media portrayals of their respective roles, so academics are inclined to take a quizzical view of university life as represented on television. Yet few would-be students are in a position to be so sceptical. For the school leaver who has little idea of what to expect, TV soap operas, news bulletins, films and even the campus novel, may function as rich sources of information on how to behave on arrival. It has sometimes been suggested that for children in primary schools 'Grange Hill' offers anticipatory socialization into secondary school life; in much the same way, new entrants to the tertiary stage of education may rely heavily on media images to provide at least initial guidance on what is expected, not just in the sense of how to comport themselves, but perhaps even more importantly how to feel, how to experience student life.

Some of them, of course, will have other, more reliable sources of information on which they can draw to construct ideas of what it is to be a student. They may have older brothers and sisters who are or who have recently been students; they may have mixed socially among students before they enrol on courses themselves. The point has already been made that much of higher education's insulation from the rest of life has broken down. Yet it still remains an unfamiliar environment to many. Expansion of higher education has ocurred unevenly, with some of the newer institutions developing very quickly indeed and filling many of their places with first-generation undergraduate students, with the result that the character of student life has altered out of all recognition. The general public from which students are recruited has very little understanding of these changes.

Explaining change

How are we to understand these complex processes of change? There is something odd about discussing the student experience as if it were a discrete, distinct entity which changes over time. Take, for example, the point that has been noted about students travelling home more frequently then they ever did in the past. Why do they do this? Is it because of close ties with parents and kin? Or is it often because of well-established relationships which were formed prior to leaving home? To understand student life as it is actually lived we need to know such things. Are many students effectively not 'living' on campus at all, but treating it as a workplace from which to return 'home'? What defines 'home'? Is it the parental home? Is it some form of group life, shared with a few friends? Or is it, increasingly, a shared living arrangement with a partner, entered into on a fairly permanent basis? The parental home can be a rather problematic notion for many students, since their parents may be divorced or separated, and the question of locating the 'home' is a matter of choice or decision. Large numbers of students elect to be treated as home-based students in the city or town where they have come to study. They find somewhere to live independent of their parents, whom they simply visit from time to time, meanwhile defining their own accommodation, however temporary, as their home.

It is clear that the student experience is not simply one that is undergone or lived through; it is, in some ways, constructed by those living through it. There is a sense in which we get the institutions we deserve. It can be objectively observed that a modern polytechnic is no longer an academic 'community' in the sense that a medieval college was (though new forms of academic community can be discerned in networks of colleagues working in similar fields, linked by the occasional conference and the fax machine) yet that is to reckon without the feelings of those who would find the latter intolerably claustrophobic. Those whose formative educational experiences at secondary school have been in quite large comprehensive institutions are unlikely to be looking for an intimate, collegiate atmosphere for their higher education; on the contrary, they may prefer the familiarity of private friendship networks alongside relative anonymity in public. If offered the kind of collegiate experience not untypical a generation ago they might shrink from it, or, perhaps more likely, transform it by the way they lived it. It is necessary to assert, then, that students today do not just encounter a world of individualism and instrumentality in higher education, they bring a great deal of individualism and instrumentality to it. These characteristics belong within and may partly be explained by reference to our broader cultural and political life.

Solidarity and diversity

Given the wider age-range at the point of entry, we cannot assume that today's students will have a great deal in common. Even among those who come straight from school we should not, perhaps, expect any very strong group identity. Is it possible that those who continue their studies immediately after leaving school, unlike young working people who often develop a strong sense of group life, become committed to a highly individualized and competitive lifestyle which undermines student life as a shared experience? Does such a contrast mirror the familiar distinction between working-class solidarity and middle-class 'educated' values?

That way of putting it might prompt the reply that, on the contrary, all young people may be seen as a coherent group. From the 1950s onwards they have been explicitly targeted as a key market, a class of consumers. Do they not, then, from this perspective, constitute a group with certain shared values in common, their group identity promoted and sustained by the mass media so as to create a youth culture which transcends social class? This kind of sociological account (Eisenstadt, 1956) may be taken further. Those whose youth is spent in education can, nonetheless, identify themselves closely with those whose youth is spent at work; they might, indeed, have less money, but they can still choose to spend it on the same sorts of things. Campus culture may then be seen as much like youth culture anywhere else, with student life actually coming in due course to epitomize the experience of the young.

While that kind of description might appear to fit student life in the 1960s, it is now hopelessly out of date. The student experience is spoken of less in terms of fun and freedom, and more in terms of anxiety and constraint. Nowhere is this more clearly seen than in the economics of student life; students are once again becoming very poor. As is often pointed out, this is not quite the same poverty as that endured by other disadvantaged groups, in that for many students it is both a voluntarily chosen and a temporary state. Nonetheless, it remains true that to be a student is once again to be relatively and perhaps absolutely poor, unless there are countervailing circumstances such as wealthy parents or industrial sponsorship. Nor is the poverty as voluntary or as temporary as is sometimes suggested. We are now worlds away from the situation in the 1950s and 1960s, when the middle-aged viewed young people uneasily and perhaps enviously as they confidently and cheekily led the way in fields such as fashion and entertainment. Now, the older generation is more likely to look upon young people with a genuine concern; they seem a vulnerable group who deserve and demand our help and support.

Widespread youth unemployment and the consequent reorganization of the transition from school to work mean that the predicament of the young worker is in many ways similar to that of the student (Frith, 1984:65). Both can mean having one's adult status postponed. 'Young worker' status is no longer to be understood as a step towards the adult world of work. It is possible that those who have no choice but to participate in training schemes may increasingly be treated like, and perhaps even thought of as, in a rather derogatory sense, 'students'. It is also possible that students in higher education who fail to secure employment on graduation will come to be seen as occupying an extended student status, rather like the untrained underclass whose lifestyle they largely share. Considerations of this sort might lead us to suppose that, with the development of training schemes and further education opportunities for virtually all school leavers, there could be a renewal of the student experience as a common, shared experience for almost all young people.

The view taken here, however, is quite the opposite: that it is the divisions in the student experience which will prove to be most pervasive. Certainly, the introduction of student loans, coupled to the pegging of student grants at existing levels, marks a new downturn in the fortunes of the average student; as the value of the grant steadily diminishes we shall inevitably see greater hardship and increased levels of debt. In such a climate, students who have alternative sources of income will become increasingly conspicuous. The student state, once one of amiable and tolerable poverty, experienced as a unifying predicament over a relatively short period, will act as an amplifier of social as well as intellectual differences, so that the student experience becomes increasingly fractured and fragmented.

In reviewing the student experience it has become abundantly clear that it has changed dramatically within a short space of time. What until quite recently operated as a unifying and cohesive force and offered a common, shared experience based upon tradition and settled commitment, has given way to an open and competitive system, which not only exposes social divisions, but is itself inherently divisive. There have been changes to the composition of the student body, changes in the size and character of higher education institutions, changes in their staffing, changed purposes and, above all, a changed context. It is hardly surprising, then, that higher education has come to mean different things, to serve different purposes in society and to reflect different sets of priorities. The student state is experienced differently according to family tradition, parental support, prestige of institution, selectivity of subject, credit-worthiness, industrial sponsorship and so on, as well as along lines of gender, race and social class. The fact is that students now have very different experiences in higher education.

This suggests that those who, in whatever capacity, would offer help and support to students have to be prepared to tackle a much wider range of matters than previously. It is no longer just a matter, if it ever was, of seeing students through their homesickness, the ups and downs of their girlfriend/boyfriend crises, and worries about their forthcoming examinations; professional student advisers and counsellors today deal routinely with marriage problems, with debt, with homelessness and family violence. Tutors, too, are affected by these changes and in their support role can easily become involved in matters which seem more appropriate to the case-load of a social worker than to the tutorial responsibilities of an academic. Yet tutors are, and are likely to remain, the front line of student support in higher education institutions. The role of the tutor needs urgent reconsideration and it is to this that we now turn.

Notes

1. I am indebted to Dr Ronald Barnett of the Centre for Higher Education Studies, University of London Institute of Education, not only for this particular point, but more generally for raising issues concerning 'academic community'.
2. Jenny Corbett (1990) draws attention to the social divisions evident in the different career prospects of 18-year-olds entering higher education and those leaving Youth Training, the effects of which, she says, will be 'long term and profound'.

Part 2

Tutorial Support

5

The Tutor's Point of View

Unlike professional support staff, teaching staff may not have a very clear idea of how they are expected to contribute to the support process. Difficulties can arise both from competing definitions of the tutorial role and from conflicting demands upon anyone who tries to combine a tutorial role with other institutional roles and responsibilities.

The designation 'tutor' is notoriously unclear, yet it remains the most appropriate word to use, in the British context, for members of teaching staff in institutions of higher education in so far as they have a responsibility for helping and supporting students. As well as its root meaning of teacher, 'tutor' carries strong historical overtones of what may be called the British tutorial tradition. It harks back to the context of medieval Oxford and Cambridge where an undergraduate would be allocated to a 'tutor' who would keep an eye on him, act *in loco parentis* and possibly be as concerned to monitor his behaviour as a young gentleman as to encourage his intellectual development. At the same time it conveys an echo of the private tutor, once a familiar figure in the English country house. In current usage it continues to convey some sense of moral responsibility and of personal attention. Although in some contexts the word may be used almost interchangeably with 'lecturer', it would not as a rule be used unless there were some suggestion of pastoral care and some likelihood of one-to-one contact with each student. It is used here in preference to the term 'lecturer' which appears to suggest nothing more than a very formal teaching role.

In British higher education 'tutor' has for a long time seemed the natural way to refer to the member of teaching staff who takes a personal interest in a student; and not only in higher education. In secondary education the member of teaching staff who has responsibility for a specific age cohort is called Year Tutor. Although, in practice, this is sometimes a largely administrative function, it is usually conceived as a student-focused or 'pastoral' responsibility as distinct from responsibility for an area of the school curriculum. In higher education there are several different kinds of responsibility which commonly carry the title 'tutor': these include Course Tutor (responsible for running a complete course), Year Tutor (responsible for one year of a course), Personal Tutor (responsible for keeping a watchful eye on the student's work and progress on an individual basis) and Placement Tutor (responsible for arranging and supervising industrial or professional placements). Institutions differ as to the precise designations of these roles, both as to what they are and what they are called. However, the word 'tutor' is used fairly consistently to designate roles which go beyond a straightforward 'lecturing' role, and to suggest some supervisory role, some personal contact with the student and/or some broad responsibility that may even extend beyond the course itself.

The tutoring experience: an investigation

Given this background, how do tutors themselves view this aspect of their role? How do they cope with the demands on them? A recent study allowed tutors to talk freely about their role in helping and supporting students and invited them to comment on this part of their work (Earwaker, 1989a,b). It gave them an opportunity to voice their frustrations as well as to explain their motivation, and revealed not only an impressive commitment to their students, but considerable confusion and uncertainty about their support role.

The study was based on tape-recorded interviews with the First Year Tutors of each major degree course offered within the institution. It was recognized that the institution's policy for Personal Tutors was beginning to become unworkable in some departments, and it was suspected that there might be an extra burden on the Year Tutors as the obvious and available staff to whom students would look for support. Since it was known that students experienced more problems in the first year of their courses than in subsequent years, it was thought that First Year Tutors, in particular, might be taking a good deal of the strain. This appeared to be true, though not the whole truth.

It became clear that Course Leaders (the title given to Course Tutors of large courses) were being consulted by students even more than Year Tutors. Consequently, as the study progressed, some Course Leaders were interviewed and also other staff otherwise identified as key members of their departments by virtue of their responsibility for and/or experience of student support. The aim was to gain a bird's eye view of how support for students was operating across the whole institution.

The main results of this investigation can be quite briefly summarized. It was clear that tutors were giving a great deal of support to students. The scale and the severity of the problems revealed were surprising, even sometimes startling. There were a number of staff who were actually trying to serve as 'the first person the student turns to' for more than 100 students. Naturally, this was taking up a large proportion of their time, even when the problems were relatively trivial; but on the evidence of these interviews major problems were cropping up quite frequently, some involving acute personal distress. The general picture that emerged was that, as suspected, the bulk of the task of giving personal help and support to students was being carried out by a relatively small number of staff, and was being experienced by them as something of a burden. It was clear that, even while a personal tutorial system remained formally in place, Year Tutors and Course Tutors who made themselves readily available to students were liable to be overwhelmed by the demands on them.

The contribution of tutors to student support

The tutors were asked to give some examples of the sort of matters they found themselves having to deal with. One tutor with responsibility for a first year group of only 24 students referred to recent cases of family violence, sexual harassment, bereavement, divorce, ill-health and disability. Another mentioned problems associated with alcohol misuse, unplanned pregnancies and arranged marriages. Another, responsible for 85 students mostly aged 18 or 19, spoke of parental divorce and family bereavements, together with ill-health, and academic and study problems, as matters that cropped up *nearly every week* in some form or other. One member of staff began by mentioning relatively minor problems such as those of adjustment to the course, the problems of non-traditional students, and the need to clarify procedural matters, but then went on to cite a whole range of personal problems which included relationship difficulties, some serious medical conditions, and two cases of 'very serious' psychological problems; this young tutor had only been working in the institution for six months.

Another tutor, asked to cite some typical problems, responded like this:

> If I just list what has happened to me in the last fortnight. I've got one girl who's getting beaten up by her live-in man, and I referred her to the counsellor. I've got one who's involved in a rather nasty sexual harass-ment case in halls of residence – who's involved with the police. And also having got all that on her shoulders she's lost her grandma. So she's in a turmoil. I've got another one whose parents have just gone through a particularly nasty divorce, and both parents seem to be visiting all the problems on the girl. So she doesn't know which way is up – she just sits there. I've got one who's got a health problem, incapable of working – continual headaches. I've got another one who's got physical incapacity. And it just goes on and on and on . . .

It was noticeable that the number of serious problems dealt with seemed to remain remarkably constant from one tutor to another. Year Tutors respons-ible for 20 students told similar stories to those with well over 100. This strongly suggests that a great many student problems never come to the attention of any tutor at all, but are simply submerged by weight of numbers. Whereas within a small student group cases of illness are immediately noticed and enquiries made, the larger the group, the greater the risk of a student being completely 'invisible'. One tutor described it as dealing with the tip of an iceberg; with some 200 students in a year group, he had found on more than one occasion that a student had left the course before any staff were aware that there was any kind of difficulty. The cause of concern here was not so much that the students had dropped out, but that they had done so without any debriefing of what could have been a very negative experience.

Obviously, some tutors are much more approachable than others. It is worth recording the reluctance, even distaste, with which some teaching staff found themselves being drawn into students' personal problems, while at the same time finding it impossible to avoid. These were not, on the whole, staff who were naturally drawn to this kind of role; rather, they were conscientious tutors who were responding to students' needs as best they could.

One who expressed considerable reluctance to get involved in students' personal problems said that students came to talk to him 'with alarming regularity' and that he felt quite weighed down by this:

> I try to keep it as professional and distant a relationship as possible, and don't really want to know what their problems are unless it starts really affecting their work.

However, despite this resolve he found it impossible to carry out his teaching and administrative roles properly without the personal life of the student constantly encroaching:

> I ask them to bring their work in and we talk about it . . . When other people are around you tend to temper it, but I'll actually say I'm sorry but you're grossly underachieving – you know, put it very straight on the line. I'll say you're not working efficiently. And *why* aren't you working efficiently? Boom! Then suddenly you find you're talking about their parents' divorce and the sordid details of what's happening here. And why. And you think 'Do I really want to know this?' I suppose the answer is I shouldn't ask the question 'Why aren't you working properly?'. But it's not sufficient just to say 'You're not working', is it, from a professional point of view?

Here was tutor who, without any eagerness on his part, was becoming involved in a large number of quite complex personal problems. Most of the tutors interviewed were similarly able to reel off a long list of recent cases requiring support. One of the more experienced tutors responded like this:

> Illness, yes. Somebody has something like glandular fever – to start with they probably don't realize they've got it – and what they've got is this lethargy, this inability to drive themselves. Very often they see themselves as being lazy, and that's not good, because of their own esteem. They get worried thinking 'I'm lazy', and getting behind and getting more worried. Other problems are things like an Asian student – he had problems with his hearing at one time, but his biggest problem seemed to be that his family were trying to marry him with someone else who he

wasn't at all sure about . . . There are some problems with home life. Parents ill. And the daughter is always expected to go back and help – to some extent, you know. They worry about things like that. We had problems with one student – his wife decided to move, and he was wanting to do this course here. I was never sure of the truth of the situation. I didn't know whether he was telling me the truth. There's another student – not very happy about being failed on his first year and had to resit it. For a long time he was very bitter about that. So generally speaking he just . . . I think he called in to see a lot of different people, to tell them what he didn't like about it!

The picture which emerges is of tutors being routinely drawn into a whole series of thorny human problems, all of them potentially quite serious for the people concerned. This kind of evidence from tutors, as well as supporting the contention that tutors play a major role in student support, also shows clearly why they cannot possibly meet every need. Several tutors confessed that they were at times quite overwhelmed by the scale and severity of the problems which were brought to them.

Tutors' feelings about their support role

The evidence of this study is that most of the tutors were operating under considerable pressure. Nearly all of those interviewed expressed some anxiety about this part of their work. Most felt very unsure of themselves in this area, and sought reassurance that they were dealing with these matters appropriately. The majority admitted to feeling 'out of their depth' at times. Some also wondered whether they were becoming too deeply involved in supporting students, so that the students' problems got out of proportion; others worried about the effect their commitment to students was having on the rest of their work. Clearly, for these tutors their role in support was undertaken with a good deal of uneasiness and uncertainty.

In view of the kinds of problems they were attempting to deal with, it is hardly surprising that they should have felt themselves somewhat inadequate at times. More than one male tutor described himself as completely nonplussed when a female student wanted to talk with him about her unplanned pregnancy; this was something for which, as young academics, they were totally unprepared. One of them voiced his anxiety like this:

Every year there will be two, three, maybe four pregnancies, that people on the course come and tell me about. It surprised me when it first happened, the first year I was here, that they would come and tell me about it, but they do. Very regularly. I found that very difficult to deal with . . . These are not problems I've encountered much in the past . . . At first I just didn't know where to go. It was an aspect of the job I hadn't anticipated. As I've been longer in it I think I've perhaps thought it out a bit more. But I still recognize my need for support of some sort. Certainly the first pregnancy, the first girl who came to tell me she was pregnant, I didn't know what to say.

If some feel somewhat out of their depth through lack of experience, others feel disqualified from discussing certain matters for the opposite reason, that they are too close to home. On the same subject, one woman lecturer said:

The thing that I'm actually dreading arising, and I would have to step back from this immediately, is if I had a girl coming to say that she was pregnant. I would find that extremely difficult because my own personal feelings about abortion would be very difficult I think – to actually lay objectively all the options out, and I think I would have to act immediately to step back from that, and say 'Look you must go and see somebody else for advice on this'.

Some of those interviewed, while keenly aware of their own lack of appropriate skills, were nonetheless rather ambivalent when asked if they would like opportunities for further training. Some were already feeling under such pressure that they did not see how they could do anything more. Nor, in most cases, did they want to jeopardize their academic careers by settling into a student support role. Typically they were asking for more 'back-up'. Several staff suggested the production of some written guidelines for all staff on how to operate in a student support role, together with basic information about the institution's support services. Others wanted help to think through their support role and to develop their support skills. It was very clear from this that, as well as needing information and training, these staff were themselves in need of support. They were acutely aware of the tensions and ambiguities in their roles, struggling to do justice to tasks which they felt often pulled them in different directions.

Some, indeed, saw themselves as the unsung heroes of the institution, keeping courses operating smoothly, ensuring that students remained, as far as possible, satisfied customers and going out of their way to help individual students with particular problems. Their impression was that the work to which they were devoting themselves was undervalued by the institution, consistently taken for granted and invariably eclipsed by the publicity given to new initiatives. While some claimed the moral high ground, suggesting that the institution's obligations to students should come first, others argued more pragmatically that it was not in the institution's long-term interests to put at risk the personal attention to students on which its reputation with its clients ultimately depended.

There was no sign of resentment that conscientious performance of a student support role generally went unrewarded; rather, there was a wry recognition that, as one tutor said, 'I must be mad to do it.' They blamed themselves for getting into what could easily become, they frankly recognized, a career cul-de-sac. Their anxiety on this score was not without justification. One might suppose that the staff most closely involved in supporting students would be relatively experienced staff, but in fact the opposite proved to be the case. Tutors with specific responsibility for the first year of each major degree programme were in some cases the most junior and least experienced members of their departments. This seems to be a reflection of the low status implicitly accorded to the student support role. The exceptions were a small number of very experienced staff who continued to give priority to student support and who had remained in positions such as First Year Tutor for many years. These staff appeared to recognize, in some cases quite explicitly, that in so far as they devoted themselves to students they could be putting their professional careers at risk. This was, to be sure, a choice quite wittingly and uncomplainingly made, but it is hardly right that it should have confronted them in this form.

The study was specifically concerned with tutors who had taken responsibility for student support and were conscientiously trying to offer students the help they needed. Such tutors are almost certainly untypical, and one should be cautious about drawing generalized conclusions from this evidence. Nonetheless, this study shows not only that these tutors were making a very substantial contribution to student support, but that this was being done at considerable personal cost. They were sometimes overwhelmed by the scale and severity of the problems brought to them. They appeared to be unsure about where their responsibility ended, doubtful about how much their institution valued this aspect of their work and confused about where to get further help. On the evidence of this study, then, tutors need help in all these ways if they are to continue to operate as key supports for their students; it is essential that the limits of the role should be clearly marked out, that the role be publicly recognized as important, and that sources of back-up and support be clearly identified.

Sources of role strain

It must, nonetheless, be recognized that there are certain elements of role strain that are inescapable whenever members of teaching staff are expected to act in a support role. This kind of role is inherently problematic and potentially stressful with or without adequate back-up. Various sources of role strain can be identified.

First, tutors appear to be uncertain how to reconcile the development of a personal relationship with the performance of a professional task. As already indicated, the promotion prospects of staff could be adversely affected by their willingness to take their student support function seriously. This might occur directly, either in straightforward discrimination against those who were seen as student-centred rather than research-centred or by drafting into the support role those who were of lowest status, thereby making their career progression more difficult. It might also occur indirectly, in that staff who devoted more time to helping and supporting students could easily fall behind in research and consultancy, which might then be used as indicators of their performance when it came to promotion or upgrading.

Many of those interviewed spoke of their 'open door' policy. They tried to be available to students whenever they were free of timetabled commitments, and would deliberately signal this availability by working with their office door propped open. The cost of this to an academic can be very high. In a context in which staff are expected to develop their own research projects, to publish, to engage in consultancy and to generate income, not to mention preparation of lectures and assessment of students' work, one can hardly expect staff to tolerate, let alone encourage, interruptions from students throughout the whole of the working day. What can happen is that, as the majority of staff are gradually compelled to reduce their availability, those who do not do so risk being overwhelmed not only by their own students, but by everybody else's as well. This not only puts an intolerable burden on a small number of staff; it leads to a culture in which the only staff who have time for students are those who have effectively given up on some of their other responsibilities.

However, devoting time to students should not have to mean being constantly interrupted. Cannot students be seen by appointment? Staff who are working with a model of higher education that expects a friendly tutor to be on hand at the point of difficulty are inclined to say that problems cannot be timetabled and that crises are, by definition, unexpected. Indeed, it is precisely this kind of relationship which characterizes higher education as such – flexible arrangements, individual attention and pastoral concern. Yet behind this approach lies an unspoken assumption about the amateur nature of the encounter; it is of the essence of the tutorial intervention that it is unscripted and *ad hoc*. It seems important to challenge both this kind of amateur tradition and the professionalism that would transform the role of tutor into that of counsellor.

Tutors sometimes find it difficult to operate both as a source of support and as an arbiter of standards. Tutors may be privy to all kinds of confidential information about the student's personal circumstances which colour their judgement of the student's performance. In particular, they are torn between their responsibility as tutors to act in the best interests of the student and their responsibility as examiners to make an objective assessment of the student's work. Because it has been felt that the tutor may be required to act as a kind of advocate on the student's behalf, it has sometimes been suggested that, as a matter of principle, students should be allocated personal tutors who have no examining or assessment role in their course. However, in practice it is not always possible or sensible to separate the two roles. Staff are normally involved in the assessment of the students they teach, so the application of this principle means allocating students personal tutors who they will not meet in the ordinary way. Yet it has been found that to allocate students to tutors they never meet in the classroom is to put both in an almost impossible position from which a relationship may never get started.

It surely has to be acknowledged that if the role of tutor includes both teaching and support then it must involve a certain amount of role strain. Tutors cannot offer total independence or impartiality. What they can offer is a different kind of service in which their experience, their knowledge of the course, and their advice may all be extremely valuable. Unless they renounce their teaching role and all that it implies, including assessment, they cannot operate as if they have no responsibility except to their client. This is to suggest that the role of tutor needs to be carefully distinguished from that of counsellor. It does not mean that tutors have to operate amateurishly, but that appropriate professional standards, in relation to confidentiality for instance, have to be worked out.

One might add here that there are particular difficulties in reconciling the tutor's responsibility towards the student with the student's right to privacy. Just as assumptions are often made concerning the tutor's ready availability to the student, so the willingness of the student to enter into a personal relationship with his or her tutor is sometimes taken for granted. However, people differ as to how much of their personal lives they are willing to share with others. The possibilities of misunderstanding here are very great, especially in a relationship which is not between equals, and cannot be, given the institutional context. Well-meaning attempts to help others may fail or even be personally damaging if elements of bullying or patronizing are allowed to creep in.

Third, tutors are far from clear about the limits of their responsibilities in respect of their students, often only turning to other agencies as a last resort. In the study referred to above, tutors were mostly rather reluctant to refer their students to anyone else. There were also a few rather disturbing cases when the back-up had apparently not been available when required. As a result, teaching staff faced with a case of acute mental distress had been unable to contact any other support agencies and they readily admitted that on these occasions they had felt extremely vulnerable. While it cannot be stated too strongly that student support is not just about coping with crises, there clearly has to be a reliable system of emergency cover on which tutors know they can rely. It is not fair to ask teaching staff to take on support roles which may expose them to difficult situations without either the necessary training or effective back-up support.

Hardly any of the tutors in the study made use of the full range of institutional provision. The usual pattern was that they would make contact sooner or later with, say, the student counsellor or one of the chaplains, and thereafter return again and again to the same person for help. It was as if tutors were finding their own way through the system, and then sticking to known and reliable routes. Whether a student was referred to the counselling service or to the chaplaincy might then depend not on careful attention to the student's specific needs or wishes, but rather on the contacts their tutor happened to have made in the past. Thus, despite the wide range of resources on offer within the institution, tutors were operating with quite a narrow repertoire of responses.

Yet there are many sources of support available. As well as the formal agencies provided by institutions and the numerous agencies available within the community there are the informal relationships within the student group, and contacts with family and friends, which for many students are the most effective supports. Yet teaching staff are often insufficiently aware of all these other sources of help. Because they often do not have any sense of how their role complements, and is complemented by, other sources of support it assumes an exaggerated importance and becomes a burden which cannot be laid down. The effect is not only to impede referral, but to reinforce tutors' feelings of personal responsibility, that they alone can provide the support the student needs. This may not be the best way of helping the student; worse, it may be very unhelpful to the student if the relationship becomes such that either the student or tutor finds it difficult to let go.

The three chapters which follow develop these three sets of issues further. Chapter 6 explores the nature of the tutorial relationship, insisting that it is no simple friendship between equals, but a professional relationship, yet at the same time resisting the conclusion that it is to be characterized as counselling. Chapter 7 tackles the question of confidentiality, especially as it confronts the tutor who has responsibilities for both support and assessment. Chapter 8 discusses the tutor's role within the overall support network with a view to clarifying questions about the limits of the tutor's support role and about referral to other helping agencies.

6

The Tutorial Relationship

We have seen that teaching staff in their support role have to cope with a range of ambiguities, tensions and conflicting responsibilities. They are, therefore, in quite a different position from that of professional support staff. On the other hand, their position needs to be distinguished from that of a friend. For a member of staff in an institution of higher education to give help and support to a student cannot be equated with one student helping another. Why not?

It is the institutional context which sets limits to the nature of the relationship. A tutor and a student may belong to the same institution, but they belong there on different terms. For both it is their workplace, but whereas for one it is the place of employment, involving a commitment to deliver a service according to a contract, for the other it is the place where the particular services they seek are to be obtained.

It is not just that each occupies a distinct role; the roles are related to each other in such a way that the tutor is presumed to know things that the student does not yet know. This is a necessary consequence of setting up social encounters of this sort where two people come into contact in order that one shall learn from, and with the help of, the other.

This does not, of course, mean that each cannot respect the other; a context of mutual respect is often required for optimum learning. Nor does the student's tacit acknowledgement of the tutor's status with respect to a specific context have to be generalized to cover any more than is covered by the course. It might be possible to think of the teaching/learning relationship as quite detached from everything else, a purely functional affair, so that one consults one's tutor rather in the way that one goes to get one's hair cut. Clearly, this is affected by the subject and level of study; it is very hard to conceive of higher education as narrowly as this. Consequently, there will almost certainly be elements of role strain when tutor and student meet informally outside the classroom and especially when they meet on the specific understanding that the tutor is to offer the student some kind of personal help, whether in the form of advice, guidance or support, since it is the teaching relationship that will be the determinative one. They meet *as* tutor and student in what is essentially a working relationship, not a social one.

Interviewing, counselling and tutoring

Surprisingly little has been written about tutoring and, in particular, the one-to-one tutorial (Bramley, 1977; Lewis, 1984; McMahon, 1985; Lublin, 1987; Jacques, 1989), but there is, of course, a considerable body of literature both on interviewing and on counselling, either of which might be expected to yield useful insights. The fact is, however, that these two bodies of literature take very different approaches. A good interviewer has a clear idea of where the conversation is going, keeps firm control of it, and dictates its direction. A good counsellor, on the other hand, is one who allows the client to determine the content, the direction and even the pace of the conversation. Indeed, according to one very influential theory (Rogers, 1973), counselling skill lies precisely in *not* being directive; the aim is to be, as far as possible, client-centred, never to dominate or to control, but always to enable or to facilitate the functioning of the other. Thus, the best counsellors are those who can draw out of even the most reticent and inarticulate client what it is that the client genuinely feels or wants. Whereas the skilled counsellor is one who keeps an open mind and can follow the lead of the client, the skilled interviewer is one who wastes no time in getting to the point, and who has no doubt about what the point is since it has already been predetermined without reference to the other person.

So is individual tutoring to be understood as a sort of interviewing or as a sort of counselling? If we think of tutoring as a kind of interviewing we shall expect the skilled tutor to have a clear idea of the purpose of the tutorial, and to make this clear to the student. We shall regard as somewhat unprofessional the tutor who approaches tutorials unprepared, who offers students a completely open agenda, whose tutorials range widely over a number of different matters and rarely come to a tidy conclusion. On the other hand, if we think of tutoring as a kind of counselling we shall expect the skilled tutor to be a good listener who allows the student to talk freely without interruption, and who can elicit from the student with a minimum of prompts whatever it is that the student wants to say. We shall regard as somewhat unprofessional the tutor who has a fixed idea about the function of the tutorial, its content or its form, or both, and who tries to help the student by giving clear and firm guidance or a clearly defined set of procedures to follow. By polarizing the issues in this way it is possible to see that the activity of tutoring is, of course, not quite like either interviewing or counselling, even though it may usefully be compared to both, and at different times and in different contexts it may be appropriate for tutors to draw on either interviewing or counselling skills. Tutoring may be conceived as occupying the middle ground between the two, occasionally verging on one or other, but to be identified with neither.

Although little has been written specifically about tutoring, there are other interpersonal encounters, especially professional-lay consultations, which have been quite extensively studied. This work could be relevant to the tutorial in that many of the same issues are present. One interesting study of doctor-patient interaction (Strong, 1979), found that doctors operated in a number of different modes, two of which were termed the 'clinical' and the 'collegial'. Occasionally, the doctor was able to talk to the patient or the patient's relatives on something like an equal footing, using the correct medical terms, and discussing the case in much the same way as with a colleague. This 'collegial' style of interacting was, however, relatively rare. Mostly, the doctors in the study adopted the 'clinical' approach, offering patients crude oversimplifications of their diagnosis and prescribing treatments dogmatically and without any discussion. This may be a useful distinction for tutors to consider. Are there different ways of conducting tutorials? Do some students somehow manage to qualify for a more 'collegial' relationship, in which they are treated as at least potential equals, so that problems are tackled jointly ('What are we going to do about this?') and within a relationship of trust? If so, this might contrast quite starkly with a mode of interacting with students in which the tutor, instead of negotiating the next step with the student, feels it necessary to tell the student what to do.

Among health professionals it is a commonplace to say that we relate to other people differently according to how we define them, as 'well' or 'sick'. This has sometimes been used as a way of distinguishing between psychotherapy and counselling (Arbuckle, 1967): the former starts from the supposition that the client is 'sick' or in some way needs help to recover the status of a normal human being; the latter tries hard to grant 'normal' status from the start, to respect the client's wishes and to involve the client in his or her own treatment as a matter of principle. Whether or not that holds as a distinction between psychotherapy and counselling, it certainly offers a useful way of distinguishing different ways of relating to the people we are trying to help. If we treat them at the outset as people worthy of our respect we shall behave quite differently than if we regard them as people who, however temporarily, or in however limited a context, have no sensible opinions to offer, since their predicament disqualifies them from engaging with us on that footing.

Similarly, among social workers it has been noted that effective provision of help appears to depend on whether or not the client is perceived as 'worthy', i.e. worth helping (Rees, 1978:107). The client, it is said, has to project and the professional has to recognize what has been called 'a moral character'. It appears, then, that the tutor's initial assessment of the student may be crucial. It is not just, or mainly, in terms of ability (brightest in the class) or academic status (a fourth year Honours student) that the student is assessed, but in terms of what might be termed 'moral status'. The tutorial will be conducted very differently according to whether the tutor judges the student to be generally a worthy person, well-intentioned, honest, reliable and hard-working, or whether the tutor suspects that the student is rather lazy, likely to make excuses and that the excuses could be invented.

In these encounters and interviews (patients consulting their doctor, clients being interviewed by a social worker) the patient or client will often be at a severe disadvantage. Similarly, the student going to see his or her tutor is in a weak position. The question of who controls the interaction is, therefore, a crucial one. The interview format suggests that the interviewer is in control: the counselling format suggests, more interestingly, that while the counsellor potentially has considerable influence in the situation this status is being deliberately renounced in favour of giving the client their say and trying to make sure it is heard. It is here that the idea of an agenda may be helpful. For the distinction between interviewing and counselling is not, of course, that one has a clear agenda while the other does not, but that in one case the agenda is determined by the professional helper while in the other it is determined by the client. Who then determines the agenda when tutor and student meet?

The tutorial: its agenda and its management

Will there be an agenda at all? Both teaching and support can appear as no more than just chatting to students; but if a tutorial is being conducted properly there will be nothing casual about it and its purposes might well be made explicit. The tutorial can then be seen as a professional task carried out by the tutor in the course of his or her professional duties and not something done out of kindness or because of a personal interest in the student.

It might, in any case, seem obvious that the agenda of the tutorial, whether dealing with an academic or personal problem, is set by the student and that it should take shape around the student's expressed needs – a question to be answered or a difficulty resolved. Yet this is to return to the remedial model criticized previously. If tutorial contact is seen not as trouble-shooting, but as fostering ongoing development, we have to acknowledge that the student may not be in a very good position to assess his or her own development, whether academic or personal, and may need help in finding the most appropriate starting-point.

Tutors may sometimes have to take the initiative in raising matters of concern, possibly setting up a tutorial which the student has not requested. Even when the initiative is entirely the student's, the tutor may wonder whether there is perhaps more to the student's agenda than has been revealed, and may probe a little to find out more. It is, of course, possible that there is more to it than they have said; there may even be more to it than they have so far realized. The student may describe symptoms without being able to determine their underlying cause. They may misdescribe or even misperceive their own problems. Ever since Freud, psychologists have claimed that there may be ways in which someone else may be able to understand you better than you can yourself. You may not appreciate the full extent or the real nature of your problem; you may not even realize that you have a problem at all. The individual is sometimes mistaken and may be helped by having this gently pointed out.

Sometimes, then, the agenda which the student brings gets altered or amended as the tutorial proceeds; the tutor focuses attention onto what lies *behind* what the student has said. If it is an academic problem, something misunderstood, the tutor may be able to convert an inarticulate question into a more pertinent one. If it is a more personal matter, again the tutor may be able to draw the student away from his or her own agenda (e.g. self-pity) and focus attention onto something else which represents a realistic way forward, a practical 'next step'. On the other hand, of course, the tutor may be clumsy, lacking the necessary skills and the agenda might then change in an unhelpful way, such as when the student wishes to talk about something and the tutor (because he or she feels insecure on that subject or because it is a personally painful matter which the tutor cannot handle) diverts attention away from this. This can happen simply by accident if the tutor is not alert to the agenda which the student has brought, and quick to identify it clearly and to bring it into focus.

However, there is another scenario which can be described in terms of 'agenda'; that is, when there is a 'hidden' agenda which the student finds it difficult to talk about. Counsellors are familiar with the case of the client who presents one problem when really there is another lurking behind, the first serving simply as a 'calling card'. The skill lies in detecting the hidden agenda, and gently bringing it out into the open so that it can be dealt with. Tutors are not usually trained to do anything like this. Often it does not occur to them that there will be more to uncover besides what the student tells them initially. Doctors are familiar with the patient who consults them about a relatively trivial problem, and then, just as they are about to leave, says 'And while I'm here, doctor . . . ' and raises a much more serious matter which is for some reason more difficult to talk about. Yet tutors, even if fully convinced that the student should supply the agenda and eager to follow the student's lead, are sometimes quite surprised at the idea that the student might not have told the full story straight out. Exercises in discovering the hidden agenda may, therefore, be some of the best introductions to training for tutors.

What these reflections seem to suggest is that it is not so much that the student sets the agenda, or that the tutor allows the student to set the agenda, but rather that the student, in a sense, *is* the agenda and that it is the tutor's job to ensure that this is so. That way of putting it seems to do more justice to the reality of the tutorial situation, though of course the student is no mere passive subject. The tutor cannot abdicate responsibility for managing the interaction.

However, if we say that the tutor has the main responsibility for managing the interaction, then how is this best done?

When two people engage in dialogue, they are doing much more than exchanging words and information. They are exchanging meanings. Skilled personal interaction involves an awareness that the words spoken and the meaning intended do not always correspond exactly. This is not only true of the inarticulate person who doesn't express him or herself very well, but also of the fluent speaker who uses language flexibly and skilfully. Conversation has to be analysed rather as a game with 'moves'. One may throw down a challenge, hold out an olive-branch or offer congratulations, while the actual words used might be in the form of, say, a question which, written down, would look like a request for information. Person-to-person discussion quickly runs into difficulties if these linguistic subtleties are not recognized. And often they are not, especially in a tutor–student conversation where a lot may be at stake, and where, if misunderstandings arise, the temptation to quote back the actual words used may be very great.

It is not only that in trying to understand what someone else is saying we have to read between the lines; we also have to read their non-verbal communication which may be more eloquent than their actual words. One of the great advantages of a tutorial is that it provides an opportunity to pay attention to one student at a time; it allows the tutor to concentrate on the needs of a particular individual and to listen to what he or she 'says' in whatever way. If the tutor simply uses it as an opportunity to talk and to teach, this opportunity has been lost or wasted.

When people are in a relatively strong position, we know how they are most likely to behave. They will initiate the interaction and they will determine when it ends; they will set the agenda, ask the questions and decide whether the answers are adequate or not; they will often address the other informally; and they will feel free to interrupt and to change the subject at any point. Non-verbal behaviour, too, will be used to establish and maintain dominance, e.g. not looking at the other so as to give little chance of feedback, ignoring any signs that the other is either agreeing or disagreeing, or is puzzled or confused or embarrassed, occasionally looking at the other too long and too hard, so that they feel their personal space is being invaded (Gahagan, 1984:62f). This could be a description of a typical tutorial. There is no doubt who is in control. The student is likely to defer to the tutor, to wait for the tutor to speak first and signal when the tutorial should come to an end, to let the tutor determine the agenda, to respond rather than to initiate, to follow any changes of direction and to give way whenever interrupted (Gahagan, 1984:74f). Taken together these are unmistakable signs of dominance and submission.

However, a tutorial does not have to be conducted like this, and it should not be conceived as something the tutor 'gives' and the student 'receives', but rather as something which happens *between* two people, an interaction. It involves collaboration and partnership. If there is an analogy with a piece of music, it is not one played by the tutor, and heard and responded to by the student, but rather a duet, played by both together and brought off jointly. Perhaps the most appropriate analogy is that of a dance (Stern, 1977). There are two parties to it; ideally, whatever happens has to be mutually understood, agreed and accepted. Often it is very far from this ideal.

What needs to be underlined here is the fact that, although we may analyse a tutorial as a social encounter, drawing on the insights and language of social psychology to interpret what is going on, nonetheless, the tutorial is a rather special example of such interaction in that it is by definition contrived. As we have seen, the tutor is in the formal sense responsible for managing the interaction. It is, therefore, not quite like a dance or a duet in which the two partners find mutually satisfying ways of performing. It is a dance in which one of the partners 'leads'. Of course, the tutor may be socially clumsy, awkward or shy in this kind of social setting; and the student may be extremely skilled at social interaction. In practice, it is possible that the student may, in effect, conduct the tutorial. Yet that is not what is meant to happen. It is the tutor's responsibility to manage, on behalf of the student, what is essentially an interactive process.

The use and abuse of power

People have different tolerances with regard to their personal affairs, and what one person regards as taking a friendly interest, another may regard as an unwarranted invasion of his or her private life. Some students may be highly sensitive on such matters, guarding their privacy quite jealously, so that an innocent enquiry about where they are spending the summer vacation will be felt to be inappropriate and intrusive, and may get a frosty response. Some may have areas of their life which are for some reason 'no go' areas to all but their closest friends, yet in other respects may be quite relaxed and open.

Apart from individual sensitivities and particularly difficult personal circumstances, there are cultural and gender differences which can lead easily to misunderstanding. A female student who told her male tutor that she had to go into hospital for a few days might not expect to be quizzed for details as to exactly what was wrong; yet a male student in the same circumstances would probably interpret such questions as friendly concern. There are wide differences in the amount of psychological space each individual expects for him or herself and habitually allows to others. The extent to which personal matters, concerning family life for instance, are spoken of outside the home can vary greatly. Cultural and religious inhibitions sometimes render whole areas of life 'taboo'. To receive confidences from someone else is to have power over them; by confiding in you, the other person becomes vulnerable to you. While it is only within a safe relationship that such a risk can be contemplated, it is always a risky procedure.

What happens when the tutor tries to share the student's vulnerability by choosing to come off his or her pedestal, admitting to human failings and offering to engage with the student as a fallible human being? A willingness to expose oneself and to let one's own vulnerability show can go some way towards redressing the imbalance of power. Professional counsellors sometimes use disclosure of bits of themselves as a deliberate tool in helping the other. Tutors, by referring only sparingly to their personal lives, not in a self-indulgent way, but with careful control and self-discipline, may enhance their performance of their helping role. A skilful and thoroughly professional performance does not rule out relating to people in a very personal way.

Of course, people who come seeking help with their problems do not want to hear about anyone else's. Yet within a long-term relationship it may be quite natural for the helper to reveal things about him or herself as a way of getting alongside the other. So while as a general rule tutors need to refrain from talking about themselves, it is possible to make discriminating use of one's own personal history to enhance one's effectiveness in helping. A tutor anxious to encourage a student who has just failed an examination, for instance, might reveal the fact that he or she once had to resit an important examination. Such a disclosure might enable the student to relate to the tutor as a person rather than simply as a representative of the institution or of a class of people who do not have problems.

The essential point, though, is that this is still a very 'powerful' thing to do. If the disclosure is done deliberately, not inadvertently, it falls into place as part of the tutor's attempt to act responsibly to 'manage' the encounter for the benefit of the student. Tutors may allow some of their own vulnerability to show, but that does not mean breaking down in tears with someone who is emotionally upset; the aim is to engage with the experience of the other, but without totally identifying with it so as to have no detachment left to offer them.

We can now identify three aspects of interpersonal power as it affects the tutorial relationship.

First, it is not just that in the context of higher education tutors are on a different footing from, and respected by, students, but that they are *entitled* to be. They have the major responsibility for managing the interaction *and rightly so*.

Yet the student is not necessarily disadvantaged by being the weaker party. Within the tutor–student relationship there are built-in assumptions which act in the student's interests. For instance, a tutor cannot legitimately respond to a student's request for help with a shrug, or say 'There's nothing I can do; I have no more influence here than you do.' Within this professional context the power of the tutor is supposed to be available to the student. It is an abuse of this professionally-bestowed power if it is exercised irresponsibly or selfishly. It is, indeed, a kind of breach of contract, in the sense that the student as client is, indirectly, buying a service from the tutor. The fact that what students are buying is tutelage, which implies putting themselves under the tutors's guidance, makes no difference. They are entitled to get what they bargained for, no more and no less.

Of course, the difficulty with buying a higher education experience is that the client can often have only a rather hazy idea of what he or she wants in advance of getting it. That is why a great deal of trust is required. What precisely is involved may only gradually become clear as the course proceeds. It may pose sharp challenges to beliefs and commitments, and be experienced as a process of personal as well as intellectual upheaval. It may involve specific experiences which the student finds uncongenial or initially threatening, e.g. an industrial placement, a presentation to the rest of the class, participation in a role play exercise, which the tutor is entitled to insist are essential if the student is to gain full benefit. At the same time, the student, by enrolling on a course, is not giving the tutor a blank cheque; in a tutorial relationship students do not have to follow wherever the tutor leads. There are certain procedural principles which are generally presupposed within this context by virtue of being written into the shared understanding of the educational process: the student is not contracting to be bullied into learning, or to be frightened into agreement. By enrolling for a course the student is not giving permission to be harassed, sexually or otherwise.

The tutor is in a very different position, able to enter the contract with both eyes wide open. By undertaking to deliver a service for payment, the tutor implicitly acknowledges that it may involve uncongenial tasks, inconvenient duties and tiresome responsibilities. Yet it is understood to be a professional engagement, limited to a specific context; it does not have to impinge upon the tutor's private life. Its content lies to a very large extent in the tutor's own hands, since it is the tutor's own expertise that is to be passed on to the student. It cannot be said to the tutor, as it can to the student, that participation in a particular activity is for his or her own good. That is not why the tutor is there. The enterprise is for the student's good, an altruistic activity in which the tutor has voluntarily undertaken to take part.

One could put this another way by saying that, on the tutor's part, the norms of behaviour are largely set by the notion of professional responsibility, including the responsible use of power and the deliberate sharing of knowledge in a way that respects the other. The tutor's commitment to the course is a professional one; there would have to be extraordinary, overriding reasons to warrant opting out of such an obligation freely entered into. On the student's part, on the other hand, the key concepts are trust and evaluation; enrolment on a course entails an element of surrender to the judgement of others, yet this is constantly checked, retrospectively, by an ongoing process of evaluation. The student's commitment to the course is necessarily provisional, conditional upon satisfactory answers being given to questions like 'Am I getting what I want out of this?' The student is, therefore, not without power, but it is of a different sort from that of the tutor. It is the power of the client to take custom elsewhere, not the institutional legitimacy enjoyed by the tutor.

Second, we should observe that the balance of power in the real world of social relationships may be very different from that predicted by an analysis of the formal role relationships. Those who occupy the most powerful positions do not necessarily have everything under control. On the contrary, they may feel trapped, with very little room for manoeuvre. So while we may say, formally speaking, that the tutor carries responsibility for managing the interaction with the student, we must recognize that, in practice, it may be the student who takes the initiative. Sometimes students will effectively run their own tutorial, may indeed run rings round the tutor. It is even possible that, in the course of what is ostensibly a tutorial conducted by the tutor for the benefit of the student, the student might give the tutor some valuable advice, in much the same way as he or she might occasionally teach the tutor a thing or two.

Of course, students, too, may misuse their power. It is not only tutors who may harass students; students may harass tutors. It needs to be said that students can sometimes be disturbingly manipulative in their dealings with their tutors.

Third, then, is it possible to distinguish different kinds of power? Given that the tutor's power is legitimately, even if not always effectively exercised, where does it get its legitimacy from? What bestows power in this context is not just the recognition from the outset on the part of the student that the tutor is a potential examiner; it is that the tutor is on the inside of the institution in a way that the student is not. The tutor's involvement in the management of the institution and its procedures, however uninterested he or she may actually be in these matters, necessarily skews the relationship and renders it asymmetrical.

Like Stanley Milgram's white-coated experimenters (1974), tutors operate within a social framework in which there is an in-built presumption that they know what they are up to. They may not actually be able to get away with murder, but they undoubtedly derive considerable power from their official position. Tutors sometimes show little awareness of this, and are inclined to play it down, encouraging the use of first names and other signs of informality. However, students are rarely fooled by this into thinking of the relationship as an equal one, for they know that in the last resort the tutor could have a great deal of influence on their future. What they seek is not a pretended renunciation of power, but its responsible exercise on their behalf.

In view of what has been said, how do tutor and student go about coming to terms with each other within an institutional context which, as we have seen, puts them on an unequal footing? For both parties it would be very easy to slip into a relationship which was in some way exploitative, which took unfair advantage of the tutor's position vis-à-vis the student, or in which, more simply, the student relinquished responsibility to the tutor. Tutors need to be clear that, even when there are matters on which they have to insist, such as the meeting of course requirements, there must always be room for the student to make his or her own decision, and to take the consequences for good or ill.

Students in higher education are legally adults and, therefore, the normal assumption must be that they are capable of taking charge of their own lives. Where, exceptionally, their ability to do this has broken down, any interference by others will be by agreement, as temporary as possible, and minimal. It will be designed to get the student back on his or her own feet, functioning independently. This general principle applies to all helping, but it is particularly important where the helper is in a position of authority or influence, or where other factors may intrude upon the situation so that one cannot be sure whether the take-up of offers of help is genuinely voluntary.

It may now be clear why it is necessary to claim not only that the tutorial relationship is an asymmetrical one, in that there is more power on one side than on the other, but that it is *inherently* asymmetrical. The way tutor and student relate in a teaching/learning setting governs the way they relate in other situations within the institutional context. Thus, the inequality of the tutor–student *helping* relationship is intrinsic to the tutor–student *teaching* relationship, and analogous to it. The problem for the tutor is much the same in each case; it is to exercise power responsibly and professionally, to help without helping too much. Those reputed to be the best teachers may actually leave least room for the student to discover anything for themselves; similarly, the tutors who appear most concerned and conscientious may be so quick to anticipate the student's needs that they provide help before the student has had time to ask for it or realized the need for it. Both may be a misuse of the tutor's superior power in this situation. Just as one should avoid spoon-feeding in teaching so one should avoid dependency in support and for much the same reason.

The paradox of helping

In any helping relationship there is always the problem of overdoing it. To help too much is, paradoxically, *un*helpful. That there is a danger of inducing helplessness cannot be denied. Martin Seligman (1975), in his book *Helplessness*, develops an ambitious theory about the ways in which people may learn to be helpless. He offers his theory as an explanation of a range of very different things: slow development in childhood learning, the institutionalization of old people, states of mental depression and the high mortality rate of men whose wives have recently died. All of these may be interpreted as forms of 'learned helplessness'. It would seem a small step to add to this list students who, once given a great deal of support, seem subsequently to be unable to manage without this help and become chronically dependent upon their tutor. Could this be another manifestation of the same phenomenon?

In view of what is sometimes made of the idea of a 'dependency culture' as a reason for dismantling welfare provision, one should be wary of drawing general conclusions from quite limited evidence in other areas. Yet there is no reason to deny that the provision of well-intentioned help can reduce the motivation to help oneself. It is certainly possible that tutors sometimes inadvertently encourage an unhealthy dependency in students who are already somewhat insecure. However, it may not be the sheer *amount* of help which is experienced as disabling but rather the *kind* of help and the *way* it is given.

An over-dependent, clinging relationship creates problems of its own and is difficult to terminate without damage. But who is clinging to whom? Busy tutors, conscious of the needs of their other students as well as all their other responsibilities, may still find themselves devoting an excessive amount of time and attention to one student. This has to be seen not simply as the student's problem (e.g. socially insecure, struggling with the course), nor as the tutor's problem (e.g. pathologically lonely, eager to feel needed), but rather as a problem of the relationship and how it has developed. That said, it must still be reasserted that the tutor has to take responsibility for managing the relationship. The tutor has the difficult and perhaps paradoxical task of assuming most of the responsibility for ensuring that the relationship is not one in which the tutor dominates the student; or, for that matter, one in which the student dominates the tutor.

Occasionally students may pester a tutor for help and support, or perhaps, more subtly, find ways of manipulating the tutor into giving an inordinate amount of time to them. It might appear that for the student to manipulate the tutor was simply the opposite case of the tutor exploiting the student, control having effectively passed out of the tutor's hands and into the hands of the student. Yet a more careful analysis might reveal that the manipulation was another form of dependency; that for the student to try to manipulate the tutor was a sign of weakness not strength. The student is more likely to be wanting to cling than to dominate. The relationship has become so personally important that the student dare not let go, and is constantly manoeuvring the tutor into a helping position for fear that the tutor will not otherwise be available.

Yet there is something of a paradox here too. For when the relationship has become one in which the tutor is virtually on the end of a string, at the student's beck and call, this does not satisfy, for what the student really wants is a voluntary relationship. Constantly asking for help creates a situation in which help is only given in response to demand and can hardly ever be freely offered.

By looking briefly at some of the ways in which helping relationships can become dysfunctional it has been possible to show that helping is a paradoxical activity. So, of course, is teaching. As already pointed out, tutors in higher education normally discourage students from becoming over-dependent for basically the same reason that they resist spoon-feeding in teaching; because in both causes to overdo it is ultimately self-defeating.

This discussion has shown up more than just the unequal status of tutor and student. It has revealed the extent of the tutor's responsibility for managing the helping process and how the tutor's power lies in being on the inside of this process in a way that the student is not. It has also exposed a fundamental principle of helping, that most people most of the time are perfectly capable of helping themselves once their situation can be viewed objectively, and that to provide this objectivity is often the best way, sometimes the only way, they can be helped without being in some way diminished.

Thus, ideally we might think of the tutor who helps a student not so much as a helping agent, but rather as instrumental in facilitating the helping process. It is not that the tutor brings to the encounter a superior wisdom with which to solve the student's problems, but rather that the tutor, by virtue of the role occupied, the human qualities shown and the professional skills deployed, enables the helping process to occur.

There are, indeed, skills which individuals possess or may acquire so as to be more effective helpers. Yet tutoring is not reducible to a set of skills, still less to knowing about interpersonal behaviour. The fact is that tutors are professionally required to be supportive and helpful to students, without necessarily sharing or even fully understanding their point of view. What matters is not whether they know about empathy, only whether they show it.

The trouble is that we can all behave considerately and humanely when we are not too busy, when we are feeling in a good mood, relaxed and un-hurried, when the student is someone we know and like, when we are on a 'safe' subject, etc. In such circumstances it is not too difficult to respond to students' needs calmly, thoughtfully and sensitively. However, often it is not like this. Students may ask awkward questions, introduce a very different perspective with which we have very little sympathy or patience; they may surprise us, shock us, or in some way 'put us on the spot' or challenge us, perhaps quite unintentionally; worse still, they may disagree with us, or actually complain to us about something, or perhaps unwittingly touch on what is, for us, a rather sensitive area. On these occasions we may find ourselves responding defensively. In addition to skill, therefore, we need qualities which have traditionally been defined as 'moral': patience, respect for the other, a willingness to put the other's interests above our own, altruism, caring. The tutorial relationship, like any other relationship, works best when these qualities are dependably present; without them it may all too easily lapse into some form of exploitation, manipulation, dependency or harassment.

7

Confidentiality

As the previous chapter was concerned to show, a good working relation-ship between tutor and student depends not on intimacy, but on mutual respect and trust, providing a secure framework within which both can get on with their respective tasks of teaching and learning. It is a mistake to suppose that discussion of more personal matters, possibly of a confidential nature, presupposes a relationship that is closer, warmer or more intimate. An effective tutorial relationship will not be a cosy one. On the contrary, if it is to allow and even perhaps facilitate the offer of criticism and its accept-ance, it is essential that the relationship is straightforward and businesslike, and is characterized by frankness and mutual respect. The crucial factors are the tutor's reliability and consistency in providing a safe and supportive relationship.

Dealing with sensitive information

One might think that the problem of confidentiality had more to do with the difficulty of keeping other people's secrets than with not knowing what one should do with them; the actual *idea* of confidentiality might seem rela-tively unproblematic. However, as consideration of a couple of examples will quickly show, a tutor may find that in practice it is extremely difficult to know how to handle sensitive information about students. Suppose a tutor asks a student about his poor attendance at a Thursday class, and gets the reply 'Well, as a matter of fact I haven't been coming to *any* of the classes on Thursdays. I have a part-time job that clashes with that part of the programme, and I can't afford to give it up.'

Here is a case where there might be a difference of opinion as to how the tutor should react. It depends to some extent upon the course and the con-text. Many courses have a formal attendance requirement and in this case the student is not only failing to meet that requirement, but is stating that he has no intention of meeting it. If the student is in receipt of a grant on the understanding that he is a full-time student, the grant-awarding authority wants to know that the student is, in fact, following the course full-time as prescribed, and is entitled to be told of any failure to meet course requirements. Yet few tutors would immediately inform the grant-awarding authority that this student was not meeting course requirements. Many would, on the contrary, have a good deal of sympathy for a student who was trying to hold down a part-time job and, in spite of this disadvantage, intended to fulfil exactly the same coursework commitments and to pass the same end-of-course examinations as other students. The student might have hoped that persistent absence on Thursdays would go unnoticed. Yet, once it is revealed to the tutor, what is an appropriate response?

Much depends upon whether the student is, in fact, infringing any formal regulation; this a technical matter. Some tutors (and courses and institutions) take the view that in higher education it is up to the student as to how regularly he or she attends lectures and classes. With recent moves to permit more flexible modes of attendance and towards competency-based assessment in which learning outcomes are more important than the processes by which the learning has taken place, it might seem particularly inappropriate at the present time to penalize a student who might be both able and conscientious for no other reason than that one part of the course has been missed. This student has, after all, been honest about the situation. When challenged, the student could easily have simply promised to attend more regularly; instead, the full story has been frankly revealed. How many more students are there, perhaps following the same course, who are holding down part-time jobs without ever revealing the fact to their tutors because they do not want to jeopardize their status as full-time students?

Yet perhaps the section of the course missed was part of the compulsory core of the course? Possibly attendance has been made a course requirement not for some formal or bureaucratic reason, but because the course being followed does, in fact, depend crucially upon full participation? What if it is a course of professional training which has no final examination, but in which the experience of practical exercises is absolutely essential to the course as a whole?

Enough has been said to show that in this case, the question for the tutor of how to handle the information the student has volunteered is not a straightforward one.

Here is another example. A married woman is deserted by her husband immediately prior to her first year examinations. She informs her Course Tutor of her circumstances, but insists that she wants to carry on as if nothing has happened. She is anxious that none of the other students should know about it. 'I think I can cope with the exams', she says, 'but I don't think I can cope with other people knowing.'

How might the tutor respond to this request? It seems perfectly reasonable and one would hope that in such circumstances most tutors would feel able to give her the reassurance that she seeks. Unlike the previous example where the demands of the part-time job conflicted directly with the requirements of the course, in this example the information has strictly speaking no bearing upon the course as such. The state of a student's marriage, domestic arrangements or family relationships is an entirely private matter which does not normally need to concern a Course Tutor. This student is under no obligation to tell anybody about her private affairs.

So why has she done so? The most obvious explanation is that, in spite of her resolve to carry on as normal, she fears that she may not manage this, so she wants the Course Tutor to speak up for her in the Examination Board. This seems very sensible of her and is surely a reasonable request? However, there are some further considerations involved. The Examination Board can hardly take into account mitigating circumstances unless it knows what those circumstances are. Is she willing that the Examination Board be told? Can the Course Tutor guarantee that information given to the Examination Board will not, in due course, reach her fellow-students? When dealing with a distraught student on the eve of her examinations many tutors would unhesitatingly accede to her request, anxious to put her mind at rest, promising that the personal information she had given them would be revealed to no one. Later, after she had, say, performed very badly in some of the examinations or perhaps failed to attend for one of them, the tutor might regret having given such an unequivocal promise of secrecy.

On the other hand, the Course Tutor might have explored the issues with the student a little further. For instance, is this information which is to be passed to the Examination Board as a matter of course, on the understanding that it is confidential? Or is it, on the other hand, information which is only to be passed to the Examination Board if necessary, i.e. if she is in danger of failing the course? The latter situation is sometimes formalized by a procedure whereby the student provides the Board with a letter in a sealed envelope, only to be opened in case of failure. However, this procedure is not universally adopted, and the student may have to choose between either keeping the information confidential, in which case it cannot be taken into consideration, or asking for it to be taken into consideration, in which case it must be revealed.[1] Revealed to whom, though? Sometimes a small sub-group of the Examination Board will vet confidential disclosures. The precise details of these procedures could make a crucial difference to how a case might be handled. In this particular instance there may be a further consideration. Under the immediate impact of such a domestic crisis the point may not be that nobody else must *ever* know, but rather that the student would find it difficult if it became known in the immediate future. The student's request might be interpreted as 'Please don't tell anyone *just yet*'. Again, this needs to be clarified.

A cynical view might be that the student wants, in effect, to take out an 'insurance policy'. One can hardly blame her for trying; to ask that confidentiality be preserved intact while at the same time offering an excuse for a possibly below-par performance is, in effect, an insurance that costs nothing. Some tutors might justifiably point out that, if special consideration is to be given to a student and especially if a lower standard of work is to be accepted or condoned, it is reasonable to insist that there is some publicly-available evidence; more must be required than telling one's tutor privately. In the case of medical conditions which are offered as 'mitigating circumstances' it is usual to insist on evidence in the form of a medical certificate from a doctor. What would be the appropriate 'proof' in this case? Or are there occasions when a student's own word may be accepted as proof enough without any independent verification? In this example, it is hardly the sort of story which a student would invent, yet students *do* invent stories, and those who are the guardians of standards are right to want to check.

Consideration of these two examples brings out some of the complexities here. What is quite apparent is that one cannot simply distinguish between two sorts of information: that which may be spoken about and that which may not. Confidentiality cannot be sensibly conceived as a kind of 'news blackout'. There is real difficulty in the notion that if something is confidential then absolutely no one should be told. It is not as if there were a two-way switch which could be either 'on' or 'off' when one is listening to the various things a student may say; rather, there is a sliding scale, ranging from ordinary information on which there need be no embargo and which can be spoken of openly, to matters which have to be kept hidden and even actively concealed because rightly or wrongly one party regards them as 'top secret'. Clearly, this is an area in which a great deal of discretion has to be exercised and in which careful judgements have to be made.

A private conversation between two people might be regarded by both as 'off-the-record' and not normally to be relayed to anyone else without the other's permission. Yet there are special circumstances surrounding the tutorial encounter where a student and a member of teaching staff have a private conversation: confidences are likely to be passed from the student to the tutor and not vice versa; the student is, therefore, in a specially vulnerable position. Because most tutors are well aware of that they are often very strict with themselves where confidentiality is concerned. Yet confidentiality is not the same as secrecy and does not lend itself to the rigid application of a rule; rather, a great deal of discretion has to be exercised. The tutor who tries to safeguard the best interests of the student may perhaps find that they conflict with the student's stated wishes. Moreover, as we have seen already, the role of tutor is not simply that of advocate; teaching staff have a wide range of responsibilities, of which upholding the interests of the individual student is only one.

Privacy, secrecy and confidentiality

It helps to distinguish between the concepts of privacy, secrecy and confidentiality. Although the terms are sometimes used very loosely, even interchangeably, their meanings are slightly different.

Privacy has to do with the circumstances or the context of the tutorial relationship. Tutors may be able to offer students very little privacy if by that is meant a guarantee that they are seen individually and may speak without being overheard or interrupted. The central idea of 'privacy' is that of being 'set apart' or 'put on one side'. It is the seclusion of the setting, rather than the intimacy of the relationship or the sensitivity of the information, that is signalled by the use of the word 'private'.

Secrecy has more to do with the actual material that passes from one to another, as to whether it should be 'classified' information or not. Within the context of a private conversation, certain bits of information may be considered secrets, not to be disclosed. The root meaning of 'secret' is 'sifted', i.e. discerned or distinguished as different and, therefore, to be kept separate. As classified information, a secret is not just kept separate, it is kept concealed; it therefore carries the suggestion of being somewhat mysterious, legitimately arousing some curiosity. Material that is secret has restricted circulation confined to those who are 'in the know', effectively excluding others. Thus, while privacy is primarily about avoidance of publicity, secrecy is about the avoidance of disclosure. If something is private it is removed from the public domain; if it is secret it is hidden from view.

Confidentiality is perhaps more complicated than either privacy or secrecy, since it is centrally concerned with the actual relationship between the two parties; not with the environmental conditions (which will often though not necessarily be private) nor with the material that passes from one to the other (which will often though not necessarily be secret), but with the trusting nature of the relationship. The basic idea is that of being able to trust the other. It suggests a relationship in which one person regards the other as trustworthy and is willing to entrust him or her with things that are not being entrusted to others. Confidentiality indicates a privileged relationship in the literal sense that it has its own rules; normal rules do not apply. A relationship of this sort is characterized by integrity and respect; it is one that can be relied on with complete assurance. There is a commitment to the other which means that whatever is passed on will be kept safe.

In the light of this analysis, then, we may say that an individual tutorial may sometimes be a private conversation; that within this private conversation it is possible that the student might reveal some secret information; and that it is expected that tutors in whom students have confidence will sometimes be entrusted with information on the understanding that they will keep it safe. Thus, there are basically three different things here and it helps if they are not confused.

Our concern here is with confidentiality. Unlike privacy, it is not easy to recognize whether or when the appropriate conditions are being met. Unlike secrecy, it is not something which operates at certain times and not at others, or in relation to certain categories of material and not to the rest. There may, perhaps, be degrees of privacy, and degrees of secrecy; there are certainly degrees of confidentiality. How might we characterize them? Are there perhaps a number of different variables involved? In the proposed model that follows, five dimensions of confidentiality are identified: levels of sensitivity, of seriousness, of relevance, of permission and of disclosure.

Confidentiality: a five-dimensional model

First, there are *levels of sensitivity of information*. For instance, in normal circumstances it would not occur to most students to think of their name and address as confidential information, though one could imagine a situation where even these basic facts about a person could become extremely sensitive – e.g. if the student is being pursued by a debt-collecting agency or by a jilted lover. By contrast, a person's sexual orientation would be generally regarded as highly sensitive information, and not at all the sort of thing to be divulged to anyone else. Between these two extremes lie matters such as one's age, marital status, academic qualifications and health record. Sensitivity, however, is a very subjective affair; some students may be very sensitive about their age; others about an unusual middle name. Different people want different things kept confidential in different contexts.

So we have to indicate a second, more objective distinction between *matters which are serious in their effects and those which are relatively trivial*. Facts about a student's past may have very little significance ('she once lived in Bolton') or may be potentially very damaging if revealed ('he was once on heroin'). A student's financial difficulties may have far-reaching consequences including forced withdrawal from the course; but other matters which are felt to be serious by the student and about which the student is extremely sensitive (e.g. going bald) may be of no consequence whatsoever.

Third, there is the question of *how far these pieces of information might have a bearing on the student's work*. There are certain facts, such as a student's previous experience and qualifications, which for a student on a vocational course can hardly be treated as confidential. For part-time students on courses paid for by their employers their current job may be an important part of the total experience. For students on sandwich courses their placement may be of central significance. So these are not by any stretch of the imagination irrelevant facts about a student which might be kept quite separate from the course itself. The tutor may wish to refer to the workplace experience, or encourage the student to illustrate the application of some theory. It is possible, then, to imagine another sliding scale, running from information about the student that may be regarded as a purely personal matter and in which tutors have no strictly professional interest since it is *irrelevant* to the course (e.g. their marital status, their hobbies, their political commitments), through information that may be *indirectly relevant* to the course (e.g. their inability to concentrate following a family bereavement), to information that is *directly relevant* to the course (e.g. their coursework marks, their entry qualifications, etc.). It is worth noting that even in the latter case this is private information, not to be spoken of freely without the student's agreement. It is also worth noting that for certain courses a physical disability might be directly relevant to student's ability to continue the course. Clearly, a tutor needs a great deal of tact and discretion not simply in deciding whether these matters are appropriate to mention, but precisely when, how and to whom.

Fourth, there is *the extent to which the student gives permission* for information to be revealed. This might seem a little odd; surely, the student either does give permission or does not? If fact, of course, it is not like that. One experiences the full range of attitudes, from 'If you tell anyone I'll kill you' to a specific request: 'I would be grateful if you would tell the other students; it will come better from you.' It is not often that a student swears a member of staff to secrecy. More often, the student reveals some information first and only subsequently (perhaps prompted by the tutor?) considers the question of how confidential it is, and who else, if anybody, should be told. Students sometimes say they don't mind if you tell X, but please don't tell Y. Or they may say that they know the information will leak out eventually, but they don't want anyone to know just yet. Quite often what a student says is at odds with what he or she seems to want; for instance, the student may feign nonchalance or apathy and say 'I don't care who you tell', which barely disguises quite strong feelings that it is none of anyone else's business.

This analysis would not be complete without identifying a fifth variable: *different levels of disclosure*. It is not often noticed that there are many different ways in which the recipient of confidential information can handle it. One response is simply to say 'My lips are sealed.' This appears to offer a very strong form of secrecy which may sometimes be quite hard to maintain, i.e. that even under close questioning from a trusted colleague the tutor will give away nothing – not even the fact that he or she is privy to some information which could conceivably shed light on the student's performance. Many tutors would feel that little harm could come (and perhaps some good be done) by revealing to colleagues that there are more facts available about a particular student, and that they are aware of some of them even if they are unable to divulge them. Sometimes the burden of others' confidences is quite hard to bear and it may help to share the burden with someone who is quite outside the situation, telling the story, but without mentioning the student's name. More commonly still, having given the student the assurance that what they have told you will go no further, the tutor realizes that it is very much in the student's interest that one or more colleagues should be alerted to the situation. Clearly, this should not happen; the student's permission should be sought first. Yet the motive here is very much to safeguard the student's interests, and it is not at all the same as disclosing confidential information inadvertently, for no other reason but one's own carelessness. Worse still is deliberate and indiscriminate broadcasting of confidential information, orally or (worst of all) in writing.

Professional responsibility

Like many other professional people, teachers in higher education cannot do their job well without knowing a good deal about those they teach, more than just information about their previous attainments in the subject. Within a good teacher–student relationship it is inevitable that other matters will come to light, such as illness or difficult domestic circumstances, and not always because they have some bearing on the student's work. These items of information will not have been sought out, nor perhaps deliberately 'confided'. There may have been no opportunity to negotiate the terms on which the information was passed on. It can happen, say, that two separate pieces of information reach the tutor from different sources; it may be the merest coincidence; yet once in possession of these two facts the tutor cannot help putting them together and drawing a conclusion. Neither of the informants knows what the tutor knows or that the tutor has this knowledge, so the question of gaining their consent cannot apply.

How does a professional person deal with this sort of information? There is really no simple answer except to say that it has to be handled with discretion, i.e. keeping things in separate compartments. It is a matter of judgement, the kind of judgement of which professional people are deemed capable and with which they are entrusted.

Tutors have tended to look to other professions to see how they handle matters of confidentiality; in particular, the influential ideas of pastoral care and of counselling have suggested that the priest's confessional or the counsellor's consultation might serve as an appropriate model.[2] However, the tutor operates very differently from either, often dealing with more than one 'client' at once. Also, it is often not realized that the priest who hears confessions will also go to confession himself or that the counselling profession has developed strict rules about 'supervision', the point being that it is simply unprofessional to attempt to carry the burden of others' secrets on the basis that one serves as the place where the buck stops and where information is simply collected. The attempt to operate as blotting paper, single-handedly soaking up other people's troubles, is misguided, even dangerous, and one is entitled to be suspicious of anyone who offers that service, to ask questions about their motivation and, indeed, their mental health. Chaplains and counsellors operating professionally within higher education institutions are reluctant to act as a kind of sump to the whole system and will seek to operate more like a safe pair of hands within a safe system, i.e. one on which one can rely because there is mutual trust enabling private and confidential information to be handled sensibly and sensitively. This seems a better model for tutors, too.

The relationship between student and tutor may be quite personal, but is not exclusive. Within an institution of higher education students may establish relationships with several members of staff, some of whom work together; so there is quite likely to be a network of relationships. In such a context, it may not be helpful to think of confidentiality simply in terms of the one-to-one relationship, or to apply rules of procedure which have been developed by counsellors, psychotherapists or chaplains. A more helpful model might be that of the social worker who, while having an individual case-load, often works closely with colleagues. In the social work context, the case-conference, where a number of professionals share information about a particular case, is now quite common. When case-loads are adjusted or when members of the team leave and are replaced, there are relatively straight-forward procedures for briefing one's colleagues and passing over the relevant file of information. Nor is it simply a matter of determining formal procedures, but rather of creating an institutional climate in which both the sharing and the withholding of information may be done appropriately.

The teaching profession has generally been much less good at dealing with sensitive information. Within higher education it is not unknown for confidential information to become common knowledge; equally, there are occasions (notably in examination boards) when secrecy is perhaps taken too far. While teachers in higher education routinely pass each other information about students' marks and grades, they are very wary of sharing more personal information. There is, indeed, a real difficulty for tutors who are responsible both for helping students and assessing them. However, the problems are not insuperable; it is better described as role strain than role conflict. There are ways of acting responsibly and professionally, and it is a mistake for staff in higher education to think that they are caught on the horns of a hopeless dilemma.

This chapter has been concerned to show the complexity of the idea of confidentiality, to distinguish it from simpler notions of keeping secrets, to unpack some of the variables involved, and to put the concept in the context of professional responsibility. Of course, the ground rules should be as clear as possible, yet in the end there are bound to be difficult cases where one has to make a judgement about what is best to do. The key to confidentiality, it is suggested, is trust. It has more to do with the quality of the relationship than the nature of the material confided or the fact that others are excluded.

Tutors may feel that to possess confidential information about a student imposes an intolerable burden and, especially if unsure of how to react, be glad of an opportunity to share it with someone else who can be trusted. This serves two purposes: it acts as a safety-valve and it widens the range of expertise available to the student. It is a mistake to regard this as a reprehensible breach of confidentiality; on the contrary, it is responsible professional behaviour. Of course, it is advisable to find one's own support outside the immediate situation and to consult someone who is not personally involved, not least because they may be able to see things in a more detached way. In a sensible professional context staff should not feel they have to offer support to students while feeling unsupported themselves. It ought to be possible for a tutor to involve colleagues and especially to be able to refer students to others who can offer specialist help when required. The next chapter addresses the question of the limits of the tutor's role, and the point at which referral may be appropriate and advisable.

Notes

1. The situation here is somewhat different from, say, an application for financial assistance, where there might be no need for anyone other than the student adviser or personal tutor to know the full details of the student's circumstances and where it might be enough for the member of staff simply to vouch for the fact that the necessary conditions (e.g. of hardship) were met. However, awarding a qualification is not like helping someone out of a hole. An academic award becomes a lifelong possession affecting job opportunities, social status and long-term career prospects. Something which confers public recognition in this way requires a criteria be met publicly.
2. A recent article (Phillips, 1991) exposes, with unusual frankness, the uncertainty which, even for professional counsellors, often surrounds this issue.

8

The Tutor's Role

If students are required to explain why they have not completed course requirements they are bound to reveal some details of their personal circumstances. So even a tutor who does not find this part of the job particularly enjoyable or rewarding and who is reluctant to get involved in students' personal lives, nonetheless, finds it impossible not to do so. Yet, interestingly, even when tutors feel overburdened with students' problems they rarely react with criticism of the students ('they should learn to stand on their own two feet'), but nearly always with self-criticism ('perhaps I should draw the line at this'). Thus, tutors are constantly blaming themselves for not drawing a clear enough line between academic assistance and personal support, or for not drawing it firmly enough, or for not drawing it in the right place. All this suggests that the boundaries of the role need to be marked out much more clearly.

Front-line support

The value of the help and support which tutors give students is rarely spelt out. What is their distinctive contribution, and how does it relate to the other supports available? The image is sometimes used of tutors acting as the 'front-line' of student support, with other more specialized supports available and waiting in the wings ready to become involved if necessary. Before we can see whether this picture makes any sense or not, let us consider just what can usefully be done by a tutor who has no special training in counselling or in social work, but who wants to be helpful to his or her students.

One might suggest as a minimum requirement that tutors should to be willing to listen carefully to what their students care to tell them about themselves. Those who lack specialist training often have no idea how useful it can be to simply offer a listening ear. They sometimes allow themselves to feel de-skilled by the fact that there are others with special skills in these areas. It is, therefore, worth noting just how much help can be given simply by allowing someone to talk and offering them your attention. If nothing more were asked of teaching staff than that they be prepared to listen to students who chose to speak to them (no special availability, no insistence on approachability, no special training given, no skills presupposed) a great deal of help and support would thereby be offered to students. Often this is all that the student requires to find his or her own way of dealing with some problem.

Tutors need not only to appreciate just how helpful attentive listening can be, but also to know when it is unlikely to be enough. If problems go back a long way; if the student cannot articulate the problem; if the student cannot express his or her feelings adequately or appropriately; if the student blames everyone else and is unwilling to make any personal change; if the student is expecting someone else to decide the matter, or wave a wand to put it right; if the student appears to have problems in virtually every department of life; if the student either resists help or quickly comes to rely on it; if the student is isolated from others, or behaves oddly, unpredictably, or dangerously: then in all these cases tutors should probably consider involving someone else.

The investigation referred to in Chapter 5 found teaching staff dealing with a surprising number of students with quite severe difficulties. This is disturbing evidence, not only because some of these students may have needed specialist help, but because it imposes an unnecessary strain on tutors who have other things to do. Tutors need to have a fairly clear conception of their role so that they can set limits to their involvement; otherwise, as already argued in Chapter 5, they can experience student support not as a fulfilling part of their teaching role, but as a kind of bottomless pit into which they feel sucked, which takes them away from other legitimate professional concerns, and which skews and distorts their professional role. Yet the fact remains that the help and support that students need can often be provided by their tutors simply giving them their time and attention.

Roles and relationships

What is offered in a tutorial, I have been suggesting, is a relationship. From this point of view, there is no fundamental difference between an 'academic' tutorial and a 'personal' tutorial. A member of teaching staff in an institution of higher education carries responsibilities for providing both kinds of help and support, and does so most effectively by relating to the student personally. In this respect tutoring differs from both interviewing and counselling.

Interviewing is a matter of skilled performance, of putting the other at ease, of allowing the interviewee a certain amount of rope, of focused questioning and of timing; it does not offer much in the way of a relationship. Indeed, a relationship with the interviewee might be thought to get in the way of the functional task that has to be done; in job interviews interviewers may withdraw from the interviewing role if it is felt that their relationship with the interviewee could compromise their objectivity.

Counselling, in a rather different way, eschews relationships. It has long been recognized that transference can take place within a psychotherapeutic relationship. Opinions among counsellors differ as to whether this kind of situation should be avoided or used creatively, but the canons of professional behaviour tend to discourage personal relationships between counsellor and client. Counselling is sometimes described as simply offering the client a 'mirror', a process of reflecting back to the client almost mechanically; others would more readily accept that counselling offers the client a personal relationship. The fact remains, however, that counselling theory has difficulty with. the idea of a relationship between counsellor and client. Counsellors often take refuge in the distinction between a personal and a professional relationship; the latter is intrinsic to the counselling process, the former is to be avoided or at least discouraged. Tutors may take refuge in the same way, yet perhaps with less justification.

The word 'role' is important here. What distinguishes a member of teaching staff from, say, a counsellor is not that the latter has specific training (some academics may indeed have training in counselling) or deals with more serious or persistent problems (though that also may be true); it is that the two roles are different.

To show this, it is only necessary to consider what is involved in going to see someone you do not normally meet: the encounter immediately becomes a 'consultation' in which the stakes are considerably raised. While a student may be able to chat to his or her tutor quite casually, and in the course of such a conversation may raise and explore a matter of some personal import- ance, there are many opportunities for retreat on both sides. The problem can be broached obliquely, mentioned casually, even just hinted at, to see whether the tutor is observant enough to notice, willing to pick it up, con- cerned to try to help. If the tutor approached handles the matter clumsily, makes too much of it, or is overinterested, it will be relatively easy for the stu- dent not to pursue the matter. Similarly, the tutor, in asking for an explanation why a piece of work has not been completed on time, may stumble on some personal problem. In these kinds of encounter, precisely because they are ill- defined, both parties have escape-routes; it may turn into a quasi-counselling session or it may not, but at least in principle either tutor or student by opting out of the discussion at any point can ensure that it does not.

It needs to be said that academics are not there primarily for this. However important we think student support to be, and however much we would like it to be closely integrated into the teaching role, it remains a secondary function. Teaching staff are primarily there to teach; their role certainly includes helping and supporting students, but it includes much else besides. In this respect they are unlike professional support staff, for whom support is the central focus of their role, and who usually have no other func- tion within the institution but to help and support students.

Equally, students are not there primarily for this either. Higher education institutions are not therapeutic communities; they want to be able to take certain things for granted (students' health and general well-being) in order to get on with other things, such as the students' education. Sometimes the relationship between the two is very close, so that it is almost impossible to distinguish them; but often students present 'problems' the resolving of which is a prerequisite for their studies to continue rather than being itself a part of their education.

When you are 'not yourself', 'going to pieces', or in some other way diminished, less than whole, it helps to go and talk to a stranger, someone you hardly know, someone you may not normally meet, someone who is not involved in your troubles and who can respond as a whole person to you in your brokenness. This person may also have special skill is allowing you to be yourself, to speak your mind, to express your feelings. But that is not what tutors offer. An educational process, at its best, is an encounter between whole people; it is not therapy. It follows that the kind of relationship which a tutor may offer should not be seen as getting in the way of the professional task, but as an intrinsic part of it. Of course, the relationship may become complicated and there are judgements to be made about any close involvement, whether hostile or favourable to the other; but these are for reasons of professional propriety, not because the educational process is vitiated when there is personal involvement. On the contrary, relationships are the very stuff of the educational process.

Setting boundaries

Institutions may define the tutor's role differently and it may be more important that there are clearly understood boundaries than exactly where the boundaries are set. However, certain general principles can be identified here which, if borne in mind, serve at least to rule out certain styles of helping and supporting by teaching staff.

First, the student is an adult. Of course, he or she may be pathologically immature at any age and, consequently, in need of special support, yet as a general principle members of teaching staff ought to treat students as adults. Students have the right to be so treated, even if they do not behave in a consistently adult way. They have a right to make their own decisions and not to be pestered by staff trying to be helpful. Indeed, they have a right to be left alone even when apparently making a mess of things.

Second, tutors have a right to their own lives, their own privacy. It is not appropriate that teachers in higher education should be at the student's beck and call; this is not the professional role which higher education institutions employ tutors to fulfil. Indeed, that professional role requires a measure of detachment from the student's situation in order to offer the kind of help and support which *is* appropriate.

Third, colleagues have rights in this matter also. We are not entitled to involve other staff in what may turn out to be, in effect, a social work or counselling role, even if this is a role they want to adopt. This is another reason for caution and for careful limits to the role. Wherever the line is drawn, it must hold good for colleagues too. Any tutors who wish to go beyond what is formally required need to be clear that this is what they are doing and to recognize that they cannot expect others to do the same. It is also important that professional support staff should be called in at an appropriate stage; delaying referral can put support staff in the difficult position of having to pick up problems at a point where they have become chronic and intractable.

Fourth, it is not just a question of 'rights', but of good practice. It is in the long-term interests of all involved to avoid, say, setting up a relationship of dependency, or getting into a situation in which the tutor is meeting his or her own needs through helping the student.

Fifth, any member of teaching staff who becomes heavily involved in supporting one or more students will need strong support him or herself. This is often not appreciated until too late. Where is this support to come from, and who will provide it? To face this question is to begin to answer the question of the limits of the tutor's role. The more deeply tutors become involved, the stronger their supports need to be; so the resources available for tutor support may serve to set limits on what tutors may safely undertake.

Sixth, there are matters of which most teaching staff have no knowledge or experience: legal issues, such as the threatened deportation of an overseas student, require legal advice; matters such as violence, crime or drug abuse, may have to involve the police; suspected mental illness probably needs to be referred to a doctor. Most tutors quickly become out of their depth on all these matters.

All of the above considerations have the effect of restraining tutors from becoming over-involved and suggest ways in which the role of tutor might be limited to more manageable proportions. There is no intention here to prescribe precisely how the role should best be carried out, but to make it more straightforward, less of a blank cheque. Because it has been ill-defined, the tutor's role has sometimes been too easily equated with some other role, for instance that of 'advocate', which has seemed to offer a clearer specification. However, the role of tutor does not necessarily require that one takes sides with the student against the institution, or against an Examination Board, though of course it might. It is a truism to say that the interests of the student are paramount, yet the fact remains that tutors have responsibilities to the other students, to their institution, to their profession, to their discipline, to themselves and their own integrity. The role of tutor is *sui generis*, not to be defined in terms of one or more other roles.

It will be argued in Part 3 that two models in particular, pastoral care and counselling, have had a powerful influence on the tutor's role and how it has been conceived, and that the contradictions between them have contributed to current confusion about the tutor's role. It should also be noted, however, that in certain respects these models have pulled in the same direction in that they have jointly had the effect of opening up the role and raising expectations of what tutors might do for students.

What is important is to establish a more realistic conception of the role that tutors might reasonably be expected to fulfil. It is necessary to insist that it is above all a *professional* role which, however defined in particular contexts, has a territory of its own. It does not allow, still less encourage, amateurish dabbling in a range of other professional roles such as counsellor, social worker or pastor. Clarification of the role benefits all concerned, but especially perhaps tutors themselves who often feel uncertain of what is expected of them. Like anyone asked to fulfil an ill-defined role, tutors sometimes get into very deep water because they do not know where to stop or where to draw the line; alternatively, fearful of not knowing where to stop, they are over-cautious and reluctant to get involved with students at all. Both these states of affairs are seen as symptoms of an underlying confusion about the role and about where to set its boundaries.

Referral

One way to clarify this further is to consider when and how tutors should pass students on to someone else for help and support. What might seem a relatively straightforward matter becomes, on closer inspection, something of a minefield. A tutor who feels out of his or her depth will no doubt be relieved to be able to hand over responsibility for the student to someone else; but how will the student feel? What may be done sincerely in the interests of the student and to ensure that the student is given the support he or she needs may be experienced as precisely the opposite – withdrawal of support just when it was most needed. Is the student being 'fobbed off' onto someone else as a way of shifting responsibility, passing the buck, or allowing the tutor to wash his or her hands of the matter? Or is the tutor admitting to some personal inadequacy? The student is entitled to know why it is thought necessary to go and see someone else, to tell the story all over again, and (apparently, at least) to delay still further the solution of the problems. If the tutorial relationship is as important as has been suggested there will need to be very strong reasons for setting it aside in favour of some other arrangement.

Anyone with a tutorial responsibility needs to have a clear idea of their own personal limits. What is the territory on which they feel 'at home'? This will indicate areas of competence which they know they can handle readily, because they have been prepared by their experience, qualifications, skills and interests. For most tutors this will include matters concerning their own professional role, their own specialism, the courses they teach, advice on study skills and a certain rather narrow range of career options with which they are familiar.

There will be other areas on which they feel less secure, more uneasy, and a few where they feel unable to cope at all. This may be because they lack relevant experience or because the personal impact of their experience has been such as to make it impossible for them to respond to students in similar circumstances in a dispassionate or disinterested way. Examples might be the experience of a broken relationship, bereavement or termination of pregnancy. It is perfectly understandable if some tutors feel that experiences of this sort effectively disqualify them from dealing with such matters, at least until they have personally come to terms with them more satisfactorily. Whereas trained counsellors can be expected to have worked through their own personal experiences, the same cannot be asked of tutors, only that they should opt out at the appropriate point.

However, what is the appropriate point? Even the minimal list of 'safe' areas given above will pose problems for some relatively inexperienced staff. Yet institutions are surely entitled to expect tutors to operate within the boundaries of their own professional context? The confusion here arises, again, from too wide a conception of the tutor's role, which necessitates the acknowledgement that tutors may find it necessary to 'opt out' of certain bits of it. On the contrary, if we have adequately defined the tutor's role there will be no question of opting out of it; rather, we shall allow the possibility that many teaching staff, for much of the time, will be able and willing to 'opt in' to an engagement with their students which goes a long way beyond this. Even so they will do so not out of a desire to dabble in counselling, but from a commitment to their tutoring role which they recognize must engage them fully and as 'whole' people if they are to give maximum help and support to their students.

Ideally, then, given that sort of commitment, why will tutors refer their students to others? Generally, it will be because this strategy looks as if it will offer the student better help and support. This may be because the tutor lacks the time, the expertise, or perhaps the neutrality that is required. In every case the tutor should know precisely why this referral is considered necessary or desirable, and it should be possible to explain this to the student. By putting it in this way, issues of referral may be seen within the context of a support system which accommodates these needs, rather than as exceptional cases which require special treatment. Where an effective support network exists, referral can be understood as part of the regular service that is available to students, not as signalling either some sort of breakdown in the system or some overwhelmingly severe problem.

Sometimes the reason for referral will be simply that the student needs more time than the tutor could reasonably be expected to spare. Often it will be a matter of putting the student in touch with specialist expertise. The student may need information to which the tutor does not or could not possibly have access, or skills which the tutor does not or could not reasonably be expected to possess. At other times it may be that there are issues involved in which the tutor has an interest which could get in the way of the kind of help and support the student needs. Sometimes, of course, all these reasons may apply.

Some students are undoubtedly particularly hard to help, perhaps because they are reluctant to ask for help or to accept the help that is offered. Sometimes they fight shy of coming to see their tutor, fail to keep appointments, or when they do come are reluctant to say very much. There are others who cannot express what they think or feel, or who cannot accept that they need help. It is particularly difficult to help those who blame everyone but themselves, who are looking for instant solutions to their problems, or who refuse to take the next step. These are cases where quite difficult decisions have to be made, bearing in mind the principles set out above. It might be possible for a skilled counsellor to coax a better response out of the student and, in many cases, a referral will be appropriate. Yet higher education institutions are not therapeutic communities and it is questionable whether every student who is difficult to help should for that very reason be given further help. Tutors are not obliged to 'leave no stone unturned' in their efforts to help students. At some point it has to be recognized that enough effort has been expended, enough time given. In an institution in which everyone is adult, and treated as such, relationships have to be made mutually; they cannot be constructed single-handedly. So there are limits not only to what tutors themselves might do for students, but also to what they might ask others to do.

There is a wide range of agencies to which students might be referred, both within higher education institutions and outside them. However, so far as one can tell, tutors usually rely on personal contacts of their own, few using anything like the full range of services available. Often it does not occur to tutors to make contact with agencies outside their institutions, within the wider community. Most staff recognize that referral to a particular named person who is known to them personally is preferable to simply putting a student in touch with an organization.

How the referral is actually done is critical. Unless the issues have been thoroughly thought out and talked through with the student, then the student may feel that the tutor is walking away from the problem (which could, indeed, be true). As well as the student feeling somewhat 'fobbed off', there may well be residual feelings of guilt or inadequacy on the tutor's part. The tutor will in many cases want to continue to keep in close touch with the situation, not simply to 'drop' the student. This needs to be clear to all concerned. It helps the student if the referral is presented in terms of an extra resource being made available, rather than of a source of help being withdrawn or exchanged. The tutor needs to make it as clear as possible that he or she has not lost interest in the student.

The tutor also needs to make quite sure the student is being sent to the most appropriate place, that the person to whom the student is referred is willing to receive the student and is adequately prepared. This does not necessarily mean passing on all the information the tutor has about the student; it may be better if the student has a fresh start with someone who can listen with no preconceived ideas. However, it is essential that the student knows what has been said. Ideally, the student should be asked what information should be passed on, so that the transfer is accomplished by tutor and student together.

One way of summing up what is said here is to use three different terms to indicate three different types of process. 'Referral' suggests a process managed entirely by the tutor; the student's role is simply to *be* 'referred'. 'Transfer' may be a slightly preferable concept in that it may be possible for a transfer to be effected jointly by tutor and student acting *together*. However, the idea of 'calling in' a third party suggests something else: it implies that the tutorial relationship remains intact, but that it is to be enriched by the addition of an extra dimension of, say, expertise.

All these considerations have a bearing on how referral might actually be done. It can now be seen that simply to suggest to the student that he or she should go and see someone else instead might be felt as very dismissive. At the other extreme, tutors might actually arrange the first appointment for the student. Generally speaking, it will be best to do rather more than the former and less than the latter. It will be helpful to talk to the student about why you are suggesting they go and see someone else. It will be helpful to make sure the student knows exactly where to go and to point them in the right direction. Yet, if possible, they should be left to arrange their own first appointment, so that they take responsibility for it, feel they 'own' it and that it is not just something done *for* them. Again, it will be helpful for the tutor to liaise as closely as possible with the person to whom the student is being referred. Whether it is a good idea to check up on the student to see if they went will depend on many factors; the student might feel it showed the tutor's continuing interest; alternatively, it might be felt as unduly intrusive.

This chapter has explored the need for clear thinking about the tutor's role. Is it that of counsellor, adviser, supervisor, advocate, friend or what? Unlike counsellors, tutors do not simply have to respond to situations which arise independently of them. Their job requires them to provoke such situations: to have a word with a student whose attendance is irregular; to explain to a student that his or her work is unsatisfactory; to challenge the student who may be trying to pass off as his own the work of someone else. Thus, tutors are helpers, but not *just* helpers. They do not only deal with students' problems, they sometimes create them. They may even be themselves part of the problem, because of what they have done or because of what they represent, and so become the target of the student's anger, envy, frustration or disappointment.

While it is good for tutors to have counselling skills, students look to their tutors for, and are entitled to expect, informed advice based on knowledge and experience. Personal tutors are expected to stick up for their students when necessary, but not to defend them regardless of the circumstances. There may sometimes be difficult judgements to make, one of which might be the development of a personal friendship. It is important to be clear that friendship with tutees is not what is asked of a tutor and is quite likely to create additional difficulties as a matter of fact. Rather, the tutorial relationship needs to be a businesslike, working relationship. Institutions of higher education may reasonably expect their teaching staff to carry out a thoroughly professional job of helping students through their courses; this entails making responsible judgements, always with the student's best interests at heart.

Questions remain, of course, as to how institutions might allocate and differentiate staff responsibilities, how they might manage the overall provision of student support and, indeed, how they might conceptualize the process. These questions are addressed in the remaining chapters.

Part 3

Institutional Policy

9

Patterns of Provision

Institutions of higher education generally acknowledge some responsibility for student support and for the most part make formal arrangements to ensure that this responsibility is discharged. Yet even if they did nothing of this sort it would still be necessary to discuss the institutional dimension. It has already been argued that student support cannot sensibly be discussed without taking its context seriously. If, as Chapter 4 was concerned to show, the student experience is not just a personal, but a social experience, it follows that the nature of the institution in which higher education takes place will bear crucially upon the student's need for and experience of help and support.

Higher education institutions in Britain are by no means uniform in size, structure or mission; nor do they have a common pattern of student support provision. We need to look, in this chapter, at the varieties of institutional provision, so that we can highlight some of the underlying ideas and issues. In the next chapter, two sets of ideas will be identified as particularly influential; I want to suggest that they have shaped our perception of student needs and coloured our institutional responses. Chapter 11 will consider some other ideas and approaches which might be helpful, and which could or should have more influence. Finally, we shall confront afresh some key questions which underlie the provision of student support. Such questions are rarely faced explicitly. Most institutional arrangements are based on unexamined assumptions which do not stand up very well to careful scrutiny.

Examples of institutional provision

Readers who are not very familiar with British institutions of higher education, or whose familiarity is confined to one type of institution, may like to be reminded of the diversity of higher education in this country. Let us look briefly at six different institutions to see what provision each of them makes for student support. Of course, these sketches are stereotypes, but they may serve their purpose which is to illustrate a variety of contexts.

Institution A caters for 8,500 full-time students, and another 4,000 part-time. Its courses include a full range of Arts and Sciences, Technology, Business and Management. It occupies a single city-centre site, but has very little residential accommodation for students: just two small halls of residence (each of 450 places) some distance from the main site. The vast majority of students are home-based, either living with their families or in (mostly shared) self-catering accommodation rented from private landlords. The institution is effectively closed at weekends (except for the Students' Union building), but is open from 9 a.m. to 9 p.m. most weekdays.

Student support is organized in various ways. First, there is a Department of Student Services, which includes a student medical service, a counselling service, a careers advisory service, a student housing service, and the wardens of the two halls of residence. Second, each academic department is responsible for providing every student based in that department with a 'personal tutor'. The precise role of these tutors has never been very clearly defined, and there is a great deal of variation in how members of staff understand and perform this role. Indeed, it varies to the extent that some staff make it their business to become the student's personal friend and confidante, while others do nothing unless or until the student presents him or herself with some sort of problem. Third, there are a number of more informal channels of help. The Students' Union employs one welfare rights and advice worker who may be consulted in the Students' Union building most days without an appointment.

Institution B was founded in medieval times and consists of a number of constituent colleges. The colleges are tourist attractions and are open all the year round to visitors. The whole university has approximately 10,000 students, but some of the colleges are as small as 400. The university arranges lectures, assesses students' work and awards degrees, but it is in the colleges that the real life of the institution goes on. Every student belongs to one of the colleges, each of which includes students studying a wide variety of subjects: in fact, a complete cross-section of the university. As a rule students spend their first year in residence in college and subsequent years in privately-rented accommodation. First degree courses are almost all of a standard length (three years). The only part-time students are those working for higher degrees or enrolled on short courses through the 'extra-mural' department.

Traditionally this kind of institution has relied on the college to meet the student's needs for social life and support. Many of the colleges are religious foundations and have a full-time chaplain who, though not an academic, is a member of the college community and whose responsibilities include the pastoral care of students. The chaplain is, in every case, an ordained priest of the Church of England and, therefore, male; a few colleges have appointed, in addition, a woman as a chaplaincy assistant. There is no other formal provision within the colleges, though the tuition provided is often more like private coaching and effectively means that students have frequent tutorial contact with at least one member of academic staff. In recent years the university has set up a small counselling service, with two full-time counsellors available to students by appointment.

Institution C is a specifically technological institution. Therefore, it has a distinctive ethos associated with the pursuit of excellence in a relatively narrow range of studies. It has 5,500 students, most of whom are following courses in technology or business. The main building is adjacent to the site of a regeneration scheme for the inner city. Links with the industrial and commercial world are strong. Nearly every course includes some kind of industrial placement. There is no student accommodation. Students are almost all home-based. Many are mature students, the average age being 25, and they are predominantly male.

What little social life there is, is centred on the Students' Union building. In this context, most students in trouble would go first either to their doctor or to the welfare office in the Students' Union. The institution has appointed one counsellor for staff and students. In practice much of her time is spent with staff.

Institution D occupies an out-of-town purpose-built campus, constructed on a green field site in the 1960s. It is a small (3,000 students) institution with a high academic reputation in a small number of (mostly arts) subjects. The proportion of female/male students is 70/30. The majority of students come straight from school at 18 and are accommodated in purpose-built study-bedrooms on campus, each block having a resident warden drawn from the lecturing staff. There is also a significant minority of international students, some of whom are generously supported by their governments. Many students have cars, without which they would be rather stranded at weekends. The women students frequently express concern about the risk of being attacked, since the campus is extensive and the pathways are poorly-lit at night.

The institution provides the usual range of health and advisory services, but a great deal of day-to-day advising is done by the wardens of the halls of residence. In many cases this role is undertaken by single people who see it as an important part of their job, and conscientiously try to get to know their students and to be approachable to them. Faced with a personal problem, many students would find it easier to talk to their hall warden than to one of their lecturers. The university counsellor (there is only one) deals mostly with very serious problems, e.g. where a student has attempted suicide, and is qualified to offer long-term psychotherapy when necessary.

Institution E which has only 1,650 full-time students, is located on the outskirts of a large town. Founded for the purpose of training teachers, it diversified its courses in the 1970s and now trains social workers and a small number of health professionals such as occupational therapists. However, the overwhelming majority (1,000) of its students are intending to enter the teaching profession and 80% are female. Most of the full-time students are accommodated in the college or in rented accommodation nearby. A substantial proportion are mature women who live locally. As well as providing initial training for teaching, the college acts as a centre for in-service training, which provides another 750 part-time students.

The college has a well-developed personal tutorial system whereby every student is allocated to a personal tutor for the duration of their course, which for the majority of students is four years. The tutor is likely to build up a strong relationship with his or her students. Time is set aside for regular personal interviews to review progress and to plan ahead. The personal tutor is responsible for monitoring the student's course work marks and, when the student leaves, for consulting with colleagues and writing the student's reference on behalf of the college Principal. The senior management team of the college includes a Dean of Students whose job description includes the pastoral care of all students. Nonetheless, in recent years some students have been sharply critical of the close attention they receive, saying they find it intrusive and sometimes not very supportive. The college authorities, however, are proud of this strong 'pastoral care' tradition which they see as modelling good practice for the teaching profession.

Institution F is far and away Britain's largest provider of higher education. Originally conceived as the University of the Air, it quickly developed innovative techniques of distance learning using radio and television programmes, correspondence texts, summer schools and some face-to-face tuition in local study centres. It caters for mature students who wish to study at home on a part-time basis. Most students pay their own fees. No qualifications are required for admission; entry is completely open access. The majority of its teaching staff work part-time and many are full-time members of staff of other higher education institutions. The degree programmes offered are all modular, based on the accumulation of credits.

From the first, it was recognized that counselling would have to be an important part of the university's provision, partly because it aimed deliberately to recruit a high proportion of students who were unprepared for higher education and partly because of the nature of the courses, which required student choice at every point. It was argued that students were going to need help to find their way through the system. (Of course, this is hardly 'counselling' in the technical sense; more like 'academic advice'.) Provision was initially made for every student to be allocated to *two* members of staff, a tutor and a counsellor. Before long these two roles were combined into one, so that the tutor-counsellor acted as tutor for the foundation stage and subsequently kept in touch with the students when they moved on to later stages of their programmes. What is important to notice here is that the idea of support (embracing academic support in subject-matter, study-skills support and personal support) was built into the system from the start.

Discussion

These six cameos of higher education institutions are offered simply to bring out some useful points. There is, in fact, more variety than this, partly because individual institutions sometimes differ greatly from others nominally of the same type and partly because some institutions, especially the larger ones, incorporate within themselves a range of different types. Polytechnics, for instance, which have been formed by college mergers sometimes operate on a number of different sites including nearly all the types suggested above, i.e. city centre, leafy suburb, countryside campus, etc. The support they offer students may be similarly varied according to context.

However, with those provisos, it is possible to see here some striking differences in provision which can now be underlined. We can see that institutions may:

1. rely heavily on appointing specialist professionals to provide for student welfare;
2. rely almost entirely on academic staff to respond to students in trouble or difficulty;
3. rely on voluntary and informal arrangements and make very little specific or formal provision to help and support students.

One might be forgiven for thinking that these striking differences in provision are hardly surprising, given the wide range of organizational frameworks, varied sizes of institution, distinct traditions, unique mixes of clientele and contrasting missions. More than that, one might suppose that it does not matter very much exactly how student support is organized so long as students get the help they need. Is not the chief concern the *amount* of provision, not how it is organized or who provides it?

On the contrary, it matters a great deal. It is far from clear that different kinds of provision fulfil the same function only in different ways. There are, in fact, a number of rather different needs being met. To some extent this is a function of the provision itself; the different kinds of safety-net catch different sorts of problem. To pursue the metaphor one might add that if the mesh is wide enough some problems will simply slip through unnoticed.

A number of common themes can now be distinguished. Consciously or not, each of the institutions described above has adopted policies which imply particular answers to a set of key questions. Institutions have to make strategic decisions on the following issues, each of which may be considered as a pair of contrasting emphases, as follows:

1. Is student support to be seen as *prevention* or as *cure*?
2. Is the institution prepared to *take initiatives* or only to *respond to expressed needs*?
3. Is the support provision understood as *integral* to the educational task, or as *ancillary* to it?

Prevention or cure?

It will already be evident how easily discussion returns to consideration of students who have problems, even when one is trying to focus more on the development of student potential. Even to polarize 'prevention' and 'cure' might be taken to imply an orientation towards dealing with problems. Much of the institutional provision outlined above has been designed, apparently, to provide a safety net for students, the aim being primarily to cope with those who fall by the wayside, not to ensure that they stay on the path and progress along it with all speed. It is as if the student support system is merely there in the background ready to come into action if and when something goes wrong.

If we resist this view and insist that student support, far from being a remedial mechanism, is properly part of the normal arrangements in the experience of every student, not just when he or she is failing, this would seem to imply that institutional provision of student support belongs with all the other institutional arrangements which seek to ensure that the student's experience is positive, enriching and rewarding. Its aim is not simply remedial, but it exists to promote the general welfare of the whole student body. Like the provision of a college library, it is something to which everyone is entitled and from which all may gain. Its aim is not to rescue students with problems and enable them to 'survive' or to 'cope', but to enhance the student experience for the benefit of all.

As an ideal, this would doubtless be widely supported, yet in practical terms it is often hard to secure resources for developing student support activities against rival priorities. The sketches above illustrate the extent to which contemporary higher education institutions may be finding it impossible to live up to their own high ideals. British higher education as a whole acknowledges the importance and value of student support, yet appears not to be resourcing it adequately. The result is that the curative model wins over the preventative. This is no abstract or theoretical point. It actually means that in many of our institutions students may have to attempt suicide before they qualify for serious attention.

Initiatives or responses?

It is likewise salutary to consider the extent to which the approaches outlined above are purely reactive. It is easy to suppose that all that such an institution need provide is an adequate response to articulated need. Yet it must be very obvious that, in dealing with such a vulnerable group of people, to wait for the cry for help may be to wait too long. Students sometimes do not know exactly what their problem is; they just feel vaguely unhappy, unwell, unable to concentrate. They may not even recognize that they have a problem at all. Or their problem may be that they are too shy or too embarrassed to seek help. It may not be sufficient to wait for the student to take the initiative; a helpful and supportive institution may have to be much more pro-active. A regular tutorial to review progress is likely to serve students better than an open invitation to pop in for a chat whenever they feel like it. In many institutions, however, the existing arrangements leave it to the student to take the initiative.

A further point related to this is that while students' needs are, of course, unequal, this does not justify a system of support which allows a small group to monopolize the help that is available. A demand-led system will favour those who are most demanding; but needs are not the same as demands, and an institution with a commitment to fairness has a responsibility to ensure that its resources are devoted to those whose needs are greatest, not those whose demands are loudest.

A support system designed simply to respond to need is likely to end up responding to demand unless it retains some sense of purposeful direction and is prepared to target its efforts and resources towards particular individuals or groups. Otherwise, just as there will be some students who get more than their share of what is available, so there will be other students who, perhaps because their problems are relatively minor and their coping skills relatively good (or possibly because they are shy about asking for help when they need it, or perhaps obstinately, even pathologically, independent), make minimal use of the support that is offered.

Low take-up is sometimes cited as a reason for dismantling support arrangements. However, if there are students who gain absolutely nothing from the offer of a personal tutorial relationship, that should be understood not as an indication of their admirable self-sufficiency, but rather as an implicit criticism of what is offered. As with teaching, some students may be able to manage on their own – may even prefer to do so; but it is important to note also that when the teaching is excellently done it is the most able students who are quickest to appreciate its value. Exactly the same might be said of student support. A lack of demand may signal not an absence of problems, but a low evaluation of the help offered.

Ancillary or integral provision?

A further tension, closely related to the others, concerns the extent to which the implementation of student support policy is seen as an integral part of, and organized within, the institution's teaching arrangements. Institutions vary as to whether personal tutorials are formally timetabled, or at any rate have a statutory amount of time that is supposed to be devoted to them, or whether it is left to individual tutors and tutees to make arrangements as required. They also differ as to whether the personal tutor is someone with whom the student comes into regular teaching contact, or is a member of staff who stands outside the teaching relationship and is to some extent independent of it. In a small college, of course, it may be quite difficult to ensure that every student has a personal tutor who is not involved in his or her teaching.

What is at issue here is the extent to which it is desirable that the student support system should operate, as far as possible, independently of the teaching, or whether there are strong arguments for integrating the two. As a rule, counselling services operate very much at the margins of institutions

– inevitably and quite properly – so that the student, as client, can be offered a personal service to meet his or her needs. It is important, too, from the professional counsellors' point of view, in that they should be able to function in a kind of insulated space, into which the internal politics of the institution cannot intrude and where the student can be offered a safe haven in which to speak freely, personally and confidentially. Yet it is clear that in many institutions there is a recognition that students may need different kinds of support; that 'ancillary' provision may meet only some needs, not all; and that the resources of teaching staff need to be mobilized to provide a much more general kind of safety net.

What is clear is that, when both kinds of provision are made, the more integrated provision is likely to have a primarily preventative function whereas some parts of the ancillary provision may be thrust into a purely curative role. That is to say, a student counselling service is liable to be seen very much as a student rescue service rather than as a support service; its clients will often be in serious trouble, having already exhausted their own support networks of family and friends, and having probably also sought help from more immediately available sources such as their tutors.

The point to notice here is that the functions of prevention and cure will tend to line up with the division of provision into integrated and ancillary. It is much easier for members of teaching staff, who may be in regular, possibly even day-to-day contact with the student, to provide a supportive relationship which enables the student to carry on, and prevents the student's problems getting out of control. It is when this is impossible, ineffective or inadequate, that more therapeutic or remedial help seems appropriate. That is more readily provided by someone who stands outside the normal business of a higher education institution, and can therefore offer both a more detached perspective and a safe, uncompromised relationship.

Improving current provision

While it is widely recognized that there is room for great improvement in this area, it is usually supposed that the problem is simply one of resourcing. It is true that the student support function of higher education institutions is currently under-resourced, whether in the form of student support services or personal tutorial systems. Many large universities employ only one or two counsellors, for instance, and there have been some steep rises in staff–student ratios. It is, therefore, likely that in the experience of the individual student the availability of support from either of these sources will have been significantly reduced. At the same time there are concerns about the quality of the support offered. To some extent this may be related quite simply to pressure of numbers. A careers adviser, say, may find that it is no longer possible to offer hour-long interviews, but instead may set aside 30 minutes only. However, as far as personal tutorials are concerned there is the serious possibility that not only is the student's share of the tutor's time quantitatively reduced, but the tutor, subject to many demands and conflicting pressures, reaches the point where to offer a ready availability is to invite more informal student contact than can be coped with. At some critical point teaching staff may find it quite impossible to make themselves available to students in the way they once did *at all*, so that a personal tutorial arrangement which once included casual and informal contact is reduced, at best, to another appointment system. Clearly, a support system which simply pairs a student and a tutor, defines an entitlement of time for the student, specifies a minimum commitment for which the tutor is required to be available and then leaves it to the two of them to get together as best they can, is hardly likely to be adequate in present circumstances.

In a number of institutions the fact that the student support system is under great strain has led to some kind of review. In most cases this has been a matter of finding a more workable arrangement by which students may have access to teaching staff. It has been widely assumed that the professional support services, albeit in many cases understaffed, underfunded and possibly overworked, are perfectly clear about their role within an institution of higher education. Discussion has, therefore, focused on the support given to students by teaching staff, and concern has been expressed that they often do not have time or opportunity to help their students in the way they wish and students need. To this is sometimes added the suggestion that if student support functions are not always performed effectively, it may be a matter not simply of general resourcing, but of specific training. Unlike professional support staff, lecturers may have no training in interpersonal skills; possibly they need guidance and help in how to fulfil this aspect of their work. Courses of training, handbooks of guidance and institutional reforms have all been suggested in recent years with a view to improving this aspect of higher education.

These moves are, of course, to be welcomed and encouraged. However, effective remedies are dependent upon accurate diagnosis. It will not be helpful, for instance, to organize courses to help teaching staff to be better personal tutors if the problem is not so much that they lack skills, but that they are already so overloaded that they cannot do the job adequately, still less find time to attend a course. It is possible that some of our efforts in this direction are misconceived. While it is certainly true that the student support function needs to be given a higher priority, more staff time, a bigger share of resources, tighter organization, clearer goals, closer monitoring and better training, the fact remains that a fundamental reconsideration of the nature of the task is long overdue. Without this it is likely that whatever resources we commit, whatever new appointments we make or whatever training programmes we launch will still have disappointingly little effect.

The diagnosis which I want to offer here is really quite simple, but its implications are far-reaching; it is that we are working to the wrong model. Student support has been wrongly conceived. It is not so much that there is confusion over what support students need and how help should be offered (though there is), but that we have often made wrong assumptions and so looked in the wrong kinds of places for answers.

It is certainly possible to find examples of higher education institutions with vague and woolly student support policies, but even where there are quite well-defined notions of what is required problems still remain. For policies are sometimes derived not from a fundamental rethink, but from firmly-held convictions based on traditional assumptions. It will, therefore, be necessary to examine the origins of some of the ideas which have given rise to these assumptions. The argument to be put forward here is that both vague confusion and false clarity need to be challenged by a much more radical critique than has so far appeared. The issue is not simply a matter of developing systems of student support that are more effective and less costly, but of identifying more precisely what is supposed to be available through the support of academic staff, who needs it and what it is for.

10

'Pastoral Care' and 'Counselling'

The account of institutional provision in the previous chapter, while bringing out the variety of arrangements in different institutions, has also shown that, where provision is made, very broadly the arrangements fall into one or both of two categories. On the one hand, there is a reliance on academic staff to take a great deal of interest in those they teach and to interpret their role as including a great deal more than just teaching. On the other hand, there is a recognition that if student support matters it must be carried out by those who are specially trained, properly qualified and specifically appointed to the task. Thus, underlying the variety of provision it is possible to discern two sets of assumptions which inform and inspire the arrangements made. The first might be called the *amateur* tradition, the second the *professional*. These two very different sets of ideas apparently exist side by side; they must now be explored further if we are to understand why student support has been organized in this belt-and-braces fashion.

It should be noted that this is to approach the matter in a peculiarly British way. In North America, where student advising has developed into a distinct profession, institutions usually make extensive provision for student counselling and advice from people who have made it their specialism. It is, therefore, not seen as a shared responsibility where some kind of balance has to be struck between the professionals and the amateurs, but much more straightforwardly as a professional job to be done by its own qualified practitioners. The style of dealing with these matters in the rest of Europe is even more strikingly different; as a general rule, institutions of higher education on the continent do not share the British sense of responsibility for every aspect of the student's life, and are less inclined even to attempt to provide institutionally for the student's every need. The point to be made here is not to commend one tradition over another, and certainly not to suggest that one offers a model to be emulated by the other, but simply to highlight a contrast of educational attitudes which may go very deep. Nor is there any need to explain such a contrast here. It would be absurd to suggest that in the lands of Rousseau and of Froebel educators are somehow less concerned with treating the learner as a whole person, or that education on the continent is pervaded by a narrow academicism whose influence has somehow failed to spread across the English Channel. It is more a matter of how the teacher's role has come to be understood and of how teachers are generally expected to behave.

To have strong amateur and professional provision side by side in the same institition is, then, a peculiarly British phenomenon. A characteristic North American reaction might be to ask why we did not leave it to the specialists. A characteristic French or German rejoinder might be to question whether it was necessary to make this kind of provision at all. Neither, perhaps, finds it easy to understand why we in this country accept the existence, side by side, of two very different approaches to student support.

That said, it must immediately be acknowledged that one of these approaches is much older than the other and, within British higher education, represents the mainstream tradition. The idea that 'pastoral care' is part and parcel of the teacher's task has been present from the beginning, whereas professional approaches to counselling in educational contexts have made their appearance only relatively recently. Nonetheless, the situation now appears to be that in many institutions these two contrasting approaches, amateur pastoral care and professional counselling, are seen as the two main ways of giving students formal and organized support. Thus, while institutional managers may prefer one approach to the other, or may treat them as complementary, or may find original ways of weaving the two strands together, in most cases they constitute the institution's whole repertoire of support provision. Other ideas exist and will be discussed in the next chapter, but there can be no doubt that these two dominate our thinking on student support.

Where have these ideas come from and why have they been so influential in shaping the kind of arrangements we have made for student support? We now need to trace each of these ideas to its source.

The British tradition of higher education

Some traditional assumptions embodied in British higher education, precisely because they are so familiar to us, are liable to go completely unnoticed; we need to bring them out into the open so that they may be critically reviewed. For the opposite reason, anyone who is not very familiar with the history of higher education in Britain needs to pay special attention to this background which has shaped British perceptions more than we usually admit.

The earliest universities were established as religious foundations, with a very clear brief to train the sons of gentlemen for the professions of law, medicine and the church. The young men were much younger than present-day students, sometimes only 14 or so. So the medieval university had more the character of a boarding school, with the teachers taking an explicit moral responsibility for their charges; hence, the idea of a Moral Tutor, a title which still survives. University teachers were quite explicitly stated to be *in loco parentis*, and were clearly expected to keep control over their students. This disciplinary oversight was understood as having a religious as well as a moral dimension, by virtue of the fact that teachers would all be, as a matter of course, ordained clergymen. Thus, the young student was entrusted to the charge of someone older and supposedly wiser to act explicitly as a moral guide and father-figure, both 'governor' of behaviour and religious mentor; all this in the context of an academic community that was single-sex, residential and quasi-monastic.

This goes a long way to explain why student support has been conceived in terms of 'pastoral care', with strong religious and moral overtones. As is well-known, the oldest universities were groupings of small self-governing colleges, each of which was organized as a community. The living accommodation, dining hall, library and chapel were typically clustered round a cloistered quadrangle, so that the four elements of shared residence, shared scholarship, shared religion and even shared leisure were practically and symbolically linked. That model has had a most powerful influence on the development of British higher education. It holds up an ideal in which staff–student relationships are built around intimate and relaxed one-to-one tutorials, and student–student relationships are encouraged by extensive opportunity for peer support. It is impossible to understand current higher education provision in Britain without recognizing the extent to which it has been moulded by this tradition, partly by building on it and partly by reaction against it.

At first glance it may appear that a polytechnic, formed in the 1960s by amalgamation of existing local-authority colleges with a primarily vocational emphasis, is quite free from the Oxbridge tradition, ordering its student support provision in a way that owes nothing to the medieval university and its elite, independent, small-scale, single-sex, religious-foundation colleges. A polytechnic has, after all, quite a different set of priorities, which include comprehensive higher education, equal opportunities for all, links with and service to the local community, and responsiveness to the needs of the national economy. In any case, successive waves of higher education expansion have moved the tradition on. Civic universities founded at the end of the 19th century ('redbrick'), post-Second World War developments ('plateglass'), out-of-town 'campus' universities, city-centre 'technological' universities – each of these types added its own distinctive ethos, while yet retaining elements of continuity with the past. The foundation of 30 polytechnics at the end of the 1960s represented an explicit break with the university tradition. The whole point was that they should be a quite different kind of institution, offering a new kind of 'public sector' higher education. The designation of several new polytechnics at the beginning of the 1990s might be thought to confirm this radical shift away from traditional forms of higher education.

Yet, in practice, it has not worked out quite like that. The so-called binary system obscured the extent to which some of the same traditional ideals reappeared in public sector institutions in a new guise. Part of the significance of the title 'university' is that it stands for the continuity of this tradition. It is true that the polytechnics were meant to start with a clean sheet and develop their own identity. However, the binary system exaggerated the differences between the two sectors and the similarities within them. Old ideals were often transformed out of all recognition, but that is not to say that they disappeared without trace.

Partly, this is the result of the particular mix of opportunities and constraints with which the polytechnics were faced throughout the 1970s and 1980s. As publicly funded institutions under the control of local education authorities and lacking, until April 1989, the independence of the universities, the polytechnics were subject to financial pressures and economic constraints which bore much more heavily on the public sector. Yet at the same time they were quicker to respond to political pressure to widen access. The polytechnics consequently led the way in admitting more non-traditional students, a group likely to be in particular need of help and support.

It could also be argued that the strongly vocational emphasis of polytechnics has put a higher premium on careers advice. While more traditional institutions continued to provide a specialized, but liberal education for the majority of their students (offering what careers help they could, but treating it as in the last resort the student's affair as to precisely how, or even whether, they subsequently made use of their degree), the polytechnics encouraged the idea that successful completion of a course should lead directly to employment. As that expectation has become increasingly problematic, demand has risen for a careers service which not only relates closely to the course but also develops the student's own self-understanding, adaptability and transferable skills. Another pressure has arisen from the development of unit-based course structures which, it is widely recognized, presuppose enhanced resources for student support and advice. Despite all these pressures, or perhaps because of them, the polytechnics have managed both to preserve some of the traditional features of British higher education and to pioneer modifications of them. Nowhere is this more evident than in student support.

The polytechnics quickly established Departments of Student Services offering a comprehensive service including help with accommodation, medical attention, careers advice and counselling, services which in many universities were relatively undeveloped or unco-ordinated. Yet it was also felt that every student should have a personal relationship with a least one tutor. The new institutions developed personal tutorial systems, whereby tutors each took responsibility for a small number of students and made themselves available to them for informal discussion about their work and progress. This kind of provision was clearly derived from an attempt not to abolish, but to reshape and reappropriate a very traditional concept of higher education; the personal tutor in a modern polytechnic is the successor to the moral tutor in medieval Cambridge.

One key feature of this tradition has been the emphasis on *residential* experience. It is a tradition to which the very idea of distance education is profoundly alien. A university education was conceived to be a matter of being present, not just attending classes, but dining in hall and being in residence in the college.[1] For the concept of a university education was one which involved the informal processes of education as much as the formal ones. The undergraduate was supposed to learn as much from his extra-curricular activities as from lectures; he was supposed to learn as much from his peers – probably studying quite different subjects – as from his own studies; and he was supposed to learn qualities of character from team-games. So it was that he learned to be a man, a gentleman and a scholar all at once. So long as even faint traces of this ideal linger on, we cannot be surprised if higher education, along with its residual elitism and sexism, is inclined towards a certain nostalgia for the residential experience.

Despite current growth in numbers of home-based students, the idea remains that it is good to have the opportunity to 'go away to college' and that this is part of the growing-up process which we ought to be able to offer to young people. The fact that this ideal often cannot be honoured does not diminish the force by which it is held. It is a brave polytechnic director who is willing to declare publicly that the institution has no obligation towards housing students; more typically, senior administrators express regret that they can only accommodate a small proportion of enrolled students, while seeking maximum publicity for schemes which may marginally improve their student accommodation.

Yet to see the extent to which this is a culturally and historically located idea, one only needs to look at other traditions, where quite different notions apply. There is a strong tradition, for instance, of the wandering scholar who gleans learning from many sources and whose commitment is not to a rooted community, but to a restless pilgrimage. However, there has been little of that tradition in the British context. Similarly, there is the idea of sitting at the feet of a 'master' or 'guru' – again one looks in vain for signs that this has ever been an influential idea in British higher education. As for public disputation, once a major means of disseminating knowledge and building an academic reputation throughout Europe, it survives in Britain only in the formal requirement in some universities that PhD vivas are in principle open to the public. However, the British way of doing things has never been like that. The big public lecture has never been a key feature of our system, except perhaps in the early days of university 'extra-mural' extension. Characteristically, university education has always been regarded as something that occurs between friends, not adversaries, within a community, not outside it, and preferably in the atmosphere of an all-male club, thick with tobacco smoke and leather armchairs. It is altogether a more aimiable tradition of higher education, relaxed and unhurried, where even sharp debate is invariably couched in the politest of language, and where disagreements are expressed in the mildest of terms and with a maximum of courtesy.

It is not just that, in Britain more than elsewhere, the residential experience in higher education retains a peculiar significance; it takes a particular form, i.e. provision of individual study-bedrooms on college premises, students

only exceptionally being asked to share. In the United States student accommodation normally consists of double rooms, though with some provision for
the 'oddballs' who request to be on their own. This example illustrates well
just how differently the social aspects of college life may be conceived; having
a room-mate is part of the American idea of higher education. It also
suggests an important qualification to the image of higher education as
membership of a club; while always a corporate experience involving quite
intimate relationships, higher education in Britain has made careful provision for privacy.

Themes like these lie below the surface of contemporary institutions which
only *appear* to have left them all behind. In the story of British higher
education there are threads of historical continuity running through every
chapter: Oxford's insistence that undergraduates dine regularly in hall and
the Open University's determination to retain its summer schools may be
seen as points along a line of tradition which asserts that, ideally, higher
education is a social experience as well as an intellectual one. The polytechnics with their explicit commitment to quite contrary values might be
seen as marking the end of this tradition, the point at which the medieval
vision of university education was finally laid to rest, were it not for a few
discrepant features of which the personal tutorial system is perhaps the most
remarkable. It is hard to account for this without reference to the survival of
traditional ideas such as that of pastoral care.

The idea of pastoral care

The tradition of pastoral care has proved itself astonishingly resistant to
historical change. No longer sustained by strong religious roots, it nonetheless derives much of its legitimacy from its religious connotations, persist-
ing strongly in quite unlikely contexts. Until recently it has received almost
no criticism (Pattison, 1988) and it is high time it was sharply challenged,
especially in view of the way it appears to have influenced educational policy
and provision, both for school children and for students in higher education.
Had we been less mesmerized by the tradition of which it is a part we might
have been more cautious in developing patterns and styles of student support
which, however different in details, rely on essentially the same basic
paternalistic assumptions. It does not seem too much of an exaggeration to
say that the idea of pastoral care has functioned very much like an ideology.

If we look at contemporary institutions of higher education without being
distracted by this ideology, we might be struck by the arrogance with which
one group of people (teaching staff) suppose that they can help another
group of people (students) in ways that go beyond either the specialist knowledge or the teaching expertise which their job entails. It is, of course,
understandable that this basic assumption might have arisen, and continued
unchallenged, as a result of ideas about the nature of the higher education
experience which have been current in the tradition. However, to explain is

not to justify and it certainly needs a better justification than it has so far been given.

Several key questions may now be posed much more sharply than before. Once off their subject, by what right do teaching staff presume to have any guidance to offer their students? By what right dare they offer themselves to students even in a non-directive counselling capacity? What makes them suppose that this is needed or will be appreciated? Even supposing they possess aptitude and/or skills in this area, surely someone with responsibility for teaching (not to mention assessing) the student is the very last person who should be drawn into a very personal discussion? These questions have rarely been asked and one is entitled to ask why. I suggest that the ideology of pastoral care has inhibited this discussion by implicitly promoting the idea that the assumption of tutorial responsibility for someone else was invariably benign. Some of the difficulties concerning the tutor's role and the tutorial relationship may now be refocused around and attributed to the idea of pastoral care.

Such questions pose themselves particularly sharply, of course, where a substantial proportion of students are no longer coming straight from school, where they have more experience of life, and where they may be as old as, or even older than, some of their teachers. Yet, as already argued when discussing the tutorial relationship, all students, if they are to be treated as the adults they are, must be allowed to make mistakes and learn from them; that applies both to academic learning and to practical coping with the vicissitudes of life.

Furthermore, as anyone who has counselled teaching staff could confirm, teachers in higher education today are likely to have at least as many problems themselves as many of their students. They, too, may be lonely, homesick, worried about forthcoming examinations, in debt or going through unpleasant divorce proceedings. Before blithely coupling together the student's need for support and the tutor's responsibility for the student as a whole person, we should remind ourselves of tutors whose own personal lives are in chaos, whose emotions are in turmoil and whose finances are in ruins.

Why do we always assume that the provision of help and support is all on one side? Can we not imagine a situation where a student actually helps the tutor? It is surely quite evident that some students may have longer experience, deeper understanding, fewer hang-ups, better judgement and more developed interpersonal skills than their tutors. Who then helps whom? Is there any particular reason to suppose that a member of staff acting as personal tutor is necessarily in any position to help an individual student with anything other than the course itself? In so far as questions such as these are hardly ever seriously considered, it would appear that our thinking on student support has been coloured by a concept of pastoral care which is anachronistic, leading us to make tutorial arrangements which are inappropriate.

Worse, they may be positively dangerous. Paternalistic or patronizing forms of helping can cause resentment if they are recognized by the student

as an abuse of the teacher's authority. Alternatively they may go un-
recognized by either party, thereby creating a relationship of unhealthy
dependency. This, too, is an abuse of the teacher's position of power vis-à-vis
the student. Of course, these are not necessarily objections to the whole idea
of student support being provided in a systematic way by teaching staff
through some sort of personal tutorial scheme, but they suggest a number of
pitfalls for the unwary arising from uncritical acceptance of a pastoral care
model.

The counselling model

The second main source of ideas on student support comes from counselling. This is of much more recent origin, closely associated with the development of psychology as a discipline. Nonetheless, it appears to have a similar
kind of influence on student support to that of pastoral care; that is to say, it
functions as an ideology.

One of the difficulties is that the general idea is applied so loosely that
practitioners of so-called counselling can be operating at a considerable
distance from any recognizable counselling theory. The term 'counselling' is
often used to include various kinds of advisory work, despite the fact that
according to many theories of counselling it is, crucially, non-directive, quite
the opposite of giving advice. There is, of course, a body of counselling
theory; yet there are many different approaches and while some general
principles are established and held by virtually all schools of thought, there is
as yet no unified theory of counselling.

Nonetheless, strict criteria for professional recognition have been established, together with clear guidelines for practice. Any counsellors working
in higher education are likely to be formally qualified and working to
well-established principles. They will be clear that their responsibility is
exclusively to their client, a commitment which gives a certain freedom, yet
to which they are restricted in that they have to put the interests of their
client first rather than be more generally helpful. This may not square
exactly with what the institution would like from them, but strictly speaking
these are the only terms on which a counsellor can operate professionally. If
institutions want general student welfare officers, for instance, or student
advisers, they have to appoint people specifically to those roles, leaving their
counsellors to operate exclusively one-to-one and in strict confidentiality.
Counsellors operating strictly to this understanding of the task would not
feed back information to a student's tutors (or only rarely, and with the
student's explicit permission), nor would they have any interest in discovering 'the other side of the story'. They attend only to their client, necessarily dealing with the student's experience as personal and individual rather
than as the social experience which Chapter 3 claimed it to be. We therefore need to be clear that counselling in this strict sense is only part of the
work of helping and supporting students, not the whole of it.

Yet the term 'counselling' continues to be used loosely, and is sometimes claimed by those with little or no formal training. Counselling serves as the best model, sometimes the only model, people have for one-to-one interaction. A nurse working in a student health service, or a student elected to office in the Students' Union, may say 'I have to do a lot of counselling, though I'm not really trained for it'. What they mean is that individuals come to see them privately to consult them. It is in this way that the idea of counselling has a pervasive influence on the whole provision of student support. Careers Advisers, Chaplains and Housing Officers, all at times find it necessary to describe their work as 'counselling' even though they know strictly speaking it is not. Thus, the language of counselling is used, in default of anything better, to describe various kinds of one-to-one conversations. This then misleads us into thinking of these other activities as in some way quasi-counselling, performed amateurishly by staff who have not had the requisite training.

The confusion arises like this: because these are obviously not cases of counselling in the strict sense, there is first of all an implication that these activities are not *proper* counselling, and then a suggestion that they should become so. In other words, the use of counselling language itself beguiles us into supposing that, done properly, these tasks would be *counselling* tasks. The very ambiguity of counselling assists the process, since it can initially be quite loosely applied to many different activities and subsequently tightened up to determine the sort of activities they shall be. This is part of what is meant by describing it as an ideology: a set of ideas which dominates our thinking and to which we look for guidance as to how to fulfil our role. The point has already been made that tutoring is a distinct role, not to be assimilated to counselling; the same is true of other support roles. That is not to say that counselling skills (and for that matter many other kinds of skills, such as interviewing or social work) would not be useful. However, it is important to resist the suggestion that all the various ways in which students are given help and support are some form of counselling.

An area of work like student support which does not seem to have been adequately thought through is particularly susceptible to this kind of influence from ideas which are either so well established that they appear to be immune from criticism, like pastoral care, or so little understood that they are imbued with a sense of mystique, like counselling. It is as if, in the absence of any more satisfactory theory, these more plausible candidates move easily into the vacuum, and assume an inappropriate importance and influence.

It is doubtful whether we should allow the activity of tutoring to be determined by a model of counselling, not least because counselling in the strict sense imposes a rather restrictively individual account of what is going on. We might rather conclude that our institutions should provide a range of different kinds of support, in which pastoral care and counselling would take their place alongside other forms of guidance and advice (perhaps including other forms of helping such as social work intervention), all of which would be supplementary to the provision of tutorial support by teaching staff.

We should not be unduly influenced by what is done elsewhere. For instance, many higher education institutions in the USA make very substantial counselling provision, yet appear to have nothing corresponding to the tutorial. However, this reflects a more therapeutically-based culture in which people are generally much more ready to consult a counsellor about their personal problems. In Britain people are still very reticent about personal matters and reluctant to share them with strangers, at least until their problems are beginning to become unmanageable. The needs of British students may at present best be met largely through providing tutorial rather than counselling support, not because there is anything intrinsically wrong with a counselling approach, which could become much more necessary in the future, but more pragmatically because this is not how we in Britain are used to tackling matters of this kind. This is not to say that tutors do not benefit from acquiring counselling skills, nor that counselling provision should not be steadily and substantially increased, but it is to question the wisdom of tutors taking counselling as a model for their tutoring role.

One major objection to counselling is that it can function simply as a palliative; it may serve to pacify those who are rightly disturbed at some injustice, thus colluding with the institution's establishment by defining any dissenter as 'sick'. It operates in any case according to a medical model, with consultations in a consulting room, by appointment, aiming to help people with *their* problems. However, what if the problems are not their private hang-ups, but more general problematic situations that affect many others? The counsellor who sees students one at a time has no means of knowing whether their complaints are just, still less of taking remedial action. The 'complaint' can appear rather as a quasi-medical symptom, the problem being located within the individual, not in any of the other people involved, nor in the social system.

Few counsellors would recognize that description except as a caricature. Yet it cannot be denied that the counselling model tends to pull us back to the discipline of psychology and to neglect the social dimension of student life which was pointed to in Chapters 3 and 4. Suppose, for instance, a student has quarrelled with a flat-mate. Counselling may, indeed, be helpful to the one who comes to seek help, but it is only by stepping outside the counsellor role as strictly defined that it would be possible to deal with this as an interpersonal rather than as a personal problem.

This criticism of counselling carries weight to the extent that counselling is allowed to dominate the provision of student support by being appropriated as a model by all those involved. As one resource among many, a counselling service may perhaps legitimately focus on the psychological needs of the individual. However, problems arise if all student helpers begin to use the language of and to define their role in terms of counselling. This has the effect of privatizing students' problems and leaving nobody to challenge such a 'diagnosis'.

What is being resisted here is the suggestion that the idea of counselling, any more than the idea of pastoral care, provides on its own an adequate model for student support. Yet it has to be admitted that it is a powerful and influential model which is as likely to distort the work of, say, careers advisers as of personal tutors. Just as the idea of pastoral care has permeated British higher education to the point where it appears to cover almost anything a tutor might do to help a student, so the idea of counselling has more recently come to be seen misleadingly as all, not part, of what student support offers.

What stands out clearly from this discussion is the extent to which student support provision is culturally and historically located. It belongs in a context; lifted out of that context it may be wholly inappropriate. What was once a sensitive and caring approach may now appear intrusive and inter-fering. The kind of help given and the manner in which it was offered by a scholastic clergyman in medieval times to his young gentlemen may be wholly inappropriate for a polytechnic lecturer acting as personal tutor to a group of mature women of his own age. The psychotherapeutic help sought and received by a young American psychology student from her student counselling service cannot serve as a model for a British engineering student in consultation with his personal tutor. There is no short cut to working out for ourselves what is appropriate in our own situation.

We might ask, first, whether we have the best balance between these two kinds of help: whether we should seek to develop a more extensive student welfare service or whether we should focus more on the informal help that can be given to students by members of academic staff. We might also ask whether we want to encourage this dichotomy in our provision, keeping student welfare quite distinct from the teaching function, as in the USA, or whether we want to encourage maximum integration of the two. However, there is a more radical question waiting to be asked, which is whether we are perhaps using the wrong models altogether.

I believe we may have been overestimating the help we can get by relying on these twin traditions of pastoral care and counselling. Under the influence of these two powerful sets of ideas we may have been thinking of student support in ways that are not particularly helpful, even misleading.

Some tutors' ambivalence about becoming personally involved with stu-dents could be attributed to the operation of these twin ideologies. On the one hand, lacking counselling skills, they feel unqualified to undertake this kind of role; on the other, they feel a sense of moral obligation to do what they can; yet because the role is ill-defined they remain fearful of being drawn in too deep. Tutors are, thus, often caught up in the contradictions between these two views of the support role. If it is counselling it requires special skills; but if it is pastoral care there is a moral obligation on every member of teaching staff to attempt it. It is small wonder that tutors have felt they were attempting to square the circle: that some have apparently looked for ways to avoid this kind of responsibility, and that others have devoted a dispro-portionate amount of time to it and sometimes, lacking training, got out of their depth. The tutors' problems can now be seen to be, to a large extent, the result of the dominance of these two models, neither of which is adequate on its own and which, taken together, are impossible to reconcile.

Note

1. I believe that in Scotland and elsewhere there has been a longer tradition of home-based students and rather less emphasis on higher education as a residential experience.

11

Alternative Models of Support Provision

Two models of student support have been outlined. The first derives from a very traditional view of higher education and is characteristically expressed in the provision of personal tutorial arrangements. It attempts to embody ideals of pastoral care and moral responsibility as inseparable from the teaching function, thereby betraying traces of the medieval, collegial and strongly religious context in which it originated. I have suggested that this model has exerted a powerful hold on our imagination; it reflects what, according to a conventional account, higher education quintessentially *is*. Despite the very different picture of higher education presented in the campus novels of, say, Malcolm Bradbury and David Lodge, it is the world captured in the novels of C. P. Snow, the cloistered quadrangle, that still provides the most widely understood image of what is meant by a university education. Provision for student support in many contemporary institutions of higher education relies very substantially on and is largely sustained by this vision.

Alongside that model, which fits less and less well into a modern higher education system with its large, looser and pluralistic institutions, is a model of student support based on professionalism and the idea of service. This is most clearly seen in the development, in some institutions, of highly organized Departments of Student Services. There is a clearly felt need in every institution to establish a central resource, staffed by professionals and readily available to all students. Development along these lines has actually been quite modest by comparison with some American institutions. However, where a strong central resource is established to operate independently of teaching departments it can offer a service to clients which is clearly understood to be ancillary to the main task of the institution, which asks of teaching staff only that they know about it and from time to time make appropriate referrals to it. On this model, for lecturers to dabble amateurishly in counselling is dysfunctional when the institution employs professionals who have specialist expertise in the necessary areas.

Thus, the two models pull in different directions. An institution which tries to combine elements of both models must expect a certain amount of tension between them. In so far as there is adequate ancillary provision accessible to all, teaching staff may feel relieved of their 'pastoral' responsibility for their students; and to the extent to which there is a well-established and effective system for personal tutorials, this may be seen as diminishing the need for a central service staffed by professionally qualified support staff. Institutions may find that they are sending out contradictory messages in seeking to affirm the value of both kinds of provision.

It may be objected that this is to misunderstand the complementary nature of these two kinds of provision. The fact is, however, that there is generally a very poor understanding of exactly how these roles complement each other and from a management point of view they frequently appear to be alternative ways of fulfilling the same task. Indeed, where teaching staff are expected to exercise 'pastoral care' without specific resourcing, it will seem as if they can offer virtually the same service at a fraction of the cost of employing specialist support staff.

However, it is actually more complicated than this. There is, of course, some overlap of function, but it is greater with some kinds of support than with others. If it is a matter of listening to a student's account of a personal problem, for instance, there may in fact be very little difference between what a tutor and a professional counsellor might each do. However, as soon as we consider, say, the central provision of a medical service, it is fairly clear that it would be rather irresponsible for a member of teaching staff to recommend a favourite remedy of his or her own when there is a student health service from which the student could get expert professional medical advice and treatment. If, on the other hand, we consider careers advice, many would say that teaching staff have a positive duty not just to respond when asked, but to initiate discussions with students about their future, especially when, as is often the case, they have knowledge and experience that is relevant to the particular career in which the student is interested. Provision of a central careers advisory service would never, one hopes, discourage teaching staff from helping students in this way. Institutions need to be quite clear about what is being asked or expected of staff with regard to the different kinds of help and support they may be able to give to students.

It must be clear from the two previous chapters that existing provision can generally be described not as the implementation of carefully worked out and self-consciously chosen policies, but as derived from some fairly conventional and for the most part unexamined assumptions. Institutions have tended to respond to perceived student needs within their own particular frame of reference. Thus, notions of pastoral care have been deeply embedded in the tradition of what higher education has been understood to be, and the arrangements made have arisen from, worked within and contributed to sustaining that set of assumptions. The development of tutorial arrangements has to be seen within a broader framework in which certain assumptions were being made about the students and about the nature of the higher education experience. That kind of provision belongs within and only makes sense against that background.

In the context of late twentieth century Britain, however, that picture becomes increasingly implausible. Universal participation in a shared religious tradition has given way to overt pluralism, strident individualism and an aggressively instrumental approach to higher education. Consequently, it has seemed 'natural' to reach for a very different set of ideas to underpin student support provision: specifically, counselling help offered in privacy and by appointment by professionally qualified specialists. It has not been sufficiently noticed that this kind of approach sharply contrasts with the former. Perhaps partly because of this lack of analysis, the newer model has not, in practice, come to replace the older one, but has overlaid what is left of it.

So far, it has been suggested that these two models of student support, in many ways polar opposites, are both present in our contemporary institutions. The task of this chapter is to extend the analysis further by drawing attention to a number of other models which seem to be implicit in current practice.

Support provision via the curriculum

One approach which appears to have been gaining ground in recent years puts the emphasis on the curriculum itself and attempts to provide support through the actual courses which students follow. Helping and supporting students then appears not as some extra-curricular activity for which time has to be found, but as a normal part of the course. There are a number of quite practical reasons why, in the British context, this might seem a sensible way forward.

First, the sheer size of many modern institutions has meant that they cannot any longer be thought of or experienced as communities. For the most part they are no longer the sort of institutions where members may expect to recognize nearly every face they meet. Reliance on casual encounters is, therefore, likely to be ineffective; anything important has to be programmed into the timetable, not left to chance, simply because the odds of that chance have been dramatically reduced.

Second, the complexity of organization makes it increasingly difficult to fit in unscheduled meetings of any sort. Most students in most institutions now commute daily to college rather than living on campus, and institutions quite commonly occupy a number of widely-spaced sites, with staff moving regularly between them. The inclusion of work experience and new developments in franchising courses, not to mention the growing research and consultancy profiles of many developing institutions, provide many more reasons why members of staff may be unavailable to students. Some institutions in any case employ a substantial proportion of teaching staff on part-time contracts whose personal availability may be limited to a few hours in the week.

Third, academic departments which were once focused on a single academic discipline and often primarily concerned with the teaching of that subject at undergraduate level for a degree in that same discipline now find themselves engaged in a much wider range of activities. This effectively means that students increasingly find their academic home not within their department, but their course. For many students, extra-curricular provision is effectively no provision at all; if they are to be offered support it has to be as part of the course. It is hardly surprising, therefore, that there has been a growth of interest in alternative ways of providing support to students through courses rather than through academic departments or whole institutions.

Yet it can sometimes happen that even the course is no longer a common experience for all students. The fact is that students themselves are less likely to be permanently residing in or regularly attending the institution in the way that was once taken for granted. Institutions increasingly deal not with a settled population of students who work alongside each other over a substantial period of time, but with a range of very different individuals whose needs coincide for certain quite specific purposes and for a limited period, e.g. for the completion of a particular unit of work. Through credit accumulation schemes and mixed-mode attendance students can now proceed through their courses at their own pace, perhaps even constructing their own personal programme from what the institution has on offer. As courses are broken up into distinct units, students need even more help in making sense of their varied experiences and in seeing things as a whole; yet the modularization of courses can render this practically difficult if not actually impossible.

Example 1

It is worth describing one particularly influential innovation along these lines: the 'Freshman Seminar' as originally developed at the University of South Carolina. This course, code-named *University 101* in the University's programme of courses, carries credit and runs throughout the Fall Semester every year.[1] It is chosen by about half the students, though students with a weak academic background are specifically recommended to enrol for it.

The aims of University 101 are: to introduce students to the institution, to show them what is expected of them, to help them towards a better understanding of their own learning processes, and to encourage them to help themselves, to help each other by functioning as a mutually-supportive group and, when necessary, to seek expert help and advice. The following are regarded as essential elements of the Freshman Seminar: reading set books or articles; writing critical reactions; study skills and time management; library skills; information about careers and course requirements; awareness of resources available on campus both for individual help and social contact; understanding of policies and regulations about such matters as grading and assessment; insight into the working lives of teaching staff; consideration of the purposes of higher education; and group-building exercises. Although the principles are clear, there is no set syllabus; teachers develop their own courses with their particular group of students. The course, therefore, relies heavily on the interest and enthusiasm of its teachers. Staff are recruited to teach University 101 on the basis that they are willing to receive training, which is given through Faculty Development Workshops to promote the aims of the programme and provide training in teaching methods.

The course has now been running for nearly 20 years and has been widely imitated throughout the United States and elsewhere. It has led to a great deal of attention being given to the First Year Experience; the staff of University 101 have established, at the University of South Carolina, a National Center for the Study of the Freshman Year which organizes regular conferences and produces a steady stream of publications on this theme.

What is interesting about this development is that it starts in a quite different place from either of the two models discussed above. It arises not from any impulse to perpetuate an ethos of pastoral care, nor from any idea of solving individual students' problems by adding some sort of supplement in the form of individual counselling, but simply from a sensitivity to the predicament of the incoming student. The approach of the Freshman Seminar is straightforward and direct; it assumes that the way to meet students' needs is to provide a course. Staff are, therefore, encouraged to identify needs that are common to incoming students and to design a course that meets those needs.

Although developed originally in the USA, the Freshman Seminar suggests a direction in which some British institutions of HE might like to go. As we have seen, it is extremely difficult to avoid student support provision appearing as merely ancillary to the main task of the institution. This is true whether it be the province of a separate department of 'support services' or whether it rests on conscientious and caring members of teaching staff. What a curriculum model offers is a way of affirming and demonstrating the institution's commitment to student welfare not as some sort of extra, but as part of its central concern. Furthermore, it shifts the focus quite decisively away from helping those students who have particular difficulties in surmounting specific obstacles to optimizing the experience of students whether they have problems or not. It makes this provision, quite literally, *as a matter of course*. Institutions which go down this road have signalled unmistakeably that student support belongs on their agenda not as an appendix, but as part of what they are centrally about.

In the USA the natural way to express this is through the provision of a credit-bearing course; participation remains optional for students. In Britain it might be more appropriate to identify such units or modules as part of a common core, to be followed by every student; this would ensure that student support was, and was seen to be, integral to the course as a whole. Again, it might seem preferable to put less weight on the provision of actual classes and more on individual tutoring arrangements which are more in keeping with British traditions of higher education. However, the central point remains: if student support is an integral part of what the institution provides rather than simply bolted on to it, and if it is understood to be fundamental to ensuring maximum value in the higher education experience rather than simply a safety net to catch those who fall, then whatever form or forms the institution's provision takes will have to include elements that are firmly built into the formal structure of courses.

Example 2

One way in which this is beginning to be done is in the use of portfolios. This kind of provision lends itself to adaptation for a specific course rather than implementation across a whole institution and there have been a number of experiments along these lines. One particularly interesting scheme may serve to illustrate the possibilities of this kind of strategy (Morton and Steele, 1991). It involves students in regularly completing a short questionnaire which invites them to assess their own progress and to identify any areas of perceived difficulty. Completed questionnaires then become the basis for a short interview with the tutor, in which the student's perceptions can be compared with those of the tutors. Experience of operating a scheme of this kind suggests that there is often a mismatch between the student's anxieties and the concerns of teaching staff. Students may be worrying needlessly; alternatively, staff may be making unwarrantable inferences, perhaps on the basis of high test scores, about the student's ability and understanding. This kind of scheme provides a way of exposing these discrepancies which can then be discussed with the student. Apart from the practical usefulness of this kind of information to both parties, it is believed that the very process of completing the questionnaires is of intrinsic value to the students, in that it encourages them to reflect on, and to become more aware of, their own learning processes, which is itself conducive to more efficient learning.

Although such a scheme focuses on the course itself and ostensibly comprises a regular review of progress, its value is understood to extend much more widely. Either on the written questionnaire or in the subsequent interview students may be invited to offer reasons for non-completion or late presentation of work. The interview provides a relatively safe format within which any personal problems can be raised, not as matters to be discussed for their own sake, but as factors which may be affecting the student's work. The whole procedure is clearly understood to be a course-related tutorial, rather than counselling. In such a context, members of teaching staff who would be wary of involvement in the latter are encouraged to provide support to their students as a matter of routine, by procedures which serve to demystify the process. Courses which have adopted this kind of system report not only that students appreciate it, but that teaching staff feel it provides them with a workable framework within which to operate. One key factor seems to be the provision of clear guidelines, so that teaching staff do not feel they are being asked to get into a totally unscripted and open-ended personal discussion, but that they are being given, in effect, a formal agenda to follow. Once the task is defined as clearly as this, it is reasonable to expect all teaching staff to take part; it is not in any sense a counselling role for which staff might volunteer their services, it is simply a way of performing the teaching role. It might be described, without disparagement, as provision of student support by numbers, in that the tutor simply follows a prescribed step-by-step procedure with back-up and referral options explicitly available.

The two examples just described are very different indeed. Yet they have in common a determination to build student support into the student curriculum itself and contrast quite sharply with more traditional forms of support, whether provided by teaching staff or by support professionals, which in either case are essentially extra-curricular.

Workplace welfare

Another approach to student support is that which sees it very much through the eyes of a manager of personnel. Educational institutions, according to this account, may be viewed as much like any other kind of institution; they contain a large number of people who perform different functions within the organization. Their arrival and their departure (hiring and firing) need to be managed skilfully; likewise, the time they spend within the organization must be put to optimum use. To this end, effective management will be concerned, for instance, about occupational health and will institute regular medical checks; it will seek to ensure good morale by the provision of recreational provision and sports facilities; it will promote an explicit corporate concern for the organization's clients through a programme of customer care; it will aim to identify and meet staff training and development needs, and to extend them in new directions. In much the same spirit, it will wish to make comprehensive welfare provision for everyone on the premises.

The value of high quality welfare provision is fully recognized in many large institutions, simply as a matter of good management. Naturally, it is only in the largest of firms that counselling provision can be included, yet it is worth noticing that 'employee counselling' is already coming to be recognized as an established profession with its own formal networks.[2] Higher education institutions now see themselves as operating, for many purposes exactly like any other large organization, with the same requirements for good management practice. This can be seen, for instance, in the new importance given to training, and particularly in the way that academic staff development and the training needs of ancillary staff, once seen as quite distinct, are beginning to be brought together under one head. For management purposes, the distinct roles occupied by individuals within the institution are often fairly irrelevant. Nowhere is this more obvious than in welfare needs. The likelihood of someone on the premises having an accident, for instance, is no greater for a member of the teaching staff than for a student; in either case the same provision needs to be made. Where creche facilities are available they are sensibly seen as available to students and staff alike. By extension, it can be argued that individuals who are somehow prevented, by some distressing personal circumstances, from fulfilling their roles within the institution, whether that role be teaching, learning or administration, are all entitled to the same consideration and care.

To argue like this is to inaugurate a Copernican revolution in thinking about student support. The issue has usually been framed in terms of how staff can best support students. This approach asks a very different question: how the institution can best ensure that everyone, students and staff alike, is given the help and support they need. The issue shifts from being about the mobilization of one group of people within the institution to help another group, to being about the provision of effective help to all, not because of their specific role or status or position, but simply because they are present in the workplace.

This approach begins from the thought that no businesslike undertaking dare neglect the welfare of either its workforce or its clients. This makes it quite different from any of the three approaches outlined above: the traditional tutoring model starts from moral responsibility; the service model starts from the idea of a professional expert with specialized skills; the curriculum model starts from what might be called an educator's concept of using curricular time to enhance students' life-skills. The workplace welfare model, by contrast, rests on considerations of effectiveness. It derives from good management practice, and embraces the notions of personnel management and customer care. It is, frankly, based on utilitarian rather than humanitarian motives.

Peer support and group-building

Once the point has been made that support is needed not just by students, but by everyone in the institution, staff and students alike, another reformulation suggests itself. There is nothing intrinsically wrong with mobilizing one group to help another group; what is wrong with the traditional tutoring model, under the influence of the idea of pastoral care, and the new service model, under the influence of the idea of counselling, is that they both assume, quite unnecessarily, that help for students comes from staff alone. Yet, of course, students get a great deal of support from each other. Can we not imagine ways in which this might be systematically encouraged?

A generation ago it was quite common in all-female teacher training colleges for incoming students to be attached to a final-year student who was known as their 'college mother'. Her role was initially to help the newcomer to settle in and find her way around, and subsequently to be on hand to help with any personal difficulties. It was hoped that she would develop into a confidante and friend, and undoubtedly the system often worked extremely well. It is hard to imagine the continuance of that system in larger, mixed, pluralistic and multi-purpose institutions of higher education. It carries overtones of paternalism and social control which would now be inappropriate and quite unwelcome in the British context. In the USA such one-to-one pairings are sometimes adopted as 'college buddy' systems. Cultural differences make possible an unselfconscious friendliness which might, in the British context, be simply embarrassing. Yet there may be ways in which the principle of peer support could be effectively applied.

So far as individual peer support is concerned, it can be rendered more acceptable if structured in the form of one-to-one tutorials with a specific *teaching* function. Students who take time to explain something to someone else often find that they come to understand it better themselves. Provision of supplementary tutorials, although ostensibly designed to help students with their studies could have considerable potential for developing relationships within which other kinds of help and support could be offered as well. Many students are, in fact, already greatly helped in this way, quite informally. There are also student-run services, such as 'Nightline', which explicitly offer help with personal difficulties, either by telephone or in a drop-in advice centre.

Rather than attempt to organize artificially induced one-to-one friendships, British higher education institutions have tried to encourage a sense of general group solidarity when students first arrive on campus, usually through some kind of induction programme; often these are best arranged by the students themselves through the Students' Union. Much more could be done by teaching staff to promote peer support within the course itself through the use of group-building exercises early on.

These sorts of activities presuppose a rather different role for teaching staff, as facilitators rather than providers of help and support. They are required to ensure, so far as they can, that each class for which they are responsible becomes a cohesive and mutually supportive group. Of course, this is something which good teachers often do without any special bidding, sometimes without consciously trying, and certainly without thinking of it as something extra they should do, but rather a by-product of creating the kind of atmosphere in which both effective learning and mutual helping are made to seem easy and natural.

In all these ways it is possible to give recognition to the acknowledged fact that a great deal of help which students actually receive comes from other students, something often missed by more traditional models of helping. It is important to see students not simply as problems, but as a major resource. On the whole, British higher education has not been very good at getting students to help each other. The Open University's 'self-help' groups have few parallels elsewhere.

This chapter has muddied the waters somewhat by pointing to some alternative ways in which the provision of student support can be conceptualized.

One is the attempt to offer help and support to the student through the course itself. Increasingly, course units are being devised which aim to help students to develop their study skills, to reflect on their own learning, and to understand their own strengths and weaknesses, all of which echo the aims of the pioneering *University 101* course.

Quite a different approach comes from looking at higher education institutions from a management perspective. On this view, what drives student support is the idea that welfare pays. It is not based on any sort of moral

consideration, as in the tutoring model; nor on the idea of professional expertise, as in the service model; nor on the educator's concept of using curricular
time to produce more rounded, more autonomous, more socialized individuals, as in the curriculum model. It is based on the principle that every
efficient enterprise will sensibly pay attention to the needs of everyone in the
workplace.

Lastly, the recognition that students are all the time helping and supporting each other suggests another approach. From this perspective the task of
helping and supporting students could be conceived as one of harnessing this
effort, or as tapping this rich resource. We have seen that there are various
ways in which institutions might encourage this process of mutual support by
helping students to learn to rely on one another.

All these models have now been discussed, and there may well be others.
What has been shown is a range of alternatives available to institutions when
framing institutional policy. Yet the contradictions here should be noticed.
Not only are there obvious tensions between the tutoring model and the
service model; there are also tensions between the curriculum model and
the models that rely on extra-curricular provision. What is more, there are
tensions between the promotion of group solidarity and attention to the needs
of vulnerable individuals, and between the mutual support of one student
for another and institutional attempts to make use of this. It should be
noted, too, that the workplace welfare model (and its associated managerial
style which treats students and staff in an identical way) sits uneasily with
attempts to build student support into courses, or to give unity and coherence to the whole of the student's experience.

Thus, what is offered here is neither a simple list from which to choose, nor
an *à la carte* menu from which various selections may be freely made. Rather,
it is an analysis which pulls apart various distinct strands which, in reality,
are often tangled together. It can now be seen that institutions have, for the
most part, neither adopted a coherent and consistent policy based on one
of the models outlined above, nor have they picked their way through the
alternatives and developed an eclectic approach of their own. Mostly, they
do not appear to have been operating according to any thought-out strategy
in this area, with the result that institutional provision has often been ill-
considered and unexamined.

In terms of the range of alternative models suggested here, most institutions have been operating a mixed economy, not as the result of making careful choices between various alternatives or weaving them together to form a
coherent support structure, but, rather, through the push of traditional
assumptions about pastoral care and the pull of more recent suggestions
about counselling. This perhaps explains why so much discussion about helping and supporting students continues to be couched in the language of
pastoral care and moral responsibility even while institutional practice is
increasingly governed by professional requirements on the one hand and
utilitarian considerations on the other.

The diversity of institutional provision, with a range of approaches evident to some degree in almost every higher education institution, may now be seen as evidence of confusion rather than sophistication. All these different approaches represent radically different ways of looking at student support. This suggests that we should resist the temptation to move quickly towards definitive solutions in this area. Rather, we should hope for a period of imaginative experimentation, allowing and encouraging a great deal of diversity of provision. Meanwhile, we should try to open up much more rigorous discussion about the underlying issues. The final chapter of this book seeks to initiate such a discussion by setting out the basic issues as clearly as possible.

Notes

1. Information about University 101 is available from The National Center for the Study of the Freshman Year Experience, 1728 College Street, University of South Carolina, Columbia, SC 29208, USA. See also Gardner and Jewler (1989).
2. See, for example, the journal *Employee Counselling Today*, launched in 1989, which is available from Employee Assistance Resource, Brunel Science Park, Kingston Lane, Uxbridge, Middlesex UB8 3PQ.

12

Rethinking Student Support

Now that we have a clearer sense of the strengths and weaknesses in conventional approaches to student support and the various kinds of provision that have been made, we can confront afresh the basic questions with a view to drawing some positive conclusions. Do we now have clear answers to the following three questions?

1. Why do students need support at all?
2. What is the responsibility of higher education institutions for student support?
3. How might we now begin to rethink the provision of student support within a higher education institution?

Students' need for support

Students enrol on courses of study to be intellectually stretched. The whole experience of higher education is meant to be stimulating and challenging. Students should not be shielded from the rigours of debate, criticism and controversy; they will not thank us if we wrap them in cotton wool and contrive to ensure that they may undergo the experience without coming to any harm. Risk is of the essence of the experience. A student who is given immunity from risk may, indeed, learn a certain amount, but will not be getting a truly higher education experience. It is a necessary part of this experience that the student is put 'on the spot', challenged to work things out for him or herself, encouraged to live dangerously.

Higher education of this sort will not be experienced as easy. Moreover, because the higher education experience is all of a piece, it will not do to say that one may experiment in the laboratory, but not in one's own personal life, or that one may be riskily creative in the library or in the studio, but not in one's relationships. One of the central purposes of higher education is to encourage students towards increasing autonomy so that they may find their *own* way through problems, both intellectual and personal. It follows that institutions of higher education have an obligation to provide and students are entitled to expect courses which are both intellectually demanding and personally challenging.

Is there then a fundamental mismatch between the idea of higher education and the idea of support? One offers challenge and risk; the other offers security and safety. Couched in these general terms, it is a fair point and serves as a salutary reminder that there are kinds of support which have no place in the context of higher education. Protectiveness, for instance, can hardly be appropriate where the task is to expose students to uncomfortable facts and difficult ideas.

The question might be restated: How do we balance the elements of support and stimulus? Acknowledging that the task is not simply to offer encouragement and help but to make demands on the student and perhaps even administer some kind of shock in the interests of the student's development, how do we reconcile these apparently conflicting responsibilities? Yet it is not really a matter of reconciling or of balancing. The issue is not about whether the element of challenge in higher education should be in some way modified or mitigated. The higher education experience is bound to be a taxing one for the student and properly so. The point is not to make fewer demands, but to set them in a supportive context.

Students may be invited, for instance, to question everything they have previously learned, but not all at once. The task of teaching involves not protecting or shielding the student, but sensibly sequencing the experiences so that the student is not overwhelmed by trying to tackle too much at once. Tasks are broken down into small steps and risky procedures undertaken one by one, always within a supportive framework that renders them manageable. This is not to compromise either the challenge of higher education or the attention to the needs of the student; both are held together in a teaching process which has to be carefully renegotiated every time. The purpose is to help the student towards maximum autonomy, but to do so within a controlled environment. The teacher's task is to manage the process in such a way that the student is free to explore precisely because the teacher has provided boundary markers that make such exploration safe. They can be let off the leash and allowed to roam freely about the territory, but only because the teacher has chosen relatively safe terrain, where if there are any minefields they are very well signposted.

It has often been noted that the most radical ideas come from those who are most firmly rooted in a tradition. Higher education at its best provides students with platforms of safety and security from which free enquiry can be launched. Students who feel themselves to be standing on solid ground can begin to get a purchase on all kinds of other questions. In due course they may wish to raise further questions. They may ask whether the ground beneath their feet is quite as solid as it at first appeared; they may even wish to see what happens when they cut off the branch they are sitting on. However, none of this would have been possible without security in the earlier stages of enquiry.

Advocates of student support too often seem to want the demands of higher education to be softened, the experience to be rendered more comfortable. It seems necessary to assert strongly that higher education can be a very uncomfortable process, in which cherished ideas have to be abandoned and old assumptions challenged. It involves the cut and thrust of debate and argument, not just cosy chats with friendly tutors. There can be no compromise on this point.

My argument is quite different. A good and challenging higher education experience necessarily involves an element of careful management of that experience by the teacher, who arranges the challenges according to a structure, following a sequence, against a background or within a frame, all of which is designed to facilitate the student's exploration and learning. By doing this the teacher is supporting the student. Thus, the key to thinking about what support students need is to be found in the very nature of the educational process. To lead students through a jungle of experiences in a way that renders those experiences intelligible is a task which cannot be effectively done without the exercise of care and concern towards the student. Perhaps this is not what is usually meant by pastoral care, but it is care. It is hardly counselling, but it does involve listening to the student, taking the student seriously and treating the student with respect.

Thus a great deal of what students need is actually provided through their courses. Teaching staff have a crucial role in helping and supporting students not by virtue of some extra responsibility for which they may volunteer, but because of the nature of the teaching task. Providing help and support is as much a part of the teacher's role as giving stimulus and challenge. From the student's point of view, a good higher education experience will be one that is both demanding and fulfilling. Ideally, these two strands, far from contradicting each other, will be experienced as indistinguishable, integral to the whole student experience.

But, of course, students have much more straightforward needs as well. If the courses are difficult, so is studying itself. A great deal of self-discipline is required; students are putting themselves to the test. Higher education is almost always highly competitive. Even if there were no element of competition, there would be no escaping the fact that every student is judged against a set of criteria in a social context where a great deal depends on the student's performance and the results are going to be taken as significant for years to come. The rewards of success may be substantial, the consequences of failure unthinkable. It is, by any standards, a recipe for stress.

To this should be added various difficulties which although they have no necessary connection with studying do as a matter of fact beset many students in our society as it is at present. These attendant difficulties, for many if not all students, will compound their problems. There are elements of hardship and strain imposed by the student state itself. As we saw in Chapter 4, by no means all students have financial difficulties, but very many do. The strains of studying are magnified when attempted without adequate resources. To be able to purchase textbooks, photocopy notes or just travel to the library, without always having to consider the cost would be of more help to many students than any amount of counselling. Possession of a word-processor, or a car, can save precious hours of time for those fortunate enough to have them. Those with young children often have complicated domestic arrangements which enable them to squeeze in a few hours of study at a time, but these arrangements will be precarious, vulnerable to the slightest alteration or breakdown. What has to be put into the equation here is not simply the inconvenience or the occasional absence, but the insecurity of these arrangements. Few of us do our best work in time snatched for study.

These are all rather special needs which are peculiar to students. They are put under pressure by the course and by the whole student experience; in both these respects they are liable to be comprehensively taxed and tested. However, there is a third way in which students need help and support which must not be overlooked. For students are, in many respects, just like every-body else. They have lives outside the lecture room and, indeed, outside the institution, and have needs that are much like everyone else's needs. They get ill; their families and friends have accidents and injuries; their relationships founder; they have difficulty in finding accommodation; their possessions are stolen. Like the rest of the population, too, students are sometimes unwise: they mismanage their affairs; they get into debt; they drink too much. Sometimes it may justly be said that they have brought their problems upon themselves. Nonetheless, they need help and support in these circumstances.

One can conclude this section, then, by saying that students require support partly because anyone needs support as they go through life and especially when going through a big change, and partly because as students they are subject to some unusually difficult pressures, some of which are contingent upon being a student and others of which are inherent in the activity of studying at degree level. Yet in all these areas the *kind* of support they need is not that which removes the element of challenge or in any way reduces or even compensates for it, but that which tries to ensure that the difficulties are met, managed and used as learning experiences.

The institution's responsibility for provision

As we have seen, there are different traditions as to how much responsibility higher education institutions should take for providing help and support to students. The oldest traditions of British higher education stem from institutions which took full responsibility for their students' lives. However, the model of an enclosed, self-sufficient institution no longer fits the institutions we have. Few students today (and very few staff) live their lives within the institution. Reconsideration of this issue is long overdue.

The present position is inconsistent, some institutions making more extensive welfare provision than others. However, there is a discernible trend to look increasingly to the wider community for resources which were once provided specifically for students and handled by the institution itself. Two examples will serve to illustrate this: medical care and student accommodation.

There is some kind of medical service in virtually every institution of any size. However, whereas some years ago it was not uncommon to find institutions employing nurses of their own (and doctors in some cases) and even providing quite extensive sick-bay facilities, these arrangements have mostly been dismantled, and in some cases the medical services have been privatized. Many students will, in any case, register with a local medical practice and attend its surgery like anyone else. For the institution to provide, on campus, a comprehensive medical service (sometimes complete with beds allowing overnight stay in what was effectively a mini-hospital) now seems unnecessary and inappropriate, as well as expensive and wasteful.

Provision of student accommodation has likewise shifted from a situation where many institutions provided residential accommodation for a substantial proportion of their students to one in which most students now find their own accommodation, with or without assistance from the institution. While few institutions have actually reduced the number of residential places they can offer and some have undertaken considerable expansion, the rapid growth of higher education has meant that, overall, only quite a small proportion of students are accommodated in halls of residence. There has been a significant switch to self-catering and a growing reliance on private landlords and local housing associations. Institutions which once felt they had to make substantial provision for students' accommodation needs are inclined to leave much more to the students to arrange for themselves. Staff once employed primarily to allocate residential places are now busy putting students in touch with local landlords who have private flats to rent. What was once quite a close supervision of the residential life of the institution has become part of the institution's routine administration.

While in these two instances one could perhaps see evidence that an institution was shedding certain responsibilities, there are other student services which seem to be relatively free from this sort of pressure. Few doubt the need for institutionally based careers advice, for instance, or for an on-campus counselling service. However, the issue has to be faced: much of what institutions provide by way of student support appears to be indistinguishable from or to overlap with what is already provided in the local community. Specific provision, paid for and controlled by the institution, has to be justified on the grounds:

1. that it offers something which is not available elsewhere;
2. that students' needs are significantly different from those of the rest of the population;
3. that students are entitled to a better service than is available elsewhere;
4. that a service is needed which relates closely to the rest of the student's experience.

Of these, the last is the best argument and it is the one emphasized here.

It is worth noticing that, if one were to take the view that higher education institutions should simply declare that the students must make their own arrangements in these matters, and that it is none of the institution's business, one would be colluding with those who insist on seeing student support as dealing with problems, and as something quite detached from the main task of higher education institutions. The line I have taken is quite the opposite: first, student support is not just about dealing with problems, but concerns students' ongoing development as individuals and their social relationships; and second, the task of helping and supporting students is not just ancillary to what higher education institutions are about, but a central, integral feature of their task.

The reasons just given as to why students need to be supported at all suggest a way of thinking about this. We may imagine a student of, say, history being subject to pressures of various kinds. Some of these are to do with the actual discipline being studied which imposes certain requirements, certain challenges; some are to do with the business of being a student, which involves set timetables and deadlines, decisions about courses and career choices; and some are to do with the normal business of life, which inevitably involves the surmounting of all kinds of obstacles such as illness, bereavement, having too few friends, or too many, sorting out priorities and so on. The student needs to be helped and supported through all these kinds of challenges.

Should an institution of higher education attempt to make comprehensive provision for every conceivable eventuality? Perhaps not. The following three points can now be quite firmly stated:

1. There are some aspects of the student support task which can only be satisfactorily provided for within the institution, since they are integral to the teaching itself. Support in this sense is the flip-side of intellectual challenge and only separable from it with considerable cost to the quality of the higher education experience.
2. There are other aspects of student support which would normally be much better provided on campus (e.g. academic or careers advice), since they probably require specialist help of a kind that might not be available elsewhere.
3. Support with personal or domestic problems, and help with ongoing personal development, may often be readily available elsewhere and may quite easily be provided off-campus for students who live in the community. Yet even here, either because the necessary help is not, in fact, available or because the institution considers it can offer a more specifically targeted service, a higher education institution may decide to make arrangements of its own. Besides, there remains one overwhelming reason for encouraging higher education institutions to make comprehensive provision, which is that these needs are rarely neatly separable. For instance, personal anxieties, career choices and intellectual difficulties may often be tangled up together. In fact, the chances are that they will be.

We have to conclude, therefore, that every institution of higher education must provide type 1 support, should if possible provide type 2 and may well provide some of type 3. In other words, some kinds of institutional provision are essential, some are desirable and others, admittedly optional, are often justified, not least because of the interrelatedness of the different aspects of the student's experience.

Rethinking institutional provision

The recognition that students need support and that institutions should provide much of it does not of course commit institutions to any particular *type* of provision. It is inevitable that the question will be asked: why not provide all support centrally, and put it in the hands of professionals who have been properly trained for it and who are given specific responsibility for it? Teaching staff would then be free to teach.

The issue about institutional provision, however, goes far beyond questions about the balance between tutorial support and professional support services. It is true that most institutions currently rely on this kind of dual provision; but these twin-track arrangements both reflect and serve to reinforce the polarization in our thinking, between ideas of pastoral care and ideas of counselling, which has been identified as one of the major problems in this area. Indeed, it is difficult to avoid the ideologies themselves influencing the analysis.

The crucial decision for institutions is how far they are committed to making integrated provision in which support is understood as part and parcel of the educational experience of students, and how far they are content to provide an ancillary support service. The point is not simply about the balance of provision, but about the underlying educational philosophy. My view is that rethinking support provision must mean bringing it into line with the institution's policies and priorities, rather than leaving it on one side as if it had nothing much to do with the institution's mission. Of course, if support is seen as integral to the teaching function then it is likely that tutors rather than the professional support staff will move centre stage.

This is not, of course, to argue that student support should be in the hands of tutors only, but it *is* to invert the common assumption that tutors in their support role simply do amateurishly what counsellors do properly. On the contrary, there is good reason to claim that within an educational institution it is the tutor who, when all is going as it should, does the whole job, the role of support staff being ancillary, concentrating on specific parts of it. Furthermore, it is misleading to say that specialist services are provided *centrally* within an institution. What is centrally provided is the day-to-day support through tutors; what specialists provide is necessarily peripheral. This needs to be stated quite bluntly, since what is at stake is our conception of the institution's task. An institution which has teaching students at the heart of its mission needs to affirm, both in its policies and in its structures, that tutors are the front line who carry this mission forward. It is confusing, as well as demoralizing for tutors, when ancillary units are described as 'central' provision. Tutors sometimes find themselves colluding with this kind of description, thereby implicitly consigning not just themselves, but the tutorial task to the institution's margin.

I want to affirm that tutors have a key role to play in supporting students, and one which, despite its long and distinguished pedigree, is sometimes undervalued. The explanation for this lies partly in the awkward tension, which has already been discussed, between ideas of pastoral care and ideas of counselling. Tutors do not have to move into a counselling role in order to help their students; they are already helping them as tutors. This kind of reference to counselling, besides doing scant justice to counselling itself, devalues the tutorial function.

A great deal of the normal work of tutors consists of helping and supporting students. If we conceive the educational experience as one of being stretched, as in physical exercise, then tutors who manage that experience for their students have a concern to ensure *both* that the student is exercised sufficiently *and* that the student is not hurt. So supporting students is not an additional thing that tutors do when they are not teaching them; it is a way of so managing the learning process that students are both challenged and sustained. To put it another way, students may sometimes be helped as much by the rescheduling of their work deadlines as by extra tuition. Both are examples of the tutor operating professionally as a support to students.

Higher education institutions which understand the education process in this kind of way will want to regard the tutor's work as the central core of the help and support given to students, while recognizing that the student has many other sources of help and support, and that the student's experience may include other matters which are of no relevance to the educational encounter with the tutor. Seen like this, the tutor's role in support is inseparable from the tutor's role in teaching; good teaching is always supportive.

From the tutor's perspective the task can be seen as one. However, from the vantage point of an ancillary support service it will inevitably look different, since that kind of structure must always deal, and rightly, with students' problems which, as we saw right at the beginning, constitute only *part* of the task of helping and supporting students. The tutorial context provides a much wider perspective on the whole student experience. This has implications for institutional policy. For instance, to administer and co-ordinate the work of personal tutors from within a student support unit, as is done in some institutions, while clearly indicating that student support is to be seen as a whole, is nonetheless bound to colour how the support role is perceived – to label it, in effect, as a kind of counselling.

To move the tutor to centre stage represents an important bit of re-thinking, but it leaves a great deal undone. Students have many different needs, only some of which have anything to do with their educational experience. Only when these impact upon the student's work, or affect the student's attendance, or impair the student's ability to meet course requirements, do they become part of the tutor's brief. This enables us to draw a fairly clear line around the tutor's role, with a good deal left outside it. Meanwhile, as we become clearer about the tutor's role we come to realize that much of it is about quite humdrum tasks; like, for instance, noticing when students are absent, and knowing every student well enough to be able to write him or her a job reference. These are not just little jobs which have to be done on top of everything else; they are what being a tutor *is*.

There is no reason for tutors to feel that their role is vague or ill-defined, with no clear boundaries; its main thrust is quite clear. Its focus is the day-to-day running of things in an educational establishment. It is *not* about having long heart-to-heart talks with individual students – not normally, routinely or regularly. In so far as these are necessary, specific provision must be made. So to recognize the centrality of the tutor's role is not to diminish the importance of support staff; quite the opposite. If the tutor's role is understood to be firmly locked into the central concerns of the institution, then the ready availability of staff who are relatively detached and independent of the basic structure, and to whom referrals can be made for specific purposes, becomes of paramount importance.

Finally, then, we must ask what bearing this rethinking has on the kind of student support arrangements that might be made. Can we construct an agenda for a higher education institution?

First, and most crucially, the institution has to decide to what extent it is ready to commit itself to a conception of education that embraces support, as outlined here, so that student support becomes an integral part of its educational mission.

Second, the institution needs to determine what it wants of its tutors. What is their role and responsibility, both in relation to students (e.g. treating them as adults, as 'whole', as 'worthy', 'worth bothering with') and in relation to support staff (e.g. are they there to provide a 'safety-net', a 'back-up', or what?).

Third, the institution will want to establish among tutors a clear sense of what is rightly belonging to their role and what is not. Tutors should understand that they are *not* being asked to undertake either pastoral care or counselling; there is no moral requirement for them to be extra-caring in their relationships with students, nor any technical requirement to be highly skilled in interpersonal interaction. What is required is that they be professionally concerned to tutor well. An institution which is as concerned for its staff as for its students will not want tutoring seen as an open-ended commitment, but will endeavour to make the tutoring task as clear and straightforward as possible. It will reward performance in this role in a way that corresponds with its public statements about its importance.

Fourth, in the light of this, the institution will need to undertake a radical review of its support services. This will necessitate looking closely at what students' problems actually are and then shaping the service round the problems. There is a real risk of the opposite happening, of problems falling into the shape of existing provision, unless this danger is recognized and steps taken to guard against it. If there are a lot of debt problems, for instance, serious consideration might be given to the appointment of a debt counsellor or financial adviser. However, care would be needed to ensure that the problems were correctly identified, and especially to check that existing patterns of provision did not distort by individualizing or medical-izing what in other contexts would be recognized as social problems. It might well be that the profile of student problems indicated a need for a social worker in the team rather than, say, a counsellor.

Fifth, the institution will want to encourage tutors and support staff to experiment. The alternatives suggested in the previous chapter indicate some lines for development and exploration. As has been shown, there is a great deal of confusion in the area of student support and, although some principles seem to be clear, there is still a great deal of room for different approaches to co-exist.

Last, the institution will want to find some way of developing this whole area of work so that it can be seen as a key element in the general edu-cational task. One reason why research in this area is so under-developed is that the necessary conceptual frameworks have yet to be established.

In this book I have tried to mark out the territory in a distinctive way, draw-ing heavily on my own experience of combining two roles often kept separate, and ranging across a number of different institutional contexts. In laying some foundations in relation to the social science disciplines, I am conscious that my approach might appear somewhat idiosyncratic; I do not expect what I have written to stand as a definitive statement. My hope is, however, that I may have opened up this area and claimed it as properly belonging to the study of education, not simply psychology or counselling.

While it has to be recognized that students' problems are becoming more like everyone else's problems, and may have to be dealt with in much the same way, it does not follow that helping and supporting students is just like helping and supporting anyone else. If the support provision available within an institution were virtually indistinguishable from that publicly available to all, then the only justification for making duplicate provision would be the sheer weight of student need. I have insisted that, on the contrary, there is something distinctive about the help and support students need *as students*, and that there is something distinctive that tutors can offer *as tutors*.

This is in one sense a very traditional view, for it is to return student support to its place *within*, rather than alongside, the educational process. Yet against the current tendency to think of student support almost exclusively as counselling, it may appear a quite radical proposal, offering a broad vision of the educational enterprise, with support right at the centre.

Currently, policies remain piecemeal. There is much fussing over defining roles and monitoring procedures, but no clear sense of what is at stake here. Student support seems marginal to the main thrust of what higher education is about. My purpose has been to challenge that. I want to shift the argument away from the question of how best to provide safety-nets for those who fall, and onto the question of how to enhance the quality of the whole student experience. I want to focus attention not on how academic staff should conduct personal tutorials, but on how students can be both supported and challenged within a tutorial relationship. I want to move away from questions about how students may be given 'pastoral care' by staff who are supposedly older and wiser, or how they may be given 'counselling' by staff who are specially trained and appropriately skilled in techniques of helping, and to pose as sharply as I can the question of how we can develop a shared sense of purpose which binds together all our teaching, learning *and helping* into a coherent educational philosophy.

References

Arbuckle, D. S. (1967) 'Kinds of counselling: meaningful or meaningless?' *Journal of Counselling Psychology*, 14, 219–25.

Astin, A. W. (1984) 'Student involvement: a developmental theory for higher education' *Journal of College Student Personnel*, 25, 297–308.

Bannister, D. and Fransella, F. (1971) *Inquiring Man: The Psychology of Personal Constructs*. Harmondsworth, Penguin.

Barnett, R. (1990a) 'Towards the learning academy' in 'Reflections on Higher Education' *Journal of the Higher Education Foundation*, 2, 1, 6–10.

Barnett, R. (1990b) *The Idea of Higher Education*. Milton Keynes, Open University Press.

Barnett, R. (1991) 'Break-up of a happy marriage' *Times Higher Education Supplement*, 15 March, 16.

Becker H. S. (1964) 'Personal change in adult life' in B. R. Cosin (ed.) (1971) *School and Society: A Sociological Reader*, 2nd edn. London, Routledge and Kegan Paul in association with Open University Press.

Blyth, W. A. L. and Derricott, R. (1977) *The Social Significance of Middle Schools*. London, Batsford.

Bramley, W. (1977) *Personal Tutoring in Higher Education*. Guildford, Society for Research into Higher Education.

Chickering, A. W. (1972) *Education and Identity*. San Francisco, Jossey-Bass.

Corbett, J. (1990) 'Uneasy transitions and the challenge of change' in *Uneasy Transitions: Disaffection in Post-Compulsory Education and Training*. London, Falmer Press.

Danziger, K. (1971) *Socialization*. Harmondsworth, Penguin.

Durkheim, E. (1952) *Suicide: A Study in Sociology*. London, Routledge and Kegan Paul.

Earwaker, J. C. (1986) 'Pacing occupational socialization in professional training'. Paper presented to *First International Conference on the First Year Experience*. Newcastle Polytechnic.

Earwaker, J. C. (1987) 'Different conceptions of self and role among first year students training for caring professions'. Paper presented to *Second International Conference on the First Year Experience*. Southampton University.

Earwaker, J. C. (1989a) 'Student support and tutoring: initiating a programme of staff development'. Paper presented to *Fourth International Conference on the First Year Experience*. University of St Andrews.

Earwaker, J. C. (1989b) *Student Support and the Role of Tutors*. Sheffield City Polytechnic.

Eisenstadt, S. N. (1956) *From Generation to Generation*. Chicago, Free Press.

Corbett, J., 37, 42n
counselling, 80, 110, 119
   as a model of helping, 108–11
   pastoral care and, 75, 82, 102, 120,
      122, 130–2
   service, 53, 98, 115, 128, 134
   cf. interviewing, 56, 58, 79–80
   cf. tutoring, 56–8, 79–80, 109–10,
      120
counsellor, 41, 75, 110
   cf. tutor, 52–3, 80
Course Tutor, 45–7, 70
curriculum
   support provision via the, 115–20
      passim, 120–2

Danziger, K., 24, 30
debt, 41, 132
   indebtedness, 10
   (*see also* financial difficulties; poverty)
demand-led, 97
Departments of Student Services, 104,
   113
dependency, 9–10, 65–7, 82, 108
Derricott, R., 27
development
   as a social process, 14, 20, 129
   interrelated processes of, 13, 15,
      19–20
   of personal skills and qualities, 16–17
   professional, 17–19
   stages of, 14, 26
   student, 12–13, 15–17, 19–20
   through the life course, 12–13
disclosure
   levels of, 72, 74
   self-, 61–2
Durkheim, E., 28

Earwaker, J.C., 17–18, 46
Eisenstadt, S.N., 40
Europe, 101
examination board, 70, 76, 82
examinations, 10, 16, 62, 69
   worry about, 23, 41, 107
   (*see also* stress)
expectations, 26–7, 29, 30, 32
   lack of clear, 8
   misleading, 38
   pressure to conform to others', 19

financial
   adviser, 132
   assistance, 76n
   difficulties, 73, 126
   sacrifices, 23
   support, 4, 6–7, 9
   worries, 9
   (*see also* debt; poverty)
first year experience, 117
First Year Tutor, 46, 51
Fransella, F., 30
freshman seminar, 116–17
friends, 35, 39, 61
   as a problem, 129
   as a source of support, 23, 54, 120–1
   friendship between tutors and
      students, 55, 86
Frith, S., 40

Gahagan, J., 60
gender, 10, 61
Goffman, E., 30
group-building, 121
growing up, 15, 27

Hammersley, H., 28
harassment, 47, 63–4, 67
helping, 64
   not experienced as helpful, 7
   paradox of, 65–6
helplessness, 65–6
higher education
   availability of, 36–7
   entry to, 23, 26, 28
   leaving, 25–6, 28
   wider access to, 20, 37
home
   difficulty of definition, 39
homesickness, 9, 24, 41

identity, 19, 31–2
   academic, 17
   negotiation of, 29
   professional, 17
   transition as a threat to, 24
ideology, 106–8, 111, 130
inequalities, 9, 37
institutional climate, 76
institutions (of higher education)

changed character of, 3, 35–9, 41, 113, 115, 120
commitment to student welfare, 117
effect on tutorial relationship, 53, 55, 63–4
impact on student experience, 27–8, 30, 32
policies of, 122, 131
provision made by, 92–5, 101–6 *passim*, 113–15
responsibility for student support, 80, 85, 91, 124, 127–30
support for tutors, 50–1, 132
tutors' responsibility to, 45, 82, 84, 86
integral provision, 97–8, 117, 129–30
integration, 111
interviewing, 56–8, 79

Jaques, D., 56

Kaye, K., 20

Laing, R.D., 31
Lemons, L.J., 16
Lewis, R., 56
listening, 78–9, 114, 126
loss, 25
low status of support role, 51
low take-up, 97
Lublin, J., 56

McMahon, T., 56
management of the tutorial, 59–66 *passim*
Marris, P., 25
medical service, 128
Merton, R.K., 28
Milgram, S., 64
models of student support, 113, 115, 120–2
moral aspects, 67, 111, 113, 120, 122, 132
Moral Tutor, 102, 104
Morton, S., 118

negotiation, 32
between self and role, 29–30, 32
of personal development, 19
North America, 101
(*see also* USA)

occupational socialization, 17
Olesen, V.L., 16, 21n
'open door' policy, 52

pastoral care, 101–14 *passim*, 117, 120, 122, 126
and counselling, 75, 82, 130–2, 134
as a model of helping, 106–8
Pattison, S., 106
peer support, 120–1
permission
levels of, 72, 74
Perry, W.G., 16
Personal Tutor, 45–6, 86, 97, 107, 131
personal tutorial, 79, 97–9, 104, 106, 113–14
personality
concept of, 24–6, 31
Phillips, M., 76n
Placement Tutor, 46
policy questions, 95
ancillary or integral provision?, 97–8
initiatives or responses?, 96–7
prevention or cure?, 95–6
portfolios, 16, 118
poverty, 40–1
(*see also* debt; financial difficulties)
power, 61–5 *passim*
privacy, 71–2, 106, 113
of student, 53, 61, 70
of tutor, 81
problems, 3–11 *passim*, 95–7, 117–18, 129, 131–3
contribution to personal development, 20
identification of, 6
initial, 8
students as, 121
tutors', 107
typical student, 9–11
professional responsibility, 63, 74–6
(*see also* tutor, responsibilities of)
'professional tradition', 101
professionalism, 52, 113
professionalization
deferred, 18
incremental, 18
instant, 17
provision (of student support), 94–9 *passim*, 123–4

(*see also* institutions, provision made by)

Rees, S., 57
referral, 53, 76, 83–6, 119, 132
  reasons for, 79, 84
relationships, 59–68 *passim*, 79–81, 85
  as a source of support, 31
  in interviewing and counselling, 79
  personal vs professional, 80
  (*see also* tutorial relationship)
residential experience, 104–5, 112n
  (*see also* accommodation)
resources, 82, 98–9
Richmond, D.R., 16
rite of passage, 14, 26–7
Robinson, D., 26
Rogers, C., 31, 56
role
  concept of, 26–7, 30–1
  cf. roles of tutor and counsellor, 80
  (*see also* tutor's role)
role strain, 51–5, 76

safety-net, 96, 98, 117, 132–3
Scotland, 112n
secrecy, 70–2
Seligman, M., 65
sensitive information, 68–71 *passim*, 76
  passing on, 85
  (*see also* confidential information)
sensitivity
  levels of, 72–3
service
  as a model of student support, 113,
    120–2
social workers, 57, 75, 133
socialization
  as a metaphor of change, 23, 26–9
    passim, 30–1
  occupational, 17
'sophomore slump', 16
Steele, R.A., 118
Stern, D., 60
Strauss, A., 29
stress, 22, 31
  in student life, 3, 126
  in tutor's role, 51
  related to examinations, 9, 16, 19
Strong, P.M., 57

student career, 11, 17, 19, 37
student development, 12–13, 15–17,
    19–20
student experience, 12, 30, 127, 131,
    133
  changed meaning of, 28
  changing, 33–42 *passim*
  differences in, 41
  interrelatedness of aspects of, 130
  quality of, 133
  social dimension of, 20, 91, 108
student life, 20, 33
students
  hard to help, 84–5
  home-based, 23, 112n
  mature, 3, 9, 12–13, 22, 27, 32
  non-traditional, 32, 37
  older, 107
  overseas, 3, 8, 32
  under-prepared, 10
students' union, 36, 121
support
  agencies of, 53–4
  responsibility for providing, 127–30
  students' need for, 124–7
  tutors' need for, 75, 82
  support networks, 8, 23, 84
support services, 132
  professional, 99, 114, 130
  specialist, 95

teaching styles
  discontinuities of, 8
Tinto, V., 25–6
transition, 22–32
  as a metaphor of change, 24, 29–31
  coping with, 22–3
  positive features of, 22
Turner, G., 28
tutor
  ambivalence of, 111
  commitment of, 46, 84, 132
  confusion of, 46, 51, 83–4
  meaning of word, 45
  responsibilities of, 41, 52–3, 59–63,
    65–6, 81–2 *passim*
  (*see also* professional responsibility)
  support for, 51, 53, 82
tutor-counsellor, 94

tutor's role, 51–5 *passim*, 78–87 *passim*, 131–2
  as advocate, 52, 71, 82, 86
  as counselling, 82, 114, 130–2
  as friend, 55, 86
  as pastoral care, 82, 131–2
  boundaries of, 81–4 *passim*, 132
  central, 131–2
  distinct, 109, 133
  front-line, 78–9, 130
  sui generis, 82
  cf. counsellor, 53, 75, 80, 84
  cf. priest, 75
tutorial
  academic, 79
  agenda of, 58–9, 118
  course-related, 118
  management of, 59–63, 65–6
  one-to-one, 103, 121
  (*see also* personal tutorial)
tutorial relationship, 55–68 *passim*, 79, 86, 97, 133
  dependency in, 65–7, 82
  meeting tutor's own needs through, 82
  'moral' aspects of, 67, 111, 113, 120, 122, 132

  power in, 61–5 *passim*
tutorial support, 109, 130
tutoring, 46–51 *passim*, 109, 117, 132
  as a model of student support, 120–2
  cf. counselling, 56–8, 79–80, 109–10, 120
  cf. doctor-patient, 56–7
  cf. interviewing, 56–8, 79–80
  cf. pastoral care, 109, 120
  cf. social worker-client, 57
  (*see also* tutorial, management of)

'University 101', 116–7, 121, 123n
USA, 106, 110, 117, 120
  (*see also* North America)

Van Gennep, 25
vulnerability, 61–2

welfare, 96, 111, 117, 121, 127
  workplace welfare as an approach to student support, 119–20
Whittaker, E.W., 16, 21n

Year Tutor, 45–7
youth culture, 40

The Society for Research into Higher Education

The Society for Research into Higher Education exists to stimulate and co-ordinate research into all aspects of higher education. It aims to improve the quality of higher education through the encouragement of debate and publication on issues of policy, on the organization and management of higher education institutions, and on the curriculum and teaching methods.

The Society's income is derived from subscriptions, sales of its books and journals, conference fees and grants. It receives no subsidies, and is wholly independent. Its individual members include teachers, researchers, managers and students. Its corporate members are institutions of higher education, research institutes, professional, industrial and governmental bodies. Members are not only from the UK, but from elsewhere in Europe, from America, Canada and Australasia, and it regards its international work as amongst its most important activities.

Under the imprint *SRHE & Open University Press*, the Society is a specialist publisher of research, having some 45 titles in print. The Editorial Board of the Society's Imprint seeks authoritative research or study in the above fields. It offers competitive royalties, a highly recognizable format in both hard- and paperback and the world-wide reputation of the Open University Press.

The Society also publishes *Studies in Higher Education* (three times a year), which is mainly concerned with academic issues, *Higher Education Quarterly* (formerly *Universities Quarterly*), mainly concerned with policy issues, *Research into Higher Education Abstracts* (three times a year), and *SRHE News* (four times a year).

The Society holds a major annual conference in December, jointly with an institution of higher education. In 1990, the topic was 'Industry and Higher Education', at and with the University of Surrey. In 1991, it was 'Research and Higher Education in Europe', with the University of Leicester. Future conferences include, 1992, 'Learning to Effect', with Nottingham Polytechnic, and in 1993, 'Governments and the Higher Education Curriculum' with the University of Sussex. In addition it holds regular seminars and consultations on topics of current interest.

The Society's committees, study groups and branches are run by the members. The groups at present include:

Teacher Education Study Group
Continuing Education Group
Staff Development Group
Excellence in Teaching and Learning
Women in Higher Education Group

Benefits to members

Individual

Individual members receive:

- *SRHE News*, the Society's publications list, conference details and other material included in mailings.
- Greatly reduced rates for *Studies in Higher Education* and *Higher Education Quarterly*.
- A 35% discount on all Open University Press & SRHE publications.
- Free copies of the Preceeding – commissioned papers on the theme of the Annual Conference.
- Free copies of *Research into Higher Education Abstracts*.
- Reduced rates for conferences.
- Extensive contacts and scope for facilitating initiatives.
- Reduced reciprocal memberships.

Corporate

Corporate members receive:

- All benefits of individual members, plus
- Free copies of *Studies in Higher Education*.
- Unlimited copies of the Society's publications at reduced rates.
- Special rates for its members e.g. to the Annual Conference.

Membership details may be obtained from
Society for Research into Higher Education
344–354 Gray's Inn Road
London WC1X 8BP
Tel. 071–837–7880   Fax. 071–713–0609